The Complete Idiot's Reference Card

Compact Chronology of the 20th Century

1901 Queen Victoria dies.

1901 Marconi sends the first trans-Atlantic radio signal.

1903 The Wright brothers fly at Kitty Hawk, North Carolina.

1904–1905 Russo-Japanese War is fought.

1905 Freud publishes his theories of sexuality.

1905 Einstein proposes the theory of special relativity.

1908 Henry Ford launches the Model T.

1909 NAACP is founded.

1911 Sun Yat-sen leads the Chinese revolution against the Manchus.

1912 *Titanic* sinks.

1913 Western art is revolutionized by Stravinsky's *Rite of Spring* and paintings at New York's Armory Show.

1913 U.S. income tax is born.

1914 Austrian Archduke Francis Ferdinand and wife are assassinated, beginning World War I.

1915 D.W. Griffiths's *Birth of a Nation* gives birth to modern movies.

1917 The United States enters World War I.

1917 Lenin leads the Bolshevik Revolution.

1918 The world is swept by an influenza pandemic.

1919 Prohibition begins in the United States.

1920 The 19th Amendment gives women the vote.

1920 Mohandas Gandhi launches nonviolent protest against British rule in India.

1922 Benito Mussolini becomes dictator of Italy, bringing Fascism to Europe.

1926 Robert Goddard launches the first liquid-fuel rocket.

1927 Charles A. Lindbergh solos across the Atlantic.

1928 Louis "Satchmo" Armstrong's "West End Blues" marks the early maturity of jazz as "America's classical music."

1929 The stock market crashes, initiating the Great Depression.

1933 Adolf Hitler becomes chancellor of Germany.

1933 Hitler establishes Dachau, first of the German concentration camps, marking the beginning of the Holocaust.

1933 Franklin Roosevelt launches the New Deal.

1936 Spanish Civil War begins—dress rehearsal for World War II.

1939 World War II begins.

1941 The United States enters World War II after Japan attacks Pearl Harbor, Hawaii.

1942 Enrico Fermi directs the first sustained nuclear chain reaction.

1943 Jean-Paul Sartre's *Being and Nothingness* launches the philosophy of existentialism.

1944 The Allies begin to retake Europe with the D-Day invasion.

1945 The United Nations is chartered.

1945 Atomic bombs are dropped on Hiroshima and Nagasaki, Japan.

1946 The first entirely electronic computer is built.

1947 Chuck Yeager breaks the sound barrier in the Bell X-1 rocket plane.

1947 The Marshall Plan for the recovery of Europe is announced.

1948 Physicist George Gamow proposes the "Big Bang" theory of the creation of the universe.

1948 USSR blockades Berlin, initiating the Cold War.

1948 Comedian Milton Berle's popularity gives Americans a reason to buy television sets.

1948 The transistor is invented.

1949 China becomes a communist nation.

1950 Senator Joseph McCarthy launches the anti-communist "witch hunts."

1950–1953 The Korean War is fought.

tear here

alpha books

W9-CBT-288

Compact Chronology of the 20th Century...continued

1953 Scientists Watson and Crick describe the double-helix structure of DNA, inaugurating the modern science of genetics.

1955 Rosa Parks refuses to "go to the back of the bus" in Montgomery, Alabama; the modern civil rights movement begins.

1955 Jonas Salk successfully tests a polio vaccine.

1957 The USSR launches *Sputnik*.

1960 The birth control pill goes on sale.

1961 Russian cosmonaut Yuri Gagarin becomes the first man in space.

1962 The Cuban Missile Crisis brings the world to the brink of thermonuclear war.

1963 John F. Kennedy is assassinated.

1964 The Civil Rights Act of 1964 is passed.

1964 The Gulf of Tonkin Resolution is passed, launching the major phase of U.S. involvement in Vietnam.

1968 Martin Luther King Jr. is assassinated.

1969 American astronauts Neil Armstrong and Edwin "Buzz" Aldrin walk on the moon.

1969 The U.S. Defense Department creates ARPANET, forerunner of the Internet.

1971–1972 The United States establishes détente with China and with the USSR.

1973 The "energy crisis" begins when OPEC embargoes oil to the West.

1974 The Watergate scandal culminates in the resignation of Richard M. Nixon as president of the United States.

1975 The fall of Saigon to the North Vietnamese ends the Vietnam War.

1980 Communism is dealt a blow by the Polish "Solidarity" movement.

1981 IBM introduces the "personal computer."

1983 The AIDS virus is identified.

1986 A nuclear reactor explodes at Chernobyl, Ukraine, in history's worst nuclear accident.

1989 China's Deng Xiaoping cracks down on the democracy movement at Tiananmen Square, Beijing.

1989 The Berlin Wall falls.

1990–? Ethnic wars rage in Yugoslavia.

1991 Led by the United States, a U.N. coalition goes to war with Saddam Hussein's Iraq.

1992 Racially motivated rioting breaks out in Los Angeles after the acquittal of white police officers charged with beating a black man.

1992 The election of Bill Clinton ends the Reagan-Bush era.

1994 Nelson Mandela becomes South Africa's first black president.

1995 Domestic terrorists bomb an Oklahoma City federal building.

1995 The "trial of the century" ends with the acquittal of O.J. Simpson on charges of murder.

1998 Scientists in England clone a mammal, a sheep named Dolly.

1999 The Senate acquits Bill Clinton of "high crimes and misdemeanors" in the first presidential impeachment trial since 1868.

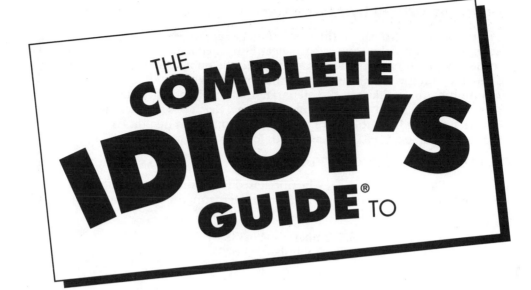

THE COMPLETE IDIOT'S GUIDE® TO

20th-Century History

by Alan Axelrod, Ph.D.

alpha
books

A Division of Macmillan General Reference
A Pearson Education Macmillan Company
1633 Broadway, New York, NY 10019-6785

Copyright © 1999 by Alan Axelrod

All rights reserved. No part of this book shall be reproduced, stored in a retrieval system, or transmitted by any means, electronic, mechanical, photocopying, recording, or otherwise, without written permission from the publisher. No patent liability is assumed with respect to the use of the information contained herein. Although every precaution has been taken in the preparation of this book, the publisher and author assume no responsibility for errors or omissions. Neither is any liability assumed for damages resulting from the use of information contained herein. For information, address Alpha Books, 1633 Broadway, 7th Floor, New York, NY 10019-6785.

THE COMPLETE IDIOT'S GUIDE TO and design are trademarks of Macmillan, Inc.

Macmillan Publishing books may be purchased for business or sales promotional use. For information please write: Special Markets Department, Macmillan Publishing USA, 1633 Broadway, New York, NY 10019.

International Standard Book Number: 0-02863385-7
Library of Congress Catalog Card Number: 99-62049

02 01 00 99   4 3 2

Interpretation of the printing code: the rightmost number of the first series of numbers is the year of the book's printing; the rightmost number of the second series of numbers is the number of the book's printing. For example, a printing code of 99-1 shows that the first printing occurred in 1999.

Printed in the United States of America

Alpha Development Team

Publisher
Kathy Nebenhaus

Editorial Director
Gary M. Krebs

Managing Editor
Bob Shuman

Marketing Brand Manager
Felice Primeau

Acquisitions Editors
Jessica Faust
Michelle Reed

Development Editors
Phil Kitchel
Amy Zavatto

Assistant Editor
Georgette Blau

Production Team

Development Editor
Phil Kitchel

Production Editor
Tammy Ahrens

Technical Editor
Walton Rawls

Copy Editor
Kris Simmons

Cover Designer
Mike Freeland

Illustrator
Jody P. Schaeffer

Designer
Scott Cook and Amy Adams of DesignLab

Indexer
Cheryl Jackson

Layout/Proofreading
Angela Calvert
Mary Hunt
Julie Trippetti

Contents at a Glance

Contents

Foreword

History, said the American transcendentalist Ralph Waldo Emerson, is like a foreign country. People do things "differently" there. As the world moves headlong into a new century, the past 100 years do, indeed, appear "different."

Today's incoming college freshmen were not even born when the Vietnam War ended. And, although it made perfect sense to their parents and grandparents, the anti-Communist crusade, and the Cold War that it spawned, make little sense to "Generation X." To anyone who can say "way back in the '80s" with a straight face, democracy's century-long struggle with monarchy, fascism, and, finally, communism, seems especially odd in light of new technologies, economic advances, and more people in college than ever before. World Wars I and II, one of my students recently told me, could never happen again. "People are too smart now," she explained confidently. Her predecessors were "just plain dumb."

Every generation is convinced it is a helluva lot smarter than the one before it. The trick is not to take this conclusion too seriously. *The Complete Idiot's Guide to 20th-Century History* will remind you of that. No generation has had a monopoly on "smarts." Woodrow Wilson believed, for instance, that the World War I would forever be "the war to end all wars." Pope John XXIII claimed that racism would "disappear by 1970," and Yasuhiro Nakasone, a 1980s Japanese Prime Minister, insisted that by 1995, 50 years after World War II, America would be Japan's "breadbasket" and Europe its "boutique." All of these men represented the "brightest and best" of global politics in their day. Oops.

For years, I have told university students in America, Japan, and elsewhere that their views on history are as valuable as the so-called "brightest and best." Having had the opportunity to teach history, write history, and even *make* a little history while serving in the U.S. Congress, I learned long ago that there may be more "idiots" in government service than out of it. The common man deserves to be heard, and, since democracy has emerged triumphant over its many 20th-century challengers, the rights of the common man are most important. This is not to say that us common folk couldn't use a little brushing up on the facts. The following narrative gives you those facts, and in a welcomed, painless fashion.

For many readers, history hurts. It is the intellectual equivalent of a root canal. Like me, these readers might have had a high school history instructor who was also the football coach. (In my case, the poor man had played too many years without a helmet.) A decent education was not the result of time spent in his classroom, and discovering the challenges of the past was left to personal interest.

Without question, *The Complete Idiot's Guide to 20th-Century History* is going to make up for that lackluster teacher. The book will challenge you, interest you, and, a la Paul Harvey, give you "the rest of the story." You'll learn, for instance, in Chapter 27, "Red Sunset and Desert Flames," that the final triumph of democracy in this century is everyone's triumph; in Chapter 28, "Prosperity and Scandal," you'll discover that with triumph comes tragedy. The book in your hands is living proof that history is not just the study of dead people and old stuff. From the description of crystal palaces and sod houses to the discussion of the Internet, history is the record of how we live, want to live, and must live if we are to survive the next century. That record is relevant to us all, and its twists and turns merit your attention. Enjoy the ride.

—Tim Maga, Ph.D.

Tim Maga, Ph.D., is the Oglesby Professor of American Heritage (an "endowed chair" of U.S. diplomatic history) at Bradley University. Previously, he was a Foreign Affairs Coordinator for the U.S. House of Representatives Foreign Affairs Committee and a U.S. trade policy negotiator. He is the author of several books on U.S. diplomacy issues, including, most recently, *Hands Across the Sea? U.S.-Japan Relations, 1961–1981* (1997), *The Perils of Power* (1995), and *The World of Jimmy Carter* (1994). In 1990 he was a finalist for the Pulitzer Prize in History for his work *John F. Kennedy and the New Pacific Community, 1961–1963*. Dr. Maga earned his Ph.D. from McGill University. When not writing the "Great History Book" or involved in a diplomatic mission abroad, he can be found teaching Shotokan Karate or forever tinkering with his 1965 Corvette.

Introduction

Look at a road map. Then look at the reality it's supposed to represent. The differences between the representation and reality are much more dramatic and numerous than the similarities. The map, after all, is a little piece of two-dimensional paper, whereas the world—well, the world is the world. But, with charity toward the cartographers, we accept maps as useful things, and we forgive them for not being more like the world they represent.

In the hope of similar indulgence, here is *The Complete Idiot's Guide to 20th-Century History*. I have tried to put the emphasis on "guide" rather than "idiot," to create a map of this most exciting, terrifying, awe-inspiring, and, most of all, event-packed period of time.

This book is a guide, a map, rather than a full-fledged history. But it is also a bird's-eye view that sweeps down frequently for a closer look at this personality or that event.

Precisely which personalities and which events? They have been chosen as the ones most representative of the century—that is, for being the events and people of the century that tell us most about ourselves, about who we were, who we are, and who we may become, as well as who we may have *wished* we were or may yet *wish* to become. As with a road map, plenty has been left out, but, like a road map, enough information has been included to get you from the beginning of the journey to the end.

I just used the word *you*. Let me tell you who I think you are. You are, like me, an American. And that's important, because this book has been written from an American perspective. Much that happened in the 20th century originated in the United States or directly involved the United States, so that it is often called the "American century." Perhaps, then, there is no need to justify the fact that most of the events and people you'll meet—or, in some cases, get reacquainted with—in the pages that follow are American, and those that aren't, nevertheless directly affected life, thought, and attitude in America. In any case, America is the lens through which we'll view the century.

Part 1, "Overview and Backward Overture," begins with an overview of the 20th century, then slips back in time to the forces of pre-1900 history that set the stage for our time.

Part 2, "The Old World Dies," covers the first two decades of the 20th century, an era in which the old, familiar world came to a violent end in the "Great War" of 1914-1918.

Part 3, "Lost Generations" is devoted to the period between the wars, a time of exciting new ideas and loosening morality, a time of hope for better lives, and a time in which totalitarian tyranny began its march across Europe, and economic depression gripped the world.

Part 4, "To Hell and Back," covers World War II and the rapid evolution, afterward, of a Cold War. The war brought to birth a new age, in which American scientists released the energy of the atom, creating a weapon that ended the most destructive war in history, but bequeathed to the people of the planet the means of their destruction.

Part 5, "American Dreams," traces America's journey in the world as its leading superpower as well as the journey of the American people from complacent contentment in the 1950s, through a growing consciousness of injustice in 1960s, and their aspiration to build a "Great Society."

Part 6, "A New World," takes America out of the Vietnam nightmare, then contrasts the generally upward struggle of democracy, between 1970 and 1989, with the downward spiral of Soviet communism.

Part 7, "Unfinished Century," explores the final decade of the century, an era of intensive and extensive change, then looks forward, briefly, to the centuries to come.

Extras

In addition to the main narrative of *The Complete Idiot's Guide to 20th-Century History*, you'll find other types of useful information, including capsule highlight of major personalities and events, key quotations of the century, the century's buzzwords, and enlightening statistics. Look for these features:

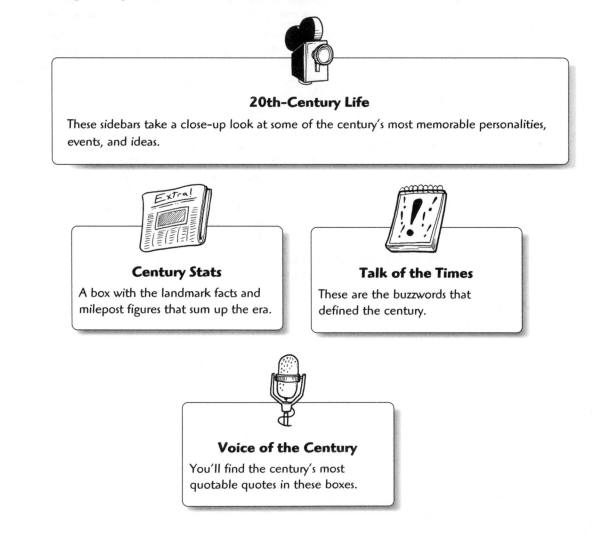

20th-Century Life

These sidebars take a close-up look at some of the century's most memorable personalities, events, and ideas.

Century Stats

A box with the landmark facts and milepost figures that sum up the era.

Talk of the Times

These are the buzzwords that defined the century.

Voice of the Century

You'll find the century's most quotable quotes in these boxes.

Part 1
Overview and Backward Overture

"Look before you leap," runs the cliché, and this section begins with an overview of the century we called home, then takes a look at what lay behind it—mostly the 19th century. We see America as the focus of growing world attention, we see the rise of the industrial age, and we pass through the crucible of civil war. We end with the United States as the cradle of inventions that made the 20th century possible, as the mecca for immigrants from everywhere on the globe, and as an emerging world power.

Chapter 1

Our Home Century

In This Chapter

➤ The 20th century as the "American century"

➤ The contest between democracy and totalitarianism

➤ Our "mediated reality"

➤ 20th century pros and cons

➤ The major themes

Out of a population of 270 million, about 2 million Americans are 100 years old or older. For a few of us, then, a century is a lifetime; for most, however, it is simply a long time. Yet we who have been born into the 20th century identify it as our time, our "home century," which we're preparing to leave as someone might leave home: with a mixture of excitement and anxiety. Whatever else it has been, the 20th century is the past and the present, whereas the 21st century is the future—an unknown.

As the American historian Frederic Harrison wrote in 1862, "All our hopes for the future depend on a sound understanding of the past"—hence the value of this over-the-shoulder glance at the 20th century. This chapter presents a snapshot of the century and says a bit about how we'll explore it.

Century in a Nutshell

Okay, fewer than 1 percent of us live to be 100 these days, but most men in the United States can at least expect to reach 72 and most women 78. This is a lot better than what folks living at the beginning of the century, in 1900, could bank on. Men were lucky to hit 48 and women 51.

This single statistic suggests that in a mere 100 years, the conditions of life have greatly changed. It is true: Medical science has advanced tremendously. The development of antibiotic medicines, beginning with the discovery of penicillin in 1928, transformed the role of physician from a person who diagnosed diseases, and then made death from them a little easier, to a practical scientist who could successfully combat illness. (Check out Chapter 12, "Victims and Heroes.") But most of the improvement in longevity is the result of better food and better sanitation, the result of a strong economy and technological advancement, two gifts of industrialization in the 20th century.

Back in 1900, the average worker put in a 52-hour week. Today, although many overachievers work 60 hours or more each week, the average is 38.9. In 1900, 42 percent of working Americans labored on farms, whereas today, agricultural workers represent under 3 percent of the workforce.

The world of 1900 was largely horse-drawn, but trains were also important for long-distance overland travel, averaging 54 miles per hour. Today, the French Train à Grande Vitesse (TGV) cruises at 160, but most of us travel by jet at about 500 miles per hour, and a few of us have been launched into space on rockets, the fastest of which skips along at 30,000 miles per hour.

Voice of the Century

"If I'd known I was gonna live this long, I'd have taken better care of myself."

—Eubie Blake (1883–1983), ragtime composer and pianist, on his 100th birthday, five days before his death

Century Stats

Combined, the three major U.S. airlines, Delta, United, and American, carry an average of 245,000,000 passengers a year.

When we're not in a plane (or on a spaceship), chances are we're in a car. American auto plants turned out almost 7 million passenger cars in 1998. In 1903, when Henry Ford was financing his new auto-making concern, a bank president advised Ford's own lawyer to avoid investing in his client's enterprise: "The horse is here to stay, but the automobile is only a novelty." If this seems shortsighted, consider that in 1901, just two years before he and brother Orville took flight at Kitty Hawk, North Carolina, Wilbur Wright declared that "man will not fly for 50 years."

The people of 1900 were just becoming accustomed to the wonders of electricity—the telegraph, the telephone, electric light, and electric motors—but most folks in that day and age had been born into a world of candles and kerosene lamps, a world in which most communication was handled by letter or shouting, and if heavy lifting had to be done, it was not a motor that did the job, but a strong back and a brawny pair of arms.

Today, few of us know life without electric power. Electricity is essential not only for light and heat and physical labor, but also for comfort (air conditioning), for communication (radio, television, and *cellular* telephones), and even for thought (computers and personal computers).

The Yanks are coming! Americans marched to their first world war in 1917.
(Image from the author's collection)

Well, this "nutshell" in which we're putting the century is getting pretty big, and all we've looked at so far is the surface of technology. The fact is, just about everything has changed in 100 years. Consider the geopolitical globe. In 1900, the greatest world power of all was the British Empire. An aged Queen Victoria presided over 11 million square miles, about a fifth of the surface of the planet, and 400 million people, a quarter of the world's population. Today, "Great" Britain has shriveled to a European island and a handful of "independent territories," mostly small Atlantic island states.

The year 1900 was the high-water mark of the British Empire. Its holdings receded and dwindled from there. Through the century, the United States has emerged first as a world power, then a leading world power, then a superpower, and, with the collapse of the Soviet Union, *the* superpower. Some have gone so far as to call the 20th century the "American century."

There is certainly economic justification for this because the United States, through most of the century, has produced, consumed, and spent more than any other nation on earth. But there is also ideological justification. In the 19th century, Abraham Lincoln called America the "last best hope of the world," and, in the 20th century, our nation did indeed become the torchbearer and defender of that experiment in government begun so hopefully in the 18th century: democracy.

A Hundred Violent Years

Much of the century was a contest between democracy and various forms of totalitarianism, either communism or fascism. Rarely in the history of the world have the lines of conflict been drawn along such sharp ideological divides. The two cataclysmic world wars, surely the most momentous features of the century, seem like some vast and bloody drama enacted between forces of good and evil, liberty and tyranny. After World War II, a series of smaller conflicts and the long, heavily armed, always tenuous truce known as the Cold War continued the drama, the last act of which loomed, but, perhaps miraculously, was never played out. World War III, the unplayed final act, promised to be, indeed, the final act of humankind. "What would World War IV be fought with?" a reporter once asked Albert Einstein. "With sticks and stones," replied the physicist, whose equation of energy-mass equivalence, $e = mc^2$, had unlocked the awful energy of the atom.

The century was populated by many powerful figures. Josef Stalin, who ruled the Soviet Union from 1929 until his death in 1953, was one of the most powerful—and most terrible. He died with the blood of perhaps 35 million or more of his countrymen on his hands. (Image from arttoday.com)

Talk of the Times

Ethnic cleansing is the program of genocide waged chiefly by Serbs against Muslims in Serb-occupied Bosnia, and Kosovo against Albanians in the 1990s.

The Great Boer War, the Russo-Japanese War, the Balkan Wars, World War I, the Spanish Civil War, the Sino-Japanese War, World War II, the Korean War, the Vietnam War—these were the major conflicts of the century, and they fill many of the pages that follow.

The wars of the century, beginning with the Great Boer War of 1899–1902, were not exclusively contests between armies. They were total wars, wars waged against combatants and noncombatants alike. Some were genocidal wars, aimed at nothing less than the destruction of an entire people or race or religion. We think of the Holocaust, Adolf Hitler's program of death that killed 6 million Jews during the era of World War II, but Hitler was neither the first nor the last practitioner of genocide in the 20th century. Sultan Abdulhamid II of the Ottoman Empire was responsible for the deaths of at least 650,000 Armenians before and during World War I. Some 35 million deaths may be attributed to Josef Stalin of the Soviet Union from the 1920s through the 1930s. Pol Pot, communist dictator of Kampuchea (formerly Cambodia), caused the deaths of at least a million Cambodians in the 1970s. Most recently, Saddam Hussein of Iraq has waged genocidal war against the Kurdish people in the northern reaches of his nation, and in the Balkans, the cauldron from which World War I emerged, *ethnic cleansing* came to describe a genocidal campaign waged by Serbs against Muslims in Bosnia during the 1990s.

The Thousand Natural Shocks...

If war, *world* war, was the great curse of the 20th century, it was not the only shock humanity endured. Shakespeare's Hamlet spoke of "the thousand natural shocks that flesh is heir to," a phrase that might be used to describe the natural disasters that befell the century.

There were earthquakes, such as those in San Francisco in 1906, in Tokyo in 1923, in Chile in 1960, in Alaska in 1964, in T'ang-shan, China, in 1976, and in Mexico in 1985. There were great floods, among them the flood of Paris in 1910, of Frankfurt in 1930, of Hilo, Hawaii, in 1946, and of Warsaw in 1964. Famine has been chronic in the *Third World* throughout the century. Drought is a frequent plague in many parts of the world; in the United States, the great Dust Bowl of the 1930s, combined with the economic hardships of the Great Depression (see Chapter 13, "The Party Ends"), ruined many thousands of farmers.

There have been plagues of disease: The great flu *pandemic* of 1918–19 might be the most devastating pandemic in history, resulting in 30 million deaths worldwide (Chapter 10, "Saving Democracy"); AIDS (Acquired Immune Deficiency Syndrome) was first reported in 1981, has killed more than 6 million worldwide since then, and infected millions more (Chapter 26, "Years of Plague, Years of Hope").

Remarkably, despite the devastation of war and these natural shocks, the population of the world has mushroomed. In 1900, 1,600,000,000 people occupied the planet. Today's figure is somewhere near 6 billion. The *population explosion* has strained resources in many areas, and, in most of the world, hunger and poverty are ways of life.

Not all the natural shocks of our time have been immediately physical in their effect. Most scientific discoveries have been made in the 20th century.

Talk of the Times

The **Third World** describes underdeveloped nations politically aligned neither with more developed capitalist nor communist powers.

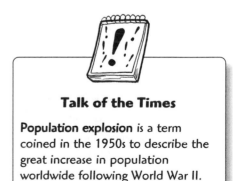

Talk of the Times

Population explosion is a term coined in the 1950s to describe the great increase in population worldwide following World War II.

Astronomers, for example, tell us that most of what we know about the universe has been learned in the past 40 years or so.

The effect of all these discoveries has been by turns glorious and, well, shocking. At the very beginning of the century, the Viennese psychiatrist Sigmund Freud told us that much of the thought and activity that occupies our lives is beyond our conscious awareness, let alone control. (See Chapter 5, "Through the Golden Door.") A series of physicists, beginning with Max Planck and Albert Einstein, created a picture of the universe on both the smallest and largest scales that is beyond the ability of most human beings to fully understand or even to imagine. (See Chapter 6, "First Years.")

In general, the science of the 20th century has greatly expanded our picture of reality, yet it has also tended to sever us from a relationship with reality based on what our senses tell us. We've come to feel alienated—as philosophers such as Jean-Paul Sartre and Albert Camus pointed out—not just some of the time, but most of the time. For many, alienation, not belonging, has become "normal"—the way you can expect to feel.

As we see in Chapter 11, "Jazz Age," after World War I, Gertrude Stein, an American writer and art collector living in Paris, a friend and confidant of such younger writers as F. Scott Fitzgerald and Ernest Hemingway, called the rising crop of intellectuals and artists a "lost generation." The phrase haunted the century, describing many people who, as a result of war, science, philosophy, or all three, had lost faith in society, government, and God.

In the West, religion was never so distant from official power as it came to be during the 20th century. Few Western governments had powerful state religions. The Catholic pope, once a powerful monarch, was now merely a "spiritual leader"—for many, little more than a figurehead. Yet religion has played an important role in our time.

Mohandas Gandhi—called the Mahatma—was an Indian lawyer who, transformed by powerful spiritual belief, led India to independence from the British rule that had dominated it since the mid-18th century. Driven by religious faith, the Jewish state of Israel was born in 1948 out of the ashes of the Holocaust. In the United States, the Reverend Martin Luther King, Jr., and—in a very different way—the "Black Muslim" minister Malcolm X were among the many religious leaders who shaped the civil rights movement that did much to end the oppression of African Americans.

Nor has religion been the province solely of great leaders. The overwhelming majority of 20th-century Americans—96 percent, according to most polls—believe in God. Some have wedded this belief to political conservatism. Others, especially in the 1960s, turned from traditional Judeo-Christian religions to the faiths of the East in search of a spiritual fulfillment they could not find amid the technological and economic trappings of everyday America.

Voice of the Century

"[Existence has] neither cause nor reason nor necessity."
—Jean-Paul Sartre, 1961

Mohandas Gandhi—called Mahatma, the "Great Soul"— led India to independence from Great Britain and taught a century devastated by two world wars and innumerable lesser conflicts that the most momentous change could be effected peacefully.
(Image from arttoday.com)

...and Even More Unnatural Shocks

Some of the nontraditional religious passion that swept the United States during the '60s was fueled in part by illicit drugs, including marijuana and the *hallucinogen* LSD. Sometimes religious longing, perhaps combined with drug use, has led to an alarming cultism. In 1969, cult leader Charles Manson presided over the brutal murders of seven people in Los Angeles, including the actress Sharon Tate, coffee heiress Abigail Folger, and supermarket chain president Leno LaBianca. Manson apparently controlled his so-called "family" with a combination of religion, sex, and drugs.

In 1978, religious leader Jim Jones, who had established Jonestown, a commune in Guyana, Central America, ordered the murder of Congressman Leo J. Ryan and a fact-finding party, who had come to investigate Jonestown. Jones also ordered the mass suicide of his followers; 911 died. In 1993, Vernon Howell, calling himself David Koresh, led his followers to their deaths after a standoff at the compound of his religious commune in Waco, Texas. Federal agents attempted to raid Koresh's "Branch Davidian" community, which had stockpiled a massive arsenal of firearms and explosives. In addition to 80 Branch Davidians, including 24 children, 4 federal officers were slain.

Cultism represented the lunatic fringe of a spiritual movement that, in a broader sense, signaled a dissatisfaction in some quarters with what the

Talk of the Times

A **hallucinogen** is a drug or other substance that produces hallucinations and distorts the perception of reality often in extravagantly fantastic form.

Talk of the Times

Smart bombs are weapons that may be electronically controlled or programmed to find their designated targets. **Cruise missiles** are essentially pilotless aircraft, steerable to their targets by remote guidance.

Talk of the Times

The **Y2K bug**, or "year 2000 prob-lem," is a glitch in certain computer programs and hardware incorporat-ing programming code that records years with only two digits and, therefore, cannot recognize whether the date "00" is 2000 or 1900. Y2K problems might cause massive breakdowns in computer systems.

rebellious American writer Henry Miller called in a 1948 book "the air-conditioned nightmare." In a word, the 20th century was *artificial*. More than at any time before, the world we inhabited was the work not of nature, but of human hands. Founded in the 18th century as an agricultural republic, the United States was now an urban nation. Today, most of us grow up not with grass beneath our feet and trees above our heads, but on concrete and asphalt, among the steel and glass of skyscrapers.

A buzzword of the latter half of the century has been *media*—radio and television, in particular—through which much of our knowledge of the world is received. In an even broader sense, however, our lives are mediated: We often speak to each other electronically, we are accustomed to doing business without face-to-face contact, and we even fight wars in an impersonal way. The *smart bombs* and *cruise missiles* employed against the forces of Iraq's Saddam Hussein during the Gulf War of 1990–91 found their targets electronically, and the people at ground zero never saw their attacker.

Perhaps the most dramatic measure of the degree to which we have created our own reality is the *Y2K bug*, the quirk of certain computer programs and hardware that, by refusing to recognize the year 2000, threatens to bring various aspects of our society to a crashing halt. It is as if time itself, which the Greek philosopher Heraclitus compared to a ceaselessly flowing river, has joined the ranks of the artificial and, like any other human-made machine, is subject to mechanical break down.

Promises, Promises

You know the old line about the difference between an pessimist and an optimist: Show both of them a half glass of water, and the pessimist will tell you that it is half empty, the optimist half full.

So it is with the 20th century.

It is a century of scientific leaps and technological wonders. It is, after all, the century in which humanity harnessed sufficient energy to achieve "escape velocity," the speed required to overcome the earth's gravitational field, and, in 1969, send a manned spaceship to the moon. It is also the century in which the energy of the atom, the "strong force" that holds together the atomic nucleus, was liberated, resulting in a force that can be used to electrify a city or, as in Hiroshima and Nagasaki in 1945, to destroy one.

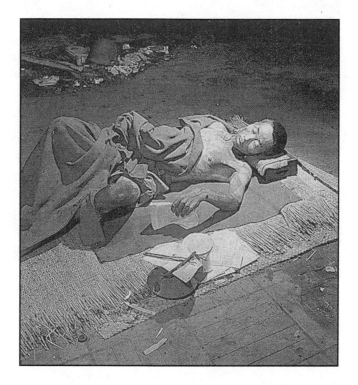

A U.S. Navy photographer documented this victim of the atomic bomb dropped on Hiroshima, August 6, 1945. In the 20th century, humankind suddenly found that it had acquired the ability to destroy itself. (Image from the National Archives)

It is a century in which a United Nations was created, offering perhaps humankind's first truly viable alternative to war for the settlement of international disputes. It is a century in which human rights and universal justice became serious causes. It is a century in which efforts to protect and preserve the natural environment were coordinated on sweeping national and international levels.

Yet it is also a century that has seen warfare of unprecedented destruction, that has seen powerful dictators direct the imprisonment, torture, exile, and murder of untold millions, and that has seen the natural environment assaulted by industry, automobiles, and unchecked population growth as never before.

An American historian was quoted at the start of this chapter to the effect that in order to prepare for the future, we must understand the past. Another historian, E.J. Hobshawm, wrote at the end of his *The Age of Empire: 1875–1914,* "The only certain thing about the future is that it will surprise even those who have seen furthest into it." Yet the prevailing sentiment at the end of this century is that the present has laid the foundation for a most promising future.

Whatever problems, political, physical, and spiritual, science and technology have created, it seems as if even more have been solved, and science and technology promise to create yet more solutions. Whatever our moral failings—and this century has shown them in some cases to be beyond all imagining—the ideal of human rights is no longer something that has to be argued. Human rights are, of course, by no means

11

universally won, but we at least feel and believe the rightness of such a concept, and in the collapse of totalitarian regimes in Russia and the nations of eastern Europe, the liberalization (however imperfect) of China, and the end of government-sanctioned, institutional racism in South Africa, we see the promise of the continued realization of human rights.

On July 20, 1969, at 4:17 P.M. Eastern Daylight Time, two American astronauts, Neil Armstrong and Edwin "Buzz" Aldrin, landed on the moon. This footprint, left by one of them, may well be our species' most enduring monument. Barring meteor impact, it will remain undisturbed on the airless, windless, and waterless lunar surface for many millions of years.
(Image from arttoday.com)

Maybe it's "only human," but most of us, in leaving the 20th century, feel that we are going on to a better time, yet a time whose improvements have been made possible by what was thought and done in the preceding hundred years.

Some Themes and Variations

Let's face it. It's not easy to take a tour, quick though it may be, of a period so packed—and so fraught—as our home century. I confess that there is a great temptation to dwell on the leaps and bounds of science and technology on the one hand and on the unremitting devastation of war on the other. This is understandable because these events are the period's most dramatically visible features. As this overview has hinted, however, there is much more to the century than what immediately meets the eye.

The chapters that follow are less an attempt at a narrative history of the century than they are a sampling, a selective inventory of the leading themes that have shaped our time.

Taking Inventory

We begin, in the next four chapters, to fill in the background of the 20th century, concentrating mainly on the 19th century, in many ways as dramatic a period as our own time. As you read these chapters and then the rest of the book, you will find it helpful to think about the following:

➤ The theme of conscious awareness versus the discovery of the unconscious mind

➤ The theme of mass production and industrial culture

➤ The theme of tyranny and totalitarianism

➤ The theme of scientific exploration, culminating in the dawn of the space age

➤ The theme of environmentalism

➤ The theme of democracy, the ascension of freedom, and the assertion of human rights

These, in one form or another, are the guideposts that appear and reappear along the many roads through our time.

Point of View

I should probably add another major theme to the list. Very early in the century, in 1905, to be exact, Albert Einstein published his theory of special relativity, the first part of the theory of relativity. We'll get into that in Chapter 7, "Rising and Sinking," but, for now, it alerts us to an issue that assumed great importance in the 20th century. The concept of reality, once conceived as an absolute (even if our knowledge might be imperfect and therefore only relative), emerged in the 20th century as itself relative. That is, reality came to be understood not as an imperfectly known absolute, but as the meeting place between a perceiver and what is perceived. Reality became not a "thing," but a point of view—or what Einstein would call a frame of reference.

Let me own up to *my* point of view in this book, lest anyone suffer irritation or disappointment. I tell the story of the 20th century from a distinctly American point of view. Most of the events recounted here are American in origin, albeit global in scope—because by the 20th century, what happened in America usually affected the world. Those events I inventory and recount that did *not* happen here are nevertheless examined primarily for their effect on America— an effect that may or may not have been immediate or direct, but that nevertheless influenced American thought, belief, sentiment, or action.

I could defend my point of view by repeating what was said earlier in this chapter: that many have called the 20th century the *American* century. I could also suggest that our nation figures so importantly in the life of the world that to take an American point of view is really to take a global view.

But I won't resort to these arguments. The rationale behind the point of view of this book is simpler. My assumption is that most who will take up this book are Americans and their interest in their home century is, at least in part, bounded and defined by their interest in their home country. In short, the American focus of this book comes from a desire to write a story that is both of most interest and of most use to those most likely to read it.

Now, let's get started.

The Least You Need to Know

➤ That people generally live longer today than at the beginning of the century is a fact; whether they live better lives is open to discussion.

➤ The 20th century is sometimes called the "American century" because it has seen the rise of the United States to become the most powerful and influential nation in the world.

➤ The most important theme of the 20th century is the contest between democracy and totalitarianism.

➤ The century has been marked by the most destructive wars the world has ever known and by the greatest progress in science and technology, as well as a broadening of the ideals of international justice and human rights.

Chapter 2

A Nation Rises (1700s–1840)

In This Chapter

➤ The American background

➤ Forging the nation

➤ The Louisiana Purchase

➤ Early technological developments

➤ The Erie Canal

Centuries are artificial things. Really, there's nothing special about a given period of a hundred years. Yet we're so accustomed to thinking in terms of centuries that we even tend to endow at least some of them with a distinctive personality, as if they were human. We call the 18th century, for example, the "Age of Reason," and we think of it as a period in which scientists (called "natural philosophers" back then) went about the business of reducing nature and natural phenomena to sets of equations, and "political philosophers" attempted to distill government to similar sets of rational principles.

In many ways, the 19th century continued this trend but went further, taking it beyond the realm of thought and translating it into the iron realities of the Industrial Age. Whereas the 18th-century *thinkers* sought to *understand* nature, the 19th-century *inventors* sought to *transform* it, to bend it to their will. These efforts produced a host of wonders, as well as a burden of discontents, as we will see in this chapter and the two that follow it, all of which introduce the 20th century by filling in the background of the 19th.

Westward the Course of Empire

George Berkeley (1685–1753), British philosopher and Anglican bishop, was also a staunch booster of the spiritual, political, and economic possibilities of the New World. He wrote a popular poem that begins, "Westward the course of empire takes its way," arguing that the westward movement of civilization was inevitable, natural, and even divinely ordained. Berkeley expressed the feeling of many leaders of his age: The future lay in the West, in the New World.

The Old World Reaches Out

Ever since the end of the 15th century, when Columbus sailed for Asia and hit America instead, Europe had been gazing more hungrily to the New World. By the middle of the 18th century, all of North, Central, and South America had been colonized by one European power or another—although Spain, England, and France predominated. In North America, France and England squared off, fighting a series of wars, with the aid of Indian allies, that culminated in the French and Indian War (1754–63), an extension of the Seven Years' War that engulfed Europe and the colonies of Europe.

After a bitter struggle, Britain won the French and Indian War but, in the process, began to lose its North American colonies. For most of the war, colonial leaders bore the brunt of the fighting yet were the butt of royal contempt. For their part, provincial military men saw how ineffectual the British regulars were at wilderness warfare, and the "Mother Country" began to seem unresponsive, uncaring, arrogant, and even incompetent. The colonies, traditionally competitive with one another, emerged from the French and Indian War feeling stronger bonds among themselves than with an aloof and unfeeling government across the sea.

Then, in an effort to put an end to Indian hostilities, Britain's King George III issued (on October 7, 1763) a proclamation setting the limit of colonial western settlement at the Appalachian Mountains. The Proclamation of 1763 pacified the Indians, who felt protected from white invasion of the trans-Appalachian West, but it enraged settlers, who flouted the proclamation and continued to settle across the forbidden mountains, which sparked renewed Indian warfare. When the settlers appealed for aid to royal authorities, it fell on deaf ears because they had violated the Proclamation Line and were entitled to no protection.

Voice of the Century

"Who would have thought it?"

—Dying words of Gen. Edward Braddock after the defeat of his British regulars by French colonials and Indians at the Battle of the Wilderness, July 9, 1755

Talk of the Times

The **Proclamation of 1765** by England's King George III forbade settlement west of the Appalachian Mountains. This outraged and alienated frontier colonists and helped create the political climate in which the independence movement was born.

The gulf between the Old World and the New thus widened, and when Great Britain introduced into its American colonies a series of taxes and other regulatory measures—without granting the colonies true representation in Parliament—the seeds of outright revolution were sewn.

All Eyes on America

To the shock and dismay of the British government, the rebellion in America quickly proved to be more than a provincial spat. Intoxicated by the democratic political ideas of philosophers as diverse as John Locke (1632–1704), who wrote of the "inalienable rights" of humankind, and Jean Jacques Rousseau (1712–78), who made liberty an object of almost universal aspiration, all of Europe eagerly watched the American Revolution. Some, such as the Marquis de Lafayette, Casimir Pulaski, the Baron de Kalb, and others—European noblemen all—did more than watch. They fought.

When the colonies won their independence by the Treaty of Paris on September 3, 1783, the world kept watching. Cynics waited for the revolutionary government to go the way of all revolutionary governments: to tyranny.

But it didn't happen. Elected by virtually universal acclamation to the office of president, George Washington refused to be a tyrant, thereby fostering a truly republican government. The course of empire had indeed taken its way westward but had been transformed in the process from empire to democratic republic and, in this form, became increasingly powerful and influential in the world.

Century Stats

Population of the United States in 1780: 2,780,400.

20th-Century Life

After the Revolution, George Washington (1732–99) returned to his beloved plantation, Mount Vernon, hoping to retire from public life. But in May 1787, he headed the Virginia delegation to the Constitutional Convention in Philadelphia and was unanimously elected presiding officer. Upon ratification of the Constitution, he was unanimously elected president in 1789 and was reelected in 1792.

By March 1797, when Washington left office, he left a well-established government and a stable financial system. During his administration, the principal Indian threat east of the Mississippi had been neutralized, and a pair of 1795 treaties with Spain had enlarged U.S. territory and averted potential diplomatic friction.

Jefferson Gets a Bargain

At the end of the 18th century, the United States was hardly a world-class military or economic power, but it was an ideological force to be reckoned with: a shining example of the government to which many people in many nations earnestly aspired.

A first step toward achieving something more than moral standing in the world of nations was made early in the 19th century.

Following the French and Indian War, France ceded to Spain the Louisiana Territory, a vast expanse of some 90,000 square miles west of the Mississippi River and including the city of New Orleans. In 1800, Napoleon reacquired the territory by secret treaty in exchange for parts of Tuscany (which Napoleon pledged to conquer on behalf of Spain) and a promise to maintain Louisiana as a buffer between Spain's North American settlements and the United States. Once the secret treaty was concluded, Napoleon promptly abandoned his Tuscan campaign, and France and Spain fell to disputing. During this period, beginning in 1802, Spain closed the Mississippi to American trade.

Thomas Jefferson, third president of the United States, knew that the fledgling nation could not tolerate an interruption of western trade, but neither did he relish the notion of Napoleon at his back door. Even if France itself did not pose a threat, the ongoing "Napoleonic Wars" between France and England would likely result in the English seizure of the Louisiana territory. To resolve the crisis, the president dispatched James Monroe to France with orders to make an offer for the purchase of the port city of New Orleans and Florida. Jefferson's plan was not only to reclaim the right to Mississippi River navigation, but also to capitalize on a discovery that had been made years earlier, in 1790, when Captain Robert Gray found and named (after his ship, the USS *Columbia*) the Columbia River on the Northwest coast. With a presence established at the mouth of the Mississippi, and with the Columbia claimed for the United States, Jefferson could also lay claim to the vast territory lying *between* the rivers. Buying New Orleans was, therefore, a very good idea. Developing circumstances made it even better.

A large French army was bogged down in the disease-infested West Indies. Rather than lose his forces to illness, Napoleon decided to withdraw from the hemisphere and focus his campaigns of conquest on Europe. Louisiana was suddenly a military liability. Even as Monroe was crossing the Atlantic, Napoleon's minister Talleyrand asked U.S. Foreign Minister to France Robert R. Livingston how much Jefferson would offer not just for New Orleans and Florida, but for the entire Louisiana Territory. Negotiations proceeded after Monroe arrived, and the bargain was concluded for 60 million francs.

Well before the purchase, Jefferson had been fascinated, like so many others, with the idea of finding a *Northwest Passage* connecting the Mississippi with the Pacific, and he persuaded Congress to appropriate funds for an expedition through the hitherto unexplored wilderness. Jefferson chose his trusted secretary Meriwether Lewis (1774–1809) to lead it, and Lewis, in turn, asked his close friend William Clark (1770–1838) to serve as co-captain.

The expedition left St. Louis on May 14, 1804, and reached central North Dakota in November. They wintered there among the friendly Mandan Indians, from whom they gathered information on what lay ahead. Accompanied by a remarkable Shoshoni woman, Sacagawea (c.1784–1812), who served as translator and guide, they explored the Rockies and reached the Continental Divide on August 12, 1805. Now convinced that the Northwest Passage did not exist, the expedition nevertheless pressed on, reaching the Columbia River and the Pacific in November 1805.

The Lewis and Clark party spent its second winter here and then set off eastward in March 1806. They returned to St. Louis on September 23, 1806. It is a testament to the skill of the two leaders that only a single man died in the course of the expedition—and his death was due not to recklessness or accident, but to a ruptured appendix.

If the expedition failed to find the Northwest Passage, it did supply a wealth of information about what had been a great blank space on the map of North America. It began the transformation of the American Far West from a place of myth and conjecture into a land of real opportunity.

Talk of the Times

The **Northwest Passage** was a water route believed to exist across the North American continent, joining the Atlantic and Pacific. Many expeditions of American exploration were formed from the 17th through 19th centuries in search of this passage.

Visionary though he was, even President Jefferson did not at first grasp the full scope of what it meant to have acquired the Louisiana Territory. He saw the purchase as nothing more than a means of avoiding war and also as convenient space for the peaceful relocation of the Indians from east of the Mississippi to west of the river in order to make room for more white settlers.

Many of the president's fellow citizens, however, saw something more: cheap land and an opportunity to make their American dreams a reality. The Louisiana Purchase was overwhelmingly popular: It catapulted Jefferson to a second term and ensured that the United States would dominate its continent—and, by the 20th century, the Western Hemisphere.

Fulton Puts on Steam

The Louisiana Purchase gave the United States one of the primary qualities that would identify it throughout the 19th century: space—room enough for everyone and for their dreams as well. (At least, such was the rapidly evolving myth.)

But the history of the 18th century showed that the vastness of American space could also be a curse. A far-flung nation was difficult to govern, as the British crown had discovered, and the allegiance to any central authority seemed to vary inversely to the distance from that authority. The Mississippi River and beyond were a very long way from the eastern seaboard.

The burgeoning technology of the new century met the challenge of national distances. Robert Fulton was a gunsmith, jeweler, and artist who had studied in London with the leading American painter of the day, Benjamin West. Fulton was soon attracted to the ultra-modern profession of engineering, and in 1796, he published a *Treatise on the Improvement of Canal Navigation*, hoping to interest the U.S. Government in his patent for a double-inclined plane, used to raise and lower canal boats from one level to another in an age when canals were the chief means of transporting cargo.

Robert Fulton invented neither the steam engine nor the steamboat, but he was the first to make steam navigation commercially profitable.
(Image from arttoday.com)

When American officials turned him down, he introduced his schemes to the French, who likewise demurred. Undaunted, Fulton next proposed to the French admiralty a plan for a submarine. Once again, he was disappointed. But, in Paris, he had made a valuable friend in American minister Robert Livingston, who provided the financial backing for a Seine River steamboat. It wasn't the world's first steam vessel, but it was the best one yet built: the first truly practical steamboat. Impressed, and jealous of the French, the British admiralty invited Fulton to England to continue his steamboat experiments. Then came Lord Horatio Nelson's triumph over Napoleon's fleet at Trafalgar, which, in a flash, convinced the admiralty that they were in no need of naval innovation.

Fulton returned to the United States with Robert Livingston, who obtained a monopoly of steamboat navigation on New York waters. Using Fulton's designs, the two men commissioned a boat to be built and ordered a steam engine from the company of steam-engine pioneer James Watt in England. The vessel was launched on August 9, 1807, and, on August 17, steamed from New York City to Albany in 32 hours. At an average of about five miles an hour, this was faster than any vessel under sail. Even more important to commercial navigation, steam power made accurate and regular scheduling possible; captain, crew, passengers, and cargo were no longer at the mercy of fickle winds.

In 1808, Fulton rebuilt his vessel, made it longer, and christened it *The North River Steamboat of Clermont,* which public and press shortened to the familiar *Clermont*. The partners then built other successful Hudson River vessels and also operated ferries between Manhattan and New Jersey and between Manhattan and Long Island.

The *Clermont* propelled Fulton (and Livingston) to hard-won success, but, far more important, steam power made large-scale, regular navigation of the nation's rivers and inland waterways possible, thereby promoting trade, national industry, and, ultimately, the westward settlement of the United States.

Century Stats

The paddle wheels of *Clermont* were powered by an English Boulton and Watt engine with a cylinder 24 inches in diameter and a 4-foot stroke. The vessel was 133 feet long and 18 feet in the beam, with a 7-foot draft and a smoke stack 30 feet high.

20th-Century Life

James Watt (1736–1819), a Scottish inventor, was one of the several "fathers" of the steam engine, the first practical machine for converting heat into mechanical energy. The Englishman Thomas Newcomen (1663–1729) had improved a 1698 steam engine invented by Thomas Savery and made from it a commercially successful water pump. Watt was repairing a Newcomen engine when he devised a series of improvements that ultimately resulted in a new, more efficient engine, which he patented in 1769. To make his engine more appealing and comprehensible to industrialists and farmers, he invented a unit of power expressed in terms of the work a horse could do. Thus, the concept of *horsepower* was born, and the Age of Steam was launched.

The steamboat Clermont.
(Image from
arttoday.com)

Big Ditch to the West

For generations, American schoolchildren were taught that the War of 1812 was nothing less than the "second War of American Independence," a righteous conflict fought because the British, at war with Napoleon and in need of sailors for the Royal Navy, insisted on boarding U.S. vessels in order to "impress" (kidnap) American sailors into His Majesty's service. The United States, not about to be pushed around, had no choice but to fight a war.

Actually, the U.S. declared war on Britain on June 19, 1812, three days *after* that nation agreed to stop impressing seamen from American vessels. The real cause of the war was not on the ocean, but in the trans-Appalachian West. Westerners saw war with Britain as an opportunity to gain relief from British-backed hostile Indians and as a chance to snatch up what was then called Spanish Florida—a "parcel" of land extending from Florida west to the Mississippi River. Spain, which held this land, was allied with Britain against Napoleon. War with Britain would therefore mean war with Spain, and victory would mean the acquisition of Spanish Florida. This would complete an unbroken territorial link from the Atlantic, through the recently purchased Louisiana Territory, clear to the Pacific, so that the United States would reach from "sea to shining sea."

Once war came, however, it proved mostly disastrous for the United States, especially the West, which suffered one defeat after another. Nevertheless, a few notable

Talk of the Times

Impressment was the British practice of boarding foreign vessels, identifying (often doubtfully) British nationals, and "pressing" them into involuntary service in the Royal Navy.

victories—especially those of Oliver H. Perry on Lake Erie (September 10, 1813), William Henry Harrison at the Battle of the Thames (October 5, 1813), and Andrew Jackson at the Battle of New Orleans (January 8, 1815)—gave Americans the *feeling* that they had decisively won the war, and it raised national pride and a sense of national identity and solidarity to new heights. More than ever, in particular, westerners clamored for more links with the East.

But President James Monroe opposed using Federal funds to build roads for the West. Never mind. His opposition served only to spur development of the nation's first great commercial link between the East Coast and the vast inland realm. Gouverneur Morris, U.S. senator from New York, proposed in 1800 something more practical than a mere road. He spoke of digging a great canal from New York City to Buffalo on Lake Erie. The project was approved by the New York legislature in 1817, and it was completed in 1825. Running 363 miles, it was a spectacular engineering achievement and a testament to American labor.

Voice of the Century

"We have met the enemy and they are ours."

—Oliver Hazard Perry announcing victory over the British fleet on Lake Erie. (In the 1960s, the popular comic-strip character Pogo converted this classic to "We have met the enemy, and they is us.")

It was also a stunning commercial triumph that quickly repaid the $7 million it had cost to build and returned an average of $3 million in annual profits—all without the assistance of the Federal government. The success of the canal, which truly inaugurated the *commercial* opening of the West, touched off a canal-building boom, linking the Northeast with the western system of natural waterways. By 1840, the United States boasted 3,326 miles of canals. The result was a trend toward commercial strength that helped pull the nation out of a postwar economic funk. The canals also tied the Northeast more securely to the West, thereby making deeper the growing division between North and the South, which had few east-west connections.

Ties That Bind

A government of high ideals, national pride, space to live and dream, and the stirrings of technology all contributed to create a great republic that was making its mark on the 19th century. They were the ties that bound a vast country into a nation.

But there were other ties as well: the bonds that held almost four million Americans in slavery's chains. Before the century was out, these bonds would be broken as the nation itself was torn apart. Once again, the world would watch and wait.

The Least You Need to Know

➤ America, the central actor in much of the 20th century, was the focus of world attention since its discovery in 1492.

➤ The vast territory acquired in the Louisiana Purchase, one of history's greatest real estate bargains, was initially seen as a place in which to segregate the Indians from the Euro-American population.

➤ The American identification with liberty is in large part the product of the country's physical vastness.

➤ The great distances of American space have helped to mold an American character and have spurred the development of technologies to span those distances effectively.

Chapter 3

Century of Iron (1844–1859)

In This Chapter

➤ Invention of the telegraph

➤ The U.S.-Mexican War and its aftermath

➤ The age of Victoria

➤ Political turmoil in 1848

➤ Darwinism and Social Darwinism

America and the world approached the midpoint of the 19th century with a mixture of hope and despair. The times were marked by burgeoning technology, miraculous invention, and relentless industrialization—all of which promised to make life better and easier.

In 1823, the Merrimack Manufacturing Company, a modern textile mill, had opened its doors in Lowell, Massachusetts, among the first modern factories in the United States. Soon, the new factories of the North were providing an unprecedented array of goods, making items of necessity as well as the trappings of luxury available to more people than ever before. But they also transformed pleasant rural hamlets into grim mill towns. Providing employment to many, that employment was typically grueling, grim, and soul numbing.

Grueling? Grim? Soul numbing? These would be mild adjectives applied to "employment" in the agricultural South. Black slavery, which had come to North America as early as 1619, continued to flourish in a land founded on the precepts of liberty. Some whites favored slavery, many opposed it, but few realized that, black or white, *all* were enslaved—dragged by iron chains into a war as terrible as it was inevitable.

This chapter looks at some of the 19th century's most intensely promising and turbulent themes.

More Revolutions

The 1840s was a decade of ferment, of technological, political, and social revolution. Typically, technology, politics, and social change were closely linked. For example, in the 1830s, Cyrus McCormick patented a new reaper and John Deere a new steel plow. By the 1840s, these products were being manufactured on a full-scale industrial level, and they revolutionized American agricultural life, making large-scale farming possible at a time when huge tracts of land were opening in the Midwest and West. Without the Deere plow, it is doubtful that the stubborn prairie soil could have been made profitable, and without an efficient reaper, no one farmer could harvest sufficient acreage to take advantage of the cheap land west of the Mississippi.

Talk of the Times

A **plow** is an implement for breaking up the ground and cutting the furrows in which seeds may be sown. A **reaper** harvests the mature crop.

The new farmers of the Midwest and West, established by the reaper and plow and controlling so much land, became a powerful political force, wielding more clout than frontier settlers had before. To be sure, the centers of political and economic power were still concentrated in the East, but more wealth and power than ever before was moving westward. The nation was truly democratizing.

Dots and Dashes

Once again, issues of coping with space and distance became pressing. With population spreading, how would the nation be held together? As solidarity along the nation's North-South axis was progressively eroded by the slavery issue, Americans looked for other ways to bind the nation.

Enter Samuel F.B. Morse. The son of a prominent clergyman, Morse was born in Charlestown, Massachusetts, in 1791, was educated at Yale University, and traveled to Europe to study the history of painting in the grand tradition. He quickly became an accomplished artist but found little demand for his work when he returned to the United States.

Talk of the Times

Telegraph means "distant writing," or writing over distance, and was coined by Samuel F.B. Morse to describe his 1844 invention, which revolutionized communication in the United States and the rest of the world.

He went back to Europe in 1829, hoping that artistic recognition there would boost his career at home. That did not happen, but on the voyage back to the United States, he chatted with a fellow passenger, a scientist named Thomas Jackson. As a result of these conversations, Morse hit upon the idea of using electrical current as a medium through which communication might be transmitted. He abandoned his artistic career and set about inventing the telegraph as well as devising a coded system of "dots" and "dashes" for transmitting language with the device.

After much labor, Morse perfected his instrument, essentially an electromagnet that when energized by a current, drew down an iron armature that inscribed on a piece of paper the dot and dash symbols of "Morse code." He next persuaded Congress to finance a wire between Washington, D.C., and Baltimore, and, on May 24, 1844, he transmitted the first telegraphic message over that wire: "What hath God wrought?"

Samuel F.B. Morse, bearing medals representing some of the many honors the world conferred upon him.
(Image from arttoday.com)

Within a decade, the 40 miles of wire strung between Washington and Baltimore had grown to 23,000 miles of network crisscrossing the nation. Instantaneous communication was suddenly a reality, and space and distance, always the nation's blessing and burden, promised now to become an unalloyed boon.

In the Halls of Montezuma

The wires of Morse's new invention would soon have something to hum about. Texas, which had been settled in the late 1820s by Stephen Austin as what amounted to an American colony of Mexico, won its independence from Mexico after a brief war in 1836. The new Texas Republic sought annexation to the United States, but Congress demurred; annexation would add another slave state to the union, bringing the nation a step closer to dissolution and civil war. Moreover, annexation would surely ignite war with Mexico.

Then, France and England made overtures of alliance with Texas, and, fearing the arrival of Europeans and European armies on the American doorstep, outgoing President John Tyler urged Congress to adopt an annexation resolution. Tyler's successor, James K. Polk, admitted Texas to the Union on December 29, 1845.

Voice of the Century

"If a thousand men were not to pay their tax-bills this year, that would not be a violent and bloody measure, as it would be to pay them and enable the State to commit violence and shed innocent blood. This is, in fact, the definition of a peaceable revolution, if any such is possible."

—Henry David Thoreau, *On the Duty of Civil Disobedience* (1849). Thoreau refused to pay his poll tax, a gesture of protest against the U.S.-Mexican War.

Talk of the Times

Manifest Destiny is a phrase coined by *Democratic Review* editor John L. O'Sullivan in 1845, which came to describe the sense, shared by most 19th-century Americans, that the United States was divinely destined to encompass the entire continent.

In the meantime, England and France also seemed to be eyeing California, held so feebly by Mexico that it looked ripe and ready to fall into the hands of anyone there to catch it.

President Polk offered Mexico $40 million for California. The Mexican president not only turned down the offer, but also insultingly refused even to see Polk's emissary, whereupon Polk commissioned the U.S. consul at Monterey (California), Thomas O. Larkin, to organize the territory's small but powerful American community into an active separatist movement. In the meantime, John Charles Frémont, intrepid explorer surveying potential transcontinental railroad routes, fomented the so-called Bear Flag Rebellion, and California's independence from Mexico was proclaimed.

California's independence fueled the flames of a smoldering dispute over the boundary of the new state of Texas, and from this, the U.S.-Mexican War began on May 13, 1846. The telegraph came alive with the news.

In the Northeast, especially in New England, the war was unpopular. People saw it as an unfair and un-American war of aggression. But in the South and West, the U.S.-Mexican War was greeted with wild enthusiasm. Recruiting offices in these regions were overwhelmed with volunteers and had to turn eager men away.

Those who supported the war were animated by one of those instantly famous phrases that ring and echo through American history. In 1845, *Democratic Review* editor John L. O'Sullivan wrote, "It is our manifest destiny to overspread and to possess the whole of the continent which Providence has given us for the development of the great experiment of liberty and federated self-government entrusted to us." Under the banner of *"Manifest Destiny,"* the American West would be won—notwithstanding the obstinate prairie soil, the harsh elements, the lives of the Indians, and the rights of Mexico.

The war itself was one-sided. Led by a series of incompetent commanders and, finally, by the dictator Antonio López de Santa Anna—the boldest and most inept of all—the

Mexican army suffered defeat after defeat against U.S. forces that possessed fewer numbers but were under the command of such skilled generals as Zachary Taylor and Winfield Scott.

Contemporary sketches of scenes from the U.S.-Mexican War. Few U.S. soldiers of the period were so neatly uniformed as these.
(Images from the author's collection)

Although a U.S. "Army of the West" conquered what had been Mexico's northern provinces in California, New Mexico, and Arizona, and an "Army of the Center"

29

secured the Texas-Mexico borderlands, Taylor led an "Army of Occupation" deep into Mexico itself. He attacked Monterrey (Mexico) on September 20, 1846, taking the city after a four-day siege and then facing a January 1847 offensive led by Santa Anna with 18,000 men, some 15,000 of whom he hurled against Taylor's 4,800-man army at Buena Vista. After two days of bloody battle, the outnumbered Taylor forced Santa Anna's withdrawal on February 23.

At this point, President Polk, distressed lest Taylor's victories make a military celebrity out of a potential political rival, replaced him with Winfield Scott, who had no political ambitions. On March 9, Scott invaded Vera Cruz, ultimately pushing the Mexican forces all the way to Mexico City. On September 13, Chapultepec Palace, the seemingly impregnable fortress guarding Mexico City, and now defended by a force that included teenage cadets (celebrated in Mexican history as "Los Niños," the children), fell to Scott. On September 17, Santa Anna surrendered, and the Treaty of Guadalupe Hidalgo (ratified by the Senate on March 10, 1848) was negotiated, whereby Mexico ceded to the United States New Mexico (which also included parts of the present states of Utah, Nevada, Arizona, and Colorado) and California. The Mexicans also renounced claims to Texas above the Rio Grande.

Century Stats

As wars go, the U.S.-Mexican War was comparatively cheap. In dollars, it cost the United States 4 percent of its gross national product. Compare the cost of World War II: 188 percent of the GNP.

Voice of the Century

"Other nations use 'force'; we Britons alone use 'might.'"

—Novelist Evelyn Waugh (1903–66) on the British attitude toward imperial conquest

Victoria Triumphant

The United States emerged from the U.S.-Mexican War with a vast western empire. But the new American empire was still a distant second to the greatest and most admired empire of all.

By the middle of the 19th century, Britain had extensive colonies that included Canada and the islands of the Caribbean, as well as holdings in the Far East and Africa. The Indian subcontinent was the giant "jewel in the British crown." And the British Empire—so vast, it was rightly said, that the sun never set upon it—would expand even more through the end of the century.

England was (and remains) a parliamentary monarchy, essentially democratic, though ostensibly subject to a king or queen. The monarch who reigned over most of the 19th century, from 1837 to 1901, was Queen Victoria. Not England alone, but most the world, saw Victoria as the leading symbol of the century.

Just why Victoria was personally identified with so much of the century is one of history's mysteries. She bore nine children but was a cold, emotionally distant mother who earnestly disliked infants and youngsters; yet the "Victorian Age" idealized motherhood. The latter two thirds of her century were marked by profound social reforms; yet an arch conservative, Victoria either resisted them or greeted them with studied indifference. Queen of a nation in the forefront of science, industry, and technology, Victoria lost no opportunity to voice her distaste for innovation of any kind.

20th-Century Life

Born in 1819, Victoria ascended the throne as queen of Great Britain and Ireland in 1837 and was subsequently crowned empress of India as well. In 1840, she married her first cousin, Prince Albert, to whom she was intensely devoted and after whose death in 1861 she plunged into three years of deepest mourning. The widowed queen never remarried.

Victoria lacked great intellect, wit, or charm. Yet she was immensely popular, not only with Britons, but with peoples of many countries. Her reign, ending with her death in 1901, was the longest in English history—and among the most eventful, witnessing the rise of industrialism at home and imperialism abroad. Her image and presence so thoroughly pervaded the last two thirds of the 19th century that it is universally known as the Victorian Age.

Queen Victoria was a motherly presence to England and the world—although she, despite being the mother of nine children, personally detested motherhood. (Image from arttoday.com)

The Year 1848

Perhaps it was the aura of serene—indeed, aloof—stability Victoria projected that accounts for her enormous popularity, for never had the Old World's old guard more reason to feel threatened. Much of the continent was swept by revolution.

Take the year 1848. At the time, France, like England, was a parliamentary monarchy. But the right to vote was enjoyed only by well-to-do property owners. Discontent had simmered for years, and on February 22, 1848, a large protest banquet was arranged to demand *universal manhood suffrage*. Francois Pierre Guillaume Guizot, the French premier, caught wind of the planned event and issued a decree forbidding the banquet.

Bad idea.

Talk of the Times

Universal manhood suffrage is the right of all male citizens, above a certain minimum age, to vote.

Guizot's provocative decree touched off a popular revolution that forced Emperor Louis Phillippe to abdicate just two days later. Although radical, socialist, and even anarchist voices made themselves heard, the people of France steered a very conservative course, electing Louis Napoleon Bonaparte, nephew of the late Emperor Napoleon I, as president of the "Second Republic of France. Ultimately, Louis Napoleon would make himself emperor as well.

The tumult in France touched off Italian rebellion against their Austrian overlords. In 1848, Hungary also rebelled against Austria, to which it had been subject for some 150 years. Austrian Emperor Ferdinand I, on April 25, granted Hungary representation in the imperial government, whereupon the Czechs, also under the Austrian thumb, clamored for a measure of independence. (Hungarians continued to fight for full independence, but the movement was crushed by the intervention of Russia in 1849.)

Revolutionary winds swept throughout Germany as well in 1848, sparking a movement for unification of the disparate German states. It, too, soon fizzled.

Darwin Looks at Life

Thanks to liberal reforms peacefully enacted in the previous decade, Great Britain weathered the political storms ravaging the continent. But one of the empire's subjects was about to stir a revolutionary tempest of a different kind.

Charles Darwin was born in Shrewsbury in 1809, the son of a prominent physician. When young Charles proved uninterested in medicine, his father pushed him into training for the ministry, but Charles nevertheless found time to pursue his interest in biology. He was befriended by botanist John Stevens Henslow, who secured Darwin an unpaid position as naturalist on board the HMS *Beagle,* which set sail on a survey of the east and west coasts of South America and the Pacific islands. Darwin embarked in 1831 and spent the next five years observing and collecting specimens of plant and animal life. He was especially fascinated and disturbed by what he observed on the Galapagos Islands. The birds and tortoises of the islands nearest the mainland clearly resembled species found on the nearby continent, whereas those of similar islands farther out were quite different.

He wrestled with this puzzle, at last concluding that species changed from one place to another and from one era to the next. This in itself was revolutionary because the Bible (and many naturalists) said that all of the animal and plant species had been created at one time and by one God. But Darwin's conclusions went even further into revolutionary territory, as he wrote in his *Autobiography*, "Favourable variations would tend to be preserved, and unfavourable ones to be destroyed.... The result of this would be the formation of new species."

This was the core idea of the book he published in 1859, *On the Origin of Species by Means of Natural Selection, or the Preservation of Favored Races in the Struggle for Life*. The title and subtitle summarize his controlling idea: Only organisms best adapted to their environment survive the struggle for life and produce offspring. Those less well adapted do not survive; their line ends, and the species becomes extinct. The surviving species, in all their variety, are the plants and animals we know.

Many found this view not only sacrilegious, but also simply disturbing. The poet Alfred, Lord Tennyson, was revolted by Darwin's picture of "nature red in tooth and claw," a natural world in a state of continual revolution, far more disturbing than the political events of 1848 had been. For survival was seen not as the product of divine plan, but as a matter of competitive edge. Variations—in structure, in agility, in keenness of senses, in food requirements, and so on—exist between species and between members of the same species. On average, those species and individual organisms possessing variations that better suit them to compete will survive and reproduce. On average, those lacking these qualities will die and fail to reproduce. Over time, the most useful variations will tend to be perpetuated and developed because more individuals possessing these variations will survive to reproduce than individuals that do not possess these variations.

"Natural selection," as Darwin called the prime mover of species evolution, is all about *random* variations that prove useful over time. Things average out. What works lives. What doesn't dies. Without plan. Without morality. Without mercy.

Talk of the Times

Developed as a theory by the biologist Charles Darwin, **natural selection**, the principal vehicle of species evolution, describes the operation of random variation that enables a species to survive in its environment.

Hard Times

Not since the end of the Middle Ages, when Copernicus unseated the earth from the center of the solar system, had a scientific idea provoked more anguish and controversy yet advanced knowledge further than natural selection.

Religious leaders denounced evolution. Scientists found the idea intensely exciting. Certain social thinkers and industrial capitalists used it to justify brutal and exploitive business practices. If nature was ruled by the principle of survival of the fittest, they argued, why shouldn't the same "natural" principle govern society?

Social reformers called for government money to help the poor. They called on industrialists to pay higher wages, to shorten working hours, and to humanize the tedium and ceaseless toil of their factories and mills. Backed by philosophers such as Herbert Spencer, some of the capitalists responded to such pleas with *social Darwinism*: In society as in nature, the fittest would survive (as they should), and the weak (as *they* should) would die.

Ebenezer Scrooge, capitalist protagonist of Charles Dickens's *A Christmas Carol* (1843) turned away a plea for charity by saying that if the poor would die if he did not help them, they'd "better get on with it and decrease the surplus population."

Talk of the Times

Social Darwinism is the use of Charles Darwin's concept of survival of the fittest in nature to justify—in society—the economic success of one class at the expense of another.

Dickens (1812–70) became the most popular storyteller of his age in part by portraying the dark, heartless side of the Victorian era. The very worst aspects of life in the industrial 19th century he summed up in *Hard Times* (1854), a portrait of life and death in Coketown, a fictional portrayal of one of the industrial hell holes that pocked the face of Victorian England.

The scars of Coketown were some of the uglier physical manifestations of the changes that, for better as well as for worse, were sweeping the world. In the United States, those changes would take the particularly devastating form of a great civil war.

The Least You Need to Know

➤ As political and economic issues divided the people of the 19th century, technology, in the form of the telegraph, brought them together.

➤ The U.S.-Mexican War polarized the nation: Some thought it was an unjust act of imperialism, whereas others believed it was the righteous realization of the United States' "Manifest Destiny" to rule the continent.

➤ England's Queen Victoria, in so many ways out of touch with the dynamism of the 19th century, came to be so closely identified with the era that two thirds of the century is called the Victorian Age.

➤ The mid-19th century was rocked by political and scientific revolution. In 1848, governments in France, Italy, Austria, and Germany were threatened, and in 1859, Darwin published his *Origin of Species*.

Chapter 4

A Nation Torn and Reborn (1860–1869)

In This Chapter

➤ The Civil War

➤ Homesteaders and sodbusters

➤ The age of the cowboy

➤ Completion of the Atlantic Cable and the Union Pacific

As hard iron realities dimmed England's vision of a Victorian golden age, so slavery, in the United States, ate away at the American dream of the universal rights to life, liberty, and the pursuit of happiness.

Liberty Compromised

The U.S. Constitution had failed to abolish slavery, and, year after year, the integrity of the union came to depend on somehow maintaining a tenuous balance between the interests of slaveholding states and states that were free. Between 1818–19, the Missouri Territory petitioned for statehood as a slaveholding state, threatening to tip the balance in favor of slaveholding interests.

Representative James Tallmadge of New York responded to Missouri's petition by introducing an amendment to the statehood bill calling for a ban on the further introduction of slavery into the state and for the emancipation of all slaves born in the state when they reached 25 years of age. Thus, gradually, slavery would be eliminated from Missouri. The House passed the amendment, but the Senate rejected it. When Congress reconvened the following year, a tortured debate ensued. At last, in March 1820, a complex compromise was reached: Missouri would be allowed to join the

Union as a slave state, but simultaneously, Maine (hitherto a part of Massachusetts) would be admitted as a free state. Looking toward the future, the Missouri Compromise provided that a line would be drawn across the Louisiana Territory at a latitude of 36° 30', north of which slavery would be forever banned, except in the case of Missouri.

John Quincy Adams, recoiling from the bitter debate, called the Missouri Compromise the "title page to a great tragic volume," and the aged Thomas Jefferson said that the furor over Missouri, "like a fire bell in the night, awakened and filled me with terror."

More compromise would follow over the years, but inexorably, the nation drew apart. With the election of Abraham Lincoln—a "black Republican," as Southerners called him—in 1860, the Southern states began seceding from the union, declaring themselves the Confederate States of America.

In the North, opinion was divided. Lincoln's own secretary of state, William H. Seward, advised the President to "let the erring sisters go," but Lincoln insisted that federal authority and property would be protected, and he refused to order the evacuation of Fort Sumter in Charleston Bay. Accordingly, on April 12, 1861, at 4:30 in the morning, a Capt. George S. James fired a signal shot, and one Edmund Ruffin, a 67-year-old rural Virginia newspaper editor and rabid defender of slavery, pulled the lanyard on the first artillery piece directed against Sumter. The Civil War had begun.

After 4,000 rounds had been fired through Saturday the 13th, the fort's commandant, Maj. Robert Anderson, at last surrendered. He was accorded full military courtesy by his Confederate opponent, Gen. Pierre Gustave Toutant Beauregard, and, incredibly, no one had been hurt in bombardment.

Edmund Ruffin (1794–1865), a rural Virginia newspaper editor and ardent advocate of secession, claimed credit for firing the first shot against Fort Sumter, 4:30 A.M., April 12, 1861. (Image from the National Archives)

The fiercely chivalrous spectacle gave no hint of just how horrible and costly the rest of the war would be: at least a half million battle deaths; many more lives shattered by wounds inflicted by the weapons of an industrial age; untold poverty, misery, anguish, and illness; and, finally, the martyr's death of the Union's leader, Abraham Lincoln, the victim (absurdly enough) of an egomaniacal actor.

Although the population and industrial might of the North far outweighed the technology and numbers the South could muster, the cream of the U.S. Army officer corps felt allegiance to the Southern states, and the Confederate forces were, in the main, more ably commanded than those of the North, especially early in the war. The Confederates stunned Union loyalists with victories:

➤ Bull Run, or Manassas, as the Confederates called it, July 21, 1861. Spectators who'd driven out to picnic and watch a Union victory were chased back to Washington along with their beaten soldiers.

➤ The so-called Seven Days battles, during Union commander George B. McClellan's Peninsular Campaign, an attempt to take Richmond by sailing down the Chesapeake and marching upon it from the south.

➤ The Second Battle of Bull Run, or Second Manassas, August 29–30, 1862.

➤ Fredericksburg, December 13, 1862, a costly defeat in which Gen. Ambrose E. Burnside ordered repeated Union charges against an impregnable Confederate position.

➤ Chancellorsville, May 2–4, 1863, Robert E. Lee's "masterpiece," a brilliant victory achieved by dividing his army twice and sending Stonewall Jackson to march around Gen. Joseph E. Hooker and surprise him from the rear.

It was not until Antietam (Sharpsburg), on September 17, 1862, that the Union was able to claim something approaching a victory—albeit one purchased at tremendous cost. The outcome of the battle gave the Union military effort sufficient credibility to enable Lincoln to issue, from what he felt was a position of strength, the preliminary Emancipation Proclamation. For the Union, the Civil War now took on an added moral dimension, officially becoming more than a struggle to save the Union. It was now a crusade to abolish slavery. When General Robert E. Lee invaded Pennsylvania, Union forces under General George G. Meade turned back the Confederate army at Gettysburg (July 1–3, 1863), the largest battle ever fought on American soil, also at great cost.

Gettysburg was the turning point of the war in favor of the Union. Not only was an invading army

Voice of the Century

"In giving freedom to the slave, we assure freedom to the free—honorable alike in what we give and what we preserve."

—Abraham Lincoln (1809–65), Annual Message to Congress, December 1, 1862 repulsed and Northern morale lifted, but also the Southern defeat discouraged both England and France from supporting the Confederate cause, the cause of slavery.

Yet the war bled on. Union General Ulysses S. Grant scored important triumphs in the conflict's western theater, at Shiloh (April 6–7, 1862), Vicksburg (under siege from October 1862 to July 4, 1863), and Chattanooga (November 23–25, 1863). Union control of the lower Mississippi River began with the victory of Admiral David Farragut, who captured New Orleans in April 1862. In 1864, after running through a series of well-meaning but variously mediocre commanding generals, Lincoln finally appointed Grant as the Union's general-in-chief.

Not until the fourth year of the war did Abraham Lincoln find a general capable of decisively defeating the Confederate army and the Southern cause: Ulysses S. Grant. (Image from the Library of Congress)

Copyright, 1891, by M. P. Rice, 1217-19-21 Penna. Avenue, Washington, D. C.

GENERAL U. S. GRANT.

From the only original unretouched negative, made in 1864, at the time he was commissioned by Abraham Lincoln Lieut. General of all the Armies of the Republic. It was suggested that this negative (with that of Abraham Lincoln) be made in commemoration of that event.

Talk of the Times

Total war is the policy of waging war against an entire people, combatants and non-combatants alike, with the object of destroying the enemy's will to fight.

Slowly and with the spilling of much blood, Grant forced Lee's army back toward the Confederate capital of Richmond, fighting the bitter Wilderness Campaign through May and June of 1864.

Meanwhile, Grant's chief lieutenant, General William Tecumseh Sherman, advanced through Tennessee and Georgia to Atlanta, which he captured, occupied, and finally burned (September–November 1864) before continuing on his infamously punitive and destructive "March to the Sea."

A brilliant strategist, Sherman introduced a concept that would become a terrifying hallmark of warfare in the next century. He didn't use the term himself, but it would be called it *"total war"*: battle waged not just against the opposing army, but against the civilian population as well, with the object of reducing the nation's will and means to support the fight.

If the means of the South were always slim at best, its will was not easy to break. Fighting continued as Union General Philip Sheridan defeated Confederate General George E. Pickett at Five Forks (April 1, 1865), and Grant took heavily fortified Petersburg after a long siege that stretched from June 1864 to April 2, 1865. On that date, Grant at last took Richmond. A week later, at Appomattox Courthouse, General Robert E. Lee surrendered his Army of Northern Virginia to General Grant, effectively ending the Civil War.

Century Stats

By the end of the war, 2,128,948 men had served in the Union army, of whom 359,528 are known to have died. The strength of the Confederate army was probably a little over a million, of whom at least 200,000 died.

20th-Century Life

Grant's description of the surrender in the McLean house at Appomattox Courthouse has a warmth that belies the bitterness of the war:

"What General Lee's feelings were I do not know. As he was a man of much dignity, with an impassable face, it was impossible to say ...; my own feelings, which had been quite jubilant on the receipt of his letter [of surrender], were sad and depressed. I felt like anything rather than rejoicing at the downfall of a foe who had fought so long and valiantly, and had suffered so much for a cause, though that cause was, I believe, one of the worst for which a people ever fought ....

"We soon fell into a conversation about old army times .... Our conversation grew so pleasant that I almost forgot the object of our meeting. ... General Lee called my attention to the object of our meeting, and said that he had asked for this interview for the purpose of getting from me the terms I proposed to give his army. I said that I meant merely that his army should lay down their arms, not to take them up again during the continuance of the war unless duly and properly exchanged."

Healing the wounds of war and reuniting the nation were heartbreakingly formidable tasks that would require the wise and charitable judgment and strong leadership of

Abraham Lincoln. His assassination on April 14, 1865, at the hands of John Wilkes Booth, a fanatical Southern sympathizer, was the crowning tragedy of the Civil War.

The unpopular Andrew Johnson was thrust into office, and the process of Reconstruction—bringing the late Confederate states back into the Union—became a struggle as vindictive as it was opportunistic. The "Radical Republicans" who controlled Congress wanted not only to punish the South, but also to keep Southern Democrats out of power as long as possible. The heritage of Reconstruction greatly prolonged the sufferings of the South, crippling its economy so severely that the ill effects were felt well into the 20th century. Worse, the process left behind a virulent strain of racism that would prove nearly as great a national curse as slavery had been.

Two faces of war: Confederate private Edwin Francis Jamieson, 2d Louisiana Regiment (killed in 1862), and a Union drummer boy, also from Louisiana, known to history only as "Taylor," 78th U.S. Colored Troops.
(Images from the Library of Congress and the National Archives)

Frontiers

Even as war clouds gathered and during the worst of the conflict between North and South, the great American West remained a vision of virgin land, a promise of a new start in a place as yet unspoiled. The first important western migrations were fueled by religious fervor: In 1843, the missionary Marcus Whitman led 200 families in the "Great Migration" to Oregon. In 1847–48, the Mormon leader Brigham Young led far more religious seekers to the Great Salt Lake in present-day Utah. Also in 1848, James Marshall, an employee of Northern California rancher John Sutter, found gold in Sutter's millrace. Within a year, the discovery triggered a great "Gold Rush," as people from all walks of life in all parts of the country quite literally dropped whatever they had been doing and made the arduous trek to California in search of their fortune.

An Empire of Sod

Few struck it rich in the California gold fields, but the influx of seekers swelled California's population to a quarter million. Still, the Gold Rush migration left much of the vast space between California and the Mississippi unsettled. On May 20, 1862, at a low point for the Union in the Civil War, President Lincoln signed the Homestead Act into law, authorizing any citizen (or immigrant who intended to become a citizen) to select any surveyed but unclaimed parcel of public land up to 160 acres, settle and improve it, and, by living on it for 5 years, gain free title to it.

Thanks to John Deere's steel plow, it was possible for a *"sodbuster"*—as the homesteaders were often called—to break up and farm the stubborn prairie soil. How the sodbuster's family coped with the harsh elements of the prairie— the raw winter cold, the parching summer drought, and the isolation in all seasons—was a matter of faith, will, and character. The important point was that the sodbusters were, in overwhelming numbers, *families*. Up to this time, most westerners had been solitary trappers, bachelor soldiers, lone trailblazers, or unattached prospectors. Sodbusters came to stay and to build.

First thing, the sodbuster usually "built" little more than a hole in the ground, called a *dugout*. A rectangle was laid out on a rising slope of land, and sod was excavated to a depth of about six feet. Next, using "bricks" cut from the sod, walls were raised to a height of two or three feet, and the structure was roofed over with boards or thatch and more sod. Later, as the family became more settled, it would build a more substantial house above ground, complete with windows, but still using sod for bricks. "Soddies," as the houses were called, were filthy and vermin infested, but they were cool in summer and warm and secure against the brutal prairie winters.

Talk of the Times

Sodbuster was the name given to settlers of the prairie, who typically built their first houses, or **dugouts**, out of the material most readily available: the prairie sod.

And an Empire of Cows

The saga of the sodbusters is full of grit (*plenty* of grit) and heroic determination. It is an important part of the nation's western heritage. Yet it hardly fires the imagination the way another of the era's agricultural laborers does.

The story of the cowboy starts this way: Young Texans went off to fight the Civil War on the side of the Confederacy, leaving behind their livestock to roam the grasslands freely. At the end of the war, with the Southern economy shattered, the men—no longer quite as young—returned to their homes. Some were Texas natives; some were Southerners from other states who came west. Either way, they had precious few opportunities and even fewer possessions. They came to Texas to round up strays—millions of head now—brand them, and drive them to market up north.

The trail-drive cattle industry was born, and if any one man can be said to have started the enterprise, it was Charlie Goodnight. Born on a southern Illinois farm in 1836, Goodnight came to the Brazos River country of Texas with his family in 1845. There, in a land of longhorns running wild, he learned to be a cowboy. With his stepbrother as partner, he put together a small herd, only to leave for the war. Mustered out of the Texas Rangers a year before the war ended, Goodnight and his stepbrother delightedly discovered that the 180 head they had left now numbered 5,000.

At this time, most ranchmen were starting to drive their cattle to Kansas railheads for shipment east. With Oliver Loving, an old-time cattleman, Goodnight decided to move in the other direction, pioneering a trail to Colorado, where mining operations and Indian-fighting military outposts were creating a tremendous demand for beef. In 1866, Goodnight and Loving gathered 2,000 of their longhorns and, with 18 riders, followed the Southern Overland Mail route to the head of the Concho River, where they liberally watered their stock for the long, dry trip across the desert. They lost some 400 head on the trail—300 of thirst, 100 trampled to death in a water-hole stampede—but the first drive along what became the Goodnight-Loving Trail netted the partners $12,000 in gold.

The Goodnight-Loving Trail was one of four principal cattle trails, which also included

➤ The Chisholm, from Brownsville, Texas, to the Kansas railheads of Dodge City, Ellsworth, Abilene, and Junction City.

➤ The Shawnee, from Brownsville to Kansas City, Sedalia, and St. Louis, Missouri.

➤ The Western, from San Antonio, Texas, to Dodge City and then on to Fort Buford, at the fork of the Missouri and Yellowstone rivers, deep in Dakota Territory.

Between 1866, when Loving and Goodnight cut their trail, and 1886–87, when a single horrific winter virtually wiped out the range-cattle industry, almost 100 million cattle and 10 million horses traversed these great trails.

But the trail drives produced more than beef. It gave birth to the trail-drive cowboy, surely the most beloved and celebrated worker in American history, an American knight, noble and brave, and, most of all, beholden to no one, in a country far from politicians, plutocrats, and police.

Or so goes our cherished myth. Seen another way, cowboys were typically the poorest of the poor—men like the Confederate veterans, who had been dispossessed of family, friends, and all they had owned. Some were loners or misfits, who could hold no other job. Many were African Americans, Indians, and Mexicans, who occupied the lowest rungs on the nation's racist socioeconomic ladder. Yet these realities hardly dim a powerful romance that refuses to fade.

Atlantic Cable

While cowboys rode the range roping strays, visionaries in Europe and the United States were considering a different kind of rope—a cable to carry telegraph messages across the Atlantic Ocean. Within a few years after the telegraph had been invented, telegraph cable had been laid under the Hudson and Mississippi Rivers and even under the English Channel and the Irish Sea. In 1854, the American oceanographer Matthew Fontaine Maury concluded that the Atlantic was shallower in the center than on either side. He concluded that this was due to the existence of a central plateau, which he dubbed the Telegraph Plateau, identifying it as an ideal perch for a cable connecting Europe with America.

Within four years, ships reeled out a cable, which did function—for a time—but it wasn't until 1867 that the *Great Eastern*, first of the new steam-driven ocean liners (almost 700 feet long), laid a permanent cable, financed largely by U.S. entrepreneur Cyrus West Field.

Talk of the Times

Isolationism is a national policy of avoiding political ties with other nations.

The cable was a great engineering feat and a boon to communication. It also had profound political consequences as an important step toward ending the attitude of *isolationism* that had prevailed in the United States ever since President George Washington had cautioned against becoming involved in "foreign entanglements."

Union Pacific

Back on dry land during this period, the transcontinental railroad, a project dreamed of almost as soon as railroads had been introduced to America, was nearing completion. With the North and South torn apart by war, President Lincoln and Congress were anxious to bind the nation together East and West. The Railway Act of 1862 granted huge tracts of land to the railroad and made mammoth construction loans. Subsequent legislation gave the railroads even more, but the project seemed to falter.

Lincoln summoned to his office a multimillionaire congressman popularly known as the "King of Spades." Oakes Ames had built his family's shovel-making business into a giant industrial concern.

Lincoln called on Ames to rescue the railroad. In response, Ames created a corporation to build the railroad and another corporation to finance construction. The latter was named Credit Mobilier, after the company that had successfully financed the French railway system 10 years earlier. Credit Mobilier, *run* by the directors (principal investors) of the Union Pacific, was *paid* by the Union Pacific to *build* the Union Pacific, the directors making a profit on the railroad as well as on the cost of building it. The scheme got the railroad built, but it was an open door to fraud and created one of the great scandals of the 19th century.

No scandal could diminish the heroic dimensions of building the transcontinental railroad. Under the leadership of Grenville Mellon Dodge and another ex-army general, John Stephen Casement, the Union Pacific began laying prodigious lengths of track—266 miles in 1866 alone—set into place mostly by unskilled Irish immigrants, who received, in addition to their pay, room and board. On the Central Pacific, the bulk of the workforce was Chinese, who were paid at about the same rate but had to furnish their own tents and their own food.

Laying and spiking 500-pound rail sections was difficult enough, but these men—some 25,000 in all—faced other perils as well: summer floods, winter blizzards, and avalanche; attack from Sioux and Cheyenne, as the rails penetrated their hunting grounds in western Nebraska and southeastern Wyoming; and simple exhaustion. Bosses had no love for Irish immigrants and even less for Chinese "coolies" and drove their workers relentlessly, heedless of life and limb.

At last, the ceremonial union of the two lines at Promontory Summit was set for May 8, 1869. Leland Stanford, CEO of the Central Pacific, almost failed to arrive because of a train wreck, and Thomas C. Durant, head of the Union Pacific, was kidnapped en route by tie cutters his company had not paid for months. Durant telegraphed for money and was released, delaying the ceremony by two days.

Century Stats

Construction of the transcontinental railroad took seven years; the Union Pacific laid 1,086 miles of track, and the Central Pacific (which faced the most difficult mountain terrain), 689.

It was on May 10, 1869, that workers and executives alike prepared to savor their great moment. It did not go quite as planned. Chinese laborers, acutely aware of how Caucasians felt about them, were lowering the last rail into place when a photographer hollered, "Shoot!" They dropped the quarter-ton rail and ran.

Then, Leland Stanford himself stepped up to join the last eastbound and westbound rails. He poised himself to drive home a commemorative Golden Spike, wired to the telegraph, so that each blow would be transmitted across the nation. He raised the heavy sledge, brought it down—and clean missed. Laborers assisted him, and the deed was finally done. From sea to shining sea, the United States was bound by bands of iron.

Director Cecil B. De Mille recreated the driving of the Golden Spike in his 1939 epic film Union Pacific. The original event took place on May 10, 1869. (Image from the author's collection)

The Least You Need to Know

➤ Promoting settlement of the West by means of the Homestead Act of 1862, in the midst of the Civil War, was seen as a means of strengthening the Union.

➤ The cowboy, one of the most enduring figures of American popular culture, was born in the great trail drives that followed the Civil War.

➤ The sodbusters, gritty settlers of the Great Plains, never claimed the cowboy's share of romantic myth, but were even more important than the cowboy in the settlement of the West.

➤ The Atlantic Cable was an important technological step toward ending any possibility of U.S. isolationism.

➤ Construction of the Union Pacific, plagued by political and financial scandal, was nevertheless a heroic achievement, which helped reunite a nation that had been torn apart by civil war.

Chapter 5

Through the Golden Door (1870–1899)

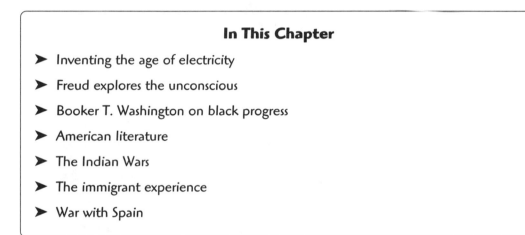

In This Chapter

➤ Inventing the age of electricity

➤ Freud explores the unconscious

➤ Booker T. Washington on black progress

➤ American literature

➤ The Indian Wars

➤ The immigrant experience

➤ War with Spain

The closing years of the 19th century were packed with change: epoch-making inventions that harnessed the force of electricity, new insights into the human mind, and new, sometimes profoundly disturbing, ideas of what it meant to be an American. This final chapter of Part 1 takes us to the doorstep of the 20th century.

Flipping Switches

We think of electricity as a hallmark of modern times. Yet electricity was known to the ancient Greeks, who were fascinated by how a piece of amber would attract small bits of straw if it were rubbed with animal fur. The very word *electric* means amber in Greek. Nevertheless, it wasn't until the late 19th century that inventors seized this strange force and made it do some useful work.

"Mr. Watson, Come Here"

Alexander Graham Bell (1847–1922) had been born in Scotland into a family of celebrated teachers of speech. Young Bell specialized in teaching the deaf to speak, and in 1872, he opened a school for the deaf in Boston, becoming a professor of speech and vocal physiology at Boston University the following year.

Bell had one of those minds that refuse to be confined to a single profession. His work with speech broadened into a more general interest in sound and the recording and transmission of sound. He began to reason that if he "could make a current of electricity vary in intensity precisely as the air varies in density during the production of sound," he could "transmit speech telegraphically."

Alexander Graham Bell. (Image from arttoday.com)

The vexing question, of course, was precisely *how* to convert sound waves into electrical impulses, but in 1876, after two years of work, Bell was sufficiently advanced in the development of a microphone and a speaker to apply for a patent. He filed the application before any speech had been actually carried across the wires.

Then, Bell suffered a minor laboratory accident. While making adjustments to his prototype, the inventor knocked a beaker of battery acid into his lap. As the sulfuric acid burned clothes and flesh, Bell called into the instrument on his workbench, summoning his assistant, Thomas Watson, who was bent over the receiver in another room: "Mr. Watson, come here. I want you."

Talk of the Times

The word **telephone**, made up of Greek roots meaning "afar" and "voice," was actually in use before Bell's invention. As early as 1835, it described a megaphone-like instrument.

So it was that the first words spoken over the telephone were a call for help, as if to demonstrate, from the very beginning, just how indispensable the instrument would become.

"Mary Had a Little Lamb"

Although Bell had to fight off a number of legal challenges to his telephone patent, he prevailed, grew rich, and commanded the admiration of the world. Yet he did not ignite the popular imagination quite so brilliantly as his contemporary, Thomas Alva Edison.

Whereas Bell was highly educated, a distinguished professor at a major university, Edison, an indifferent student, socially awkward and isolated in part because of partial deafness resulting from a childhood injury, had dropped out of grade school. As a youth, he made his way as a "news butcher," selling candy and newspapers to railroad passengers—newspapers he printed himself on a press mounted in the baggage car.

Thomas Alva Edison, the "Wizard of Menlo Park." (Image from the Henry Ford Museum)

As a boy, he was always a tinkerer, but what fascinated him most while working on the railroad was not the mechanics of the mighty locomotives, but the action of the telegraph key. He learned to send and receive code with prodigious speed and accuracy, which secured him a position as a railroad telegrapher, a job that turned his tinkering to electrical experimentation.

Edison's first invention was a practical success, but a commercial failure. He offered to the United States Congress a simple electric device for counting and recording votes.

49

The machine worked, and the congressmen were duly impressed—but, it turned out these politicians were in no hurry to have their votes efficiently counted and recorded. The old way of crying out the yeas and nays, followed by a show of hands, it seemed, bought the representatives the extra time they needed to persuade their colleagues to vote one way or the other.

Voice of the Century

"Genius is 1 percent inspiration and 99 percent perspiration."

—Thomas Alva Edison

After this experience, Edison vowed to make certain there was a need for a thing *before* he invented it. He turned next to the creation of an electric stock ticker, which the house of J.P. Morgan purchased for a sum lordly enough to allow Edison to pursue inventing full time. In 1874, he sold financier Jay Gould the rights to improvements to the telegraph, which netted Edison $100,000—the most that had ever been paid for an invention.

Edison set up a full-scale laboratory and workshop in Menlo Park, New Jersey. No doubt, he was a success, but he was an indifferent businessman, and his enterprise was always in need of fast cash. In 1876, Bell's newly invented telephone caused great excitement, but no one really thought of anything so wild as installing telephones in people's homes and businesses. No, the idea was to treat the telephone like the telegraph, residing in a central office in each city or neighborhood, with messages jotted down and delivered to the intended recipient. One summer day in 1877, Edison, pressed for cash as usual, was attempting to rush to fruition an idea for a machine that would transcribe these telephone messages graphically. He used a stylus-tipped carbon transmitter to make impressions on a strip of paper that had been coated with paraffin wax. Quite by accident, however, Edison discovered that, when the paper was pulled back beneath the stylus, the indentations that had been made by the original sounds would reproduce those sounds—more or less.

Talk of the Times

Like telephone, the word **phonograph** was used before the invention of the device that bears the name. Earlier in the 19th century, phonograph was used as a synonym for hieroglyphs or other written characters that represented sounds. It was also the name of an 1863 device that electromagnetically transcribed notes played on a piano or other keyed instrument.

Edison hastily drew up plans for a machine that applied the stylus not to wax paper, but to a cylinder wrapped in tin foil. He handed the plans to an assistant, and, without telling him what it was supposed to do, directed him to put the machine together. It was a laughably simple device: little more than a cylinder attached to a crank. What *could* it do?

When the prototype had been cobbled together, Edison bent over a funnel-shaped object attached to a diaphragm, which was attached to a stylus touching the cylinder. While cranking the cylinder, Edison spoke into the funnel: "Mary had a little lamb. It's fleece was white as snow." He then moved the stylus to the beginning of what he had recorded and played it back—to the stupefaction of his assistant, the rest of the workers in his laboratory, and, soon, the world.

The prototype of the Edison phonograph did not look very promising. (Image from arttoday.com)

Edison had invented the phonograph. More to the point, he had *recorded sound*. It was as if he had defeated time itself, rendering permanent the most ephemeral of human products—the voice—which, after all, was nothing more than vibrations in the air.

The Incandescent Age

Not only did the phonograph pull Edison out of his financial crisis, but also it earned him the title of the "Wizard of Menlo Park." Newspaper reporters made his New Jersey workshop part of their daily beat. The world wanted to know what he would do next.

What he did was move from the realm of sound to that of light. The principle of the arc light, produced by a bright electric spark, had been known since 1800. But arc lights were harsh and dangerous, impractical for most applications, save, perhaps, lighthouse beacons and searchlights. Edison decided to pursue the idea of *incandescence*, running a current through a filament, which would glow with a sustained, safe, and usable light.

The problem was the filament. Edison tirelessly experimented with thousands of materials, including a whisker plucked from the beard of a workshop assistant, all to no avail. At last, on October 21, 1879, he tried something very simple. It was described as "carbonized cotton"—but was really nothing more than a piece of thread that had been scorched black. He put the thread in glass bulb, pumped the air out to create a vacuum, and ran a current through it. For 40 hours, it provided steady, usable, safe illumination.

Edison demonstrated his incandescent electric lamp publicly on December 31. He improved it so that it burned longer, and with financing from J.P. Morgan and the Vanderbilts, he established the Edison Electric Light Company. He realized, after all, that it wasn't enough to have invented an electric light. He now had to invent the generators and power-transmission systems to allow the people of entire cities to benefit from—and purchase!—his invention. In 1881, Edison opened the world's first electric generating plant, the Pearl Street Station in lower Manhattan. Within a remarkably short time, all of the urban United States was being wired for electricity. By the early 20th century, rural communities would follow suit.

20th-Century Life

The incandescent light was a tough act to follow, but Edison kept right on inventing, personally securing 389 patents for electric light and power, another 195 for innovations related to the phonograph, 150 for the telegraph, 141 for storage batteries, and 34 for the telephone. This hardly scratches the surface: Edison also invented a practical means of making and projecting motion pictures—making movies—and he even invented wax paper!

But electric light put Edison into everyone's lives and made him a full-fledged cultural hero. When he died on October 18, 1931, the nation looked for some way to honor his passing. President Hoover suggested a nationwide shutdown of electricity for a minute. Nice thought but it was rejected. People depended on electricity too much to turn it off, even for a minute.

And More Light

The inventions of Bell, Edison, and others were seen as triumphs of the imagination and the will, as well as proof of the superiority of "Yankee ingenuity" or "good old American know-how." (Nevermind that Bell was born a Scot; he was a naturalized U.S. citizen.) There was a feeling, at century's end, that the human mind would, sooner or later, penetrate all mysteries.

Opening the Unconscious

The greatest mystery of all, however, was the human mind itself. It had been the object of intellectual speculation at least since the philosophers of ancient Greece and, doubtless, earlier. By the end of the 19th century, psychological theories abounded—but, judging from the grim fate of patients in mental institutions and sanitariums, to little avail.

Sigmund Freud, born to middle-class Jewish parents in Freiburg, Moravia, and raised in Vienna, had been a brilliant student of Greek philosophy and even considered a career studying and teaching the classics. But medicine soon attracted him more, and, within medicine, the study of the mind.

As a young practitioner, Freud became a partner and collaborator with Josef Breuer (1842–1925), a physician who specialized in treating a mental disorder known at the time as hysteria. A patient he called Anna O suffered from a host of "hysterical" symptoms, including occasional paralysis for which there was no physical cause. Using hypnosis, Breuer was able to alleviate her symptoms. Breuer concluded that certain mental ailments were the result of the workings of what he called the *unconscious mind*. If the feelings and fantasies trapped within the unconscious could be liberated by getting the patient to talk about them, a cure might be found.

Together, Freud and Breuer published *Studies in Hysteria*, which began the systematic analysis of the normally submerged wellspring not just of mental disorder, but of human behavior and motivation. Disagreement over basic issues of therapy ended the Freud-Breuer collaboration, but Freud, at the threshold of the 20th century, went on to map the geography of the unconscious mind in *The Interpretation of Dreams* (1900)— which treated the material of our dreams as a "royal road" into the unconscious—and *Psychopathology of Everyday Life* (1904) and *Three Essays on the Theory of Sexuality* (1905).

Unleashed into an age that prided itself on the progress of civilization—on telephones, phonographs, and electric lights, on great empires and high Victorian morality—Freud's ideas ignited a firestorm. Not only did he declare that the part of our personality we think of as our self, the *"ego,"* was separate from the part that directs our morality, the *"superego,"* he also held that both were in varying degrees in thrall to the unconscious, the *"id"* (a Latin word meaning simply the *it*). As you'll see in Chapter 7, "Rising and Sinking," even more provocative was his idea that the goal of the id is to pursue the *pleasure principle*, based in gratification of sexual desire—and not just in adults, but in children and infants as well.

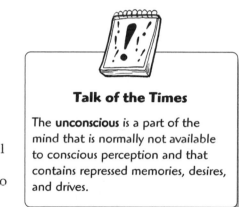

Talk of the Times

The **unconscious** is a part of the mind that is normally not available to conscious perception and that contains repressed memories, desires, and drives.

A Place Called Tuskegee

In the darkest recesses of America's collective soul was the lingering racist legacy of slavery. The Emancipation Proclamation had ended the institution of bondage that all other civilized nations had done away with years earlier. But in the North as well as the South, African Americans were still treated not just as second-class citizens, but hardly as citizens at all.

The lot of Booker T. Washington (1856–1915) was no different from that of any other poor, rural black of his day. But he had a vision of making his life better and perhaps the lives of others, as well. Born to a slave and a white father, he attended school while working at a salt furnace and in a coal mine in Malden, West Virginia. He excelled and became an educator himself, drawing the attention of the Alabama state legislature, which officially appointed him principal of Tuskegee Institute, an industrial and agricultural school for African Americans that he had founded on a shoestring. Soon, Tuskegee became renowned as a center of black education.

Booker T. Washington.
(Image from
arttoday.com)

From its initial emphasis on agriculture the institute moved toward professional and business education in the 1920s, becoming a full-fledged college in 1927, with, by 1943, a graduate program as well.

Voice of the Century

"No race can prosper till it learns there is as much dignity in tilling a field as in writing a poem."
—Booker T. Washington, address to the Atlanta Exposition, September 18, 1895

The faculty and alumni of Tuskegee have included George Washington Carver, whose work with the peanut brought a measure of prosperity to southern farmers, both black and white, and Ralph Ellison, one of the most highly acclaimed African American novelists. Although Tuskegee showed white America what blacks could accomplish, Washington's emphasis on black achievement of economic self-determination rather than attainment of political and civil rights created controversy.

"In all things that are purely social," Washington declared, "we can be as separate as the fingers, yet one as the hand in all things essential to mutual progress."

The NAACP (National Association for the Advancement of Colored People), founded in 1909, would be among a new order of African American organizations that would oppose Washington's pragmatic approach and demand full civil rights. Yet, at the close of a century of oppression for black Americans, Tuskegee was a start.

Mississippi River Tale

For all its technological progress and material prosperity, 19th-century America could be a hard, cold place. Not only were the majority of Americans indifferent, at best, to such issues as racial injustice, most also turned their backs on any aspect of culture that did not immediately serve a practical purpose or contribute to the bottom line.

A minority of Americans did produce and appreciate art and literature. George Caleb Bingham (1811–79) portrayed life on the nation's rivers, Albert Bierstadt (1830–1902) revealed the magnificence of the western landscape, and Thomas Eakins (1844–1916) penetrated human character with his powerful portraits.

In literature, there were the likes of Washington Irving (1783–1859) and James Fenimore Cooper (1789–1851), the first American authors to gain international reputations; then in mid century came Edgar Allan Poe (1809–49), Ralph Waldo Emerson (1803–82), Henry David Thoreau (1817–62), Walt Whitman (1819–92), Nathaniel Hawthorne (1804–64), and Herman Melville (1819–91). Although popular recognition of Melville didn't come until the 20th century, the others were universally regarded as great authors.

Most 19th-century Americans did not look at American art or read American books. To the degree that they cared about such things at all, they looked to Europe for their culture.

In 1884 came a book about an illiterate little boy who takes a raft journey down the Mississippi River with a runaway slave. Years later, Ernest Hemingway would observe, "All modern American literature comes from one book by Mark Twain called *Huckleberry Finn* … it's the best book we've had…. There was nothing before. There has been nothing so good since."

Samuel Langhorne Clemens was born in 1835 and spent his childhood in Hannibal, Missouri, where he witnessed frontier life at its most idyllic and its most brutal. He realized his boyhood ambition to become a Mississippi riverboat pilot, and it was from that experience that he took his pen name. The call of "mark twain!" indicated a river depth of two fathoms—safe passage for a riverboat.

The Civil War brought an abrupt end to Twain's piloting days, and he became a miner, lecturer, and journalist, traveling to California, where he wrote his first popular work in 1865, a sketch entitled

Voice of the Century

"Can we never extract the tapeworm of Europe from the brain of our countrymen?"

—Ralph Waldo Emerson, "Culture" (1860)

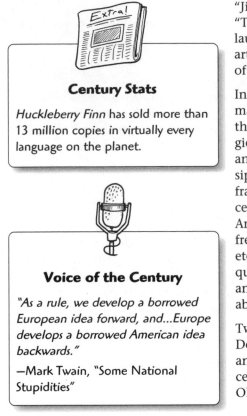

Century Stats

Huckleberry Finn has sold more than 13 million copies in virtually every language on the planet.

Voice of the Century

"As a rule, we develop a borrowed European idea forward, and...Europe develops a borrowed American idea backwards."

—Mark Twain, "Some National Stupidities"

"Jim Smiley and His Jumping Frog" but better known as "The Celebrated Jumping Frog of Calaveras County." It launched his career. But who would have expected an artistic masterpiece like *Huckleberry Finn* from an author of such a humble and checkered background?

In Huck, Twain created a great hero-narrator and commanded a staggering range of American dialects among the other characters while balancing episodes of nostalgic romanticism, unflinching realism, moving pathos, and outrageous comedy. Most of all, there is the Mississippi River itself, evoked as a mythically powerful framework for the whole tale, involving a true innocent's adventures in a pre-Civil War slave-owning America, where to befriend a slave and help set him free is to accept—as Huck has been taught to believe—eternal damnation. Huck willingly accepts the consequences in embracing fugitive Jim as a human being and not a slave. It is a story about America, but also about humanity.

Twain's masterpiece may be seen as the nation's artistic Declaration of Independence, which allowed the artists and authors of the United States to enter the 20th century on a more equal footing with those of the Old World.

Land of Liberty

If America had to struggle to win recognition for the productions of its artists and authors, its role as what Abraham Lincoln had called "the last best hope of the world" was clear and unmistakable as the new century approached. In 1886, the Statue of Liberty, created by the sculptor Frederic August Bartholdi and presented to the United States as a gift of the French people, was unveiled. Standing 151 feet high in New York Harbor, the coolly majestic female figure (modeled after the artist's mother), holds in one arm a tablet inscribed with the date of American independence and, in her other hand, raises a torch of liberty and hope. The poet Emma Lazarus (1849–87) composed a sonnet for inscription at the base of the great statue. "Give me your tired, your poor," the concluding portion begins...

> *Your huddled masses yearning to breathe free,*
> *The wretched refuse of your teeming shore,*
> *Send these, the homeless, tempest-tost, to me,*
> *I lift my lamp beside the golden door!*

The Vanishing American

It is a cliché to say that ours is a nation of immigrants, but it is also a hard fact that, from the perspective of America's first inhabitants, the people Columbus miscalled Indians, the first immigrants came as invaders. The first armed conflict between "invaders" and Indians erupted in 1493, the year after Columbus's first landing, and warfare continued, with little interruption, for the next 400 years.

In 1830, at the urging of President Andrew Jackson, Congress passed the Indian Removal Act, which authorized the financially compensated but forced "relocation" of tribes east of the Mississippi to "Indian Territory," land encompassing present-day Oklahoma and portions of other future states. The removal of the Cherokee was especially horrific, resulting in the deaths of 4,000 of the 15,000 who embarked on what came to be called the "Trail of Tears." Despite the "removal," conflict between whites and Indians continued and intensified as more settlers moved farther west. The period 1866 to 1891 saw the most intensive and deliberate U.S. military campaigns against the Indians of the West.

Contrary to the claims of some Indian as well as white activists in the 20th century, it was never the federal government's *official* policy to commit genocide against the native peoples of the West. Rather, the government hoped to "concentrate" Indians on strictly defined reservations. Once consigned to such a reservation, Indians became wards of the federal government, which pledged to provide them with rations and other necessary goods. In practice, this pledge was rarely honored, at least not adequately. United States Indian policy was beset by almost universal indifference on the one hand and outrageous corruption on the other. Reservation Indians suffered varying degrees of starvation, and hostilities were aggravated.

Talk of the Times

Indian removal was the federal policy, inaugurated by the Indian Removal Act of 1830, of "relocating" Indians living east of the Mississippi to "Indian Territory" reserved for them in the West.

The U.S. Army in the West, after the Civil War, was puny: some 20,000 officers and men, poorly paid, poorly fed, poorly educated, poorly equipped, poorly trained, and often poorly led. On the prairies, this force confronted Indian warriors who excelled in horsemanship and guerilla tactics and whose culture exalted warfare.

For all their physical and spiritual advantages, Indians were handicapped in warfare by the very features of their culture that prized individual strength, cunning, skill, endurance, courage, and honor. War chiefs were hardly the equivalents of generals and did not command their braves so much as they "led" them through example and personal influence. Truly coordinated strategy was usually impossible. Moreover, after the Civil War, the white population in the West outnumbered Indian population by a factor of 10. Against such odds, no warriors, regardless of skill and commitment, could long prevail.

By the 1880s, most Indian resistance had been crushed. Yet if the body of defiance was dead, its spirit lingered. A religious movement swept through some of the reservations. Based on a belief that generations of slain braves would come back to life, that the buffalo (nearly hunted to extinction by the end of the 1870s) would again be plentiful, and that Indians would once again prevail, the religion called on the people to perform a "Ghost Dance" to hasten the promised salvation.

Century Stats

After numbering an estimated 60 million at the time of the first Europeans' arrival, the buffalo was hunted to the brink of extinction, effectively eliminating the crucial element in the Plains Indians' existence. By the 1880s, only 300 remained when they came under government protection.

Soon, many western reservations were alive with what white officials regarded as frenzied dancing. When leaders among the Teton Sioux at the Pine Ridge Reservation in South Dakota called for armed rebellion against the whites, reservation agent Daniel F. Royer frantically telegraphed Washington, D.C., for help. On December 15, 1890, reservation police (Native American officers) were sent to arrest the most revered of all Indian leaders, Sitting Bull, at Standing Rock Reservation. A fight broke out, and Sitting Bull, with six followers, his teenaged son, and a half dozen policemen, was killed. The old chief's body was hastily transported to the agency headquarters and buried without ceremony in quicklime.

Sitting Bull, holy man of the Hunkpapa Sioux. (Image from the author's collection)

20th-Century Life

Chief and holy man of the Hunkpapa Sioux, Sitting Bull (ca. 1831–90) assumed the role of spiritual and military leader of resistance in the sacred Black Hills of the Dakotas. Promised federal amnesty in 1881, he was instead imprisoned at Fort Randall, Dakota Territory, until May 1883, when he was released to the Standing Rock Reservation on the present border of North and South Dakota. Between 1885 and 1886, he toured with Buffalo Bill Cody's famed Wild West Show and then returned to the reservation, where he exercised great influence in the Ghost Dance movement.

In the meantime, another chief, Big Foot of the Miniconjou Sioux, was making his way to Pine Ridge. U.S. army commander General Nelson A. Miles assumed that Big Foot's purpose was to fan the flames of a rebellion that now had so compelling a martyr. He dispatched the 7th Cavalry to intercept him and his followers. The troops caught up with the Indians on December 28, 1890, at a place called Wounded Knee Creek, on the Pine Ridge Reservation.

As it turned out, Big Foot's purpose was to persuade the Pine Ridge Indians to surrender in order to avoid further useless bloodshed. Neither Miles nor Colonel James W. Forsyth, commander of the 7th, knew this, and Forsyth quietly surrounded Big Foot's camp, deploying four Hotchkiss guns (deadly rapid-fire howitzers) on the surrounding hills. On the 29th, the soldiers entered the camp and began to confiscate the Indians' weapons. A hand-to-hand fight developed, shots were fired—it is unclear whether these came from the Indians or the soldiers—and then the Hotchkiss guns opened up, firing almost a round a second at men, women, and children.

Nobody knows just how many died at Wounded Knee. The bodies of Big Foot and 153 other Miniconjous were found, but it is likely that 300 of the 350 camped beside the creek ultimately lost their lives. After a brief fight with the 7th Cavalry on December 30, the Indians withdrew. Two weeks later, on January 15, 1891, the Sioux formally surrendered to U.S. Army officials. So ended the "Indian Wars" and, with them, four centuries of warfare on the American continent.

Ellis Island

While the Indians of the West were being transformed into what one popular writer called the "Vanishing American," newcomers from Europe poured into the nation's East Coast ports. Immigration had been steady through the 18th and early 19th centuries, but, in 1841, as Ireland was starving in the great potato famine, millions of new Irish immigrants sought new lives in the United States. The influx of Irish Catholics into what was principally an Anglo-Protestant nation prompted many to worry that "their" American culture would crumble, and the Irish immigrants were openly abused and exploited, given the most menial work to do at the lowest possible wages.

By 1880, as American factory-based industry grew, so did the demand for cheap labor. Spurred by economics, the government opened America's doors not only to northern European immigrants (hitherto the favored group), but to those from southern and eastern Europe, as well. Italians, Greeks, Turks, Russians, and Slavs came in large numbers, as did Jews—hitherto a rarity in the United States.

Although the cities of the East and the Midwest tended to assimilate the new immigrants readily, resistance to immigration remained strong in the West and Southwest. It wasn't that employers in these regions didn't want the cheap labor—they most certainly *did*—but they didn't want the workers to enjoy citizenship. In the Southwest, migrant labor from Mexico provided a scandalously cheap source of temporary farm workers. Asians were prized as hard workers but were barred from attaining U.S. citizenship by naturalization laws. In 1882, the first of a series of Chinese Exclusion Acts were passed, blocking importation of Chinese laborers.

From Europe, however, the immigrants came in such a flood that in 1892, the United States Immigration Bureau opened a major central facility to "process" them. The massive compound was erected on Ellis Island, within sight of the Statue of Liberty in New York Harbor. Here, newcomers were examined for disease, evaluated as fit or unfit for entry, and either admitted to the mainland, quarantined, or deported. For more than six decades, Ellis Island became the symbol of immigration into America's promised land. It was an icon, a place of fear as well as hope.

Century Stats

When the potato famine swept Ireland during 1841–51, the country's population fell from 8.2 million to 6.6 million due to starvation, disease, and emigration.

Century Stats

During its 62 years of operation, from 1892 to 1943, Ellis Island processed immigrants at rates as high as a million people a year.

The Other Half

The influx of immigrants was making American cities deeply divided places. There were neighborhoods of more established citizens, decently clothed and adequately fed and housed, and there were the warrens of newer arrivals: overcrowded, dilapidated, and crime-plagued slums. The middle-class reaction to this "other half" of America was to ignore it—at least until Jacob August Riis (1849–1914), a New York journalist, published an eye-opening study in text and photographs of his city's slum life. His *How the Other Half Lives* (1890), Theodore Roosevelt declared, came as "an enlightenment and an inspiration." It heralded reform movements not only in New York, but also across the nation.

Although Riis's book and the work of other reformers brought gradual improvement to the cities, many looked away from urban America to the dream of wide-open western spaces. At noon on April 22, 1889, government officials fired signal guns, sending hundreds of homesteaders racing across the border of Indian Territory to stake claims. The last great tracts of western land, formerly pledged to the sole possession of the Indians, were opened to white settlement.

Remember the *Maine*!

Although there was much to divide Americans at century's end, it was also true that a sense of national identity seemed to be growing stronger. A dramatic demonstration of this came at the close of the last decade of the century, and the issue was the fate of a small Spanish colony off the coast of Florida.

U.S. agricultural companies had made major investments in Cuba, especially in sugar plantations. When rumblings of revolution against Cuba's Spanish overlords threatened to disrupt business, the major financial interests supported the idea of ousting the Spanish and installing an ostensibly independent government that would, in fact, serve American interests as a compliant puppet of the United States. Perhaps Cuba could even be annexed to the nation.

All that was needed was a pretext for war with Spain. The beginnings of one came on February 9, 1898, when the sensationalist newspaper owner William Randolph Hearst published a purloined private letter in which the Spanish minister to the United States insulted President McKinley as weak and ineffectual. The letter created national outrage. McKinley had sent a U.S. Navy battleship, the USS *Maine*, to Havana Harbor to stand ready to protect Americans in Cuba. On February 15, 1898, the *Maine* suddenly exploded, resulting in the deaths of 266 crewmen. The rival papers of Hearst and Joseph Pulitzer vied with one another to point the finger of blame on Spain, and immediately America echoed with cries of "Remember the *Maine*...to hell with Spain!"

In April, a still-reluctant President William McKinley asked a most willing Congress to authorize an invasion of Cuba and to recognized Cuban independence. In response, Spain declared war on the United States on April 24.

The war, which Secretary of State John Hay (1838–1905) would sum up as a "splendid little war," was over in 10 weeks, Spain having been humiliated at every turn.

In the Philippines, another Spanish colony, U.S. Admiral George Dewey (1837–1917) and his Asiatic Squadron sunk all 10 Spanish warships stationed in Manilla Bay. This was followed by a landing of 11,000 U.S. troops, who, acting in concert with the guerilla forces of Filipino rebel leader Emilio Aguinaldo, quickly defeated the Spanish army in the islands. In July, Spanish Guam also fell, and the U.S. gathered up previously unclaimed Wake Island. Most importantly, Congress passed a resolution annexing Hawaii.

Fighting in the Philippines during the Spanish-American War. (Image from the author's collection)

20th-Century Life

Having liberated Cuba from Spanish imperialism, the United States high-handedly annexed what had been the Spanish-held Philippines. How did America justify this action? President William McKinley rationalized neatly to a group of clergymen visiting the White House:

"I thought first we would take only Manila; then Luzon; then other islands, perhaps, also. I walked the floor of the White House night after night ...; and I am not ashamed to tell you, gentlemen, that I went down on my knees and prayed Almighty God for light and guidance more than one night. And one night it came to me this way: (1) That we could not give them back to Spain—that would be cowardly and dishonorable; (2) That we could not turn them over to France and Germany—our commercial rivals in the Orient—that would be bad business and discreditable; (3) That we could not leave them to themselves—they were unfit for self-government—and they would soon have anarchy and misrule worse than Spain's was; and (4) That there was nothing left for us to do but to take them all, and to educate the Filipinos, and uplift and civilize and Christianize them, and by God's grace to do the best we could by them .... And then I went to bed, and went to sleep, and slept soundly."

In Cuba, on May 29, the U.S. fleet blockaded the Spanish fleet at Santiago Harbor, and in June, 17,000 U.S. troops landed at Daiquiri and assaulted Santiago. The war's make-or-break land battle, at San Juan Hill on July 1, included a magnificent charge—on foot, it should be pointed out—by the volunteer Rough Riders, led by Lieutenant Colonel Theodore Roosevelt. In the meantime, Admiral Pasqual Cervera sailed into the harbor of Santiago de Cuba, where he was blockaded by the U.S. fleet. On July 3, after the U.S. victory at San Juan Hill, Cervera decided to run the blockade. Within four hours, his fleet was almost completely destroyed. Four hundred seventy-four Spanish sailors lost their lives, whereas only two U.S. sailors perished. On July 17, 24,000 Spanish troops surrendered, and Madrid sued for peace nine days later.

Teddy Roosevelt, colonel of the "Rough Rider" regiment, U.S. Volunteers.
(Image from arttoday.com)

Reflections on the White City: Looking Toward the 20th Century

Victory in the Spanish-American War ensured that the United States would enter the 20th century as a bona fide world power. Only five years before the war, in 1893, the country had already celebrated its place in the world by staging the World's Columbian Exposition.

Ostensibly this "world's fair" commemorated the 400th anniversary of Christopher Columbus's discovery of America, but really, it was an assessment of the present and a look toward the coming century. President Grover Cleveland himself opened the show by pushing a button in the White House, which set into motion a great generator in far-off Chicago and turned on all the lights, which illuminated buildings constructed in imitation of Grecian and Roman temples, gleaming white and christened a "White City."

Behind those classical facades was the future: exhibitions of the latest products and products yet to come—promising, on the cusp of a new century, a new life within the reach of all Americans.

The Least You Need to Know

➤ The last three decades of the 19th century saw the creation of the Electric Age.

➤ Invention and economic prosperity characterized much of this period, but African Americans and new immigrant arrivals suffered discrimination, economic disadvantage, and injustice. The first Americans—the Indians—were the victims of even worse, a war of aggression and concentration on intolerable reservations.

➤ During this period, American art and literature struggled for national as well as international recognition.

➤ The Spanish–American War (1898) signaled U.S. entry onto the world stage as a world power.

Part 2
The Old World Dies: 1900–1919

There is nothing inherently special about a century. The passing of one century does not bring about the end of a way of life anymore than the commencement of a new century necessarily brings a new way of life. And yet, strangely enough, the first years of the 20th century were dramatically different from the last years of the 19th. A host of new inventions appeared, ranging from the Kodak Brownie, to radio, to the Wright Brothers' airplane. In Africa, a new kind of warfare was under way; in American cities, new kinds of buildings were being raised; in the arcane realm of physics, a new picture of the universe was emerging.

As if to certify the passing of the old, Queen Victoria herself, venerable symbol of the 19th century, died. Then everything seemed to change. Japan won a great mechanized war against Russia. Revolutions swept nations as well as ideas. Even the "unsinkable" Titanic sunk. And, finally, the entire world erupted into the greatest war fought to that time.

Chapter 6

First Years (1900–1902)

> **In This Chapter**
>
> ➤ Technology comes to the masses
>
> ➤ The world shrinks
>
> ➤ A new physics brings a new picture of reality
>
> ➤ Invention of radio
>
> ➤ End of the Victorian Age
>
> ➤ Building urban America

Most people of the "civilized" world expected the 20th century to be an age of miracles. The *Ladies' Home Journal* for December 1900, for instance, predicted such wonders as hot and cold air from spigots (we'd regulate the temperature of our houses as we regulate the temperature of our baths); "aerial warships" and "forts on wheels" (sounds a lot like bombers and tanks); instruments to allow human beings to see around the world (television?); the elimination of the letters C, X, and Q from the alphabet (they'll be judged unnecessary); and strawberries and raspberries that, through selective breeding, would grow as large as apples (one fruit, one serving).

This chapter tells what *really* happened when the world dipped a toe in the 20th century.

Box Brownie and Boxers

The last years of the 19th century were packed: inventions, political upheavals, and profound changes in the population makeup of the United States. And yet much remained unchanged. The automobile had been invented (by Germany's Carl Benz in 1885) but was nothing more than a rare curiosity; the world was still horse-drawn. Telegraph wires and the Atlantic Cable linked place to place, yet the pace of information exchange was still quite leisurely. Nevertheless, change, as they say, was in the wind. Here are two instances at the very threshold of the century.

Say Cheese

By 1900, photography was familiar throughout the world. It had been introduced in 1839 by Louis-Jacques-Mande Daguerre and was used extensively throughout the 19th century by professional photographers whose purposes ranged from the artistic, to the documentary, to the commercial.

The key word, however, is *professional*. Through the 1880s, photography had been the exclusive province of professionals or very committed amateurs. The equipment was cumbersome and difficult to use. A fully equipped darkroom and a set of pretty nasty chemicals were required.

Talk of the Times

A **box camera** is a simple, cheap, fixed-focus camera for casual picture takers. Designed for average-light and average-distance situations, neither its shutter speed, aperture, nor focus is adjustable, as they are on more sophisticated cameras.

Century Stats

Kodak sold 250,000 Brownies in 1900, and the camera, with rather minor modifications, remained on the market for the next 80 years.

Then, an entrepreneur from Rochester, New York, George Eastman (1854–1932), created a simple, fixed-focus box camera, which proved popular and put photography in the hands of a growing number of amateur enthusiasts.

The real revolution, however, came in 1900, when Eastman radically simplified his already straightforward box, producing the Brownie. Named either for its designer, Frank Brownell, or after the brownie-like elf Eastman used as a trademark logo, it cost a buck, was small enough to carry anywhere, and was so simple a child could use it.

Eastman called his company Kodak, a name whose consonant-bracketed syllables sounded like the click of a camera shutter—and offered for sale not only the camera, but the film (flexible celluloid rather than the cumbersome glass plates professional photographers used) *and* the developing service.

What was so revolutionary about the Brownie is that it suddenly offered anyone a share of high technology and the ability to record the world in a personal way. The Brownie elevated and celebrated the family, whose history could now be pressed into another new product, the photo album. It documented the otherwise anonymous passing of any number of individual lives.

The 20th century, which would be marked by mass production and mass warfare, thus began in an intensely personal way, by providing a machine that glorified the individual.

A woman using a Kodak Brownie during the early 1920s. This incredibly popular camera had hardly changed since 1900 and would remain pretty much the same, except for cosmetic changes now and then, through the end of the 1970s. (Image from arttoday.com)

East Meets West

While Americans were eagerly taking *"snapshots"* of each other, events in what most Americans still thought of as "far-off" China were about to demonstrate that the world was becoming an ever smaller, ever more interdependent place.

In 1899, U.S. Secretary of State John Hay communicated with the governments of France, Germany, Great Britain, Italy, Russia, and Japan, endorsing an "Open Door Policy" in matters of trade with China. He proposed that all nations would have equal access to Chinese trade.

The Open Door Policy met with almost universal approval—except that none of the nations thought to consult China. That ancient empire, racked by internal disturbances and tenuously held by Tz'u-hsi, the empress dowager, was in the throes of intense antiforeign feeling. In the spring of 1900, the empress dowager encouraged an uprising of units of a militant secret society called the Yihe Quang, loosely translated as the "righteous harmony of fists" and called "the Boxers" by Westerners.

The Boxers rampaged throughout the country, killing foreigners as well as Christian Chinese, and in the capital city of Beijing, the legations of European nations and Japan were laid under siege.

Talk of the Times

Before 1900, the word **snapshot** was a hunting term that meant a quick shot fired without careful aim. After the introduction of the Brownie, however, the word was universally applied to photographs casually taken with a handheld camera, and its original meaning was forgotten.

A German diplomat was slain. An international contingent of British, French, German, Japanese, Russian, and U.S. troops was sent into Beijing to put down the Boxer Rebellion. This accomplished, the coalition imposed a harsh $333 million indemnity against China, which was also forced to agree to the stationing of U.S. and other troops in the country.

The palace of the Tz'u-hsi, Forbidden City, Peking (Beijing).
(Image from arttoday.com)

Talk of the Times

The **Manchu**, also called the Qing, was the last of the Chinese imperial dynasties. The Manchus came as invaders from the northeast and seized power in 1644.

The U.S. role in defeating the Boxer Rebellion, coming as it did on the heels of its triumph over Spain, was a heady nationalist experience. It dramatized for most Americans the fact that their nation was no longer insulated from the world by two great oceans but was not expected to take an active role, even in affairs on the other side of the globe.

What no one saw at the time, however, is that the entire Boxer affair was the death knell for the rickety Manchu dynasty, which would fall in the revolution of 1911, an event that would leave China unstable and ripe for a form of government that had yet to appear in 1900: communism.

New Century, New Reality

The Boxer Rebellion was not the new century's only harbinger of a shrinking world. Very few Americans—very few people anywhere—had heard of Max Planck, an obscure physics professor at the University of Berlin. Even fewer people had ever heard of something called the "ultraviolet catastrophe." But it would have profound implications for how reality is understood.

Quantum What?

For more than 200 years, scientists had been pretty confident in their understanding of the basic laws of physics. Sir Isaac Newton had seen to that. Take light—energy, radiation. If you heat something, its molecules vibrate, producing light. Simple. According to Newtonian physics, the more you heat a thing, the faster its molecules vibrate—to an infinite range of frequencies, the light emitted rising in frequency from red, to orange, and on through the spectrum into the far ultraviolet.

The trouble was this didn't actually happen. If Newtonian physics couldn't explain this basic phenomenon, two centuries of scientific understanding might well have to be chucked.

Planck wrestled with the ultraviolet catastrophe. Then, in a leap of genius, it dawned on him: Energy had to be given off not continuously, but in discrete pieces or "packets." The size of each "packet" was fixed, inversely proportional to the wavelength of the radiation in question. Because the wavelength of violet light is half that of red light, the energy packet for violet light "contains" twice as much energy as that for red light.

Planck called each energy packet a *quantum* (Latin for "How much?") and worked out the relationship between energy and wavelength using an exquisitely small number, 6.6×10^{-34} joule-seconds (a joule second is the amount of energy corresponding to 1 watt acting for a single second), which, in effect, represented the "graininess" of energy. That is, the only permitted energies are whole-number multiples of this number (soon christened "Planck's constant") multiplied by frequency.

Again, so what? In the everyday world, it is true, Planck's constant, so infinitesimal, has little meaning. On a large-scale, "macroscopic" level, energy behaves as if it were radiated continuously, just as Newton had explained. But in special cases, as in the ultraviolet catastrophe, the graininess of energy has to be taken into account.

Planck himself did not pursue the implications of quantum theory. That, as you'll see in the next chapter, was left to another German physicist, Albert Einstein. But at the outset of the century, Planck's quantum was a seed that would change everything. It would "sprout" Einstein as well as Werner Heisenberg (who explained that Planck's constant represented an absolute limit to what is knowable about the universe). Ultimately, quantum mechanics would blossom into ideas about releasing the monumental amounts of energy that hold the nuclei of atoms together. That, before the century even reached its midpoint, would result in the most destructive weapons the world had ever known.

Talk of the Times

Quantum mechanics is the branch of physics that deals with the emission and absorption of energy by matter and with the motion of subatomic particles in matter. It did not exist before 1900 and is now a cornerstone of our understanding of the universe and our ability (for better or worse) to release the enormous energy of the atom.

Look Ma, No Wires!

Although quantum mechanics was a scientific advance far beyond the comprehension (or even attention) of all but a handful of scientists, the invention a young Italian physicist named Guglielmo Marconi (1874–1937) demonstrated on December 12, 1901, created a most dramatic effect worldwide.

Long-wave electromagnetic radiation—invisible energy waves that were soon dubbed radio waves—were described as early as 1888 by the physicist Heinrich Hertz. A number of scientists tinkered with ways in which these waves might be used to transmit information, to create, that is, a telegraph without wires. Marconi diligently worked to develop an effective transmitter and receiver (called at the time a "coherer"). In that December demonstration, he hooked an antenna to a balloon and lofted it high into the air. He then successfully transmitted a Morse code signal from his location at the southwestern tip of England to a receiver across the Atlantic Ocean in Newfoundland.

20th-Century Life

Guglielmo Marconi was convinced he had the makings of a revolution in communication. Marconi went to London in 1896 and received the support of Sir William Preece, the chief engineer of the Royal Post Office. In September 1899, he equipped two U.S. ships to report to New York newspapers on the America's Cup yacht race. This prompted investment in Marconi's enterprise, and in December 1901, he transmitted a message across the Atlantic, proving that the curvature of the earth wouldn't limit communication by electromagnetic waves to little more than 100 miles.

Marconi continued to perfect and improve radio transmitters, receivers, and antennas, was financially rewarded for his work, and, in 1909, received the Nobel Prize for Physics.

Radio—the British would persist in calling it wireless—had been invented. It allowed instantaneous communication over vast distances, wherever a receiver and a transmitter could be placed. Communication might be person to person or, perhaps, ship to ship. (In 1912, the stricken ocean liner *Titanic* was the first vessel to broadcast a genuine S.O.S.)

What neither Marconi nor anyone else predicted in 1901 was that radio would become a source of mass entertainment—the first commercial radio station, KDKA Pittsburgh, began broadcasting in 1920—and an instrument of national purpose: In the 1930s, Franklin Roosevelt would pull his nation through the Great Depression by means of his weekly radio "fireside chats," and, using radio propaganda, Adolf Hitler would pull his nation into a catastrophic war waged against the world.

A Marconi radio transmitter from the 1910s.
(Image from arttoday.com)

A Queen Dies, a War Ends

Victoria, the monarch so closely identified with the 19th century, died on January 22, 1901. It seemed the most symbolic event of a reign already laden with symbolism.

Victorian Twilight

Victoria's Britain ruled more of the geopolitical world than any other nation. During her reign, England completed its century-long conquest of India and gained dominance over what Europe called the "Dark Continent" of Africa by taking control of Egypt and the Nile in 1898.

Somehow, a small European island nation, symbolically ruled by a dowdy, stuffy old widow, held sway over the world. When Victoria died, the British poet laureate Robert Bridges declared that it was "as though the keystone had fallen out of the arch of heaven." All grieved. Even London's prostitutes, it was reported, wore the black of mourning.

Yet Victoria's death, at the outset of the century, also seemed to clear the air. Fifty-nine-year-old Edward VII, dapper, sophisticated, and much given to the pleasures of the flesh, ascended the throne of a nation that had had enough of Victorian propriety and conservatism.

Voice of the Century

"I mourn the safe and motherly old middle-class queen, who held the nation warm under the fold of her big, hideous Scotch-plaid shawl and whose duration had been so extraordinarily convenient and beneficent. I felt her death much more than I should have expected; she was a sustaining symbol—and the wild waters are upon us now."

—Novelist Henry James (1843–1916) to jurist Oliver Wendell Holmes, Jr., February 20, 1901

It was liberating. But it also presaged the end of the England of empire. Edward was so genial a monarch that he embraced the French people, whose more relaxed morality, as he perceived it, appealed to him rather more than that of the English. This soon led to the Anglo-French alliance known as the Entente Cordiale. This agreement, unthinkable during Victoria's reign, created a European crisis in the balance of power that prompted Germany to arm itself. Soon, Britain, France, and Germany were locked in an all-out arms race. As they armed themselves, they also forged a complex web of mostly secret alliances.

England's Edward VII was so portly that he was unable to close his bottom vest button; when he left it unbuttoned, the world followed his lead—and continues to do so (at least where vests are concerned). (Image from arttoday.com)

The European stage was being set for a tragedy of war beyond anything the world had yet known.

Africa: A New Kind of Combat

England's first major war of the new century took place not in Europe, however, but in Africa. Following the First Boer War (1880–81) in South Africa, the Boers—Dutch settlers, also called Afrikaners—were given partial independence from Great Britain by the creation of the South African Republic. At the start of the new century, gold was discovered in the lands of the republic, and Afrikaners sought to protect the gold fields from British exploitation. "Outlanders," as the British and other non-Boers were called, were denied political rights, resulting in a crisis that prompted the British government to send troops.

The South African Republic and its ally, the Orange Free State, seemed weak enemies, with no navy, no regular army, no industry, and certainly no empire. Between them, they could muster fewer than 90,000 men against a British mobilization of 450,000. Yet the Second ("Great") Boer War, fought with brutal *guerrilla* tactics, dragged on for almost three years, from 1899 to 1902. At last, the British commander in chief, Horatio Kitchener, waged total war on the Afrikaner people, combatants and noncombatants alike, starving them into submission.

Talk of the Times

The **Boers**, also called Afrikaners, lived in South Africa and were of Dutch descent.

Afrikaner farmers—Boers—father and son, at the time of the Second ("Great") Boer War. (Image from the author's collection)

The treaty of Vereeniging, which ended the war in 1902, compelled the Boers to lay down their arms and acclaim King Edward VII as their sovereign. In return, the Afrikaners retained their property and paid no war indemnity. Britain also agreed to postpone settling the issue of giving nonwhites the vote until after the Afrikaners had been granted full self-government. Thus, the treaty established the basis of racial oppression that would dominate South Africa for most of the century.

When the war began in 1899, Victorian England was the leading nation of the world. When it ended, Britain was drained, both economically and spiritually. Perhaps worst of all, other nations of the world—Germany in particular—had seen England's military falter. Britain no longer seemed so invulnerable. Certainly, the Second Boer War was the high-water mark of the British empire.

Talk of the Times

The Spanish word *guerra* evolved into the single word **guerrilla** to describe a limited, covert style of warfare as well as the combatants who fight such wars. Guerrilla warfare figured importantly throughout the 20th century.

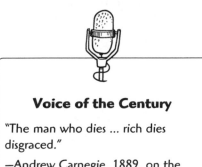

Voice of the Century

"The man who dies ... rich dies disgraced."

—Andrew Carnegie, 1889, on the reason for philanthropy

The Unnatural World

The United States at the start of the century was still predominantly a rural land, a nation of farmers, but that was rapidly changing. The American scene was becoming increasingly urban, owing less to nature and more to the hand, brain, and muscle of humankind.

Big Steel

The family of Andrew Carnegie (1835–1919) had immigrated to the United States in 1848 to escape poverty in Scotland. The boy found work in a cotton factory, then in a telegraph office, and finally with the Pennsylvania Railroad, rising quickly through the executive ranks until he became head of the railroad's western division in 1859. He resigned from the Pennsylvania in 1865 to form the Keystone Bridge Company, the first in a series of iron and steel concerns he would own. In 1899, Carnegie consolidated his holdings as the Carnegie Steel Company, which he sold to J.P. Morgan's United States Steel Company in 1901 for $492 million— the equivalent, roughly, of 5 billion of today's dollars in an era before the introduction of income tax.

Carnegie was no saint. He had built his wealth ruthlessly, strangling his competition in the marketplace and using strong-arm tactics in an attempt to destroy the American industrial union movement. As early as 1889, however, he revealed another side of himself. In a speech titled "The Gospel of Wealth," he proclaimed that the captains of industry had a responsibility to use their wealth for the clear benefit of society.

Years later, from 1901 until his death, Carnegie practiced what he had preached. Declaring that the man who died wealthy died in disgrace, he dedicated himself to philanthropy on a grand scale, donating more than $350 million to a wide spectrum of causes. He founded more than 2,500 public libraries throughout the United States; he established the Carnegie Institute of Pittsburgh, the Carnegie Institution at Washington, the Carnegie Foundation for the Advancement of Teaching, the Carnegie Endowment for International Peace, and the Carnegie Corporation of New York.

Andrew Carnegie, steel tycoon and philanthropist. (Image from the author's collection)

Carnegie's philanthropy had even further-reaching effects, as other equally ruthless tycoons followed his lead. Rail magnate Leland Stanford founded and endowed Stanford University; oil baron John D. Rockefeller endowed the University of Chicago and created the Rockefeller Institute of Medical Research, established the Rockefeller Foundation, and bought vast tracts of land that became national parks. Other industrialists and financiers did similar deeds and continue to do so today.

Building Up

It wasn't Carnegie's money alone that was building American towns and cities. His steel (and steel supplied by others) made possible a new kind of architecture, a style of building uniquely suited to the new American city. The use of steel to create a structural cage made possible buildings that could be much taller than any masonry structure. The steel supports, not the walls, bore the load of the building.

The Home Insurance Company Building in Chicago (1883–1885), designed by William LeBaron Jenney, is generally considered the first *skyscraper*, as the new structures were called. However, the major early exponent of the skyscraper style was

Talk of the Times

The word **skyscraper** goes back to the 18th century, when it referred to a lofty sail high on a ship's mast. Beginning in the early 19th century, the word was also used as a synonym for an exaggeration—a "tall story"—a high-standing horse, a very tall man, and even a rider on a high-wheel ("penny-farthing") bicycle. In 1891, skyscraper was first used (by a Boston newspaper) to describe a new, multistory building.

Louis Sullivan (1856–1924), who, in 1879, formed a highly successful and partnership with Dankmar Adler. Their practice was based in Chicago, an ideal place for architects at the time because the city had been devastated by the Great Fire of 1871 and was ripe for rebuilding. The invention of the elevator suddenly made buildings of more than five stories practical. By the early years of the 20th century, architects in Chicago, New York, and other major American cities were vying with one another for claim to the world's tallest building.

As the Middle Ages in Europe were the era of the great cathedral, so the 20th century called for its own cathedrals—dedicated not to religion, but to commerce—and so the face of urban America was reshaped.

Cooling Off

The importance of innovations such as the telegraph, telephone, electric light, and radio is obvious. Less heralded is a development that took place as skyscrapers were transforming more of the outdoors into indoor spaces.

The second law of thermodynamics is one of nature's immutable laws. It states, quite simply, that heat flows from hot places to cooler places. The idea of a *cooler* temperature flowing into a *warmer* one—well, it was just unnatural.

In 1902, a young engineer named Willis Carrier accomplished this very feat. The Sackett-Wilhelms Lithography and Publishing Company of Brooklyn, New York, had a problem. They printed the popular humor magazine *Judge*, in color. Color printing requires several runs through the press, and Sackett-Wilhelms was finding that on hot, humid days, the paper would absorb moisture, expand between press runs, and cause the color printing to go out of register, becoming blurry.

Carrier's assignment was to figure out a way to control the humidity in the plant. He did so in 1902 by combining two relatively new technologies, refrigeration and electricity, using electric fans to blow air over chilled coils. The coils condensed out the excess moisture in the air while also substantially cooling the air. Four years after his work for Sackett-Wilhelms, Carrier patented an "Apparatus for Treating Air": the basis of modern air conditioning.

The idea of "treating" or "conditioning" air was especially well suited to the new century, which sought to conquer and transform nature itself. Carrier's invention made the skyscraper practical and increased the profits of retail stores, theaters, and movie houses. (People liked to shop and to be entertained in cool comfort.) Installed in hospitals, it made patients more comfortable and doubtless even saved lives. In factories, air conditioning improved productivity. Gradually, beginning in the 1950s, air conditioning became sufficiently affordable to be installed in many—and then most—American homes. By the end of the century, the majority of interior urban spaces had been air conditioned.

Heart of Darkness?

In 1940, the renegade American author Henry Miller (best known for his sexually daring *Tropic of Cancer*, 1934) wrote a book titled *The Air-Conditioned Nightmare*, creating a portrait of a civilization that had become anesthetized, removed from nature and natural impulses. Like Miller, we might think of air conditioning as a metaphor for a key theme of life in the 20th century: life lived *against* nature.

We see this theme in the work of Freud (who sought to illuminate the dark places of the mind), and we see it in the electric light of Edison (who sought to illuminate dark places, period). We see, too, how the imperialists of Britain—as well as those of the United States—sought to bring the "light" of civilization to such "dark places" as Asia and Africa.

Most people welcomed and cheered each innovation and new enterprise civilization had to offer, but there were a few who were not so sure.

Jòzef Teodor Konrad Korzeniowski was born in Poland in 1857 to a family of political activists. Raised with his father in Russian exile (his mother died during this period), Korzeniowski went off to sea when he was 17. For the next 20 years, he sailed in the French and British merchant marine. He began to teach himself English—and, at the age of 40, started to write novels, in English. By then, he was calling himself Joseph Conrad.

In 1902, Conrad published a novella about a perilous riverboat journey into the heart of the Belgian Congo in search of a missing white trader named Kurtz. Kurtz was renowned as a brilliant man, an idealist of the best sort European civilization could produce. Kurtz took a job as an ivory trader, but he resolved to educate and enlighten the natives while overseeing the shipment of ivory.

After many travails, Conrad's hero-narrator finds Kurtz, desperately ill and quite insane. The bearer of civilization's light into the heart of darkness had revealed his own heart of darkness, making himself a tyrannical chieftain and decorating his hut with the skulls of his many enemies. His diary bears a final entry: "Exterminate the brutes." As he lay dying on the river journey back to the "civilization" that had produced him, he mutters only a single phrase: "The horror! The horror!"

This would be the tenor of the century. On the one hand, it was to be marked by a deep delving into the secrets of nature, which, to a degree unprecedented in history, would indeed reveal themselves. It would be characterized by a new caring

Voice of the Century

"The conquest of the earth, which mostly means the taking it away from those who have a different complexion or slightly flatter noses than ourselves, is not a pretty thing when you look into it."

—Joseph Conrad, *The Heart of Darkness* (1902)

for life and the quality of life and the fate and well-being of the individual. It would be a century of innovation and invention, of machines to make life easier, more fulfilling, and even more fun. It would be, quite simply, a century in which people learned and did more than any other people had ever learned or had ever done before.

But it would also be a century seared and all but destroyed by war—and not just war, but genocidal war conducted under policies and with weapons of unprecedented cruelty. It would be a century marked by the exploitation of one people by another. Although celebrating the individual, it would be a century that often brought a sense of alienation, rootlessness, anxiety, and discontent.

It would be, simultaneously, the most creative and destructive period of humankind on this planet.

The Least You Need to Know

➤ The 19th century introduced a new height of technology; the 20th century began to put that technology into the hands of the people.

➤ Increasingly, through events such as the Boxer Rebellion, Americans saw themselves not isolated from the affairs of the world, but an actor in them.

➤ The creation of quantum mechanics, little recognized at the time, planted the seeds not only of a new physics, but the "atomic age," which would come to so fearful a birth at the end of World War II.

➤ The death of Queen Victoria coincided with the high-water mark of the British empire as the dominant force in world affairs.

Chapter 7

Rising and Sinking (1903–1913)

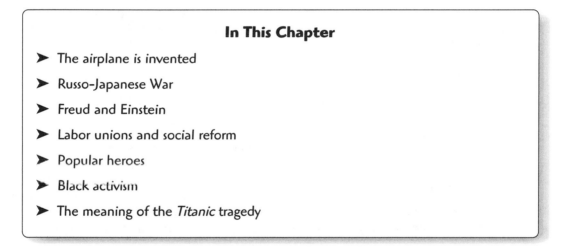

In This Chapter

➤ The airplane is invented

➤ Russo-Japanese War

➤ Freud and Einstein

➤ Labor unions and social reform

➤ Popular heroes

➤ Black activism

➤ The meaning of the *Titanic* tragedy

Picture a day in Dayton, Ohio, shortly before the turn of the century. Perhaps it's summer, the ladies in long but lightweight cotton dresses, the gentlemen in stiff collars and cuffs, a straw boater on every head. Picnic baskets all around. And bicycles. The picture of naive good times, simple pleasures. What could be simpler than a bicycle?

Well, in 1892, when the two sons of Milton Wright started making and selling bicycles in Dayton, they were considered pretty fancy machines. They weren't cheap. A bicycle was a complicated, hand-built vehicle—an adult conveyance, well beyond the financial reach of boys and girls. As bicycle mechanics, Orville (1871–1948) and Wilbur Wright (1867–1912) were skilled machinists and clever inventors. They made a fine living from their shop, with plenty of money left over to finance their hobby: aeronautics.

Quietly, together, they turned from bicycle smithing to making the century's truly epoch-making machine—out of wood and fabric and dreams.

Kitty Hawk Morning

Wilbur (1867–1912) and Orville (1871–1948) Wright were raised in Dayton, Ohio, where their father was a bishop of the United Brethren Church. The Wright brothers were inseparable, always working together, talking together, and reading together. They read a newspaper account in 1896 of the death of Otto Lillienthal, a German inventor of gliders, killed in one of his own machines. It wasn't the death that interested the boys, but the machines, and, after reading that story, they bought every aeronautical book and magazine they could find.

The Wrights were methodical. They secured the advice of the Weather Bureau (now the National Weather Service) on the best location for testing flying machines. By 1899, when they completed their first man-carrying biplane kite, they had settled on the beach at Kitty Hawk, North Carolina, for its pleasant winter climate (winter was the bike business's slow season) and gentle prevailing winds. When the 1899 glider and a subsequent machine failed to perform to their satisfaction, they concluded that all published tables of air pressures on curved surfaces were wrong. To get accurate data, they built a 6-foot wind tunnel in their shop, tested more than 200 wing designs, and drew up the world's first reliable tables of air pressures on curved surfaces. This enabled the Wrights to build a better glider in 1902, in which they flew more than a thousand times.

Century Stats

The Wrights' first plane cost less than a $1,000 to build, engine included.

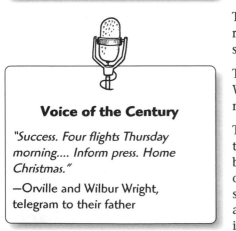

Voice of the Century

"Success. Four flights Thursday morning.... Inform press. Home Christmas."

—Orville and Wilbur Wright, telegram to their father

Their goal was not to build the perfect manned kite, however, but to mate a gasoline engine to a workable glider design and achieve powered flight. In 1903, they fitted a 170-pound, 12-horsepower motor to the *Flyer I*, a 750-pound gossamer contraption of fabric and wood, and took it all to Kill Devil Hill, Kitty Hawk, North Carolina, on the morning of December 17. They flipped a coin. It came up heads, and Orville assumed his position at the controls, lying on his belly across the bottom wing of the craft.

The engine erupted into life. The aircraft raced down a rail track laid on the beach for it. Then, it flew. For 12 seconds, over a distance of some 120 feet, it flew.

The Wrights made three more flights that first day, Wilbur managing to keep *Flyer I* aloft for almost a minute over a distance of 852 feet.

The bishop's boys returned quietly to Dayton, where they continued their experiments in a cow pasture until, by 1905, they achieved a flight of 38 minutes' duration over a distance of 24 miles. The following year, they secured a patent, during 1908–1909, they toured an astonished world, and in 1909, they began manufacturing aircraft commercially.

The first flight, December 17, 1903.
(Image from arttoday.com)

20th-Century Life

In 1908, the Wrights secured a contract with the U.S. Department of War for the first military airplane. Wilbur toured France, demonstrating the airplane and securing a French manufacturer. On September 17, 1908, a crash landing seriously injured Orville Wright (who suffered a broken thigh and two broken ribs) and fatally injured his passenger, Lieutenant Thomas E. Selfridge. The brothers carried on and were achieving considerable financial success when Wilbur died suddenly of typhoid fever on May 30, 1912. Although he never fully recovered from his brother's death, Orville continued to work in the Wright Aeronautical Laboratory until his death in 1948.

War and Peace

The airplane did nothing less than eradicate distance, bringing the people of the nation and of many nations together. But it also was one of those few human inventions that transformed not only the physical dimensions of life, but the spiritual dimensions as well. Until that winter morning in 1903, powered flight, controlled at will, had been the dream and longing of untold centuries. After that morning, powered flight was a human reality.

Having realized the dream of flight, the Wrights also realized that they did not live in a dream world. Who would buy their invention? In 1909, they decided to demonstrate the aircraft to the U.S. Army. A few years earlier, in 1904–1905, the world had seen its first demonstration of modern, mechanized war in conflict between two ancient empires, Russia and Japan. The Wrights therefore figured that the army would be interested in a weapon newer than any.

It proved a hard sell. The U.S. Army was conservative in 1909 and still looked to the cavalry for its main mobility. But in less than a decade, airplanes would be routinely shooting each other out of the skies above France, and after another 20 years of development, planes would rain down fire and ultimately drop bombs with the power to destroy cities, nations, perhaps everything.

Another New War

In 1904, war was not yet in the skies, but on the ground and on the sea. For most of its history, Japan had been, in Western eyes, a quaint kingdom of posturing swordsmen and coyly mincing geishas wrapped in gorgeous silks. Indeed, it was a small nation—but with a growing population, grand imperial ambitions, and a warrior tradition that was far more than mere posturing. Through the last half of the 19th century, the Japanese watched the Russian empire push into eastern Asia. In 1894, Japan defeated Manchu China in war, gaining many concessions, but also driving the Chinese into an alliance with Russia. The Chinese emperor granted the tsar permission to extend the great Trans-Siberian Railroad through Manchuria to Vladivostok. Four years later, the Russians secured from China a lease on Port Arthur (present-day Lu-shun) on the Liao-tung Peninsula and then decided to occupy the strategically commanding peninsula permanently—as the Japanese saw it, a dagger poised at their very heart.

Voice of the Century

"What am I going to do? I am not prepared to be a tsar."

—Nicholas II, in his diary, on the death of his father, 1894

Century Stats

Mukden, fought during late February and early March 1905, was the final battle of the land war and the costliest. Russian forces totaled 330,000 men and Japanese 270,000. The Russians suffered some 89,000 casualties, and the Japanese 71,000.

But Japan was hardly defenseless. It had been building up a modern army, equipped with the latest weapons, and a navy of modern battleships and cruisers, sporting heavy guns produced with the latest technology. What kept Japan from launching an attack was the looming presence of Great Britain, acknowledged master of the seas. Then, in 1902, that nation, also fearful of Russian expansionism, signed a non-aggression treaty with Japan.

Neither England, nor Russia, nor any other European power, for that matter, expected Japan to pose a serious threat to the armies and navies of the mighty tsar. But, on February 8, 1904, the Japanese fleet laid siege to the Russian naval squadron anchored at Port Arthur. Russia's Pacific Fleet was not merely defeated, it was obliterated, and when Tsar Nicholas II sent his Baltic Fleet into the fray, it, too, met with disastrous defeat, badly overmatched by the more advanced ships of the Japanese navy.

In the meantime, on land, the Japanese army swept across Korea, crossed the Yalu River, and invaded Manchuria. The Russian forces fought valiantly but were outgeneraled and outgunned. Nicholas, a weak and indecisive monarch tragically unsuited to the new century, turned to God and to his family's spiritual advisor, the "mad monk" Rasputin. Assured by Rasputin that the Russian will to victory was indomitable, Nicholas spurred his beleaguered forces onward to the Battle of Mukden, China. They were again cut to ribbons, although the toll on the Japanese was also great.

American Peacemaker

The West was stunned by the spectacle of the Russo-Japanese War. Despite its relative brevity, it was among the largest armed conflicts ever fought. What was most shocking was the reality of an Asian nation bringing a European power to its knees—and doing so with superior soldiery, superior leadership, and superior weapons.

Although Russia was clearly being defeated, the cost to Japan was also high, and neither nation was willing to back down. Into the deadlock stepped President Theodore Roosevelt, with an offer to mediate a peace.

The belligerents met at Portsmouth, New Hampshire, from August 9 to September 5, 1905, concluding under Roosevelt's guidance a peace that recognized Japan's conquest of Korea, its control of the Liao-tung Peninsula and Port Arthur, as well as the South Manchurian Railroad.

Japan was now a world power. Theodore Roosevelt, whom many admired and others criticized for his bellicose "big stick" policies (which you'll read about in Chapter 8, "The World Reshaped"), was awarded a Nobel Peace Prize. Tsar Nicholas II confronted a social revolution. Although this so-called 1905 Revolution was quickly crushed, Nicholas's authority was greatly eroded, and the stage was set for the "October" Revolution of 1917: the days that would shake the world by ending the reign of the czars, who had endured since the early Middle Ages.

Two Theories

It is not only war and revolution that can shake the world. Ideas, if sufficiently strong, will rock reality to its core. The new century would be rife with such ideas.

Freud on Sex

The Viennese physician Sigmund Freud (1856–1939) had already introduced the idea of a vast property of mind he called the unconscious when, in 1905, he published *Three Essays on the Theory of Sexuality*. It linked the mighty unconscious to the force of sexuality, which, Freud argued, was a drive present from infancy and through childhood and was a force that animated all thought, feeling, and endeavor and that informed each and every relationship with wife, husband, lover, son, daughter, mother, and father.

Talk of the Times

Psychoanalysis is the general term for Freud's theory of mind as well as the clinical procedures for understanding mental processes and treating mental disorders.

Freud's new book struck a nerve, deeply. The idea that "innocent" children were sexual beings evoked outrage, as did the notion that sex lay at the center of the human universe. Yet Freud persisted, and he won a growing circle of followers. In its way, the theories of the unconscious and of infantile sexuality were as profoundly disturbing of the accepted order of things as was the assertion of Copernicus, some 400 years before, that the sun and not the earth was at the center of our planetary system. Yet such ideas are ultimately liberating, and even as the 20th century would turn outward, ultimately to outer space, probing distant worlds, it would remain preoccupied with introspection as well, exploring the dark worlds that lay within us all.

Einstein on Relativity

If Freudian theory provoked outrage followed by fascination, the work of another German-speaking scientist elicited incomprehension followed by awe and ultimately by consequences no one could have imagined in 1905. Who, in any case, would have thought that anything significant, let alone earthshaking, would come from Albert Einstein (1879–1955)? He had been born in Ulm, Germany, and raised in Munich, but as a toddler, he was so slow to speak that his parents feared he was retarded. Once enrolled in school, he proved himself capable of doing well but bridled under authoritarian Teutonic teaching methods and was expelled. In 1901, he turned his back on Germany, secured Swiss citizenship, and found a job as a clerk in the Swiss patent office.

Albert Einstein, about 1931.
(Image from the University of Frankfurt, Germany)

Einstein relished his obscure government post because it allowed him plenty of time to pursue his passion for mathematics and physics. He tackled the Michelson-Morley experiment, which posed a problem thorny enough to have preoccupied physicists since it was first performed in 1881.

Using funds supplied by the telephone's inventor, Alexander Graham Bell, the German-born American physicist Albert Michelson (1852–1931) built an interferometer, a device that split a light beam in two and then brought the two beams back together. His objective was to use the interferometer to measure the earth's "absolute motion"—that is, the motion of the earth against what was assumed to be the substance of space, a "luminiferous ether," which was believed to be absolutely without motion. The interferometer would split a beam of light at right angles, sending one half in the direction of the earth's motion. That beam should complete its round trip a little later than the other beam, and by measuring the width of the difference between the two beams, Michelson could measure the motion of the earth with respect to an absolute.

It didn't work. There was no difference between the beams.

Michelson wrestled with the problem and in 1887 perfected his experimental technique with the aid of the American chemist Edward Williams Morley (1838–1923). The two were able to confirm that there was no "interference fringe." That is, the speed of light was apparently the same, regardless of the motion of the light source relative to the observer. *Why*? At the time, only two explanations seemed possible. Either the earth was motionless with respect to the "luminiferous ether," or the earth dragged this substance with it. Neither explanation made sense.

In 1905, Einstein *began* with the assumption Michelson and Morley had arrived at experimentally (though he claimed to have been unaware of their result): that the one constant in the universe was the speed of light through a vacuum. Why didn't the Michelson-Morley experiment work as expected? There is no absolute in the universe other than the speed of light. There is no absolute rest—absolute motionlessness—and, therefore, no absolute motion. Michelson and Morley were trying to measure something that didn't exist.

Einstein went far beyond explaining a "failed" experiment. He took the fact of the absolute speed of light and deduced that length contracted and mass increased with velocity while the rate of time flow decreased. That is, everything people thought of as absolutes—space, mass, and time itself—were relative to the observer's frame of reference within these dimensions. For that reason, Einstein called his formulation a *theory of relativity*. (In fact, he called it *special* relativity because it applied only to

Talk of the Times

The **Theory of Relativity** proposes a universe in which the only absolute is the speed of light and in which matter and energy are ultimately equivalent. It demonstrates that the commonsense model of the universe proposed by Isaac Newton is valid only for our particular frame of reference.

Voice of the Century

"The most incomprehensible thing about the world is that it is comprehensible."

—Albert Einstein

the "special" case of objects moving at constant velocity. He would later develop a "general" theory as well.)

For anyone who takes Einstein's relativity theory to its logical conclusions, the picture that emerges of the universe seems to defy common sense—not to mention the model of the universe as it had been understood since Sir Isaac Newton. Space, mass, and time, all of which seem so manifestly separate, are linked together in this theory, each a variable dependent on the others.

Are both common sense and Newton wrong? In *relative* terms, no. On relatively small scales, both common sense and Newton hold true, but Einstein forced the century to deal with reality on an enormous interstellar scale and dealing with velocities almost beyond imagining. At these extremes, Newtonian physics proves inadequate.

In 1907, Einstein expressed the relation among matter and energy even more dramatically, in what became the most famous mathematical expression of the century:

$$e = mc^2$$

The equation demonstrates that matter and energy are not separate entities, but readily convertible; in effect, matter must be seen as highly concentrated energy. A quantity of energy (e) is equal to an amount of mass (m) multiplied by the square of the speed of light (c).

Like the special theory of relativity, the equation changed in a profound way the theoretical view of reality itself. In the course of the century, it would do far more than change theory. The speed of light is a large number—about 984,000,000 feet per second. If you square that number (multiply it by itself), you get a tremendously large number. Multiplying the mass of a given quantity of matter by that tremendously large number yields the amount of energy that may be produced by even a small mass of matter—if a process could be found to convert matter to energy efficiently, on a subatomic level. That process would, indeed, be found, resulting in the liberation of huge amounts of *atomic energy*, which might be used to supply a city with electric power or to level that city with an atom bomb. (You'll get to that in Chapter 17, "'Now I Am Become Death'.")

Talk of the Times

Atomic energy (also called nuclear energy) is the energy released by nuclear fission (the splitting of an atomic unit into fragments) or nuclear fusion (the joining of atomic nuclei).

Saviors Wanted

Ultimately, both Freud and Einstein would become household names, icons of popular as well as scientific culture, although their theories remained obscure as far as most people were concerned. In the early years of the new century, the "average" man and woman had much more pressing needs than the stirrings of the unconscious mind or the farthest reaches of the universe. The advancement of science was all well and good, but people had to earn their bread or go hungry, and, for many, that was a struggle.

"I Won't Work"

By the closing years of the 19th century, U.S. industry, operating without government regulation, was working people hard, long, and for little pay. The Knights of Labor, a national union of skilled as well as unskilled workers, was formed in 1878 but fell victim to the anti-union feeling that followed the deadly Haymarket Riot of 1886 in Chicago. That same year, however, another national union, the American Federation of Labor, was organized by former cigar maker Samuel Gompers (1850–1924). Unlike the Knights of Labor, the AFL recognized the differing needs of different trades and enjoyed considerable success in lobbying for an eight-hour day, workmen's compensation, and the like.

Yet the AFL left the needs of one vast group unaddressed. Unskilled laborers had no union to turn to and were very much at the mercy of big employers. Eugene Debs (1855–1926), a socialist labor activist, was a prime mover in 1905 in the creation of the International Workers of the World, formed from the Western Federation of Miners and other labor organizations. Leadership of the IWW (detractors said the initials stood for "I Won't Work" and dubbed members the "Wobblies") soon passed to William "Big Bill" Haywood (1869–1928), a hard-drinking, uncompromising political radical. The charismatic Haywood wanted to transform the IWW into "one big union" for all oppressed workers, and he advocated class warfare and a revolution that would replace capitalism with an industrial democracy.

The IWW proved too radical for most Americans—and it died out during the Red Scare following World War I (as you'll see in Chapter 12, "Victims and Heroes")—but it was part of a worldwide social movement to claim the rights of the individual and to make big government and big business responsive to those rights. In some parts of the world, the movement would swell to truly revolutionary proportions, but in the United States, its effects, though profound, were less dramatic.

Urban Jungle

Not only American workers felt exploited during the single-digit years of the new century. Urban Americans of all walks of life were growing tired of big-city "machine politics," run by political "bosses" who enriched themselves and their cronies at the expense of their constituents. The closing years of the 19th century saw a parade of such bosses, including New York's William Marcy "Boss" Tweed, Pittsburgh's Chris Magee and Bill Finn, Philadelphia's "King Jim" McMahon, Boston's "Czar" Martin Momansey, and St. Louis's "Colonel" Ed Butler.

Reform-minded journalists such as Lincoln Steffens (1866–1936) and crusading politicians including Theodore Roosevelt and Robert M. LaFollette (more in Chapter 8, "The World Reshaped") did much to marshal public opinion and the collective will against the political machines, but to many Americans, the twin subjects of corruption and reform seemed abstract and remote. It took a novel, *The Jungle*, written in 1906 by socialist author Upton Sinclair (1878–1968), to bring these issues—quite literally—to the gut level.

Voice of the Century

"I aimed at the public's heart, and by accident, I hit it in the stomach."

—Upton Sinclair, speaking of *The Jungle*

Talk of the Times

Muckraker was a reference to *Pilgrim's Progress*, a Christian allegorical novel written by the British writer John Bunyan in the 17th century. The book was a fixture in many 19th-century homes and was widely taught in the schools, so most of the public was familiar with Roosevelt's reference to one of 'the characters, who used a "muckrake" to clean up the (moral) filth around him as he remained oblivious to the celestial beauty above.

Sinclair described the plight of one Jurgis Rudkus, a Lithuanian immigrant who worked in a Chicago meat-packing plant. Through the eyes of this downtrodden and exploited worker, Sinclair described in sickening detail the horrors of modern meat packing. To fatten the bottom line, packers did not hesitate to use decayed meat, tubercular meat, floor-scraped scraps of offal, and even rat meat in the manufacture of meat products.

Here was a grittily graphic tale of big business not only exploiting workers, but exploiting consumers as well. Comfortable middle-class Americans might or might not care about the fate of a blue-collar Lithuanian immigrant, but the idea of meat packers poisoning *them* and *their* families was truly nauseating. As a result of the indignation stirred by *The Jungle*, Congress enacted the landmark Pure Food and Drug Act a mere six months after the novel was published. The legislation was among the first laws that revealed a new style of American government, a government that declared itself responsible for the physical—not just political—welfare of its citizens.

Sinclair was one of a group of writers President Theodore Roosevelt dubbed "*muckrakers*." Sinclair, Lincoln Steffens, Ida Tarbell (author of a landmark exposé of Standard Oil), and other journalists exposed child labor practices, slum life, racial persecution, prostitution, sweat shop labor, and the general sins of big business and machine politics.

Heroes Wanted

Just as new-century Americans looked for social and political saviors, they also craved identification with larger-than-life popular heroes and champions. Some were real, others fictional. Some were flesh and blood, others no more than shadows flickering on a screen.

Tinsel Town (Before the Tinsel)

Thomas Alva Edison, who had already given the world electric light and recorded sound (in Chapter 5, "Through the Golden Door"), also invented a way of recording light—or, more precisely, light in motion. In 1889, Edison used strip film (invented the year before by his friend George Eastman) and devised a way to create on it a series of closely spaced photographs of moving objects. The result could then be viewed using a device that moved the film in synchronization with a flashing light. Edison quickly formed a motion-picture production company, which, in 1903, produced Edwin S.

Porter's *The Great Train Robbery*, a western that was the first movie to tell a story, using such techniques as close-ups and edited cuts.

During the first years of the "flickers" (or "movies," as the new medium was soon called), the Edison company wrangled with upstart production companies over patent rights. By 1908, however, Edison and the others joined forces in the Motion Picture Patents Company, a trust that aggressively moved to monopolize the industry through a spate of lawsuits and with a small army of strong-arm enforcers—hired thugs who "persuaded" would-be competitors into paying a hefty licensing fee to "the Trust."

As early as 1907, a handful of New York entrepreneurs left the East Coast for a dumpy suburb of Los Angeles called Hollywood. Here the real estate was cheap, the sun bright, and rainy days few—all important assets in an age when most filming had to be done outdoors. Hollywood was also a haven from the long arm of the Trust, and it soon became a company town whose product was dreams.

The Trust was ruthless not only against the competition, but also in its treatment of those who appeared in its films. Wishing to hold salaries to rock bottom, the Trust strictly prohibited giving named credit to actors, lest they become high-priced stars. Carl Laemmle, a transplanted New Yorker who started Universal Pictures in Hollywood, lured the actress Florence Lawrence away from one Trust company, Biograph Pictures (where she was known only as "The Biograph Girl"), with a hefty salary and a promise to put her name up in lights. Instantly, the Hollywood "star system" was born, and the public was given names to hang on what soon became a pantheon of film heroes and heroines.

Hollywood became the home and workplace of a galaxy of film stars. Among the first were Florence Lawrence, leading man Maurice Costello, comedian John Bunny, matinee idol Arthur Johnson, and, biggest and brightest of all the earliest stars, Mary Pickford—"America's Sweetheart" and the first American woman to earn a million dollars.

Jack Johnson and the Great White Hope

Hollywood began to weave its web of gossamer dreams, but in another arena, the dreams were made of sterner stuff. After "Gentleman Jim" Corbett defeated John L. Sullivan in 1892, boxing became a national passion—and was seen by some as a shortcut to riches. During the later 19th and early 20th centuries, driven from their country by famine and political persecution, the Irish were the most downtrodden of American immigrant groups. Prizefighting, desperate though it was, offered an escape from immigrant poverty.

Of course, the Irish were hardly the only oppressed minority in turn-of-the-century America. African Americans had little enough to hope for as well. Denied so much in the way of social and economic opportunity, black Americans were also expected to "know their place," which meant to behave in a docile, submissive, yet happy-go-lucky fashion. Few dared to violate these expectations, and of those few who did, fewer succeeded.

John Arthur "Jack" Johnson (1878–1946) was born in Galveston, Texas, and began boxing professionally in 1897. From the beginning, he refused to conform to the pattern white America tried to impose on him. He was flamboyant and outspoken, and made no secret of his taste for fine clothes, fast cars, and beautiful women—white as well as black. Johnson made his money from white audiences who enjoyed the spectacle of black boxers beating each other senseless, but then, he dared to want a shot at the best white boxers, too. Most white American prizefighters refused to fight blacks, so Johnson went to Sydney, Australia, where he fought 14 rounds with Tommy Burns in 1908. Defeating Burns, he became the first black heavyweight champion of the world.

That victory provoked white outrage not only in Australia, but also in America and much of the world. Johnson ate it up, relishing the celebrity. African Americans participated with vicarious pleasure in Johnson's victory, which put the lie to the dogma of white supremacy. Johnson's triumph also overcame white boxers' scruples about fighting a black man. Boxing promoters now conducted a sensationally publicized search for the "Great White Hope" who could defeat Johnson. Former champ Jim Jeffries came out of retirement for a contest staged on the Fourth of July, 1910. After 15 bloody rounds, Jack Johnson remained standing.

What happened to Johnson in the years after he defeated Jeffries speaks volumes about what it meant to be a black American in the early 1900s. He was twice married to white women when such "miscegenation" was not only deplored, but, in some states, illegal. In 1912, when he drove his white fiancèe out of one state and into another, he was arrested, tried, and convicted for having violated the Mann Act, which made it a federal crime to transport a woman across state lines "for immoral purposes." Johnson jumped bail and fled to Canada, and thence to Europe, successfully defending his title three times in Paris. In 1915, he traveled to Havana, Cuba, to fight Jess Willard.

Johnson later claimed that he had been told that the authorities would drop the charges against him if he lost to Willard. After an incredible 26 rounds, Johnson did go down—but the charges stood.

Century Stats

Of 114 bouts, Johnson won 80, drew 14, and lost 7. Thirteen ended in no decision.

Now the *ex*-heavyweight champion of the world, Johnson fled again, although he finally tired of life in exile and surrendered in 1920. During his year in the penitentiary at Leavenworth, Kansas, he fought exhibition bouts within the prison system. After his release, he made a precarious living in vaudeville and carnivals, even sharing billing with a flea circus.

Black Activism in 1909

The story of Jack Johnson is painful and poignant, not just because Johnson deserved better, but for what it says about the prospects of African Americans early in the century. But some black leaders saw more than the impossible long-shot opportunities prizefighting and the like offered. W.E.B. DuBois (1868–1963) was born in Great

Barrington, Massachusetts, and, with the moral and spiritual support of his family, became the first African American ever to receive a Ph.D. In 1909, with a group of white and black intellectuals and social thinkers, he founded the National Association for the Advancement of Colored People (NAACP).

The NAACP was created as an alternative not only to general black hopelessness, but to the principle of *gradualism* on which Booker T. Washington, the era's most famous African-American social leader, had founded Alabama's Tuskegee Institute in 1881. Washington's gradualism held that achieving economic self-determination (in part through education at places such as Tuskegee) had to take precedence over achieving full political enfranchisement and civil rights. Once blacks were economically self-sufficient, Washington argued, justice and equality would—gradually—follow.

Talk of the Times

Gradualism was a program of social change advocated by Booker T. Washington, who believed that social and political equality was less necessary to African Americans than economic self-determination and that such equality would come, gradually, after economic self-determination had been achieved.

20th-Century Life

Jamaica-born (1887) Marcus Garvey spoke to and for African Americans who had abandoned the hope of gaining equality in the United States. Leaving Jamaica for America in 1916, Garvey established branches of his Universal Negro Improvement Association in New York's Harlem and black neighborhoods in other American cities. By 1919, he was hailed as the "Black Moses" and claimed a following of some 2 million. He published a newspaper, *Negro World,* which aimed at instilling black pride, and he established a number of commercial enterprises, including the Negro Factories Corporation and the Black Star Line, as well as a chain of restaurants and grocery stores, laundries, a hotel, and a printing press, all with the object of helping African Americas achieve economic independence. Ultimately, he hoped to establish an independent nation for African Americans.

Garvey was the target of government probes and criminal investigations. In 1922, he and others were indicted for mail fraud in connection with the sale of stock in the Black Star Line. He was convicted and sentenced to five years' imprisonment, but his sentence was commuted to deportation to Jamaica in 1927 by President Calvin Coolidge. Garvey died there, in obscurity, in 1940.

DuBois and the NAACP were not willing to wait. DuBois lectured and lobbied widely, editing *The Crisis*, the magazine of the NAACP, and also mounting legal attacks against racist institutions and practices. The NAACP scored its first major legal victory in 1920 when it successfully fought the so-called "grandfather clauses" in certain Southern state constitutions. Many Southern states sought to bar blacks from the polls by enforcing strict literacy requirements. Because poorly educated whites were no more successful at passing literacy tests than poorly educated blacks, the states declared that descendants of people registered to vote in 1867 were exempted from the literacy requirement. This provision effectively barred illiterate blacks, but not illiterate whites.

On the basis of its success against grandfathering, the ranks of the NAACP grew, and it became the most influential African-American political and social organization of the century.

Accidents Will Happen

History is the story of careful planning and heroic striving, but it is also the story of accidents and the outcome of accidents. Some accidents of the early 20th century were extraordinarily creative, whereas others, destructive, shook the century to its soul.

It's Called Plastic

Much of our century is made of a material whose name describes its primary quality: plastic. The most important manufacturing substance of our time, it was "invented" by accident. The accident happened in 1909, but we need to look back almost a half century earlier.

In the 1860s, the billiards business was booming in America. There was only one problem. Billiard balls were made of ivory, always expensive and, with the demand for billiard balls at an all-time high, outrageously so. Collectively, the billiard industry offered $10,000 to anyone who could come up with a viable substitute. The prospect of prize money jogged the memory of a young American chemist named John Wesley Hyatt, who recalled an interesting—but hitherto commercially useless—substance called pyroxylin, developed by a British chemist in 1855. Hyatt began to work with pyroxylin and developed a method for fashioning it into a smooth, hard material resembling ivory. He called it *celluloid*, registered a patent on it, and collected his prize money.

Celluloid never took off in a *really* big way, although plenty of it was sold for the manufacture of flexible photographic film and stiff collars and cuffs for men's shirts.

That brings us to 1909. Leo Baekeland (1863–1944) was a Belgian-born American organic chemist who routinely worked with materials similar to celluloid. However, he

Talk of the Times

Celluloid was the first practical form of plastic. It is made by treating cellulose nitrate with camphor and alcohol. Celluloid was thought of as a "miracle substance" because it could be fashioned to imitate a host of costly materials.

wasn't thinking about how to make these substances more commercially useful. He had a more immediate problem: how to remove the tarry, organic gunk that accumulated on his costly experimental apparatus. To test various solvents, Baekeland created a special test "gunk" by combining phenol and formaldehyde. The substance that resulted was stubborn indeed, resistant to one solvent after another.

Then, it dawned on Baekeland: If this gunk is so durable, it might actually be *useful*. Baekeland set about making his resin even tougher, harder, and more easily worked. At last he developed a liquid that could be poured into a mold, emerging as a dense, tough solid that could even be cut and machined further. He named the material after himself, calling it Bakelite, and made a fortune with it.

It was only the beginning. This accidental substance became the basis of the dazzling variety of plastics that form so much of our world.

A Fire in Manhattan

Accident or not, Bakelite was a distinctly modern product of very modern chemistry. Yet such modernity meant little to most people in the century's early years. Many, perhaps most, Americans of this time worked under conditions that, in both technological and human terms, were downright primitive. Such was the case in the many "sweatshops" found throughout urban America. Poorly paid workers—often immigrant women—worked long hours in grim circumstances to produce clothing and other items.

One such establishment was Manhattan's Triangle Shirtwaist Factory. At the end of a workday on March 25, 1911, one of the factory's 500 employees noticed a fire in a pile of rags on the 8th floor. She alerted others, who rushed to extinguish the fire, but the blaze quickly spread out of control. Factory manager Samuel Bernstein directed workers to break out the firehose, but it proved to be rotten and useless. Indeed, the entire factory, which occupied the top three floors of the 10-story Asch Building, was a decrepit fire trap. Even the fire escape was inadequate to support the number of people who rushed to use it. It separated from the wall, and many fell to their deaths. Employees who ran to the internal stairways found locked doors. A number of workers heroically remained behind to operate the freight elevators and carry some fortunate individuals to safety. Some of the 70 employees who worked on the 10th floor clambered onto the building's roof, to which students from New York University, across the street, extended ladders.

Many employees, hopelessly trapped, leaped to certain death on the sidewalk below. Firemen could only watch helplessly: Their ladders only reached the sixth floor; streams from the hoses reached only as high as the seventh. They held nets, but the terrified workers often jumped in pairs, holding hands. The nets split under the weight.

In all, 146 people perished in the Triangle Shirtwaist fire, bringing a general outcry for laws to regulate the safety of working conditions. The public was outraged that such a disaster could occur in the midst of the nation's mightiest and most advanced metropolis. It seemed an affront to civilization, and it helped swell the wave of reform that was already gathering during this era.

Titanic Tragedy

If the Triangle fire represented the dark side of early 20th-century industrial civilization, the gorgeous passenger liner *Titanic*, queen of the British White Star Line, surely represented the best of the new century's technology. A floating palace, it was a seagoing monument to industrial achievement and financial prowess. It combined such advanced engineering and naval architecture that it was deemed "unsinkable." Its mighty double hull was divided into 16 watertight compartments; even if two of these completely flooded, the ship would remain safely afloat.

The Titanic.
(Image from
arttoday.com)

The vessel carried more than 2,200 passengers on its maiden voyage from Southampton, England, bound for New York, among them some of the world's wealthiest people, including John Jacob Astor and department-store owner Isidor Straus. Captain Edward J. Smith, the White Star Line's most senior commander, was eager to make this maiden crossing in record time and pressed his ship at 22 knots on the night of April 14, 1912, even though the waters off Newfoundland were known to be littered with icebergs.

Titanic had been designed with safety in mind, including a full complement of lifeboats—enough to accommodate all passengers. However, White Star management felt that too many lifeboats cramped the vessel's deck space, so they cut the number in half. One other item was in short supply that night: binoculars. Ice lookouts had been posted, but they were armed only with the naked eye, and the clear, cold night actually made it more difficult to detect bergs. Without wind, there were few waves that one might see or hear crashing against an iceberg.

When the massive berg was spotted, it was too late. Engines were reversed, and the ship steered hard, but underwater, the iceberg tore a great gash in the hull. Six watertight compartments flooded—more damage than the ship could sustain. The collision occurred at 11:40 p.m. After only 2¹/₂ hours, the vessel sank.

Technology might still have saved many lives. The ship was equipped with Guglielmo Marconi's recent invention—the wireless telegraph—and the vessel's radio operator heroically remained at his post, broadcasting the ship's position and the Morse code distress signal: S.O.S. It was the first time in history that this signal had been transmitted in earnest.

Not far away was the steamship *Californian*. Tragically, that vessel's lone wireless operator had turned in for the night. Nevertheless, the *Californian's* crew saw *Titanic's* lights as well as the rockets it fired. But the rockets were white, not the red signals universally understood as tokens of distress. The captain and crew of the *Californian* thought they were just a fireworks display. Another vessel, *Carpathia*, did receive the distress call and steamed toward the stricken liner. It was many miles distant, and by the time *Carpathia* arrived, 1,517 had perished.

Century Stats

The largest and most sumptuous vessel of its time, *Titanic* displaced more than 52,000 tons of water and was 882¹/₂ feet in length.

The loss of the *Titanic* has haunted and fascinated the century. It has been the subject of many books and at least three major movies, including the sensationally successful *Titanic* of 1998. The wreck itself, at the bottom of the North Atlantic, has been the object of intense study ever since its discovery in 1985 by a team of scientists led by Robert D. Ballard of the United States and Jean-Louis Michel of France.

What sustains our fascination? Perhaps we collectively interpret the death of the mighty ship, a vessel of so many hopes and dreams, as a cautionary tale about the arrogance of modern technology pitted against the eternal elements of nature.

The Least You Need to Know

➤ The early years of the century were marked by epoch-making inventions, horrific war, earth-shaking ideas, and the development of a large-scale social reform movement.

➤ The invention of the airplane not only changed the course of history, warfare, and transportation, but also it was the material expression of one of humankind's long-held dreams, the dream of flight.

➤ Freud and Einstein came to be towering figures in popular culture, even though few "ordinary" people understood their contribution to thought.

➤ Black activism reached its first true maturity in the founding of the NAACP in 1909.

Chapter 8

The World Reshaped (1908–1913)

> ### In This Chapter
>
> ➤ The "Sick Man of Europe"
>
> ➤ Revolution in China
>
> ➤ Economic motives of U.S. and European imperialism
>
> ➤ U.S. government gets bigger
>
> ➤ Ford launches the automobile age—and the assembly line
>
> ➤ Music and art pick up the pace of the century

The "old world" of the 19th century was defined by great, far-flung empires. The interests of the peoples of Asia, the Middle East, and Africa were, for the most part, controlled by Europe and, especially, Great Britain. The Second, or Great, Boer War, which ended in 1902, revealed the first cracks in the old imperial system.

At home, in the United States, it was the size more than the shape of government that was changing, and, in other ways, too, modern life was making itself universally and dramatically felt, heard, and seen.

Two Revolutions

As those living in Europe and America saw it, the Western world was filled with the wonders of science and technology; factories hummed and the wireless telegraph chirped. The peoples of the East, however, remained stubbornly mired in the beliefs and trappings of ancient times. Quaint little Japan, which had defeated mighty Russia in 1905, was an exception to the rule. Nations such as Turkey—still called the Ottoman Empire—and China were what the East was really all about: backward, stuck in time.

Or so it seemed to Western eyes.

Young Turks

At the height of its six-century history, the Ottoman Empire had controlled most of central and eastern Europe, western Asia, and North Africa. In 1908, it was very far from its height. In fact, it had been falling for the last 300 years, and now that decline was accelerating so rapidly that the rest of the world called the decrepit and corrupt empire "the Sick Man of Europe."

Yet, despite losing Cyprus in 1878, Tunisia in 1881, and Egypt in 1882, the Ottoman holdings still encompassed a vast territory, including Macedonia, Albania, Palestine, Libya, Syria, Mesopotamia, Crete, Bulgaria, and lands along the Red Sea and Persian Gulf. In the last century, Germany's dynamic chancellor, Otto von Bismarck, had been the force behind the system of interlocking alliances that characterized European politics. What remained of the Ottoman Empire would mean a great deal to that delicate balance of power, and Germany, Austria, and Russia all gazed greedily on pieces of the Ottoman pie, especially the pieces in *the Balkans*.

As the nations of Europe pondered just how the pie should be carved, it became crucial to the peace of Europe to ensure that the tottering Ottomans did not prematurely collapse, lest one overeager nation rush in and gobble up all the pieces for itself. Keeping the empire intact wasn't easy. Toward the end of the 19th century, Sultan Abdulhamid II cracked down on liberal forces within Turkey by unleashing a brutal secret police force. Most outrageous of all, in the 1890s, he ordered the genocide of tens of thousands of Armenians—an act of terror that not only presaged 20th-century horrors to come, but also provoked revolutionary unrest and brought the empire that much closer to collapse.

As early as the 1860s, a group of Turkish intellectuals had begun agitating for reform, many working from exile outside of Turkey. Over the years, the so-called Young Turks movement grew but lacked definite direction until a group of young officers of the 3rd Army Corps stationed in Macedonia's Salonika (now

Talk of the Times

The **Balkans** was a phrase frequently heard in the first quarter of the 20th century, when this geographical area included Albania, Montenegro, Serbia, Bosnia and Herzegovina, Greece, Bulgaria, and Rumania. It was a flash point of conflict and the cauldron from which World War I would emerge.

Century Stats

Some 2.5 million Christian Armenians lived within the Ottoman Empire by the late 1880s. In 1895, government-backed mobs slaughtered some 50,000. In 1915, 1,750,000 Armenians were deported to Syria, at least 600,000 dying of abuse and starvation in the course of the involuntary exodus.

Thessaloniki, Greece), frustrated by antiquated equipment, irregular pay, and no pay, formed the Ottoman Liberty Society. These military men joined forces with the intellectuals, and the stage for revolt was set.

It came first in the form of mutinies, then a general uprising in Macedonia on July 3, 1908. The rebels did not call for the ouster of the sultan, but for restoration of the constitution and representative government. Abdulhamid consented, but the Young Turks, themselves torn by dissension, could not capitalize on what they had gained. The sultan staged a counterrevolution that wasn't stemmed until 1913, when a triumvirate of Young Turks, Talat Pasha, Ahmed Cemal Pasha, and Enver Pasha, effectively seized control of the Ottoman government.

But the "Sick Man of Europe" was now on his deathbed. In the chaos, Bulgaria declared its independence in 1908, and that same year, Austria annexed Bosnia and Herzegovina. Turkish Crete proclaimed union with Greece (although threats from Istanbul kept Greece from immediately acting on the declaration). In 1911, Italy overran Tripoli (today's Libya), which inspired Serbia, Montenegro, Greece, and Bulgaria—all former provinces of the Ottoman Empire—to attack European Turkey in October 1912.

Voice of the Century

"One sees many wounded soldiers with broken noses, the result of having held their guns improperly while firing."

—Herr Wangenheim, the German ambassador to the Ottomans, on the incompetence of the Turkish army in 1912

"Young Turk" leader Enver Pasha.
(Image from arttoday.com)

The Turkish Army collapsed, and by November 3, the Bulgarians had reached Istanbul; five days later, the Greeks were in Salonika. The Adriatic port of Durazzo fell to the Serbs on November 28, and the Ottomans sued for peace on December 5.

All of Europe was stunned by the Ottoman defeat. England immediately called for a Conference of the Great Powers, which began a week later in London on December 10, 1912. Amid great dissension, the Ottoman Empire's Balkan possessions were carved and carved again as warfare erupted throughout the region during 1912–13. What alarmed the great powers of Europe was not just missing out on getting their share of the dilapidated empire, but the prospect of being dragged into a major war. For the great powers, like Gulliver among the Lilliputians, had allowed themselves to be tied down to the tiny Balkan nations by a web of entangling alliances.

Although the Young Turks did indeed reform the government of what was left of Turkey, the collapse of the Ottoman Empire had packed Europe like a powder keg. All that was required to set it off was the striking of a match. That would come in a place called Sarajevo on a day in June 1914.

Sun Rises in China

Perhaps the only old giant more vulnerable than the Ottoman Empire was China. Torn by internal dissension for years, fatally weakened by the consequences of the Boxer Rebellion (Chapter 6, "First Years"), China had been held together by the formidable empress dowager, Tz'u-hsi. With her death in 1908, it was nominally ruled by a boy emperor, Pu-Yi. Royal ministers sought to appease revolutionary forces by introducing constitutional reforms, but it was too little and much too late.

On October 10, 1911, a group of army dissidents seized the arsenal in Wuhan, central China, and persuaded the brigade commander there, Li Yuanhong, to lead a rebellion. With the Manchu, or Qing, royal court alienated from mainstream Chinese society, it was impossible to raise an effective army against the mutineers.

Dr. Sun Yat-sen, a longtime Chinese revolutionary leader whose activities had forced his exile, seized the moment to return to China and take command of the revolution—the first in thousands of years of Chinese history. In December 1911, a revolutionary congress at Nanking elected Sun president of a new republic in South China. Sun recognized that General Yuan Shih-k'ai, ostensibly loyal to the Manchus, retained the loyalty of most of the army officers in the north. Accordingly, Sun offered the presidency to the general on condition that he compel the boy emperor to abdicate and bring to an end the Manchu Dynasty. Troops marched into Beijing's Forbidden City, and, on February 12, 1912, Pu-Yi abdicated. But the Chinese Revolution was hardly at an end.

Talk of the Times

The **Forbidden City** is the Imperial Palace complex within the Inner City of Beijing (formerly Peking), China. It is surrounded by a 35-foot wall and contains hundreds of buildings—a total of some 9,000 rooms—which housed the entire imperial court.

20th-Century Life

Sun Yat-sen (1866–1925) is known as the father of modern China. Born into a family of impoverished farmers in the South Chinese province of Kwangtung, he was educated as a physician, mostly abroad, including in Hawaii, and working from Europe, Hawaii, and Hong Kong, he gained great political influence over the Chinese revolutionary movement.

The 1911 revolution gave Sun his opening to return to China, and although he was elected provisional president of the nation, his efforts to retain power involved complex compromises that ultimately resulted in betrayal of him.

Sun was perhaps the only Chinese leader of his time who might have unified the nation and averted a long, very destructive civil war. Tragically, by 1923, when he was installed as generalissimo of a new Chinese regime, his health had begun to fail, and he succumbed to cancer in 1925 before he could institute his bold programs for a unified Chinese nation.

As he had promised, Sun Yat-sen stepped aside for Yuan Shih-k'ai, now president of all China, but Yuan instantly betrayed Sun after Sun's Nationalist Party, the Kuomintang (KMT), won a majority in the nation's first parliamentary elections. Yuan responded by outlawing the KMT, dissolving parliament, assuming dictatorial powers, and sending Sun Yat-sen fleeing to Japan for his life.

By early 1916, Sun Yat-sen, backed by the Japanese government, returned to China as Yuan's regime weakened. The real powers at this time were the warlords, each of whom held sway over a province. Sun united a number of them in opposition to Yuan, who, exhausted, succumbed to illness in the spring.

This left Sun Yat-sen to contend with the warlords he had unleashed. Sun found it impossible to regain the presidency, and the struggling republic was tossed and torn by the feuding warlords. The chaos lasted through the first half of the century, and its resolution, as we shall see in Chapter 18, "A War Served Cold," would change the political and military face of the world.

Voice of the Century

"Nothing and no one can destroy the Chinese people. They are relentless survivors. They are the oldest civilized people on earth. Their civilization passes through phases, but its basic characteristics remain the same. They yield, they bend to the wind, but they never break."

—Pearl S. Buck, *China: Past and Present*

Imperial Gestures

Europe and the United States were not always unable or unwilling to intervene in the contests for power across the world. Sometimes, involvement was simply a matter of the right catalyst—even something as unlikely as oil and bananas.

The First Arab Oil

For most of human history, oil was regarded as nothing more than thick, black, ugly, noxious fluid that bubbled and oozed from the ground. In the mid-19th century, the world depended on expensive and increasingly scarce whale oil for clean-burning illumination. A few entrepreneurs realized that the oil in the ground, after it had been refined into kerosene, might be a cheap substitute for whale oil, and in 1859, drillers sunk the world's first oil well near Titusville, Pennsylvania. A boom started.

By the end of the 19th century, oil barons were finding new uses for their product, as a heating fuel, as a fuel to replace coal to power great ships, and, early in the 20th century, as a product called gasoline, which could power the internal-combustion engines of the bizarre new vehicles some were calling automobiles, but most referred to as horseless carriages.

William D'Arcy was one of those larger-than-life figures who made the Victorian age so colorful. A British soldier of fortune, he struck it rich in an Australian gold rush. In 1901, he heard about a French report claiming that vast oil deposits might be found in Persia (today's Iran). D'Arcy purchased from the grand vizier in Tehran a concession of nearly half a million square miles—an area about twice the size of Texas—and assembled an international crew to drill.

D'Arcy learned, the hard way, just how unforgiving the oil business was. He sunk his fortune into one dry well after another, but, in 1908, on verge of financial ruin, he hit a gusher.

It gushed high enough to draw the attention of British authorities. At the time, Persia was a semicolonial possession held jointly by Russia and Britain. The British crown dispatched troops from India to guard the wells of D'Arcy's new Anglo-Persian Oil Company. In 1910, the British government brought in Indian laborers to lay the world's first oil pipeline. Soon, the Anglo-Persian Oil Company became a semi-official arm of the British imperial government, and at the outbreak of World War I in 1914, Britain would purchase a controlling interest in the company, which it officially nationalized.

Oil is a fuel and a lubricant—but it served as a political and economic glue to bind the Middle East first to Britain and then to all of the West. A young Winston Churchill, as Britain's First Lord of the Admiralty, would oversee the nationalization of Arab oil in 1914 (to ensure that the Royal Navy's ships would always have enough fuel), and 40 years later, Prime Minister Winston Churchill would have to scramble to prevent a now-hostile and politically independent Iran from itself nationalizing foreign oil companies.

During the intervening years, the great powers of Europe broke up the old kingdoms of the Middle East into "independent" countries run by whichever leaders were most cooperative in supplying the West's growing thirst for black gold. The result was a permanent state of political instability, a situation that has blighted the Middle East for most of the 20th century, spawning such volatile "strong-man" leaders as Iran's Ayatollah Khomeini, Libya's Muramar Khaddafi, and Iraq's Saddam Hussein. Many such dictators replaced equally repressive rulers, such as Iran's shah, that had been backed by the imperialist policies of European nations.

America Plays in Her Own Backyard

The United States wasn't above similar meddling in the affairs of supposedly sovereign nations for its own economic reasons. If Britain had come to regard the Middle East as its oil-rich backyard, interests in the U.S. saw Central America the same way.

The United States had long held a proprietary stake in Latin America. Back in 1823, President James Monroe had promulgated the so-called Monroe Doctrine, setting up the United States as the defender of all the Americas against the designs of European colonialism. The Spanish-American War of 1898 ostensibly followed from the Monroe Doctrine but was also an exercise of U.S. proprietary interests in Cuba.

Engineering a Shortcut

Then came a proposal for one of the century's greatest projects. Recall that Columbus, in 1492, sailed for Asia and hit America instead. For some explorers, America was a destination, but, for many more, it was only an obstacle to the spice-rich lands of the Asia. Even into the 19th century, expeditions were mounted in search of a Northwest Passage that might connect the Atlantic and Pacific oceans.

In the mid-19th century, hundreds of thousands of gold seekers had to choose between an arduous overland trek west to California or an equally arduous ocean voyage, either all the way down and around the tip of South America or to the narrow Isthmus of Panama, where travelers would disembark to make a hazardous journey through the disease-ridden Panamanian jungle to a Pacific port, where they would take a ship the rest of the journey. To secure that overland passage, the U.S. government negotiated an agreement with New

Talk of the Times

Yellow fever is an infectious tropical disease caused by a virus transmitted by mosquitoes. This debilitating, often fatal disease, is characterized by high fever, jaundice, and dark vomit resulting from gastrointestinal hemorrhaging. **Malaria**, marked by severe cycles of chills and high fever, is caused by infection of red blood cells by a protozoan (of the genus Plasmodium), transmitted by the bite of an infected female anopheles mosquito.

Granada (a nation consisting of present-day Panama and Colombia) for rights of transit across the isthmus. Within a few years, the United States funded construction of a railroad across the 51-mile-wide isthmus. But that was not enough. A canal was clearly needed, and the U.S. and Great Britain concluded the Clayton-Bulwer Treaty in 1850, agreeing that neither nation would ever attempt to assert exclusive control over the canal.

But, of course, there *was* no canal. In 1881, a French firm under the direction of Ferdinand de Lesseps began construction but soon suffered bankruptcy. Twenty years later, President Theodore Roosevelt persuaded Great Britain to relinquish its claim to joint control of a Central American canal, and the New Panama Canal Company, successors to the defunct firm of de Lesseps, sold the United States its rights to the canal route for $40 million. Congress authorized construction early in 1902, and the next year ratified the Hay-Bunau-Varilla Treaty, granting the U.S. a 10-mile-wide strip of land across the isthmus in return for a $10 million-dollar cash payment and an annuity.

So far, so good. Then, the Colombian senate held out for a higher figure. At this, the Roosevelt government fanned the flames of an uprising in Panama, by means of which Panama became an independent republic. A new treaty was conveniently concluded with the new government.

Century Stats

The Panama Canal is 51 miles (82 km) long, has 6 locks, and traverses two lakes, including one 85 feet (26 m) above sea level. Today's super-tankers and certain other modern cargo vessels are too large to navigate the canal, which has therefore lost some of its earlier strategic importance.

That left nothing but the matter of actually digging the canal. The task of clearing miles of thick jungle and then moving 240 million cubic yards of earth was gigantic. But it was actually something very small that threatened to end the project before it even got under way.

The Panamanian jungle was rife with two microbial killers, *yellow fever* and *malaria*. Colonel Walter Reed, a U.S. Army doctor, realized that eradicating these plagues meant waging full-scale warfare against a tiny but formidable enemy: the mosquito. Yellow fever is caused by a virus, and malaria is caused by a parasite, but both are transmitted by the bite of certain mosquitoes.

Once this war was won, Col. George Washington Goethals, of the U.S. Army Corps of Engineers, super-vised digging the 40-mile-long channel, which was punctuated by a series of complex locks. After 8 years and $300 million, the canal was opened in 1914.

An ocean liner passes through the Panama Canal.
(Image from arttoday.com)

Banana Dictatorships

While the canal was under construction in Panama, at the southern end of Central America, maneuvering of a different kind was going on in Guatemala, at the northern end.

In 1913, the American-owned conglomerate United Fruit Company established the Tropical Radio and Telegraph Company in Guatemala, gaining a monopoly in the small, impoverished nation's communications system and asserting absolute control of this supposedly independent nation's infrastructure. The object was to completely control the agricultural resources and agricultural labor of the nation. United Fruit had the blessing of the United States government, which saw an opportunity to promote its own political interests—all in the name of free enterprise, of course—while being spared the inconvenience and embarrassment of an official policy of colonialism.

The United Fruit operation in Guatemala worked like this: The wealthy heads of local government granted United Fruit tax exemptions, vast tracts of plantation land, and ownership of Guatemala's main port. Moreover, promised further U.S. investment in their country, Guatemalan leaders turned over control of the nation's railways to United Fruit, which became, effectively, a shadow government.

United Fruit ruled the country like a company town. Workers had to buy their necessities from company stores and so were eternally indebted to their employer. Although the company built and maintained hospitals for its workers (they were, after all, useless if sick or dead), it also ran the people's lives.

In Panama and Guatemala, as well as in Cuba, the Philippines, and much of the Caribbean and Central America, resentment of U.S. imperialism festered. As British imperialism bred chronic instability in the Middle East, so U.S. policy sowed the seeds of anti-American hostility and laid the foundation for a series of brutally exploitive dictatorships that would plague our hemisphere throughout the 20th century.

Big Government

Ever since the United States Constitution was ratified in 1788, Americans cherished the ideal of minimal government: a federal authority that intruded as little as possible on local governments and on individual lives. By the start of the 20th century, however, it was clear that American government was making inroads into the lives of people in other nations, particularly in Central America and the Caribbean, and it was also penetrating more deeply into the lives of its own citizens.

The Progressives

Why did Americans permit the expansion of government? They saw it as a lesser evil than unregulated big business. During the late 19th century, the Populist political movement grew in response to abuses by railroads and other corporate giants. In Chapter 7, "Rising and Sinking," we saw how the muckraking journalism of Upton Sinclair and others moved Theodore Roosevelt's administration to endorse legislation to break up monopolies and regulate businesses where public welfare and safety were concerned.

Roosevelt was a "progressive." That became an important third political party when Wisconsin senator Robert M. La Follette founded it in 1912, but, well before then, "progressive" was a more general label pinned on anyone who wanted government to participate in a general program of moral uplift that would check the excesses of capitalism while preserving the capitalist way of life.

It worked like this: Progressives voiced support for "progress," "civic reform," and "modernization." They attacked corrupt politicians as well as the excesses of greedy railroad and utilities. They favored the break-up of monopolies, and they sought to put more power in the hands of the people through primary elections (instead of the selection of political candidates in secretive smoke-filled caucus rooms), the popular election of U.S. senators (until the 17th Amendment in 1913, election to the Senate was indirect, by state legislatures), women's suffrage, and Prohibition.

Talk of the Times

Progressivism was an American political philosophy that favored an array of reforms aimed at establishing "clean government" and giving the electorate more power—although it stopped short of anything approaching radicalism. Progressive ideas figured importantly from the beginning of the 20th century through the administrations of Theodore Roosevelt, William Howard Taft, and Woodrow Wilson.

Yet the Progressives did not speak for the poor, for immigrants, or for racial and ethnic minorities. They would have no truck with labor radicals. Indeed, the Progressives were solidly middle class.

Three presidents came out of the Progressive tradition: Theodore Roosevelt, William Howard Taft, and Woodrow Wilson. Roosevelt moved against the trusts, backed government regulation of the railroads, got a pure food and drug law enacted, and moved to protect natural resources against exploitation by private industry. Taft, although more conservative than Roosevelt, also moved against trusts and strengthened both the Interstate Commerce Commission as well as the federal court system. Wilson lowered tariffs and created a Federal Reserve system as a brake on an entirely free-market economy.

Income Tax Is Born

The reforms put forth under the banner of Progressivism accomplished much that was good, but they also redefined American government. Like it or not, government would be a partner in American business and even a member of each and every American family. It would regulate, protect, and even attempt to influence private morals. Despite periodic reactions against the trend, the role of the federal government would steadily expand as the century advanced.

But the single biggest step toward big government came all at once, in 1913. The 16th Amendment to the Constitution was ratified by the required two-thirds of the states in February 1913, and the federal government was henceforth authorized to collect a tax on income.

Conservatives considered income tax too radical an idea, yet it was hardly a new one. Tithes were levied at least as early as biblical times, and in the United States, an income tax (varying from 3 to 5 percent) was temporarily instituted to help finance the Civil War. An emergency measure, that tax ended with the war, but farmers and industrial workers continued to favor it, feeling that the wealthy should justly bear a greater tax burden than the less well off. In the spirit of Progressivism, Congress enacted a new income tax in 1894, but it was struck down by the Supreme Court as unconstitutional. That left only one option—amend the Constitution—and the income tax was born.

Century Stats

The century's two world wars would temporarily send top-bracket income tax rates sky high—as high as 77 percent during World War I and 91 percent during World War II. In 1943, Congress enacted an automatic payroll-withholding system, thereby greatly increasing taxpayer "compliance" (as the IRS politely terms it) and doubling tax revenues by 1944.

Modern Times

All that we have discussed in this chapter contributed to the fabric of early 20th century life. Certain innovations were set apart from the others, however, as imparting to the times a distinctly modern feel.

The Ford Factory

Henry Ford was born on a Dearborn, Michigan, farm on July 30, 1863. He showed an early aptitude for all things mechanical and, with his parents' blessing, left the farm to apprentice in a machinery shop. He found work as an itinerant repairman for a farm machinery company, a sawmill operator, and chief engineer for the new Edison Illuminating Company in Detroit, tending and maintaining the generators.

This work suited Ford, who was always attracted to the latest gizmo. One machine that particularly fascinated him was the "horseless carriage," which had been invented in 1885 by Carl Friedrich Benz (1884–1929) in Germany. Ford tinkered together his own automobile in 1896, completing it in his shed at 2:00 on the morning of June 4. After working for a manufacturer of custom-made automobiles, Ford built a racing car (the "999"), which driver Barney Oldfield pushed to better than a mile a minute.

In 1903, Ford organized the Ford Motor Company. He was entering the industry at an opportune time, and the company turned a profit from day one. But Ford, the eternal tinkerer, was not content. Like other auto makers, he regarded his product as a custom-made luxury item for the wealthy. In 1908, however, he decided to find a new market and developed the Model T. Ford understood that the main cost of manufacturing a car was in labor, not parts. If you could reduce the amount of time it took to build a car, you could lower the price of the car.

Ford introduced a new manufacturing technique: the assembly line. Instead of a few specialist craftsmen working on one car, each car would pass through a larger number of semiskilled (and lower-paid) workers, each one trained to do some specific aspect of assembly. The result was a car that sold for $850, significantly cheaper than a custom-made vehicle.

In 1908, $850 was still well beyond the reach of the average American. Ford introduced further modifications to his assembly line, further subdividing procedures and making each one simpler and more efficient, reducing the price to $360 by 1916.

Sturdy, reliable, homely, and humble, the Model T changed the world in many ways. It fostered a society driven (the pun is intended) by consumerism as never before. It leveled economic classes to an unprecedented degree: Rich and poor alike were now mobile. It furthered the unification of the nation by triggering construction of what would become a vast network of roads.

Century Stats

In 1908, Ford turned out 10,607 cars at $850. In 1916, he manufactured 730,041 at $360 each. By 1927, the last year of the Model T, Ford had produced a total of 15 million cars.

It also changed the face of the nation. Once divided between cities and farms, America saw the rise of suburbs, satellites of the city made accessible by automobile.

The Model T and the methods used to produce it also dramatically changed the relation of labor and management. At first, this was all to the benefit of labor. Ford, interested in efficiency and quality, paid his workers well for the times. Then, in the interest of maximizing profits, he started to demand higher levels of production from his workers. This profoundly changed the nature of labor itself. No longer were products the creation of individual craftspeople; they were the collective result of an anonymous assembly line. No longer did human beings control the nature and tempo of production. They performed the same tasks repetitively, without variation, without creativity. They did this in time with the moving machinery of the assembly line, not at any human pace.

Voice of the Century

"The idea [for the assembly line] came in a general way from the overhead trolley that the Chicago packers use in dressing beef."

—Henry Ford

Stravinsky's New Noise in Paris

For some, the assembly line represented the height of industrial civilization, providing to the masses the blessings of high technology. As others saw it, however, the assembly line was an industrial hell. It was one of modern life's unpleasant realities.

Thank goodness, in the midst of modern life's jarring cacophony, one could turn for refreshment, escape, and balm to music and art. After all, wasn't it the purpose of the arts to soothe us with images and sounds of tranquil beauty?

Not everyone thought so. Igor Stravinsky had been born into old Russia, near Saint Petersburg, on June 17, 1882. While enrolled in law school, he began to study composition with one of Russia's most eminent composers, Nikolai Rimsky-Korsakov, and he began to turn out quite creditable compositions in the lushly romantic, highly melodic Russian nationalist vein Rimsky-Korsakov and his contemporaries had been mining for some years.

Young Stravinsky soon broke with his teacher, creating the scores for three stunning ballets staged in Paris by Serge Diaghilev's Ballets Russes. There was the *Firebird* in 1910 and *Petrushka* in 1911; then, most radical of all was *The Rite of Spring* in 1913. It premiered on May 29, inciting a full-scale riot among the sophisticated Parisian audience who heard it.

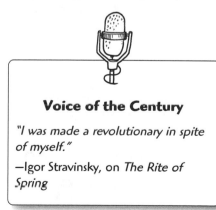

Voice of the Century

"I was made a revolutionary in spite of myself."

—Igor Stravinsky, on *The Rite of Spring*

In a way, nothing like *The Rite* had ever been heard before. Wild and exuberant, its harmonies were discordant and its complex rhythms, which shifted every few measures, were charged with an intense sexuality. Yet, for all its violent newness, the music evoked a world of primitive feeling and passion. Through eminently modern dissonances and approaches to rhythm, it reached back to the primordial past, as if to recover a set of feelings, of sensations, of values all but forgotten in modern cut-and-dried civilization.

Paris and then the world roared both approval and disgust. Some saw Stravinsky and Diaghilev as having wrought an art form equal to the demands of modern reality, whereas others accused them of bringing about the downfall of everything decent and valuable in Western art and culture.

Whether one loved or hated his work, it was obvious that Stravinsky had tapped into something essential in Western society. Perhaps it was what the eminent Swiss psychologist Carl Gustav Jung intended when he titled a 1933 book *Modern Man in Search of a Soul*. Indeed, that title might well be applied to much of the most significant art and thought of the 20th century.

Stravinsky, in the manner of such radical emerging visual artists of the period as Henri Matisse and Georges Braque, plumbed the soul-satisfying depths of primitive urges and primal rituals to create a modern, highly complex work featuring orchestrations, harmonies, and rhythmic patterns never before heard, yet nevertheless rooted in some distant, shared, and all-but-forgotten past.

To many, the artistic vision of Stravinsky and other so-called primitivists was threatening, suggestive of anarchy and uncomfortably expressive of the political climate pervading an Old World shakily balanced on the brink of war and revolution. To others, works such as *The Rite of Spring* pointed the way to an aesthetic and spiritual rebirth, an exciting new way of connecting with a challenging, discordant, and alienating world.

Art Gets Cubed—and Why

The shenanigans of a Stravinsky were all well and good in a wild place like Paris, but "modern art" would never *go* in America.

Or would it?

In 1913, at the 69th Street Armory in New York City, the International Exhibition of Modern Art—better known as the Armory Show—opened its doors. It drew 300,000 visitors in New York alone and even more as it toured to Chicago and Boston.

The purpose of the show was to introduce Americans to so-called "anti-academic" artists, whose work was usually little seen in the mainstream. Among the European artists exhibiting were Paul Cezanne, Henri Matisse, and Pablo Picasso, but the artist whose work caused the biggest stir was Marcel Duchamp. His *Nude Descending a Staircase* would become the most famous work in a style christened cubism.

Nude Descending a
Staircase, *by Marcel
Duchamp.*
(Image from
arttoday.com)

Duchamp's provocatively titled painting made no attempt to reproduce the conventional reality of representational art that most art patrons considered "true" painting. Instead, Duchamp aimed to capture relative time and motion itself, portraying his nude from a variety of perspectives and at different points in time—all simultaneously.

Duchamp had not invented the style—Picasso and Braque had—but he took it to a fascinating and scandalizing extreme. The picture made some viewers angry. One critic declared that it looked like "an explosion in a shingle factory." Others, however, saw the painting as a revelation that melded art with the newest ideas in physics and psychology, both of which stressed the relative nature of reality.

The Armory Show was exciting for some, but profoundly disturbing for others. Clearly, the new artists wanted art to venture to the frontiers that science and philosophy—and even politics—had approached. But what would be the end result of such a venture?

Voice of the Century

"I have forced myself to contradict myself in order to avoid conforming to my own taste."

—Marcel Duchamp, around 1945

After the Armory Show, Duchamp began producing what he called "ready-mades," art objects that were barely transformed items of everyday reality. His most famous was a common urinal, which he signed "R. Mutt" and titled *Fountain*.

Was it a joke? Or was it a comment on the despair and irrelevance of trying to create anything of beauty in a world, which in 1917 was consuming itself in a war that was both total and apparently pointless?

Maybe it was all of these things, and people who had looked to art for relief from the pain and alienation of an increasingly painful and alienating century were depressed and frightened.

In any case, the year of the Armory Show was the last year of anything even approaching peace the world would know for a long time.

The Least You Need to Know

➤ The decline and fall of the creaky Ottoman and Chinese empires profoundly shook and shaped the century.

➤ The U.S. government embarked on imperialist adventures in Latin America during this period while, at home, extending its reach into the lives of its citizens through Progressivism and the income tax.

➤ Henry Ford's production of the Model T and institution of the assembly line changed the face of American and world civilization forever.

➤ The art and music of the avant garde on the eve of World War I expressed new ideas about the nature of reality and also eerily presaged the destructive chaos about to come.

Chapter 9

Sarajevo Shooting (1914–1916)

In This Chapter

➤ How World War I began

➤ How Germany almost won the war

➤ World War I stalemate

➤ Feminism and birth control

➤ The movies come of age

The world embodied in the music of Stravinsky and the art of Duchamp may well have seemed chaotic to the average listener or viewer, but the apparent chaos was driven by an inner order, a logic all its own. Much the same was true of the world as it moved from 1913 into 1914.

It was, for the most part, a world armed to the teeth with the highly effective weapons of a new industrial age. Although the turmoil of Europe appeared chaotic, it was actually driven by an inner logic, a myriad of secret alliances that linked the fate of one nation to that of another. When we hear Stravinsky's *Rite of Spring* or view Duchamp's *Nude Descending a Staircase*, we sense an energy just barely under control. The music seems on the verge of explosion and the painted images about to fly apart—apt expressions of the world entering 1914.

Wrong Place, Wrong Time

Sarajevo. Today we know it as the war-torn capital of Bosnia, province of the former Yugoslavia. Early in the 20th century, however, few Americans had heard of what was then a provincial capital in the Balkans. In 1908, as the Ottoman Empire sank further

Talk of the Times

The **Hapsburgs** were the ruling dynasty of Austria-Hungary. They had held power since about A.D. 950.

to its knees, the Austro-Hungarian Empire annexed Bosnia and Herzegovina, much to the chagrin of the neighboring Serbs, who saw the region as vital to Serbian nationalist interests. In May 1911, Serbian army officers formed a secret society, the Black Hand, to train resistance forces in Bosnia and Herzegovina.

Into this troubled region ventured Francis Ferdinand, archduke of Austria, inspector general of the Austro-Hungarian army, and heir to the *Hapsburg* throne. With his wife, the Archduchess Sophie, he was determined to make a state visit to his empire's most recent acquisition.

The World as a Trap

Early 20th-century Europe was very much a family affair. King Edward VII of England, who died in 1910, was uncle to Kaiser Wilhelm II of Germany and Czar Nicholas II of Russia, and was related to many other monarchs and nobles of Europe. These family ties were further complicated by political relationships and by the personal ambitions of various rulers. England's new king, George V, desperately wanted to hold together the empire created during the long reign of his grandmother, Victoria. Germany's Wilhelm II wished to extend the might of Germany even beyond what his grandfather, Wilhelm I, had achieved. Russian czar Nicholas II ineptly struggled to suppress the growing tide of revolution in his country. The government of France, humiliated by defeat and the loss of territory in the Franco-Prussian War of 1870-1871, wanted to regain what it had lost.

In 1914, the major nations of Europe were locked into two major sets of alliances, with Germany and Austria on one side and France, Great Britain, and Russia on the other. That much was clear. Supposedly clear, too, was the purely defensive nature of these alliances, which seemed eminently prudent. In actuality, however, the pacts created an indefinable, irrational atmosphere of hostility in which the nations of Europe vied with one another to arm themselves. In 1908, when Austria-Hungary seized Bosnia and Herzegovina without first consulting Russia, the world moved to the brink of war. Russia denounced the action, and Britain and France rushed to support their ally. For its part, Germany rallied to the cause of Austria.

Russia still smarted from its ignominious defeat at the hands of the Japanese in 1905 (Chapter 7, "Rising and Sinking") and backed down. War was thus narrowly averted.

The world should have learned a lesson. The great alliances had been formed with the intention of protecting the major powers from attack. It became evident, however, that these alliances were all too capable of dragging the signatories into war, even when the disputes at issue did not directly concern them. Intended as protection, the alliances were revealed as traps.

But the world did not learn. Instead, it continued to arm.

The Trap Is Sprung

June 28, 1914, was the 14th wedding anniversary of the archduke and archduchess. They arrived in Sarajevo, where 7 young Serbs—5 were under age 20—awaited their visit, each armed by the Serbian Black Hand with a bomb, a pistol, and a vial of cyanide in case of capture.

Austrian archduke Francis Ferdinand with his wife Sophie and their children. The assassination of this royal couple set into motion the machinery of World War I.
(Image from arttoday.com)

One of the conspirators, a pale, thin, consumptive youth named Gavrilo Princip, was stationed with the others along the announced procession route of the royal couple's car. Princip was third in line. He would be called on to act only if the first two assassins somehow failed.

Indeed, Princip heard an explosion, so he assumed the bomb of either the first or second assassin had found its mark. He was so shocked to see the royal auto, undamaged, speed past him, that he forgot to hurl his bomb. Dejected, Princip melted into the crowd.

In the meantime, the archduke and archduchess were rerouted as a security measure, but the driver, unfamiliar with the new route, took a wrong turn and ended up at a dead end. He backed out, stopping the open car—by sheer accident—directly alongside Gavrilo Princip.

This time, the boy was ready. He leveled his pistol, and, at almost pointblank range, fired two shots, one into the jugular of Francis Ferdinand, the other into the gut of Sophie.

"Soferl, Soferl!" the stricken archduke moaned, "Don't die. Live for my children."

But both were dead within minutes.

20th-Century Life

Gavrilo Princip was born in West Bosnia on his father's farm on June 13, 1884. The parish priest mistakenly entered the birth date as *July* 13, 1884, in the civil register. Because Austrian law prevented execution for a crime committed when under the age of 20, Princip escaped death after he assassinated Archduke Francis Ferdinand and his wife the Archduchess Sophie on June 28, 1914.

"I do not feel like a criminal," Princip said at his trial, "because I put away the one who was doing evil. Austria as it is represents evil for our people and therefore should not exist.... The political union of the Yugoslavs was always before my eyes, and that was my basic idea. Therefore, it was necessary in the first place to free the Yugoslavs...from Austria."

Sentenced to 20 years in prison, Princip contracted tuberculosis and died on April 28, 1918. On the wall beside his bunk, he scrawled: "Our ghosts will walk through Vienna/And roam through the palace/Frightening the lords."

"The Lamps Are Going Out"

It was not known whether the Serbian government had any foreknowledge of the assassination. But that didn't stop Austria from resolving to teach Serbia a lesson. It drew up a list of demands, effectively nullifying Serbia's sovereignty. That Serbia was willing to agree to them hardly mattered. Austria wanted to go to war, presumably to secure a firmer foothold in the Balkans.

The match had been touched to the fuse, and the flame moved inexorably to the powder keg.

Talk of the Times

Mobilization is a word that echoed through the summer of 1914. It means putting a nation's military forces on a full war footing.

Russia, already pledged to aid Serbia, *mobilized*, the czar gambling that this move would cause Austria to back down. Instead, Austria declared war on Russia. Germany, tied to Austria by solemn treaty, sent Russia an ultimatum, demanding that it retract its mobilization. When Russia refused, Germany declared war on Russia on August 1.

France and Great Britain, although bound to Russia by alliance, hesitated. Germany, which had been perfecting its war plans for years, suddenly found itself with a situation the chief plan—called the *Schlieffen plan*—had failed to contemplate. The plan did not call for blundering into a two-front war. Germany could not go into action against Russia without first eliminating the threat from the west. That meant invading France. Not only were the French and British linked in alliance, but marching through Belgium, also protected by alliance with England, would bring that country into the war even sooner. Germany's hope was that England, beset by revolutionary unrest in Ireland, would be too preoccupied to honor its commitments, at least not right away.

Accordingly, on August 2, Germany sent Belgium an ultimatum: Allow free passage to the armies of the Reich or suffer the consequences. Belgium refused and did its best to defend its border.

In the meantime, on August 1, in response to Germany's invasion of little Luxembourg, France mobilized. On August 3, Germany declared war on France. On the same day, Belgium's King Albert appealed to his British allies for aid. On August 4, Germany invaded Belgium. Great Britain issued an ultimatum demanding the withdrawal of its armies. When this was ignored, Britain declared war on Germany at midnight on August 4.

"The lamps are going out all over Europe," British statesman Sir Edward Grey remarked. "We shall not see them lit again in our lifetime."

Thrust and Stalemate

"You will be home before the leaves have fallen from the trees," Germany's Kaiser Wilhelm II promised his troops as they departed for the invasion of France.

Given the lightning speed with which the German army swept through Belgium and drove deep into France, it must have seemed to the soldiers that their Kaiser's promise would hold true.

Big Plans

The Germans operated according to the plan drawn up by Count Alfred von Schlieffen in the 1890s. Schlieffen reasoned that although the Russian army was enormous, it was poorly equipped and Russia was sparsely served by rail. It would take six weeks for the Russians to mobilize. Therefore, Germany would adopt a purely defensive strategy on its eastern front, while it concentrated almost all of its

Talk of the Times

The **Schlieffen Plan**, formulated and repeatedly revised by Germany's brilliant chief of staff, Count Alfred von Schlieffen (1833-1913), prescribed a strategy for fighting a decisive two-front war against France and Russia. Deviation from the plan in the opening month of World War I stalemated the war for four unprecedentedly bloody years.

Talk of the Times

Élan is a French word meaning, roughly, spirit; however, as used by the philosopher Henri Bergson (1859–1941), it connoted an unconquerable life spirit—which the French military believed was inherent in every French soldier and would lead inevitably to victory.

119

troops in the west, bypassing France's frontier fortifications by advancing through neutral Belgium. Once inside France, the army would sweep westward and then southward through the heart of northern France, capturing Paris and knocking France out of the war within a few weeks. This accomplished, Germany could turn its full attention against Russia.

It was an intoxicating plan indeed, but France had its ideas, too. Plan XVII called for an immediate, headlong, and general offensive. It would be energized by nothing less than the French warrior spirit, called *élan*, an indefinable quality in which the French general staff placed all its faith. It would meet the German armies head on, north and south, and it would push them back.

The only trouble was that Plan XVII grossly underestimated the numbers of the German forces and never considered how few of those forces would be detailed to contend with Russia. France would be devastated.

Little Belgium

The first victim of the war was Belgium. The nation's army consisted of a mere 100,000 men, whereas the Germans were marching with almost 10 times that number. The Belgians resolved to fight it out, deploying their small numbers in elaborate fortresses, which were especially strong at Liège and Namur. But the Germans had learned to respect heavy artillery after observing the Japanese against the Russians in 1905. Gigantic artillery pieces, such as the 420-mm howitzer known as "Big Bertha," were brought to bear against the forts.

The bombardment was unprecedented in the history of war, and on August 16, the last Belgian fort capitulated. The Belgian countryside was ravaged by the advancing German army.

Voice of the Century

"The war was decided in the first 20 days of fighting, and all that happened afterwards consisted in battles which, however formidable and devastating, were but desperate and vain appeals against the decision of Fate."

—Sir Winston Churchill

Soil and the Blood of France

The first clashes between the French and German armies along the Franco-German and Franco-Belgian frontiers are collectively called the Battle of the Frontiers. They proved disastrous for the armies of France and the small British Expeditionary Force, which had been sent to France. This initial stage of the war culminated in the First Battle of the Marne, which began on September 6, and, with more than two million combatants, was not only the largest single battle of the war, but also may well have been the largest battle in history up to that time.

That battle was the result of the Germans' departure from the Schlieffen plan. Count Helmuth Johannes Ludwig von Moltke was the chief of the German general staff. He carried on his shoulders not only the weight of the

German army, but also that of his very name. His uncle, also Helmuth von Moltke, had been the chief of the general staff in service to Otto von Bismarck. He was the brilliantly decisive architect of victories over Denmark (1864), Austria (1866), and, most important, France (1871).

Although competent, the younger Moltke knew that, compared to his uncle, he was a mediocrity. The junior Moltke had driven the men of France and England back across much of France. The armies of Germany were just 30 miles from the Eiffel Tower and the Arc de Triomphe. But now a familiar lack of confidence surfaced, and Moltke felt a shudder of fear. He had moved so fast! How could he maintain his vital lines of supply? What if his vast armies were suddenly cut off? Moltke ordered his field commander, Alexander von Kluck, to halt, wheel about, and dig in.

The First Battle of the Marne resulted in a German retreat and saved Paris. But it also began a war of stalemate and slaughter. By December 1914, both sides had dug into a system of fortified trenches some 600 miles long, extending from Belgium to the Swiss border. Incredibly, for the next four years, the "Western Front" hardly moved.

Voice of the Century

"And all this madness, all this rage, all this flaming death of our civilization and our hopes, has been brought about because a set of official gentlemen, living luxurious lives, mostly stupid, and all without imagination or heart, have chosen that it should occur rather than that any one of them should suffer some infinitesimal rebuff to his country's pride."

—Bertrand Russell, Letter to Nation (London, August 16, 1914)

Helmuth von Moltke: His sudden decision to depart from the Schlieffen plan cost Germany a swift victory and plunged Europe into four years of murderous stalemate.
(Image from the author's collection)

Life in the trenches was a crucifixion of misery. Cold, wet, filthy, the men shared the trenches with rats and other vermin. The tedium of such an existence was regularly punctuated by attacks and counterattacks that resulted in nothing but death. No territory to speak of was gained.

By 1915, four million young men were living in trenches. In the first year of the war, France had lost 1.5 million men, out of a total population of 40 million.

In February 1916, acting on a plan to "bleed France white," the Germans attacked the strongest Allied fortress, Verdun, knowing that France would pour men in to defend it. For two days, 1,400 German guns lobbed some 2 million explosive shells against Verdun, but the fortress did not yield. The siege lasted for 10 months; France poured 70 percent of its army into the battle—and lost half a million men. The Germans suffered 400,000 casualties.

20th-Century Life

Although trenches had been extensively used during the American Civil War (1861–1865), never had entire armies of millions of men faced each other in a system of trenches extending from the Belgian coast all the way through northeastern France and to Switzerland. So intense was the artillery and machine-gun fire that soldiers could survive only by burrowing into the earth.

The trench networks became intricate labyrinths, containing command posts, first-aid stations, kitchens, latrines, and bomb shelters. Life in the trenches was filthy, wet, cold, and dark. Vermin of all kinds, especially rats, were abundant, and even minor wounds were subject to life-threatening infection. Most terrifying of all was the effect of poison gas, heavier than air, which would sink down into the deepest trenches, catching men unawares.

French poilus (soldiers) relax during a rare lull in the shelling at Verdun. (Image from arttoday.com)

Gas!

Whenever the war seemed as if it could get no worse, it usually did. "Humanity must be mad to do what it is doing," remarked one British soldier.

On April 22, 1915, at the second Battle of Ypres, Allied troops watched as a heavy, yellow-green vapor crept along the ground. Suddenly, men began gasping and coughing. Ten thousand troops broke and ran; within 10 minutes, half that number were dying, writhing in pain.

The Belgian town of Ypres was the scene of the first major assault using poison gas—the terror weapon of World War I. The photograph shows the town's shattered cathedral. (Image from the author's collection)

Chlorine gas was a terrible new weapon, but the Allies quickly discovered that it could be neutralized by breathing through pads soaked in hyposulfite solution. New poison gasses were manufactured: *phosgene*, which smelled like new-mown hay and then turned to hydrochloric acid when breathed into the lungs; and *chlorpicrin*, "vomiting gas," which was not deadly in and of itself, but which caused troops to remove their gas masks to vomit, forcing them to breathe in other, more deadly, agents launched with the chlorpicrin.

All pretense of the glory of war, of patriotism, of heroic sacrifice dissolved in clouds of poison gas. The war made no sense. But still, it went on.

The Russian Bear Falters

While German armies swept across France and then turned so fatefully outside Paris, smaller numbers were left to defend East Prussia (mostly modern Poland) from the dreaded Russian onslaught.

Two Russian armies, the First, under General P.K. Rennenkampf, and the Second, under A.V. Samsonov, invaded German East Prussia in August, scoring initial victories. The German commanders, Paul von Hindenburg and Erich Ludendorff, soon discovered that the invading forces consisted of semiliterate men so poorly trained that they were unable to encrypt and decrypt their communications. Orders were sent "in the clear," and the Germans eagerly listened in, hearing every Russian order as it was issued.

What the Germans didn't know is that the two Russian generals, Rennenkampf and Samsonov, despised one another. This, combined with overall incompetence and primitive communication equipment, caused Rennenkampf to fail to maintain contact with Samsonov. On August 26, Hindenburg and Ludendorff threw all their strength against Samsonov's isolated army near Uzdowo, just south of Tannenberg (today in northeastern Poland).

Samsonov's troops were routed. Thirty thousand were slaughtered in battle, and some ninety-two thousand were taken prisoner. In effect, one entire Russian army was lost. Samsonov, wheezing from asthma, was on horseback in the agonizing retreat. "The Czar trusted me," he kept repeating to his aide. "How can I face him after such a disaster?" At 1:00 on the morning of August 29th, Samsonov rode into the woods. A single shot rang out. The general had killed himself.

Tannenberg was a crushing defeat for Russia, and it only got worse. The Germans turned to Rennenkampf, whose army they defeated at Battle of the Masurian Lakes during September 1–15. This drove the Russians out of East Prussia at a cost of a quarter million men. As we will see in the next chapter, these defeats also precipitated an end to centuries of czarist rule in Russia and ushered in a new government, driven by a new ideology, which would create a new set of bloody conflicts.

For the immediate present, however, if there was a positive side for the Allies, it was that these victories kept numbers of German troops from participating in the great battles of the Western Front and helped make possible the French comeback at the First Battle of the Marne.

Empires in Flames

In the midst of it, people called it the Great War. Before long, however, with 36 nations drawn into the hostilities, it was dubbed the *World* War. The might of the British navy and the extent of British and French colonial holdings kept Germany and Austria from seeking substantial victories outside of the European continent. Nevertheless, battles were fought on the oceans, in colonial Asia and Africa, and in the colonial possessions of the Pacific.

In Africa, the Allies successfully invaded Germany's possessions, except in East Africa, where the extraordinary tactical skill of Lt. Col. Paul von Lettow-Vörbeck, a master of guerrilla warfare, cost the Allied forces heavily.

Turkey, by secret treaty, had allied itself with Germany at the outbreak of the war. The British, seeking to protect the supplies of oil necessary to fuel their navy, conducted a rapid and successful campaign against the Turkish defenders of the Mesopotamian oil fields between the high mountains of Persia (today's Iran) and Saudi Arabia.

Turkish forces also suffered against Russians in the Caucasus, the Russian-Turkish border region, in battles spanning late 1914 through the spring of 1917. In the meantime in Egypt, a Turkish bid to seize control of the strategically crucial Suez Canal was defeated by Anglo-Indian troops.

By the autumn of 1914, with stalemate established on the Western Front, the Allies decided that a major success outside of Europe would greatly improve their position. The British drew up plans to seize the straits of the Dardanelles and the city of Constantinople (modern Istanbul), which would then provide a direct route to supplying Russia. Anglo-French forces, which included large numbers of colonial troops, Australians, and New Zealanders, landed at two points on the Gallipoli peninsula but were pinned down and slaughtered by Turkish and German artillery, which commanded the heights. The battle was among the most futile of a war that consisted of a seemingly endless chain of futile battles. Losses from enemy fire, as well as disease and thirst, were staggering, in excess of 200,000, and nothing had been gained by the time the Allies were forced to withdraw.

20th-Century Life

For the British, Gallipoli was perhaps the most tragically inept campaign of modern times. Had the campaign been successful, Russia might have enjoyed sufficient success to keep it in the war, and Turkey would have been knocked out. The failure resulted not only in terrible loss of life, especially among British colonial troops, but certainly contributed to extending the war. Much as the poor performance of British military leadership in the French and Indian War in the 18th century helped create the conditions in which the American Revolution developed, so the outrage among colonial troops after Gallipoli contributed to the development of the independence movements following World War I, which ultimately resulted in the dissolution of the British empire.

Safe at Home

Democrat Woodrow Wilson (1856–1924) was the epitome of the Progressive politician. Highly educated—he had been a professor of history and president of Princeton University—he won election as New Jersey governor on a platform of government reform. Sent to the White House on the same platform, his first term saw

➤ The introduction of the Federal income tax.

➤ The lowering of protectionist tariffs.

➤ Passage of the Federal Reserve Act and currency and banking reforms.

➤ New antitrust legislation.

➤ Laws to regulate the working conditions of sailors.

➤ A Federal Farm Loan Act to provide low-interest credit to farmers.

➤ Passage of the Adamson Act, mandating an eight-hour day for interstate railroad workers.

➤ Passage of the Child Labor Act, curtailing children's working hours.

If Wilson was working to make America safer and more secure, he also pledged to keep America out of the "European war." That was just fine with most Americans.

Wilson realized that it was critically important for the United States to preserve its rights as a neutral. Germany, in the meantime, had embraced the modern technology of submarine warfare and had adopted a policy of its "unrestricted" use. This meant that German U-boat (short for *Unterseeboot*) commanders could fire torpedoes on any and all vessels, including British and French passenger liners, without warning. In February 1915, Wilson issued a stern warning to Germany that the United States would hold that nation strictly accountable for the loss of American lives in the sinking of neutral or passenger ships.

Just four months later, on May 7, 1915, a U-boat torpedoed the British passenger liner *Lusitania,* killing 1,200 people, including 128 Americans. Many in the United States—including Theodore Roosevelt—clamored for immediate entry into the war. Instead, Wilson issued a strong protest to Germany, demanding reparations and the cessation of unrestricted submarine warfare. Germany replied that the *Lusitania* carried munitions (which was true, although vigorously denied by the British), but diplomats did not want to face yet another enemy. Accordingly, Germany ordered its U-boats to give passenger ships ample warning before firing upon them.

Wilson's bellicose firmness with Germany prompted isolationist Secretary of State William Jennings Bryan to resign in protest, but the American people had faith in their president and returned him to a second term after a campaign propelled by the slogan, "He kept us out of war."

The French magazine L'Illustration *ran this sketch of the sinking of the British liner* Lusitania, *torpedoed by a German U-boat on May 7, 1915.* (Image from arttoday.com)

President Woodrow Wilson gained reelection on the campaign slogan "He kept us out of war." (Image from arttoday.com)

A War in the Bedroom

While war raged in Europe, Americans found themselves engaged in a much older battle: the one between the sexes. The Victorian age, so recently passed, had glorified motherhood above all else. "The hand that rocks the cradle," a popular Victorian saying went, "rules the world," and, "A woman's place is in the home."

In 1914, most Americans, men and women, heartily agreed with both of these sentiments. To think otherwise was to threaten the very fabric of society.

Margaret Sanger dared to think otherwise. Born Margaret Higgins in Corning, New York, on September 14, 1883, this early feminist began working as a nurse in the slums of Manhattan in 1910 and became active in radical politics, joining both the Socialist Party and the Industrial Workers of the World (IWW). As a nurse, she saw firsthand the desperation that drove impoverished women to self-induced—and often catastrophic—abortions. Sponsored by the Socialists, she began to write and speak on sexual and health-related issues in 1912. It was Sanger who coined the term "birth control."

In 1914, she began publishing a radical feminist newspaper called *Woman Rebel,* which was followed by *Family Limitations,* a how-to manual on contraception. Federal authorities charged her with using the U.S. mails to disseminate "obscene" materials, and Sanger fled to Europe to avoid prosecution. There, she studied with the pioneering sexologist Havelock Ellis and with the Dutch feminist physician Aletta Jacobs. By the time she returned to the United States in 1915, a national birth-control movement was well under way, and charges against her were dropped.

Then, Sanger upped the ante. With her sister, Evelyn Byrne, she opened a birth-control clinic in Brooklyn, a purposeful act of civil disobedience that resulted in Sanger's arrest. The resulting legal battle ended in agreement that medical practitioners had the right to dispense birth-control information to patients.

In the 1920s, Sanger would distance herself from radical politics, and she outraged former liberal allies by advocating birth control as a method of reducing the birth rate of those she deemed "inferiors." Despite this, her work in the 1910s not only promoted the cause of birth control, but also raised the consciousness of women all over the world, some of whom began to challenge their traditional social roles. This challenge, together with the subjects of birth control and abortion, would continue to figure importantly and often bitterly throughout the century.

Voice of the Century

"No woman can call herself free who does not own and control her body. No woman can call herself free until she can choose consciously whether she will or will not be a mother."

—Margaret Sanger

As we will see in Chapter 21, "From Sputnik to the New Frontier," the ideas of Sanger and others provided a foundation for the "sexual revolution" of the 1960s, but it is also true that, in later years, a backlash against feminism in general and birth control in particular developed. By the end of the century, some physicians who performed abortions would find themselves in danger of their lives; some were attacked, some murdered, and abortion clinics were bombed.

A War in the Movies

In the 1910s, the struggle for sexual equality and the controversy over birth control and abortion had not yet reached the level of violence. Nor had the "European war" reached our shores. But Americans could watch a war nevertheless.

As we saw in Chapter 7, Thomas A. Edison, the Wizard of Menlo Park, had invented motion pictures—movies—in 1889, and his company produced the first significant film, Edwin Porter's *The Great Train Robbery*, in 1903. A dozen years later, in 1915, David Wark Griffith, a onetime stock actor, traveling salesman, laborer, and mostly unsuccessful writer, directed what is still regarded as the single most important film in the development of cinema as a form of popular artistic expression.

The Birth of a Nation, three hours long in its original version, is a monumental epic of the Civil War. Not only did it summarize everything that was known about film making at the time, and introduce entirely new techniques as well, it scored a great commercial success and drew international critical praise as a significant work of art. *The Birth of a Nation* brought the film industry to a new level of sophistication and helped to bring the mass media of age.

Yet despite its technical and artistic merits, there was a highly disturbing aspect to the film. Based on Thomas Dixon's *The Clansman,* a popular novel that glorified the activities of the Ku Klux Klan after the Civil War, *The Birth of a Nation* demonstrated just how film could be manipulated socially and politically.

For Americans in much of the 20th century, movies would be a mirror, reflecting not only what we were, but also what we wanted to be, and even what we feared we might become. In the hands of unscrupulous political leaders, such as Adolf Hitler and his minister of propaganda, Josef Goebbels, film would become a sinister instrument for shaping public opinion, public attitude, public will, and the perception of truth itself.

Such thoughts were far from the minds of Griffith's audience in 1915, who were much more concerned about whether they really could afford the $2.00 admission (in an era of 5- and 10-cent tickets) seeing that spectacular film had cost them. As for the other war, the one off-screen and across the Atlantic, President Wilson would continue to keep us out of it. Right?

The Least You Need to Know

➤ World War I was *triggered* by the assassination of Austria's heir apparent but was *caused* by a series of complex, interlocking, and often secret alliances among nations.

➤ After Germany's initial advance through France, the Western Front became a static theater of slaughter in the trenches.

➤ The poorly trained, poorly led, and poorly equipped Russian army suffered devastating defeat at the hands of Germany, which hastened the coming of the Russian Revolution.

➤ In the United States, Woodrow Wilson sought to pursue a policy of strict neutrality for a nation more preoccupied with social change than a European war.

Chapter 10

Saving Democracy (1917–1919)

In This Chapter

➤ America mobilizes for war

➤ U.S. troops turn the tide

➤ The Treaty of Versailles and the League of Nations

➤ Postwar America: "return to normalcy" and isolationism

➤ The Russian revolutions

➤ The American reaction to communism

➤ Worldwide influenza epidemic

Woodrow Wilson believed that he had acted firmly but prudently in protesting the sinking of the *Lusitania* by a German U-boat on May 7, 1915. His pacifist secretary of state did not. William Jennings Bryan thought Wilson's response too provocative and resigned from the Cabinet in protest. Although Wilson won reelection in 1916 in part on the momentum of the slogan, "He kept us out of war," the national mood was turning bellicose. Influential politicians such as Theodore Roosevelt clamored for immediate entry into the fray, and the martial din beat more and more loudly.

This chapter describes how the United States entered the "European war" to "make the world safe for democracy"—and what happened in the aftermath.

Zimmermann Sends a Telegram

Faced with an ultimatum from Woodrow Wilson, the Germans did back down. They did not call off submarine warfare, but U-boat captains were ordered to surface and give warning to passenger and cargo vessels before firing torpedoes against them. In this way, civilian passengers and crew could abandon ship before the vessel was sunk. As the stalemate on the Western Front bled on, Germany groped for any advantage it could find. The destruction of British merchant and passenger vessels (most of which did secretly transport munitions and other war materiel) was just such an advantage in what had become, since General von Kluck's fateful turn away from Paris back in August 1914, a war of attrition. The targets were just too tempting. Banking on a high level of isolationism in the United States, the German high command decided to resume unrestricted submarine warfare.

On February 3, 1917, the *Housatonic,* a U.S. Navy warship, was torpedoed and sunk without warning. President Wilson responded by severing diplomatic relations with Germany. Then, on March 1, the Wilson administration made public a document known as the Zimmermann Note or Zimmermann Telegram.

Voice of the Century

"The world must be made safe for democracy.... We desire no con-quest, no dominion. We seek no indemnities for ourselves, no material compensation for the sacrifices we shall surely make. We are but one of the champions of the rights of mankind. We shall be satisfied when those rights have been made as secure as the faith and freedom of the nations can make them."

—From Woodrow Wilson's war message to Congress, April 2, 1917

A coded message sent on January 19, 1917, intercepted by British intelligence from Germany's foreign secretary Alfred Zimmermann to his nation's ambassador to Mexico, outlined the terms of a proposed German-Mexican alliance against the United States. Today, in an era of NAFTA, cooperative antidrug programs, souvenirs from Tijuana, and vacations in Cancun, such a proposal sounds more than faintly ludicrous. But recall that just a year earlier, in 1916, President Wilson had high-handedly dispatched General Pershing into Mexico with a punitive force in search of Pancho Villa, who had shot up a New Mexico town. Mexican-American relations, fraught with tension and resentment since the U.S.-Mexican War of 1846–48, were at particularly low ebb in 1917. Zimmermann proposed to Mexican President Venustiano Carranza "an understanding on our part that Mexico is to reconquer her lost territory in Texas, New Mexico, and Arizona." Carranza was also asked to "invite the immediate adherence of Japan."

The Zimmermann Telegram galvanized public opinion, and on April 2, 1917, Woodrow Wilson asked Congress for a declaration of war. It was voted up on April 6.

Alfred Zimmermann, Germany's foreign secretary: His telegram proposing terms of a German-Mexican alliance helped shake the United States out of neutrality. (Image from arttoday.com)

Mobilization: Patriots and Slackers

Germany had reason to fear the industrial might of the United States, which could, if it chose to do so, supply the British and French with unending streams of ships, vehicles, and weapons. But the threat posed by the U.S. Army seemed quite another matter. In 1917, it numbered a mere 200,000 men and had not fought in a major conflict since the Spanish-American War of 1898, a skirmish in comparison to the carnage of Europe. Indeed, the last large-scale combat the army had faced was the Civil War.

President Wilson and Congress were as well aware of this as the Germans were. Wilson had no desire to do with his army what the British had done with theirs early in the war: pour a force that was too small into a conflict that was too large. Doing so had virtually destroyed the professional core of the British army in the first year of the war.

Accordingly, in May 1917, Wilson ushered through Congress a Selective Service bill, by authority of which 2.8 million men were drafted. By the end of the war, the 200,000-man U.S. Army would swell to a force of more than 4 million.

About 2 million men would serve in the AEF (American Expeditionary Forces), which Wilson and the nation entrusted to the leadership of General John J. Pershing, a handsome, stern disciplinarian and a fine administrator, coolly distant in demeanor, yet charged with that fire in the belly that makes a great warrior. Naval forces sailed under the command of Admiral William S. Sims, whose understanding of modern naval warfare had been built in part on his service as a U.S. observer during the

133

Russo-Japanese War. (See Chapter 7, "Rising and Sinking") Sims had closely studied and reported on the effect of modern naval ordnance on armor plate, and he formulated tactical doctrine for American destroyers accordingly. Working closely with the British Admiralty, Sims would make the U.S. Navy a major presence in the war.

General John J. Pershing, commander of the American Expeditionary Force, earned his nickname, "Black Jack," because he had once commanded the Tenth Cavalry, a regiment of African American "buffalo soldiers."
(Image from arttoday.com)

"America's Sweetheart," the wildly popular silent-film star Mary Pickford, was one of a small army of celebrities who exhorted patriotic Americans to buy war bonds.
(Image from the author's collection)

On the home front, the Wilson Administration created a welter of special war agencies, effectively placing private industry entirely under federal control to turn out the hardware of war. Not only industry, but also individual citizens were subject to government regulation, as all manner of goods and products were rationed.

Germany's brutality against Belgium, its program of unrestricted submarine warfare, and the outrage of the Zimmermann Telegram were sufficient to convince most Americans to support the war effort. Nevertheless, to counter any lingering objections to American youth's spilling blood in a "foreign war," President Wilson, within a week of the declaration of war, created the Committee on Public Information and appointed newspaperman George Creel to head it. The Committee was the century's first major exercise in *propaganda*, the art of mass persuasion, which would become a hallmark of our time. The Creel Committee, as it came to be called, turned out hundreds of films, posters, pamphlets, and public presentations to portray the "Great War" as a momentous contest between nothing less than civilization and the ever-ravenous "Hun": the forces of good versus those of evil.

"A vast enterprise in salesmanship," Creel forthrightly dubbed his work, and although it was remarkably successful in forging American resolve to fight this foreign war, Wilson could always draw upon emergency war powers to plug whatever holes propaganda might leave unfilled. To "make the world safe for democracy," the press was censored and critics of the war silenced by arrest and imprisonment. Little was done to protect the rights of U.S. citizens of German ancestry, many of whom were threatened and persecuted. In many places, the use of the German language was forbidden by law, and ethnic newspapers were shut down. In some places, the public use of *all* foreign language was barred— you couldn't be too careful—and rural American towns with names such as Hamburg and Berlin changed their names to Liberty. Even sauerkraut was popularly called "liberty cabbage."

Voice of the Century

"The man who does not think it was America's duty to fight for her own sake in view of the infamous conduct of Germany toward us stands on a level with a man who wouldn't think it necessary to fight in a private quarrel because his wife's face was slapped."

—Theodore Roosevelt, speech made in April 1917

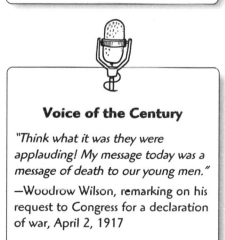

Voice of the Century

"Think what it was they were applauding! My message today was a message of death to our young men."

—Woodrow Wilson, remarking on his request to Congress for a declaration of war, April 2, 1917

"Lafayette, We Are Here!"

When Pershing arrived in Paris on June 14, 1917, he laid a ceremonial wreath at the grave of the Marquis de Lafayette, the liberty-loving French aristocrat who had come to

Talk of the Times

Propaganda, a term rooted in the Catholic church (in which it refers to the official body charged with regulating missionary preaching), is the systematic and persuasive use of selected truths in order to further a cause.

Talk of the Times

The British called their soldiers **Tommies**, the French *poilus*—literally, "hairy ones." American troops were familiarly known as **doughboys**, a term of obscure origin. Some think the word comes from the dusty appearance of troops in the American West—like they had been dusted with flour—whereas others believe the term refers to the buttons of the uniforms looking like a piece of bread dough rolled thin and fried, also called a "doughboy."

Washington's aid during the American Revolution. It was not Pershing, but Maj. Charles E. Stanton, paymaster of the AEF, who proclaimed, "Lafayette, we are here!"

As far as France and Britain were concerned, it was not a moment too soon. Although the Western Front was still stalemated, the balance favored the Germans. Every French offensive had ended in costly failure, and the demoralized French army was plagued by mutinies. Although the British had made a major push in Flanders, it, too, ended in a stalemate of mutual slaughter. As for the Eastern Front, it had collapsed in Russia's headlong charge toward a revolution that would not only end centuries of czarist rule and introduce communism into the world, but also that would bring about a "separate peace" between Russia and Germany. This would free up masses of German troops for service on the Western Front.

The first AEF troops followed Pershing to France on June 26, but it was October 21, 1917, before substantial units were actually committed to battle, and truly massive American forces would not be brought to the front until the spring of 1918.

As for Pershing, he found himself facing more than combat with the Germans. The French high command insisted that the American troops be put under its authority, a proposition that Pershing resisted in no uncertain terms. Backed by Wilson, Pershing prevailed and retained full authority over U.S. troops. They might be fighting a European war, but they would do so on American terms.

Over the Top

It was unlike any war Americans had ever fought in. The Spanish-American War had been a "splendid little war" epitomized by Teddy Roosevelt charging up San Juan Hill with his Rough Riders. Now, *doughboys* huddled in filthy trenches, trading fire with the enemy, enduring artillery bombardment, and groping for gas masks at the first faint whiff of phosgene.

Punctuating the terrible tedium of the trenches were commands to go "over the top," to clamber over the lip of the trench and advance across "no man's land," strewn with corpses, cratered by shell holes, and tangled with barbed wire, between the Allied trenches and those of the Germans.

The public liked to think of the doughboys as cheerful, comfortable— and clean, as this artwork from a 1917 Ivory Soap ad suggests. In reality, life on the front lines was grim, cramped, and filthy: Soldiers hunker down in a Marne bunker. (Image from arttoday.com)

African American doughboys are given chocolate bars by Salvation Army volunteers— France, 1918. (Image from the National Archives)

The British and French were grateful for America's entry into the fray, but they had little enough confidence in the untested American soldier. "America's power to help win the war—that is, to help us defeat the Germans in battle—is a very weak reed to lean upon," said Sir William Robertson, chief of Britain's Imperial General Staff. Yet the American army had key advantages. It was well led. It was well equipped. It was well trained. Most of all, it was new and fresh and unwearied. Between June 6 and July 1, 1918, the "Yanks" recaptured for the Allies Vaux, Bouresches, and—after a particularly bitter battle—Belleau Wood. The Americans also managed to hold the critically important Allied position at Cantigny against a great German offensive during June 9–15.

If the performance of the American army came as a shock—a welcome shock to the French and British, a terrible shock to the Germans—the horror of this "Great War" was unimaginable to the Americans. It was a sudden initiation into what Europe had known for the past four years: the world of a humanity gone mad.

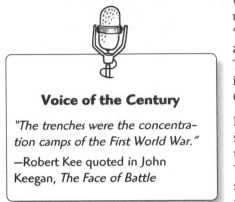

Voice of the Century

"The trenches were the concentra-tion camps of the First World War."

—Robert Kee quoted in John Keegan, *The Face of Battle*

Marne and St. Mihiel: The Stalemate Cracks

The Marne, the river and district east of Paris, where the Germans had been fought to a standstill in the early months of the war, erupted into a second great battle in the summer of 1918. In that contest, between July 18 and August 6, 85,000 American troops broke the seemingly endless stalemate of the Great War by defeating a major German offensive. Here, at last, was a battle that could be judged a genuine turning point. The Marne victory was followed by Allied offensives—at the Somme, Oise-Aisne, and Ypres-Lys during August.

In each August offensive, Americans fought side by side with the British and French. They acted independently, however, against the St. Mihiel *salient* during September 12–16. Here was a concentration of German forces desperately trying to protect their lines of supply. Against them, Pershing loosed a massive number of U.S. troops, some 1.2 million men, who pounded and then cut the German supply lines between the Meuse River and the Argonne Forest.

Talk of the Times

A **salient** is the fortified enemy area that comes closest to one's own lines.

Even as the German government was sending out peace feelers, Pershing pressed the campaign, which continued until the very day of armistice, November 11, 1918. It was a spectacular success that did nothing less than end the war, but it was also terribly costly to American units, which suffered, on average, a casualty rate of 10 percent.

A League of Their Own

The fighting skill and spirit of the American troops was formidable enough, but what overwhelmed the German forces was the health and energy of these new soldiers. It was also clear that the United States was willing to pour in as many troops as it would take to win this war. Moreover, the industrial might of the United States was matchless.

Faced with inevitable defeat, Germany sued for peace and agreed to an "armistice," a cessation of hostilities to be concluded precisely at the dramatic eleventh hour of the eleventh day of the eleventh month of 1918. Pershing pressed the attack until the very last minute.

Woodrow Wilson in Europe

The armistice was a truce only. Hammering out the official treaty of a world war took some time, and President Wilson was determined to have a leading voice in the terms of that peace; his noble and ambitious object was not merely to end this war, terrible as it had been, but to end all war. Wilson personally headed the American delegation to the Paris Peace Conference.

Century Stats

A total of 65 million men and women had served in the armies and navies of combatant nations during World War I. Of this number, at least 10 million were killed and 20 million wounded. Of the 2,000,000 U.S. troops who fought, 112,432 died, and 230,074 were wounded. The monetary cost of the war to the United States was the equivalent of $32,700,000,000 in current dollars. It was financed in significant part by a series of Liberty Loan bond drives.

Fourteen Points

On January 8, 1918, Wilson announced in an address to Congress what he hoped would be the terms of a lasting peace:

> *What we demand in this war, therefore, is nothing peculiar to ourselves. It is that the world be made fit and safe to live in; and particularly that it be made safe for every peace-loving nation which, like our own, wishes to live its own life, determine its own institutions, be assured of justice and fair dealing by the other peoples of the world as against force and selfish aggression. All the peoples of the world are in effect partners in this interest, and for our own part we see very clearly that unless justice be done to others it will not be done to us.*

Wilson continued by setting forth "Fourteen Points" as "the program of the world's peace...the only possible program." Here are the points in Wilson's own words:

    I. *Open covenants of peace, openly arrived at....*

    II. *Absolute freedom of navigation upon the seas...alike in peace and in war....*

    III. *The removal, so far as possible, of all [international] economic barriers....*

IV. *Adequate guarantees given and taken that national armaments will be reduced to the lowest point consistent with domestic safety.*

V. *A free, open-minded, and absolutely impartial adjustment of all colonial claims….*

VI. *The evacuation of all Russian territory and such a settlement of all questions, affecting Russia as will secure the best and freest cooperation of the other nations of the world in obtaining for her an unhampered and unembarrassed opportunity for the independent determination of her own political development….*

VII. *Belgium, the whole world will agree, must be evacuated and restored, without any attempt to limit the sovereignty which she enjoys in common with all other free nations. No other single act will serve as this will serve to restore confidence among the nations in the laws which they have themselves set and determined for the government of their relations with one another. Without this healing act, the whole structure and validity of international law is forever impaired.*

VIII. *All French territory should be freed and the invaded portions restored, and the wrong done to France by Prussia in 1871 in the matter of [seizing the] Alsace-Lorraine [region], which has unsettled the peace of the world for nearly fifty years, should be righted, in order that peace may once more be made secure in the interest of all.*

IX. *A readjustment of the frontiers of Italy should be effected along clearly recognizable lines of nationality.*

X. *The peoples of Austria-Hungary, whose place among the nations we wish to see safeguarded and assured, should be accorded the freest opportunity of autonomous development.*

XI. *Rumania, Serbia, and Montenegro should be evacuated; occupied territories restored….*

XII. *The Turkish portions of the present Ottoman Empire should be assured a secure sovereignty, but the other nationalities which are now under Turkish rule should be assured an undoubted security of life….*

XIII. *An independent Polish state should be erected….*

XIV. *A general association [league] of nations must be formed under specific covenants for the purpose of affording mutual guarantees of political independence and territorial integrity to great and small states alike.*

This fourteenth point was the linchpin of the entire program. If the Great War was truly to be the "war to end all war," some alternative to war had to be established to settle disputes among nations. Wilson was determined that the creation of a League of Nations would be integral to any treaty of peace.

Hall of Mirrors

In Europe, Wilson was greeted with great enthusiasm. Wilson's own enthusiasm, however, was soon challenged by his realization that the other major Allied leaders—

Georges Clemenceau of France, David Lloyd George of Great Britain, and Vittorio Orlando of Italy—were less interested in laying the foundation for enduring world peace than in vengefully humiliating and severely punishing Germany. To an important degree, Wilson prevailed in the peace conference. Hammering away at his Fourteen Points, he succeeded in welding them to the Treaty of Versailles, a document named after the former royal palace in which the signing took place.

That signing ceremony was held amid much pomp in the palace's magnificent Hall of Mirrors. The great room, as it turned out, was all too aptly named. The treaty reflected the perceived self-interest of the Allied nations as well as the single-minded—indeed, blind—idealism of Woodrow Wilson. As for Germany, it received nothing from the treaty except a levy of economically devastating reparations and national humiliation, which included almost total disarmament. It left the vanquished nation without hope and its people with nothing more to lose.

The Hall of Mirrors during the signing the Treaty of Versailles, 1919. (Image from the National Archives)

It was a document destined to fail, a tragic document that sowed the seeds in Germany of domestic revolution and international defiance. Far from bringing about a lasting peace, the unreasonably harsh terms of the Treaty of Versailles turned a dangerous nation into a desperate one and ensured the eventual coming of another war.

Betrayal

Woodrow Wilson was aware of the injustice of the Treaty of Versailles, but he felt that the document's shortcomings could be addressed later—by the very League of Nations he had created. But although he succeeded in getting the heads of foreign states to accept his League, he had neglected to develop bipartisan support for it at home.

141

Democrat Wilson was afraid that conservative Republican isolationists would resist the League of Nations. His solution was to cut the Republicans out of the loop. He chose not to appoint any prominent Republican to the peace delegation, and, even worse, he made peace and the League a political issue by appealing to voters to reelect a Democratic Congress in 1918.

Unfortunately for Wilson and the League, the war-weary nation eagerly embraced Republican isolationism as the war wound down, and the 1918 congressional contests gave the Republicans majorities in both houses. It was a ringing vote of no-confidence against Wilson and his crusade for world peace. The Constitution stipulates that although the president may make treaties, it falls to the Senate to ratify them. Henry Cabot Lodge (1850–1924) led Senate Republican opposition to U.S. ratification of the League of Nations.

Cartoon from the British humor magazine Punch *depicting the American attitude toward the League of Nations: a bridge designed by the United States but lacking "Keystone USA."*
(Image from the author's collection)

Wilson responded to this challenge not as a politician, but as an idealist. He would brook no compromise. Aiming to bring popular pressure to bear on the Senate by taking his case directly to the people, an exhausted Wilson embarked on a grueling 9,500-mile transcontinental whistle-stop speaking tour. On September 25, 1919, drained by war, by the heartbreaking labors of making peace, and by his desperate battle on behalf of the League of Nations, President Wilson collapsed after a speech in Pueblo, Colorado. His train sped him back to Washington. There, his condition deteriorated and, a week after his collapse, he was felled by a stroke that left him partially paralyzed.

An embittered shadow of himself, Wilson instructed his followers to accept no compromise on the League. Politics, especially American politics, is the art of compromise. An indignant Senate rejected the Treaty of Versailles *and* the League of Nations.

Wilson, now an invalid, served out his term, his wife, Edith, silently assuming many of his daily duties. Warren G. Harding (1865–1923), a Republican who ran on a platform of "a return to normalcy," succeeded Wilson and told Congress that "we seek no part in directing the destinies of the world…[the League] is not for us."

Red Star Rising

For all its rancor, the struggle over ratification of the League of Nations was played out, as such matters usually are in our American democracy, as an orderly political drama. The same could not be said for events in Russia.

Voice of the Century

"This war, like the next war, is a war to end war."

—Attributed to David Lloyd George (1863–1945), British prime minister

The Czar Falls

The Russian Revolution of 1917 was actually two revolutions. The first took place in March (according to the outmoded Julian calendar in use in Russia, it was still February), and the second in November (or, by the old Russian calendar, October).

Nicholas II (1868–1917) was the most hapless of monarchs in an era of hapless monarchs. He became czar on the death of his father in 1896 but was intellectually and temperamentally unprepared for the role. Although personally charming, he was shy and even timid. He had no interest in politics, and although he was fond of uniforms, his was far from a military mind. Devoted to his wife, Alexandra, he deferred to her in matters both personal and political. The defeat of the czar's armed forces in the 1905 Russo-Japanese War had triggered a revolution that created a parliament, the Duma. Since that time, bitter relations between czar and Duma created growing unrest throughout the country. It was czarist regime's incompetence in another war, the Great War, that finally brought about the revolutions of 1917, which toppled the 300-year reign of the Romanov czars forever.

Following the disastrous early battles on the Eastern Front, at Tannenberg and the Masurian Lakes (you'll find these in Chapter 9, "Sarajevo Shooting"), the military situation utterly disintegrated. As Czar Nicholas II poured more resources into the hopeless war, the Russian economy fell apart. In Petrograd (St. Petersburg, recently renamed because it sounded too German), food riots broke out in March, and the Petrograd garrison joined the revolt. As for the czar, he responded to the riots that broke out in Petrograd in March 1917 by abdicating the throne in favor of his brother Michael—who, quite prudently, declined the honor.

Talk of the Times

A **soviet** was any popularly elected legislative assembly. Soviets existed on local, regional, and national levels.

Nicholas II, "Czar of all the Russias"—and the last of the Romanovs to rule. (Image from arttoday.com)

20th Century Life

The czar's heir apparent, Alexis, was a hemophiliac, whose suffering seemed to find relief in the faith-healing ministrations of Grigory Yefimovich Novykh (1872?–1916), better known as Rasputin—"the debauched one." An illiterate peasant, Rasputin acquired a reputation as a mystic and a healer. He was introduced to the royal court in 1905 and, by 1908, began to exercise an influence first over Alexandra and then the czar. In the meantime, his sexual debauchery created a scandal throughout St. Petersburg. Worse, he insinuated himself in the administration of the state, and when Nicholas left court to take personal command of his forces in September 1915, Rasputin, through Alexandra, effectively ran the country.

Popularly called "the Mad Monk," Rasputin was the target of numerous assassination attempts until, on December 29, he was invited to visit the home of Prince Yusupov, who fed him poisoned wine and tea cakes. When the sturdy peasant showed no ill effect from these, Yusupov shot him. Wounded, Rasputin ran out of the house and was shot again. Still not dead, Rasputin was kicked in the head, bound with ropes, and cast through a hole in the ice of the frozen Neva River.

The "Mad Monk" Rasputin exercised inordinate influence over Czar Nicholas and his wife, Alexandra. He is pictured here surrounded by members of the royal family—mostly female (Alexandra is seated second from his right).
(Image from arttoday.com)

The Duma appointed a "Provisional Government," which immediately found itself challenged by the rival Petrograd *Soviet* of Workers' and Soldiers' Deputies, 2,500 delegates who had been chosen from factories and military units in and about Petrograd. When the "official" Provisional Government voted to continue Russia's participation in the war, the Soviet issued Order No. 1, directing the military to obey it and not the Provisional Government.

Between March and October 1917, the Provisional Government and the Soviet vied for control of the nation, which, during this period, continued to starve. The revolutionary leader Aleksandr F. Kerensky briefly seized the reins of government and attempted to establish a coalition of the Provisional Government and the Soviet, but the issue of whether to go on prosecuting the war continued to divide the suffering nation most deeply.

Aleksandr F. Kerensky briefly led Russia in the ways of democracy, forging a doomed coalition with the Russian Soviet.
(Image from arttoday.com)

The Triumph of Comrade Lenin

During the spring and summer of 1917, the radical forces opposed to the Provisional Government coalesced around a single intellectually forceful leader. Vladimir Illych Lenin was born Vladimir Ilyich Ulyanov on April 22, 1870 into a prosperous middle-class family. After his older brother Aleksandr, an active revolutionary, was hanged in 1887 for plotting against the czar, Ulyanov threw himself into radical political philosophy. During the closing years of the 19th century, he dedicated himself to adapting the socialist thought of the German economic-political philosopher Karl Marx (1818–83) to the conditions he perceived in czarist Russia. Whereas Marx believed that universal revolution and, hence, social justice would come from a spontaneous and inevitable uprising of the world's industrial workers, Lenin believed that, in Russia, where industrial workers identified themselves with the agricultural peasantry, revolutionary consciousness could not be left to chance but had to be raised through carefully organized political programs.

20th-Century Life

One of the most influential books in the 20th century was written in the 19th. *Das Kapital,* which appeared in three volumes during 1867, 1885, and 1894, was written by the radical German economist Karl Marx. Marx argued that, in the capitalist system, labor—human beings—was nothing more than a commodity. The capitalist pays the worker less money than his time is worth, and reaps the "surplus value"—profit. Thus capitalism depends not on the just *compensation* of labor, but on the *exploitation* of labor. Marx held that the liberation of labor could be achieved only when workers, not capitalists, owned the means of production. And that required revolution. *Das Kapital* served as the handbook for Lenin and the other architects of the communist revolutions of the 20th century.

Ulyanov—who took the pseudonym Lenin in an effort to disguise his identity from the czar's secret police—was sufficiently successful to merit arrest and Siberian exile in 1895. Five years later, he left Russia and continued his revolutionary work from abroad. His thought became increasingly radical, as he rejected mere *political* democracy as the basis for individual liberty and embraced *social* democracy, which would render society entirely classless. In 1903, he became leader of a radical wing within the Russian Social Democratic Labor Party, which he called the Bolsheviks—the "majority"—but those who didn't share his radical beliefs he labeled the Mensheviks, the minority. Even these labels demonstrated Lenin's audacity: The fact was that the so-called "minority" outnumbered the so-called "majority"!

Vladimir Lenin: master-mind of the Bolshevik Revolution.
(Image from the author's collection)

Lenin returned to Russia during 1905–1907 but resumed exile and his most intense revolutionary activity, finally returning to Russia in April 1917.

In October 1917, Lenin led the Bolsheviks in the second revolution of the year, a virtually bloodless coup that transformed Russia into a communist state. Among the first acts of the new government was the signing of a separate peace with Berlin, which resulted in the 1918 Treaty of Brest-Litovsk, by which Russia not only immediately exited the war, but also delivered either to German occupation or into the hands of German puppet governments Poland, Lithuania, the Baltic Provinces, Finland, and the Ukraine.

The October revolution did not bring harmony to Russia. Lenin was faced with splinter groups and civil war, which raged from the Black Sea to the Caspian Sea as "Whites" (monarchists) sought to defeat "Reds" (communists) in order to reinstall a czarist government.

In the meantime, the czar and his family, wife Alexandra, four daughters, and son Alexis, the heir apparent, were being held in a cellar in the Ural Mountain village of Ekatarinburg. As a White army force neared the village, Bolsheviks decided to dispose of the royal family. They were assembled and then executed at pointblank range by firing squad. When the executioners saw that some of the girls and Alexis had not perished in the hail of bullets, they finished off the children with bayonets.

Voice of the Century

"The war of 1914–1918 was imperialist (that is, an annexationist, predatory war of plunder) on the part of both sides; it was a war for the division of the world, for the partition and repartition of colonies and spheres of influence of finance capital, etc."

—Lenin, 1920

The Red Scare

With his fledgling communist state torn by civil war and racked by economic disaster, Lenin decided to compromise his Marxist absolutism by granting certain economic concessions to foreign capitalists and even reinstituting a degree of private enterprise. This might have gained his government some international support or, at least, warded off foreign interference in the civil war, had Lenin not engaged in a campaign to extend the communist revolution to the rest of the world. Through organizations called *cominterns*, he sought to create communist governments everywhere.

In the long run, this established the battle lines of the great political and ideological struggle that would be a defining feature of the century through the end of the 1980s: communism versus capitalism. In the short run, the activity of the cominterns created a worldwide "Red Scare."

Caught in the wave of anticommunism, U.S. Attorney General A. Mitchell Palmer ordered a series of raids on the headquarters of radical organizations in a dozen cities beginning in 1919. His agents summarily rounded up 6,000 U.S. citizens suspected of communist sympathies. After anarchists mailed bombs to Palmer, Rockefeller, J.P. Morgan, and more than 30 other wealthy, prominent conservatives—most of which failed to reach their destinations because of insufficient postage!—Palmer created within the Justice Department the General Intelligence Division, headed by a pudgy, baby-faced zealot named J. Edgar Hoover. Hoover quickly compiled dossiers on 150,000 radical leaders, organizations, and publications, building the core of what would eventually become the Federal Bureau of Investigation (FBI), the closest the American government ever came to creating a federal secret police force.

Talk of the Times

A **comintern** was a "local" branch of the *Comintern*, an association of *international Communist* parties established by Lenin in 1919 (and dissolved by Stalin in 1943).

Century Stats

In the dozen major American cities for which the U.S. Public Health Service kept records, 22 percent of the population caught the flu. A total of 20 million Americans contracted the disease, of whom half a million perished, not including the 50,000 soldiers who had died of flu during the war. (U.S. combat deaths numbered 48,909.)

The Plague of War: Influenza Rakes the World

Amid war and political chaos, nature suddenly took a hand. In the ancient world, war frequently brought in its wake epidemic plague. The mass movement, filth, and deprivation of World War I created the conditions in which an influenza epidemic—called the Spanish Flu—swept the world. About half of all American troop deaths were caused not by German bullets, but by flu.

After the war, the epidemic became a *pandemic*, killing 21.64 million people world-wide—1 percent of the world's population. The disease was carried back to the United States by returning doughboys. It struck first in Boston, with an alarming rate of mortality. In October and November 1918, one fifth of those infected died of pulmonary complications within mere hours of falling ill.

Flu swept the nation in three waves, through 1918–19, before it left as suddenly as it had come, bringing the era of the Great War to an even more miserable conclusion than the folly of humankind alone had wrought.

The Least You Need to Know

➤ America's isolationism was overcome by a combination of Germany's unrestricted submarine warfare and the revelation of the Zimmerman Telegram, a proposed German-Mexican alliance against the United States.

➤ It was largely the infusion of American troops that turned the tide of the stalemated war in the Allies' favor; however, the harshly punitive nature of the Treaty of Versailles created conditions that virtually guaranteed the eventual eruption of a *second* world war.

➤ Postwar America eagerly embraced what newly elected President Warren G. Harding called "a return to normalcy"—that is, isolationism—and the Senate rejected U.S. membership in the League of Nations.

➤ The conditions of World War I brought on a great worldwide pandemic of influenza, creating what some historians believe to have been the deadliest pandemic in history.

Part 3
Lost Generations: 1920–1938

It was an off-hand remark by a then-obscure avant-garde writer and art collector, Gertrude Stein, to a then-unknown short story writer and novelist, Ernest Hemingway. "You are a lost generation," Stein told Hemingway. It may even have been something she heard a garage owner say to a young and inept mechanic who had failed to fix Stein's Model T.

But the phrase stuck, and it describes as well as any the generation between the world wars. It was a time of exciting new ideas, loosening (some would say disintegrating) morals, high hopes, and low despair. The interwar period would see the rise of dictators in Europe and Asia, and the rise of a criminal underworld in the United States. It was an age of heroic deeds and scientific marvels. It was an age that saw the worst economic depression the world had ever known.

It was an age that struggled to preserve world peace and, in so doing, brought to birth a second world war, far more terrible than the first.

Jazz Age (1920–1929)

In This Chapter

➤ Women get the vote

➤ Prohibition is enacted—and defied

➤ The impact of jazz and literature

➤ African American culture

➤ The rise of cinema and radio

➤ Gangster culture

Some times and places are remembered by a particular label or phrase. In the case of the 1920s, at least four phrases come to mind. Phrase number one is what Warren G. Harding, Woodrow Wilson's successor to the White House, promised the nation: a "return to normalcy." But the next three tag lines gave the lie to Harding's promise. Gertrude Stein, the American writer living permanently in Paris, remarked to her young friend and protégé Ernest Hemingway that his was a "lost generation." Hemingway's own literary comrade, F. Scott Fitzgerald, called the decade "the Jazz Age," a reference not only to the exciting new music of the period, but also to the spirit that music embodied: moral abandon, wild energy, and daring improvisation.

Perhaps the most enduring label of all was simply this: "the Roaring Twenties." It expressed the climate of economic boom, of desperate energy, of an anything-goes ethos—and of sheer noise: the din of a decade-long party that all but drowned out the cry of despair just below the era's surface of merrymaking.

This is the first of two chapters that explore the decade between the Great War and the Great Depression.

What Is Normal?

"A return to normalcy." Just what did it mean? For most Americans, it implied a calming of the wartime madness and a return to the feeling that America was safely insulated and snugly isolated from the chaos of the rest of the world. Of course, the war and the subsequent Red Scare proved this was an illusion. But that hardly mattered now. It was a pleasant feeling, and most Americans wanted to stick with it.

The Women's Vote

For some Americans, "normalcy" also implied getting back on track with the Progressive program of reform. (See Chapter 8, "The World Reshaped") Two items on the Progressive agenda came to fruition at this time in the form of constitutional amendments: The 18th Amendment drained the nation dry—no more booze—and the 19th Amendment gave women the vote.

The latter, women's suffrage, was the culmination of a long struggle, which had formally begun in 1848 with the Seneca Falls (New York) Convention, in which 240 women and men met to draw up a list of feminist grievances, including the extension of the franchise to women. During the pre-Civil War years, the cause of women's suffrage became intertwined with that of abolition, and although pioneering feminists Elizabeth Cady Stanton (1815–1902) and Susan B. Anthony (1820–1906) espoused *both* causes enthusiastically, the result, after the Civil War, was the 14th and 15th Amendments, which extended the vote to black men. Women, however, black *and* white, were left out. The struggle dragged into the early years of the 20th century, until President Wilson approved the tersely worded 19th Amendment, which was ratified by the states in August 1920.

Extending the franchise had two apparently contradictory effects in the 1920s. First, contrary to what many men had expected, women did not vote in a unified bloc. Moreover, although the suffrage movement had long been identified with liberal and even radical causes, women did not vote for a slate of liberal candidates. Warren G. Harding, a conservative nominated by the Republican old-guard caucus in a smoke-filled room, was the first president elected after women got the vote.

The 19th Amendment did come at the opening of a decade in which women would assume a new identity in America and the world. The long-held Victorian image of the innocent girl who married for love and became a chaste wife and mother dissolved into the "modern woman": socially and sexually savvy and perhaps even capable of pursuing a career independent of husband and family. At her most extreme, the 1920s woman was a *flapper*, a sexually liberated female devoted to having a good time and beholden to no man.

Talk of the Times

Flapper was the label for the "liberated" young woman of the 1920s, whose interests were unabashedly worldly and whose inhibitions were few or none. The origin of the term is obscure but might refer to the wild flapping gestures associated with such 1920s dances as the Charleston.

Warren G. Harding, Republican, conservative, passive, and pliable, succeeded Wilson to the White House, promising Americans a "return to normalcy." (Image from arttoday.com)

The Volstead Act

The image of the flapper, both alluring and threatening to the typical American man, was also born, in part, of a new sophistication created by the war. A popular song toward the end of World War I asked the question, "How ya' gonna keep 'em down on the farm/After they've seen Paree?"

How indeed? Hemlines rose, morals loosened—and yet, simultaneously, a prudishly conservative backlash also set in. Its major result was the 18th amendment, ratified in 1919, prohibiting the manufacture, transport, and sale of alcoholic beverages anywhere in the United States. It was called Prohibition—or the Volstead Act (which was the name of the legislation passed to enforce the amendment)—and it had its origin in the temperance movements of the 19th century. By 1916, 21 states had voted themselves "dry," and they sent a "dry majority" to Congress. The lawmakers hammered out the amendment in 1917, and, over the veto of Woodrow Wilson, it was passed and sent on to the states for ratification.

President Wilson, a strait-laced moral idealist if ever there was one, objected to Prohibition on the grounds that it would create a nation of lawbreakers. He was right. In 1919, state legislatures and Congress were dominated by rural lawmakers, whose constituents supported prohibition. But the big city neighborhoods always voted against such measures, and now they flouted the Constitution itself by brewing their own beer and "bathtub gin." Nor was all of this production strictly for home consumption. Neighborhood *bootleggers* sold homebrew and booze to neighbors and even distributed the stuff through local ice cream parlors, grocery stores, pharmacies, and the like. As for the cop on the beat, well, he usually looked the other way—or, for a few dollars or a few bottles, could be *induced* to look the other way.

A poster promoting Prohibition, published during the drive to ratify the 18th amendment. (Image from arttoday.com)

Talk of the Times

A **bootlegger** made, smuggled, or sold liquor during Prohibition. The term originated not in the 1920s, but in the 19th century and came from the practice of hiding a whiskey flask in upper part of one's boot.

At first, it all seemed innocent enough. In the cities, few approved of the new law and few begrudged anyone's breaking it. Restaurants and private clubs not very surreptitiously served liquor—often in tea cups—creating a demand for something better than homemade product. Smuggling—rum running—became a profitable business, as liquor was brought in via the Caribbean islands or from Canada. As the illegal booze business grew, it drew the attention of big-time mobsters.

The great flaw of Prohibition was that it was aimed at the supply of liquor. It could do nothing to curb the demand for it, and where a demand exists, a supply will be found. Prohibition fueled crime on an unprecedented scale, as a network of mobsters organized the illegal liquor trade into an underworld big business.

The New Music

The restaurants, clubs, and back-alley dives where bootleg liquor was served were called *speakeasies*, and they purveyed more than alcohol. A new kind of popular music—*jazz*, they called it—was also served up in these places.

It had migrated north from the red-light district and French Quarter of New Orleans. Its ambassadors were such musicians as King Oliver, Jelly Roll Morton, and, paramountly, Louis Armstrong (1900–1971), the first great jazz soloist and one of the genre's greatest musicians. Jazz was rooted in African American folk music, the music of the slaves, combined with the popular dance music of European immigrants. By the 1920s, the early practitioners of jazz were both black and white, but the prime movers of the music were African American. The audience for the music, however, was mostly white; indeed, for many whites, jazz provided the first opportunity for thinking about African Americans in something other than a subservient role.

If jazz broadened horizons for black as well as white Americans, it also opened the doors to the international recognition of American culture. As the popularity of jazz ignited the States, it spread simultaneously to Europe, especially France. As you read in Chapter 5, "Through the Golden Door," American art, music, and literature had a long struggle to gain serious international attention. Even most Americans habitually gave the nod to Europe in cultural matters, ignoring homegrown works.

Talk of the Times

Jazz is a highly improvisational form of music primarily developed by African Americans who combined European harmonic structures with African rhythmic complexities. These are, in turn, overlaid with European and white American dance and march rhythms and with elements borrowed from the blues tradition. The word is probably derived from a slang term for sexual intercourse.

20th-Century Life

Louis Armstrong (1901–1971), nicknamed Satchmo (short for "Satchel Mouth"), was born into poverty in New Orleans—where he grew up fatherless, his mother working as a prostitute—and learned to play cornet at the Home for Colored Waifs, to which he was sentenced for general delinquency. Armstrong came into his own when he joined the band of King Oliver in Chicago.

Jazz lifted Armstrong from a life of poverty to wealth and fame, and he transformed jazz from ensemble music to a showcase for virtuoso solo improvisation. Recordings made with his own Hot Five and Hot Seven groups, between 1925 and 1928, are the beginning of modern jazz. Armstrong gave the music maturity, expanding its rhythmic and harmonic complexity. Armstrong was the ambassador of jazz, responsible more than any other individual for establishing it as a unique and universally popular musical art form.

Jazz changed all that. Hooked on the sounds of Armstrong, Oliver, Morton, and such European apostles of the American music as the jazz violinist Stephane Grappelli and the gypsy guitarist Django Reinhardt, Europe went wild for American music and, because of the music, became interested in American art and literature as well.

The New Literature

In fact, the most exciting new American writers, people such as the poet e.e. cummings (whose fondness for lowercase type extended to the way he spelled his own name) and the fiction writers Sherwood Anderson, William Faulkner, Ernest Hemingway, and F. Scott Fitzgerald, gravitated to Paris after the war.

Of course, that city had always attracted artists and writers. But it now harbored a new magnet, another expatriate American, Gertrude Stein (1874–1946), and a rotund, homely woman with close-cropped hair and an ever-present mousey companion named Alice B. Toklas. Stein had been born on February 3, 1874, in Allegheny, Pennsylvania, and had an education afforded to few women at the time. While attending Radcliffe College, she studied with the great American psychologist and philosopher William James before leaving school in 1903 to live with her brother, Leo, an art collector and dealer, at 27 rue de Fleuris, Paris.

The Steins amassed a highly discriminating collection of modern art and developed enduring friendships with the likes of Pablo Picasso and Henri Matisse. Gertrude Stein wrote two avant-garde works of literature in the years before World War I, *Three Lives* (1909) and *Tender Buttons* (1914). During the war, she and Toklas threw themselves tirelessly into relief work. After the war, with equal passion, she threw open the doors of 27 rue de Fleuris to Hemingway, Faulkner, Fitzgerald, and the rest. She imparted to them her sense of literature as a radical form of social criticism and her understanding of the postwar period as a time of intense creative ferment, of frenzy, despair, moral decay, and a struggle to create a new order of civilization.

To the promising young American writers who came to her, Stein gave a sense of direction. About 1925, in conversation with Hemingway and other expatriates, she told the young writers that theirs was a "lost generation." In those two words, Stein captured the mood of an era, and Hemingway's debut novel, *The Sun Also Rises* (1926), gave early voice to this lost generation, which had come of age in the Great War, even as it had been physically, emotionally, and spiritually wounded by it. Hemingway's genius lay not only in his having captured the exciting yet world-weary spirit of the times, but also in his having found an uncompromisingly lean and austere prose style that seemed to strip all pretense from his art. Instantly, he became an international literary superstar.

Hemingway was born and raised in the Chicago suburb of Oak Park (a "city of broad lawns and narrow minds,"

Voice of the Century

"I have taken as my ruling idea the determination never to write a false line."

—Ernest Hemingway, 1962 interview

he called it), and his companion in postwar Paris was another Midwesterner, F. Scott Fitzgerald, a native of St. Paul, Minnesota, but much more at home among the "smart set" of Manhattan. Fitzgerald had already secured a reputation as the novelist laureate of the Jazz Age (a phrase he coined) with the novels *This Side of Paradise* (1920), *The Beautiful and Damned* (1921), and two collections of short stories, when his first masterpiece, *The Great Gatsby* appeared in 1925.

Unlike *The Sun Also Rises*, *The Great Gatsby* was set not in bohemian Paris, but among the newly rich of New York and Long Island. It relates the fate of one Jay Gatsby, a lowborn millionaire whose desperate love for the heedless and unattainable Daisy Buchanan becomes a metaphor embodying the American dream and the corruption of innocence in a world that had passed through the crucible of war.

A Renaissance in Harlem

Hemingway and Fitzgerald gave voice to a class of young people who may have felt lost, but were nevertheless privileged. There was, however, another generation of Americans for whom these writers said nothing and whose sense of alienation had nothing to do with the late war.

African American slavery had ended with the Civil War, of course, but discrimination against blacks continued to be very much a part of American society. In the South, racial segregation was not only legal, but also it was supported by law. In the North, the law was silent on segregation, but prejudice and discrimination were no less real. African Americans had served with distinction during World War I in segregated military units. The French did not discriminate against blacks, however, and, for some African American soldiers, the overseas experience came as a revelation. They returned to the States no longer willing to accept second-class citizenship.

Many white Americans did not so much discriminate against blacks as ignore them. Excluded from most positions of power and influence, African Americans simply did not matter to mainstream white society. This began to change in the '20s. The best jazz was being played in clubs and cabarets located in New York's Harlem, a predominantly black neighborhood. Sophisticated white audiences came to hear the music of such greats as Armstrong, Fletcher Henderson (1898–1952), and the young Duke Ellington (1899–1974). They also found themselves attracted to the work of African American artists and writers who were coming from all parts of the country to live in Harlem. A lively exchange between white intellectuals and black Harlem artists developed into what became known as the Harlem Renaissance.

This literary and artistic movement drew inspiration from the black political leader W.E.B. DuBois, whom we met in Chapter 7, as editor of *The Crisis*, the magazine of the National Association for the Advancement of Colored People (NAACP). DuBois argued that blacks could not achieve social equality by merely emulating whites; they had to awaken black racial pride by discovering their own African cultural heritage. The poet Countee Cullen (1903–46), novelist Rudolph Fisher (1897–1934), poet-essayist Langston Hughes (1902–67), folklorist Zora Neale Hurston (1901–60), poet James

159

Weldon Johnson (1871–1938), and novelist Jean Toomer (1894–1967) were some of the significant American writers associated with the movement DuBois was instrumental in launching.

The Party Begins

The groundwork laid by DuBois and the writers, musicians, and artists of the Harlem Renaissance was important to a people struggling not just to overcome oppression, but to be seen and taken seriously. Yet it was groundwork only. By and large, mainstream white culture was not yet ready to focus seriously on African Americans and their culture. Indeed, most Americans had little interest in being serious about anything.

Flagpoles Are for Sitting

If a sense of being lost underlay the Roaring Twenties, its surface was frivolous. People who had never been to college became intensely interested in "collegiate life," which seemed to consist of attending football games and fraternity "smokers" and, on a dare, swallowing live goldfish.

In this era, advertising became big business. The product was seen as less important than what might be said to sell it. "Publicity stunts"—outrageous public acts sponsored by the purveyor of this or that product—were staged to attract coverage from newspapers and, also new in the era, the newsreel. People walked tightropes between skyscrapers, went over Niagara Falls in barrels, and, a hallmark of the 1920s, sat on flagpoles. There was inordinate attention paid to individuals who sought to perch atop a flagpole, usually topping some prominent skyscraper, longer than anyone else. Flagpole sitters would endure the elements, hunger, fear, tedium, and fatigue for hours and even days.

Even for some contemporaries of the period, flagpole sitting seemed to symbolize the era, in which the ideal was mindless amusement and the very notion of actual achievement seemed hollow. Did you want to be a great man? Why not just be a great flagpole sitter?

Movie Madness

The 1920s were the culmination of the American fascination with mass spectacle. In the late 1800s, the likes of P.T. Barnum and Buffalo Bill Cody provided the spectacle. In the 1920s, it was the movies. We saw the beginnings of the film industry in Chapter 7, but in the years following World War I, the American film industry grew into a national obsession.

At first, movie producers went out of their way to avoid making stars of their actors, lest salary demands become disproportionately great. But the likes of Mary Pickford (1893–1979), "America's sweetheart" and the first American woman to earn a million dollars, and comedian Charlie Chaplin soon demonstrated that the major appeal of movies was not in the stories, but in the stars. By the early 1920s, studios vied with one another to create stars, whom they cheerfully paid astronomical salaries to appear in films that, for the most part, were churned out like Henry Ford's Model Ts.

Charlie Chaplin in his most familiar and popular guise—as the Little Tramp.
(Image from the author's collection)

Hollywood, a middling suburb of the middling Southern California city of Los Angeles, had originally attracted movie producers who were looking to escape the stranglehold "the Trust" exerted on the industry. (See Chapter 7.) By the 1920s, this inexpensive and practical refuge, where the real estate was cheap and the weather always fine for shooting, was being portrayed as an enchanted land of make-believe, dedicated to the fulfillment of public fantasy.

Stars such as Rudolf Valentino, Gloria Swanson, Nita Naldi, Pola Negri, and Clara Bow—known as "the *It* girl"—fueled that fantasy with images of sexually charged romance. If the public appetite for such erotic fodder seemed insatiable, comedies were even more popular. Charlie Chaplin, Harry Langdon, Roscoe "Fatty" Arbuckle, Mabel Normand, Harold Lloyd, Buster Keaton, and the team of Laurel and Hardy, comics all, became household names.

Century Stats

By the early 1920s, about 40,000,000 Americans went to the movies at least once a week. Half this number were under age 21.

Hollywood stars became notorious for the decadence of their life styles, and the worlds of fantasy and reality sometimes clashed. The comedy of Roscoe "Fatty" Arbuckle, for example, was based on a libidinous, leering character he created. In September 1921, Arbuckle was charged with the rape and manslaughter of a young starlet, Virginia Rappe, which touched off a sensational scandal. Although Arbuckle was ultimately acquitted, his career was ruined—although he later directed movies under the assumed name of William B. Goodrich (will be good—and rich?). Soon other scandals surfaced, the murder of director William Desmond Taylor and the death of matinee-idol Wallace Reid as a result of a drug overdose.

Hollywood moguls scrambled to stave off public protests, boycotts, and, worst of all, the prospect of government censorship by instituting in 1922 the practice of self-censorship, which was administered by former U.S. Postmaster General Will Hays. The so-called Hays Office promulgated a "Purity Code" and set forth a policy of "compensating values": movie makers could show just about any salacious thing they wanted as long as it resulted ultimately in the punishment of wrongdoing.

Voice of the Century

"Strip away the phony tinsel of Hollywood and you'll find the real tinsel underneath."

—Oscar Levant

A skillful director could turn the requirements of the compensating values into what might be termed creative moral license. Cecil B. DeMille, for example, presented extravagant orgies of sex and violence in the context of thoroughly uplifting religious spectacles, the most famous of which was the 1923 *Ten Commandments*, one of the most successful movies of all time.

Radio Days

Movies were not the only mass medium to come of age in the 1920s. In Chapter 6, "First Years," we saw how Guglielmo Marconi's demonstration of trans-Atlantic radio communication created a worldwide sensation in 1901, and just five years later, in 1906, engineer Reginald Fessenden developed a transmitter capable of broadcasting not just code, but music and voice as well.

Back when Thomas Edison was working on improvements to his electric light (that was in Chapter 5), he tried sealing a metal wire in the same bulb with the filament. To his surprise, he found that current flowed across the gap from the filament to the wire. Edison patented this arrangement, called the phenomenon the Edison effect, but could find no earthly use for it. In 1906, the American physicist Lee De Forest used the Edison effect as the basis of the Audion *vacuum tube*, a device capable of amplifying weak current, such as that produced by radio-frequency signals.

Until it was replaced by the transistor—developed in 1948 and in general use by the early 1960s—the vacuum tube was the basis of all electronic circuits. Eager to demonstrate his invention, De Forest broadcast opera performances in New York between 1907 and 1909. Although a handful of amateur radio enthusiasts made similar broadcasts before World War I, sending music and speech into the airwaves, no major company materialized to develop the potential of commercial radio broadcasting until after the war.

At last, on November 2, 1920, the radio station KDKA in Pittsburgh broadcast the results of the presidential election. From this moment on, commercial radio exploded. By 1923, 556 commercial radio stations were broadcasting across the nation. When radio's popularity became obvious, station owners sought ways not only to make money, but also to reduce competition. They organized individual stations into networks, which broadcast the same show at the same time, and they started to sell on-the-air advertising. At first, a public outcry arose over the advertising. Listeners considered it an outrageous invasion of privacy. Not to be daunted, the networks adopted methods of "indirect" advertising, in which singing groups, comedians, and bands labeled themselves with a company's name, which they mentioned at every opportunity.

By the end of the decade, listener objections had been overcome, and *direct* radio advertising was big business. Radio was now poised to become the most powerful mass medium of its time—more influential than any newspaper and more intimate than any live stage performance.

Talk of the Times

The **vacuum tube** is an electron tube that acts to amplify weak electric currents or to use low–voltage currents to control higher–voltage currents. It is the basis of all electronic circuitry before the invention of the transistor in 1948.

Cops and Robbers

The first commercial radio broadcast was of election results, and, from the beginning, news was a main dish on the radio bill of fare. Some of the most sensational news in the 1920s concerned crime—not the isolated bank heist or the occasional mugging, but *organized crime*, the work of sophisticated gangs.

Ancient Traditions and Neighborhood Boys

No one knows just when the Mafia got its start, but it might date as far back as the 13th century, when groups of Sicilians organized to fight French domination of their country. The word *Mafia*, some have said, is an acronym for *Morte alla Francia Italia Anela* ("Death to the French [is] Italy's Cry"), and others have traced it to the same period, to the plea of the mother of a Sicilian girl raped by French soldiers on her wedding day: *"Ma fia! Ma fia!"* ("My daughter! My daughter!") Yet it wasn't until the Napoleonic era that the Mafia became truly powerful in Sicily, and no longer as a selflessly political force, but now as a criminal organization. By the middle of the 19th century, the Mafia was part of the baggage some Sicilian immigrants carried with them to the United States. It came to prominent public notice here on October 15, 1890, when members of the Mafia assassinated David Hennessey, the crusading police chief of New Orleans.

The Mafia was only the largest and most conspicuous of many ethnically based criminal gangs that came to dominate much of the life of immigrant urban neighborhoods by the beginning of the 20th century. Neighborhood boys, street toughs, banded together and ran gambling and prostitution operations, as well as "protection rackets"—extorting tribute from shopkeepers in return for letting them do business in peace.

Organization Men

As mentioned earlier, the enactment of Prohibition in 1919 transformed much of the United States into a nation of lawbreakers. It also upped the ante of crime exponentially. Prostitution and gambling had been profitable, but booze was *really* big business.

A key figure of organized crime in the 1910s and '20s was John Torrio. Born in Italy, Torrio began his criminal career in New York before moving to Chicago in 1909. He dreamed of making crime into a big business and was among the first to go into bootlegging in a major way. It was Torrio who brought to Chicago a Brooklyn thug named Alphonse Capone, who, with Torrio, organized Chicago's multi-ethnic gangs into a city-wide syndicate.

Not that the process of organization was peaceful. Torrio and Capone terrorized, attacked, and killed ("hit") gangs, gang members, and gang leaders who refused to get in line. Torrio and Capone conducted their violent gang wars openly, brazenly. It was not that the police were helpless to stop them; it was that Torrio and Capone *owned* the police, as well as other city officials, on up to the mayor.

In 1925, Torrio himself was wounded in a "hit" directed against him. He fled to Italy (later to return when Italian dictator Benito Mussolini declared war on the Mafia) and turned over the Chicago underworld to Al Capone, who resumed the gang wars with redoubled violence and catapulted himself to quasi-mythic prominence as a criminal czar.

The Untouchables

Throughout most of the 1920s, the public was more intrigued than outraged by the activities of organized crime. After all, Capone and his ilk supplied the demands of the thirsty, and the only people getting hurt were other criminals. However, on St. Valentine's Day 1929, Capone hit the rival gang of George "Bugs" Moran, gunning the men down with Thompson submachine guns ("Tommy guns," the gangster's weapon of choice, available in abundance as war surplus) in the Clark Street garage Moran used as his headquarters. The murder of these seven hoodlums (Moran himself had not been present) was so brutal that a shocked public at last responded with demands to clean up Chicago and the nation's other crime-infested cities.

The public outcry had two effects. The first was a response from New York crime boss Charles "Lucky" Luciano, who, together with his lieutenant Meyer Lansky, called a "conference" in Atlantic City of gangsters from all across the country. Slaughter such as Capone was perpetrating, he argued, was not merely brutal; it was bad business. Luciano and Lansky proposed a vast underworld "syndicate" that would fairly divide the nation's criminal activities into exclusive "territories." Everyone would get a piece of the action so that murderous competition would no longer be necessary. In this way, at the end of the decade, modern organized crime was born.

The second effect of the St. Valentine's Day Massacre was a concerted federal effort to fight emerging organized crime. Twenty-six-year-old Eliot Ness (1903–1957) was appointed to the government's Prohibition Bureau in 1929. Realizing that the Chicago Police Department was thoroughly corrupt and that even federal officials were suspect, Ness personally organized a tight-knit squad of nine men, so squeaky clean and unavailable to the forces of corruption that the press branded them "the Untouchables."

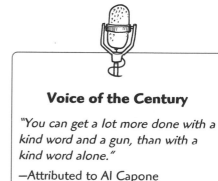

Voice of the Century

"You can get a lot more done with a kind word and a gun, than with a kind word alone."

—Attributed to Al Capone

Beginning before the decade was out, and continuing into the 1930s, the Untouchables would pursue, harass, and menace Capone and his operations. Ness and his organization assumed a quasi-mythic status on a par with that of Capone himself, as the public was treated to a contest, it seemed, between no less than the forces of good and evil.

When the climax came, however, it was all anticlimax. Capone had so thoroughly corrupted officials and so thoroughly terrorized his enemies that no prosecutor was ever able to bring him to justice for his greatest crimes, which included myriad counts of extortion, violations of the Volstead Act, gambling, prostitution, kidnapping, assault, and murder. Frustrated, Ness and his men resorted to the income tax laws. It was obvious that Capone was a wealthy man. It was just as obvious that he had not reported any of his income to the IRS. In 1931, Capone was tried and convicted for six years of income-tax evasion and was sentenced to an 11-year term in federal prison. Suffering from the irreversible late-stage neurological effects of untreated syphilis, he would be paroled in 1939, paralyzed and almost completely out of his mind. So the dark side of the Jazz Age came to its end.

The Least You Need to Know

➤ The culmination of Progressive reform in the 1920s was women's suffrage and prohibition.

➤ Prohibition, popular in rural areas but never welcomed in the cities, created the economic and moral climate that made organized crime a hallmark of the 1920s.

➤ Jazz emerged during the decade not only as America's leading popular music, but also as the first form of American art to gain enthusiastic worldwide recognition.

➤ The decade saw the meteoric rise of two important forms of mass media—the movies and radio.

Chapter 12

Victims and Heroes (1920–1929)

In This Chapter

➤ The Harding and Coolidge administrations

➤ Rise of the dictators in Italy and Germany

➤ J. Edgar Hoover and the FBI

➤ American xenophobia and its consequences

➤ High points of the decade

To see the 1920s only for its glitzy surface and its often ugly underbelly is to miss what lay between these extremes: much of the real drama of the decade and its remarkable richness of achievement. It was a period in which momentous events occurred, some squalid, some glorious, and, viewed with the hindsight of history, it was a decade that seemed to set the world stage for two of the cataclysms that nearly destroyed, but also shaped, our time: the Great Depression of the 1930s and World War II. This chapter takes another view of the Jazz Age.

Choosing Up Sides

Toward the end of Chapter 10, "Saving Democracy," we encountered Warren G. Harding's phrase, "return to normalcy," and it was repeated in the Chapter 11, "Jazz Age." The superficial extravagance of the Roaring Twenties—the desperately silly stunts, the fantasy world of Hollywood, and the amorality of organized crime fueled by an experiment in enforced morality called Prohibition—these things were anything but "normal."

That phrase was really as hollow as the Harding administration itself. Warren Gamaliel Harding (1865–1923) was a handsome, small-town Ohioan with a good speaking voice, an affable manner, and a pliant attitude. Elected state senator (1899–1902), lieutenant governor (1903–04), and U.S. senator (1915–21), he served in all three offices with no distinction whatsoever. That made him singularly attractive to the conservative Republicans, who caucused at the party's 1920 presidential nominating convention in June 1920. In those days, there were no primary elections. Candidates were chosen by party caucuses meeting at night in the so-called "smoke-filled rooms." With the convention deadlocked among three contenders, Harding, precisely because he was a nonentity, emerged as the most viable compromise.

His campaign style was laid back to the point of nonparticipation. In an age when candidates traveled the nation on whistle-stop tours, giving speeches from the rear platform of a passenger train observation car, Harding conducted a "front porch" campaign, letting the press and people come to him. He cultivated the image of an easy-going Midwesterner who would demand as little from the nation as Woodrow Wilson had demanded so much.

The promise of "return to normalcy" was really a shared fantasy of nostalgia, a desire to return to the good old days—before world war and Bolshevism, when America was a place of rural hamlets rather than cities teeming with immigrant masses.

Century Stats

Warren Harding was voted into office by a popular margin of 60.3 percent, the biggest presidential win recorded to that time.

Talk of the Times

Political patronage is the distribution of lucrative political appointments in return for political support and to pay off political debts.

The majority of Americans wanted to turn back the clock, to bury their heads in the sand. The president was happy to oblige. He took a hands-off approach to government, which extended to the running of his own administration. He gave remarkably little thought to the selection of his Cabinet, which he supervised not at all. *Political patronage*, the use of lucrative political appointments to pay off political debts, was common. For many positions, Harding simply appointed his friends.

The result was a happy-go-lucky administration rotten with corruption. The biggest of many scandals bubbled to the surface in the spring of 1923. U.S. Senator Thomas J. Walsh was beginning to make public evidence that Secretary of the Interior Albert B. Fall had secretly leased federal oil reserves to business associates in return for substantial kickbacks. The reserves were supposed to be for the exclusive use of the U.S. Navy, to ensure a reliable supply of fuel oil, and were thus vital to the nation's defense. One of the principal reserves, at Teapot Dome, Wyoming, gave the growing scandal its name.

During the "Teapot Dome" investigation, Harding set out on a transcontinental tour, hoping, perhaps, to divert himself and the nation from the scandal. He arrived in San Francisco, ill and exhausted. His condition grew more grave, and he died on August 2, 1923. The official cause of death was food poisoning, but rumors of foul play abounded and have never been laid to rest. Some believe that Harding's wife, fearful of the coming scandal—which, she knew, included her husband's chronic infidelity—poisoned him.

After Harding's death, Teapot Dome did indeed boil over, and a number of his appointees were exposed. Some were tried and convicted of fraud. Harding's personal integrity remained largely unblemished, however, and the American people welcomed his vice president, Calvin Coolidge (1872–1933), into office.

"Silent Cal"—the stereotypical tight-lipped Vermonter Calvin Coolidge, 30th president of the United States. (Image from arttoday.com)

The last president to die in office had been William McKinley, fatally wounded by an assassin's bullet in 1901. At that time, his vice president, the dynamic Theodore Roosevelt, moved into the White House. Coolidge, however, was no Roosevelt. A Vermont conservative so tight-lipped he was popularly called Silent Cal, Coolidge quietly and efficiently set about cleaning house and restoring integrity to the executive branch. As for larger domestic reform and international politics, however, Coolidge was an even stronger believer in hands-off government than Harding had been. That was fine with the electorate, who returned Coolidge to the White House in the election of 1924, propelled by the less-than-electrifying campaign slogan, "Keep Cool with Coolidge."

Mussolini Makes the Trains Run on Time

For all the frenetic activity surrounding them, it was as if most Americans were sleepwalking through the decade—at least where politics was concerned.

Not so in Italy. The nation had been floundering under years of directionless monarchical rule. The Italian economy struggled, and the nation was looked down upon by the more efficient and prosperous states of northern Europe. Then, on October 28, 1922, Benito Mussolini grabbed the world's attention by leading a Fascist march on Rome. He obtained a mandate from Italy's King Victor Emmanuel III to form a coalition government—and obtained "temporary" dictatorial powers for himself.

Mussolini had been born on July 29, 1883, into the family of a blacksmith with strong socialist and anti-church beliefs. The boy's mother was convinced—and readily persuaded her son—that he was destined for greatness. A precocious child, Mussolini grew up reading the works of philosophers such as Machiavelli and Friedrich Nietzsche, who wrote about powerful leaders who made their own morality. Trained as a schoolteacher, Mussolini became a socialist journalist, at first arguing passionately against Italy's entry into World War I and then, in a sudden about-face, urging entry on the side of the Allies.

Expelled from Italy's socialist party, Mussolini started his own newspaper, in which he advocated a political movement that would soon be called *Fascism*—a form of government that, defining the state in terms of "race," put the state at the center of life and put at the center of the state the absolute authority of a leader who the people were expected to follow, unquestioningly, to national greatness.

Talk of the Times

Fascism is a form of totalitarian government in which the state is the focus of life and, governing the state, is an absolute leader, who the people are to follow, unquestioningly, to greatness.

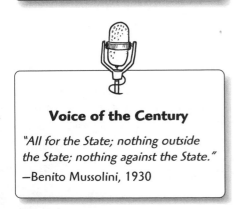

Voice of the Century

"All for the State; nothing outside the State; nothing against the State."
—Benito Mussolini, 1930

Mussolini served as a private during World War I (he was wounded in the buttocks by trench-mortar fragments), and then, after the war, worked with the popular, glamorous poet-novelist-patriot Gabriele d'Annunzio to form the *Fasci di Combattimento*—the core of what would become the Fascist party. The name came from the Italian word *fascio,* "bundle" or "bunch," which suggested union, and from *fasces,* a Latin word signifying a bundle of rods bound together around an ax with the blade protruding—the ancient Roman symbol of power. Indeed, Mussolini intoxicated his people with a promise to recreate in modern Italy the imperial grandeur of ancient Rome.

When, by October 1922, the Fascists were powerful enough to march in force on Rome, Mussolini was able to secure from Victor Emmanuel III dictatorial powers for a period of one year. In that brief span, he boldly reshaped Italy's economy, streamlining bureaucracy, slashing government expenses for public services and cutting taxes on industry to encourage production. As admirers remarked, "Mussolini made the trains run on time." Getting the notoriously unreliable Italian rail system to run on schedule was a symbol for how he had transformed the stubbornly lazy pace of Italian industry and politics.

Benito Mussolini, founder of European fascism, in a photograph from the 1920s.
(Image from arttoday.com)

Mussolini also took advantage of his dictatorial powers to replace Victor Emmanuel's palace guard with his own Fascist *squadisti* and a secret police force called the Ovra. He rattled the saber against Greece and Yugoslavia, and, at home, he brutally suppressed the kind of strikes that traditionally had crippled Italian industry.

In an elaborately orchestrated public-relations gesture in 1924, Mussolini nobly relinquished his dictatorial powers and called for new elections. He had, however, ensured their outcome by obtaining legislation that guaranteed a two-thirds parliamentary majority for his party regardless of the popular vote. Yet socialism was still a powerful force in Italian politics, and when the popular socialist leader Giacomo Matteotti voiced opposition to Fascism, he was murdered. This resulted in anti-Fascist attacks in the opposition press. Mussolini was powerful enough to respond by outlawing all parties except for the Fascists, abolishing trade unions, and imposing strict censorship on the press. Individual voices were silenced by his army of blackshirted thugs. Realizing the tremendous power of the Catholic church among the Italian people, Mussolini concluded the Lateran Treaty of 1929, which established the Vatican as a city-state within the city of Rome under the absolute sovereignty of the pope.

A Little Man in a Beer Hall

Among those in the world who had their eye on the man Italians now called "Il Duce"—the Leader—was another low-ranking veteran of World War I, a shiftless Austrian-born son of a minor customs officer named Adolf Hitler (1889–1945).

Voice of the Century

"To me those hours seemed like a release from the painful feelings of my youth. Even today I am not ashamed to say that, overpowered by stormy enthusiasm, I fell down on my knees and thanked Heaven from an overflowing heart for granting me the good fortune of being permitted to live at this time."

—Adolf Hitler, in *Mein Kampf,* recalling his reaction to the news that World War I had started

As a youth, Hitler had been a mediocre student driven by nothing more than a frustrated desire to become an artist. Twice rejected for enrollment at the Academy of Fine Arts in Vienna, he drifted, eking out a living painting postcards. Then came World War I. At first rejected as unfit for military service, Hitler enlisted in the 16th Bavarian Reserve Infantry Regiment. Wounded in October 1916, he was also gassed late in the war. Although he never rose above the rank of corporal, he proved his valor in action and was decorated with the Iron Cross, Second Class, in 1914, and, in 1918, the Iron Cross, First Class—a rare achievement for a mere corporal. In war, Hitler had found his calling.

After the war, Hitler was retained by the army as a political agent, and in 1919, he joined the fledgling German Workers' Party in Munich, determined to overturn the humiliating surrender terms the Allies had imposed with the Treaty of Versailles. Hitler quickly rose to prominence in the new party, which was renamed, in 1920, the *National-sozialistische Deutsche Arbeiterpartei*—abbreviated to Nazi Party.

Adolf Hitler.
(Image from the Library of Congress)

Economic and political chaos was rife in postwar Germany. Bavaria, Hitler's home during the 1920s, was a hotbed of political activity. Bavarians had never welcomed the rule of Berlin, and they particularly resented the present republican government—the Weimar Republic—as weak. The provincial Bavarian capital of Munich was headquarters for disgruntled veterans and members of the Freikorps, an unofficial army organized in 1918–19 from units of the German army that refused to demobilize.

With associates such as Ernst Röhm, Hitler transformed the Nazi party along the lines of Mussolini's Fascists, creating a private army of thugs, just as Mussolini had done. Hitler and Röhm clad their men in brown shirts rather than black. With the SA (*Sturmabteilung*), they crushed all political opposition.

More than his strong-arm tactics, Hitler's genius for propaganda did most to consolidate his power. A little man with a ridiculous mustache—which looked for all the world like the one made popular by film comic Charlie Chaplin—Hitler nevertheless exercised magnetic influence as a public speaker. In November 1923, he felt sufficiently confident to join with World War I commander Gen. Erich Ludendorff to kick off a national revolution against the hated Weimar Republic.

On November 8, Hitler and his men broke into a right-wing political meeting in a Munich beer hall. The leaders of the meeting agreed to join a mass march on Berlin—patterned on Mussolini's march on Rome. But the next day, the column of 3,000 Nazis was fired on by police. Sixteen party members and three policemen were killed, and the revolution was aborted. Hitler and Ludendorff were arrested and tried. Ludendorff was released, but Hitler was sentenced to five years' imprisonment—the minimum sentence for treason.

The effects of the "Beer Hall *Putsch*" did not end there. Hitler was given comfortable quarters at Landsberg prison, where he used his sentence (of which he would serve only nine months) to write the first volume of a political memoir titled *Mein Kampf*—My Struggle. In this document, Hitler distilled his own fascist ideas. He saw the greatness of Germany's racial heritage, the "Aryan people," as a birthright betrayed by the Weimar Republic,

Voice of the Century

"In view of the primitive simplicity of their minds, [the masses] more easily fall victim to a big lie than a little one."—Adolf Hitler, *Mein Kampf*, 1924

"By the skillful and sustained use of propaganda, one can make a people see even heaven as hell or an extremely wretched life as paradise."—Hitler quoted by Cyril Falls, *Ordeal by Battle*, 1943

Voice of the Century

"I set the Aryan and the Jew over against each other; and if I call one of them a human being, I must call the other something else. The two are as widely separated as man and beast. Not that I would call the Jew a beast.... He is a creature outside nature and alien to nature."

—Adolf Hitler, early 1930s

which had shamelessly capitulated to the terms of the Versailles treaty. All other races, Hitler wrote, were inferior to the Aryans and, because of this, sought to destroy the German *Volk*, the "master race." The Weimar democracy would never realize the great German destiny, the great enemy of which was Marxism (socialism as well as communism), and behind that, the Jews. Tapping into an all-too-common vein of German antisemitism, Hitler portrayed the Jews in mythic terms, as the incarnation of everything evil.

What could save Germany and return to the German people their birthright as members of the master race? Only the destruction of the democratic Weimar Republic and absolute rule under a single great leader, who would be called in German not Il Duce, but *Der Führer—the* leader.

During Hitler's nine-month absence, the Nazi party had all but disintegrated. Worse—from Hitler's point of view—a degree of economic stability had returned to Germany. A strengthened Weimar government forbade Hitler from speaking, first in Bavaria and then almost anywhere else.

Yet, slowly, the Nazi party recovered and began again to grow. When the worldwide economic collapse that brought about the United States stock-market crash of 1929 (which you'll read about in Chapter 13, "The Party Ends (1929–1934)") reached Germany, Hitler was able to plead his cause not just to the working class, but to the beleaguered industrialists and capitalists. The Nazi party soon became the second largest party in the country, polling more than 6 million votes in the 1930 election.

At the end of the decade, Adolf Hitler was positioned for power. In the elections of 1932, he would run against Germany's war-hero president, the aged and infirm Paul von Hindenburg, capturing more than a third of the votes and thereby demonstrating enough popularity to compel Hindenburg to appoint Hitler, whom he personally detested, chancellor—in effect prime minister, the number-two man in the government.

G-Men

The United States, during this period, was a long way from totalitarianism, but even here a kind of shadow government formed within the official American democracy.

You read in the last chapter how U.S. Attorney General A. Mitchell Palmer ordered a round-up of persons suspected of being Bolshevik sympathizers. The man he chose to head the Justice Department's newly formed General Intelligence Division was J. Edgar Hoover (1895–1972), a Washington, D.C., native who started out intending to become a minister. Instead, he took a law degree at George Washington University and, in 1917, joined the Justice Department.

Swept up in the Red Scare of 1919 and the early 1920s, Hoover, without benefit of warrant, freely conducted raids, searches, and seizures and made arrests. He compiled meticulous dossiers on as many as 150,000 suspected "radicals," starting a practice that became a lifelong obsession. Hoover began compiling files on just about anyone with any power or influence in government.

In 1922, Hoover was officially transferred to the Justice Department's Bureau of Investigation, at the time a feeble, disorganized outfit staffed by corrupt political hacks. Both Palmer and the bureau's director, William Burns, were ousted in the wake of the Harding administration scandals, and the new attorney general, Harlan Fiske Stone, appointed Hoover in 1924 to head the bureau. The new director revolutionized the organization, which was renamed the Federal Bureau of Investigation, the FBI. He rid the bureau of the corrupt old guard and installed a set of squeaky-clean professionals, all of whom were not only trained law-enforcement professionals, but also fully qualified attorneys.

During the balance of the 1920s, Hoover concentrated principally on issues of espionage and subversion, but, by the end of the decade, he realized that to build the FBI into a truly powerful federal law-enforcement agency, he needed to capture the *public* imagination. The national outrage produced by the St. Valentine's Day Massacre of 1929 (see Chapter 11) gave him his opportunity. He positioned the bureau as the noble and implacable foe of the underworld. Under Hoover, the FBI would not target organized crime as such (indeed, the FBI studiously avoided pursuing the Mafia and related crime organizations until forced), but the bureau did target high-profile bank robbers such as the Barker Gang, Pretty Boy Floyd, Baby Face Nelson, and, Hoover's personal nemesis, John Dillinger. To mythologize these pursuits, Hoover created the "Ten Most-Wanted List," and, as we will see in the next chapter, he enlisted the press to play up the performance of the bureau in general and of himself in particular. Soon, the entire nation was talking about the FBI and its "G-men" (government agents).

20th-Century Life

The ugliest side of Hoover's use of the FBI as an instrument of personal prejudice came to light with his zealous investigation of Martin Luther King Jr. in the 1960s. Hoover employed illegal surveillance, including wiretaps, in an effort to embarrass and, if possible, discredit King. As was often the case with the surveillance Hoover directed, the material relating to the civil rights leader was of a sexual nature. When no other federal authorities showed interest in the FBI's King files, Hoover sent compromising photographs to King's wife, Coretta Scott King. She never dignified this material with a response.

In time, Hoover would loom larger than the agency he directed. Certainly, many of the attorneys general and presidents under whom he served would have liked to remove him from office; he had become too powerful, acting independently of the Justice Department and executive authority. Yet, in the 48 years during which he ran the FBI, no attorney general or chief executive dared to move against him. His private dossiers bulging, J. Edgar Hoover simply knew too much about too many influential people. Indeed, not until 1961 was Hoover challenged by Attorney General Robert Kennedy. Hoover steadfastly resisted Kennedy's order that the FBI investigate civil rights violations and organized crime. Although Kennedy prevailed against Hoover to a significant degree, the director retaliated by compiling files on the Kennedy brothers, meticulously recording extramarital affairs and financial activity. Hoover did the same with prominent civil rights leaders, especially Martin Luther King Jr.

Hoover's eccentricities became the stuff of legend. He once dismissed an agent for being ugly. He fired another for wearing a tie he did not like and yet another for having married a "foreign woman." Hoover ruled the FBI until his death, from a heart attack, on May 2, 1972.

The Golden Door Slams Shut

In the 1920s, the notoriety created by J. Edgar Hoover's eccentricities and excesses lay far in the future. For the present, most people were happy to have the G-men keeping an eye on the masses of foreigners here. The nation was in the grip of acute *xenophobia*—a fear of foreigners. Before World War I, immigration was largely unlimited. In 1924, however, Congress passed the Johnson-Reed Act, reducing the number of immigrants to be admitted annually to a mere 150,000 and specifying that some 90 percent of this small number were to come from northwestern Europe. The doors would not reopen until after World War II.

Xenophobia could have a very human face. On Christmas Eve morning, 1919, a robbery was committed in Bridgewater, Massachusetts, 30 miles south of Boston. Witnesses said a gang of "foreign-looking men" held up the payroll truck of the White Shoe Company, killing the paymaster and a guard. On circumstantial evidence, two working men, Nicola Sacco and Bartolomeo Vanzetti, both self-proclaimed anarchists, were arrested for the robbery and murders.

Tried in 1921, the pair was convicted and sentenced to death, despite much evidence corroborating their alibis. The case captured America's attention. Although some clamored for the execution of the "foreign radicals," groups of intellectuals, writers, and even some politicians took up their cause. Not only prominent American writers, but also the likes of George Bernard Shaw, Anatole France, and even Benito Mussolini, pleaded on their behalf. The slogan "Sacco and Vanzetti Must Not Die" became a banner under which 1920s radicals and liberals united.

Talk of the Times

Xenophobia is an exaggerated fear of foreigners.

Nevertheless, through many subsequent appeals, the convictions were upheld, and the pair was executed on August 23, 1927. The case, which spanned three quarters of the decade, was a defining moment for many American liberal thinkers, awakening them from the social numbness of the Harding-Coolidge years. By raising liberal and radical consciousness in the United States, the Sacco and Vanzetti case prepared the ranks of social activists who would come to the fore when the hard times of the Great Depression would shake the *entire* nation out of its complacency.

As for the case that had started it all, in the 1970s, an underworld informant revealed that the crime had actually been committed by the notorious Morelli gang, five mafiosi brothers who had moved to New England from Brooklyn during World War I.

Flying High

It must be said that the number of people "radicalized" by the Sacco and Vanzetti case was small, compared to the number of Americans who ultimately cared little about the fate of two Italian anarchist immigrants—or, at least, didn't care enough to do anything about it. For most Americans, life was good in the 1920s. A Cole Porter song of the era asked, "How'm I flyin?" and answered its own question: "I'm flyin' high."

Far fewer Americans than had an interest in Sacco and Vanzetti had even heard of another Massachusetts event: the flight, on March 16, 1926, of the first liquid-fuel—that is, modern—rocket, launched from a farm in Auburn, Massachusetts.

Its inventor was Robert Hutchings Goddard (1882–1945). Born a frail lad in nearby Wooster, Goddard grew up captivated by H.G. Wells's science-fiction novel *War of the Worlds*, which he read in an 1898 serialization in the *Boston Post*. On October 19, 1899—as he remembered it for the rest of his life—young Goddard climbed a cherry tree in his backyard and "imagined how wonderful it would be to make some device which had even the possibility of ascending to Mars."

From that day forward, the path of his life was clear to him. Goddard earned a Ph.D. in physics in 1908 and, working in a modest laboratory, proved that thrust and propulsion can take place in a vacuum. (Isaac Newton had predicted as much back in the early 18th century, but Goddard was almost certainly the first to verify it experimentally.)

Goddard also began to work out the complex mathematics of energy produced versus the weight of various fuels, including liquid oxygen and liquid hydrogen—the fuels that would ultimately power the great rockets that lofted human beings into orbit and to the moon. The liquid-fuel rocket Goddard launched from his Aunt Effie's Auburn farm in 1926 was the direct ancestor of the *Saturn* booster that sent *Apollo* to the moon and the great engines that take the Space Shuttle beyond the pull of earth's gravity.

The 1926 launch was little noted by the world of science—or anyone else, for that matter. Nor were

Century Stats

Goddard's early rockets were little taller than a man and achieved altitudes of no more than a mile. He died (of throat cancer, in 1945) before he could develop his more advanced rocketry theories, including the use of multiple stages to achieve greater altitude.

the larger and more powerful rockets Goddard tested during the 1930s and 1940s. But Goddard forged ahead, patenting steering apparatus and the idea of what he termed "step rockets"—what would later be called multistage rockets—to gain greater altitude. Single-handedly and without fanfare, Robert H. Goddard mapped out most of the eventual range of space-vehicle technology, including fuel pumps, self-cooling rocket motors, and other devices required for an engine designed to carry human beings into outer space.

A Miracle Drug from Mold

If a Massachusetts farm was a humble arena for scientific advance, how about a Petri dish smeared with germs and contaminated by mold?

Alexander Fleming (1881–1955) was born in a small Scottish village and took a medical degree at London's St. Mary's Hospital Medical School. His special interest was bacteriology, and, during World War I, working with soldiers who had survived initial wounding only to succumb later to infection, Fleming began to search for substances that might be effective against the growth of bacteria. He made an intriguing discovery in 1921 when he isolated the enzyme lysozyme, present in human tears and mucus, which attacks many types of bacteria. But not until a laboratory accident in 1928 did his breakthrough discovery come.

Talk of the Times

Penicillin was the first important **antibiotic**, a drug that destroys harmful microorganisms, inhibiting the synthesis of murein, the substance that makes bacterial cell walls strong. Since the cell walls of nonbacterial cells do not contain murein, penicillin can destroy bacterial cells without harming body cells.

For one of his experiments, Fleming was growing staph bacteria in a Petri dish. To his great irritation, he noted that one of the staph cultures had been contaminated by a mold, *Penicillium notatum*. He was about to discard the Petri dish when he looked more closely at it. Surrounding the mold growth was a circle free from bacteria. Something in the mold had killed the staph germs.

Fleming set about isolating the substance in the mold responsible for killing the bacteria. He soon succeeded, dubbed the material penicillin, and performed further tests that showed penicillin to be effective against a wide range of bacteria. Even better, it was itself nontoxic.

Medicine had its first antibiotic. This meant physicians were no longer confined to the role of observing and diagnosing disease and then providing superficial comfort. For the first time in medical history, they were in a position to actually *fight* disease.

The Lone Eagle Soars...

The world would soon hear much about "wonder drugs," and the name of Sir Alexander Fleming would soon find its way into school textbooks. Some achievements, however, gained more immediate and universal public attention.

If the public in the 1920s gave little or no thought to the rockets that so fascinated Robert Goddard, they were fascinated with the airplane. It had come of age quickly in World War I, in which it had been used mostly for observation, some bombing, and also fighting against other aircraft. But in 1922, when Charles Augustus Lindbergh (1902–1974), son of a U.S. Congressman from Minnesota, flew for the first time, *aviator* was neither a respectable nor profitable occupation. Contrary to the wishes of his family, Lindbergh was nonetheless hooked on flying, and he eked out a precarious living as an itinerant *barnstormer*, an exhibition stunt flier who also gave passengers thrill rides at five bucks a pop.

Talk of the Times

A **barnstormer** was an itinerant exhibition aviator who performed stunts and took curious passengers aloft.

Lindbergh joined the army in 1924 to learn more about flying and was commissioned a second lieutenant the following year. The peacetime military had more pilots than it needed, however, and Lindbergh was assigned to air-mail service.

At this time, air mail was more a novelty than a reliable means of delivery, thanks to unreliable aircraft and poorly trained pilots. Lindbergh wanted to find some way of stimulating the development of aviation by proving its commercial potential. He hit upon the idea of flying solo, non-stop across the Atlantic Ocean. Obtaining financial backing from a group of St. Louis businessmen, he commissioned the Ryan Aviation Corporation to custom design *The Spirit of St. Louis*, a sleek, single-engine monoplane that was essentially a flying fuel tank.

In an era intrigued by stunts, what Lindbergh proposed to do held a natural appeal. But it went far beyond the realm of a mere stunt. America—indeed, the world—embraced the tall, modest, boyishly handsome Lindbergh as the "Lone Eagle" and anxiously awaited word of his progress and fate after he took off at 7:52 A.M. from muddy, rainy Roosevelt Field, Long Island, New York—today the site of a popular shopping mall. The fuel-burdened craft barely cleared the treetops, and, for the next 33½ hours, Lindbergh fought sleep and the elements over the Atlantic.

Lindbergh was overwhelmed by the reception when he landed at Le Bourget Field outside of Paris at 10:22 P.M. (local time) on May 21. Thousands swarmed around him, as they did in the cities of the United States, where he was hailed as a hero. No one, not the generals of World War II, not the astronauts who walked on the moon, has been so hailed since.

Lindbergh did succeed in generating commercial interest in flight, but he also, if only briefly, united the world in wonder at the achievement of a combination of mind, skill, and courage.

One of the most familiar news photographs of the boyish Charles Lindbergh, beside his Ryan monoplane.
(Image from arttoday.com)

...and So Does the Babe

The acclaim for Lindbergh demonstrated a deep hunger for heroes and leaders, a hunger that the jaded and hypersophisticated members of the 1920s "smart set" might try to deny, but a hunger that would not *be* denied. Italians and Germans were prepared to follow the likes of Mussolini and Hitler. Americans, it is true, had voted into office the nonleaders Harding and Coolidge, but they surely loved the stars of Hollywood on the screen and the Lone Eagle in the air.

On the ball field, the object of their admiration was a big, heavy man with the face of a pug dog: George Herman Ruth, known universally as the Babe. Born in Baltimore in 1895, he was deemed an incorrigible child of the slums and received what little formal education he had at St. Mary's Industrial School, an orphanage and reform school. Among the skills he learned there were the rudiments of baseball, and in 1914, he joined Baltimore's minor-league team. Later that first season, he was sold to the Boston Red Sox.

Ruth made his first mark as a pitcher. In two World Series with the Red Sox (1916 and 1918), he pitched $29^2/_3$ consecutive scoreless innings, a record that remained intact until Whitey Ford broke it 1961. Ruth was the best left-handed pitcher in the American League when he was switched to the outfield in 1918 because of his phenomenally powerful hitting.

"I like to hit home runs," he remarked casually whenever questioned about his prowess.

Century Stats

Babe Ruth led the American League in home runs for 12 years, hitting at least 50 in 4 separate seasons and at least 40 in each of 11 seasons. His single-season record of 60 was broken by Yankee Roger Maris, who hit 61 in 1961. His lifetime home-run total was 714, unbroken until Hank Aaron hit his 715th home run in 1974.

Babe Ruth signs a copy of his autobiography for future president George Bush—in 1948 the captain of the Yale baseball team. (Image from the George Bush Library)

20th-Century Life

Of the many legends surrounding Babe Ruth, the most famous is the "Called Shot" in the 1932 World Series against the Chicago Cubs. Ruth had two strikes in the fifth inning. Before the next pitch, Ruth pointed toward the bleachers and then sent the next pitch flying toward the spot. Although pitcher Charlie Root insisted that Ruth's gesture was meant for him, indicating that he "still need[ed] one more, kid!" reporters claimed that the Babe had called the shot—which Ruth didn't try to deny.

Almost equally famous is the story that Ruth visited a sick child, Johnny Sylvester, in a hospital and promised to hit three home runs for him—if he promised to get well in return. There is a grain of truth in the story: During the 1926 World Series, the desperately ill boy received autographed balls from players on the other team before the fourth game, in which Ruth hit three home runs, each longer than the one before. A radio announcer who heard about the sick boy and the baseballs improvised the story of Babe Ruth's promise.

Sold to the New York Yankees in 1920 for a record-breaking $125,000, he played outfield through 1934. It was, of course, as a hitter—the "Sultan of Swat"—and as a bigger-than-life personality that Ruth rose to legendary prominence at a time when professional baseball was struggling to overcome the cynicism caused by the "Black Sox" scandal of 1919, in which Chicago White Sox players were bribed by gangsters to throw the World Series.

Ruth shattered the major-league home-run record in 3 consecutive years, 1919 through 1921, and again with 60 home runs in 1927.

Prosperity

As the Roaring Twenties drew to a close, Americans felt great self-satisfaction in being part of a country that could produce both a Lone Eagle and a Babe Ruth. They were two of the good things about the good life most Americans felt they were living. What could possibly go wrong?

The Least You Need to Know

➤ The Harding administration was riddled with corruption and scandal, yet most Americans, pleased with the general prosperity, refused to be outraged by any of it.

➤ While America enjoyed life under the easygoing administrations of Harding and Coolidge, Italy and Germany embraced the dictatorship of Mussolini and Hitler.

➤ American isolationism deepened during this period, as evidenced in a 1924 law severely restricting the influx of new immigrants.

➤ For all its interest in mindless diversion, the 1920s produced some extraordinary achievements in science, aviation, and sport.

Chapter 13

The Party Ends (1929–1934)

In This Chapter

➤ Background of the Great Depression

➤ Hoover's response to the crisis

➤ Crisis in Europe and the failure of the League of Nations

➤ The rise of Stalin and Hitler

➤ Roosevelt to the rescue

Grace Goodhue Coolidge, wife of Calvin Coolidge, liked to tell a story about a young woman, seated next to the president at a dinner party, who challenged her husband's legendary frugality with words. She bet Coolidge that she could get at least three words of conversation from him. Without looking at her, "Silent Cal" quietly replied, "You lose."

He was equally laconic in 1928, when, vacationing in the Black Hills of South Dakota, he issued a statement on his plans for the upcoming elections: "I do not choose to run for president in 1928." America was stunned. Coolidge had cleaned house after the scandals of Harding, won election in his own right, and presided over a period of apparent tranquility and manifest prosperity. Why not capitalize on his popularity?

Privately, to his closest confidants, Coolidge had confessed his fear that the era of prosperity was about to come crashing down—and he didn't want to be in the White House when that happened. It proved a prudent decision. This chapter is about the early years of the worldwide Great Depression.

Recipe for Depression

Throughout the 19th century and into the early 20th, the stock market was unofficially reserved for tycoons, financiers, and the captains of industry. "Ordinary" folk squirreled away modest savings in banks (or mattresses). After World War I, however, America and much of the rest of the world entered into an era of unprecedented production of consumer goods—automobiles, appliances, and various luxury items—and, with this, unprecedented corporate expansion. This created many jobs, much wealth, and considerable prosperity for all classes (except, as we will see in a moment, farmers). Finding themselves with a good deal of disposable income, in an economic climate in which expanding companies were hungry for capital, people of all kinds put their savings into stocks.

Mary Petty cartoon depicting the tycoon, vintage 1920s. (Image from arttoday.com)

And not just savings. They borrowed money as well. At the time, brokerage firms welcomed the free-wheeling purchase of stock on *margin*, meaning that stocks could be acquired for pennies down on the dollar. This was a credit transaction; when your margin loan was "called," you were obliged to come up with the full value of the loan, plus interest. No problem—if the underlying stock had retained or increased its value. If it fell in value, however, where was a stockholder to get the cash to pay off his loan?

One of the trends that disturbed Coolidge—and presumably contributed to his decision not to run for reelection—was the epidemic of stock-market speculation and

Talk of the Times

To purchase a stock **on margin** is to pay a small percentage of the value of the stock and to finance the remainder of the purchase price through the stock brokerage.

margin transactions. An awful lot of stock in circulation had no cash behind it, save for the 10 percent paid up front on margin. It was as if the entire financial world had made loans backed by potentially worthless collateral.

Tremors

Only a small minority saw the economy of the 1920s as a disaster waiting to happen. Most were content to watch the value of their stocks rise far beyond anything a mere bank account could return.

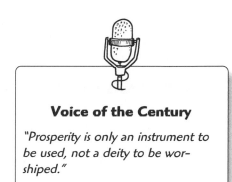

Voice of the Century

"Prosperity is only an instrument to be used, not a deity to be worshiped."
—Calvin Coolidge, 1928

There were other economic tremors, however, that shouldn't have been ignored. Take farmers. Few of them partook in the general prosperity of the 1920s. Food prices were depressed throughout the period. It is true that the 1920 census revealed that the United States was now an urban nation—for the first time in history, more Americans lived in cities than on farms—and it is also true that, for the shortsighted urbanite, low food prices were a happy thing—leaving that much more money to invest in stocks. However, farmers and agricultural laborers were still a huge segment of American society, and as their buying power shrank, so did the market for the vast quantities of consumer goods rolling off American assembly lines.

Far more consumer amenities and luxuries were produced than could be consumed. Farmers couldn't buy the goods, and even though the wages of the American industrial worker rose throughout the decade, they hadn't risen sufficiently to enable most working families to buy many of the goods now available to them. Companies continued to produce, and unsold inventories piled up in warehouses.

Crash!

The stock market was oblivious to these tremors. Through early 1929, it climbed higher and higher. With the first autumn leaves, however, the market began to falter. In September, Wall Street boarded a roller coaster, with prices running sharply up *and* down, although the trend was unmistakably downward. As stock prices fell, nerves grew taut and then frayed. On October 18, a sell-off began, with prices falling sharply. The first day of absolute panic happened on October 24—"Black Thursday." On that day, 12,894,650 shares were traded, a record number up to that time.

For the moment, however, the economy functioned as it should. Big banks and major investment firms purchased great blocks of stock to buoy up the market and stem the panic. On "Black

Century Stats

On Black Tuesday, October 29th, U.S. stocks lost an average of 40 points. Stocks trade dropped in value by more than $26 billion.

Monday" (October 28) and "Black Tuesday" (October 29), panic returned with a vengeance. On the 29th, more than 16,000,000 shares were traded—dumped—and stock prices folded beyond rescue.

Global Chain Reaction

The image we have of the 1929 stock market crash is of herds of brokers and financiers leaping out of Wall Street windows. It is true that the crash did bring on a wave of suicides as fortunes were utterly wiped out in a moment. Investors, overextended on margin, could not possibly meet calls for payment. But such leaps to the pavement were only the overture. The greater, grimmer drama was yet to come.

With the collapse of stock prices, industry sharply cut back on production, suddenly hurling workers out of their jobs. The unemployed, of course, do not make good consumers. Markets shrunk further, and even more workers lost their jobs. As industries shut their plants and workers lost their jobs, banks across the country failed. Businesses and individuals were unable to pay their loans, and families withdrew their savings en masse. In 1930, the first full year of the Depression, 1,300 banks closed their doors. Over the next two years another 3,700 followed suit. The bank failures fed into the cycle of collapse by denying people access to funds, which in turn kept those people from pumping funds into the economy.

One of the most important 20th-century trends has been the ever-increasing interconnectedness and interdependence of people and nations. By 1929, no longer was the economy of one nation independent from that of another. Industrial America had become both a major supplier to the world and a major consumer of what the world had to offer. Most recently, the United States had been the principal financier of World War I—and was now the world's chief creditor. Now that the flow of American investment credits to Europe was drying up, the Depression traveled across the Atlantic. Hardest hit were Germany and Great Britain, the nations that owed the most to the United States. War debt payments from Europe were reduced to a trickle, deepening the depression in the United States.

In a panic of self-preservation, the United States and other nations scurried to protect domestic industries by raising tariffs and import duties or imposing new ones. The result was to strangle already-suffering international trade. By 1932, the total value of world trade had been cut by more than 50 percent.

"Prosperity's Just Around the Corner"

Coolidge had chosen not to run, but his popularity paved the way for the ascension of another Republican, Herbert Clark Hoover (1874–1964). Born in Iowa and orphaned before he was nine, Hoover was raised by an uncle in Oregon and educated at Stanford University as a mining engineer. He worked internationally in this field for almost two decades before becoming involved in relief work, first in China (following the Boxer Rebellion of 1900) and then during World War I as Allied relief operations and, later, chairman of the Commission for Relief in Belgium. When the United States entered the war, Hoover was appointed national food administrator to stimulate production and conserve supplies. After the war, he once again directed European relief, and in 1921, he was appointed U.S. Secretary of Commerce. In all of these posts, Hoover earned a reputation for humanitarianism as well as administrative genius. With Coolidge a no-show, he was a shoo-in for the Republican presidential nomination in 1928.

Now, at the end of 1929, Herbert Hoover was faced with the greatest challenge of his life in public service. Determined to check the downward economic spiral and restore public confidence, he reassured his countrymen that "prosperity was just around the corner."

A bust honoring Herbert Hoover, the World War I-era humanitarian. One would be hard-pressed to find monuments commemorating Hoover's Depression-burdened presidency.
(Image from arttoday.com)

Although his secretary of the treasury advised doing absolutely nothing—let the economy bottom out naturally, he counseled—Hoover took action, devising a program for federal, state, and local government. Between 1929 and 1932, President Hoover called on businessmen to maintain prices and wages. He proposed a cut in federal taxes and in interest rates. He designed public-works programs and cooperative farming plans. Hoover asked states and municipalities to start relief programs for the unemployed. The president even proposed a plan of federal aid to homeowners who could not meet their mortgage payments.

Shanty Towns and Skyscrapers

For some conservative Republicans, Hoover's programs smacked of radical socialism. The fact was that they were hardly radical enough. Most of what the president proposed relied on state and local governments, which were already incapable of meeting

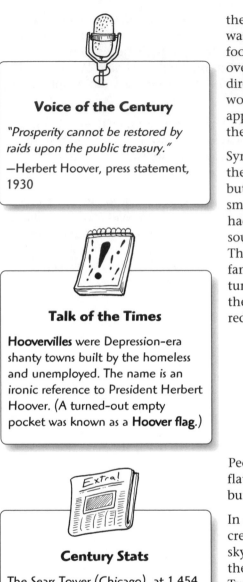

Voice of the Century

"Prosperity cannot be restored by raids upon the public treasury."

—Herbert Hoover, press statement, 1930

Talk of the Times

Hoovervilles were Depression-era shanty towns built by the homeless and unemployed. The name is an ironic reference to President Herbert Hoover. (A turned-out empty pocket was known as a **Hoover flag**.)

Century Stats

The Sears Tower (Chicago), at 1,454 feet, took the world's-tallest-building title from the Empire State in 1973. The Petronas Towers (Kuala Lumpur, Malaysia) are currently the tallest skyscrapers in the world, at 1,483 feet, but the International Financial Center, scheduled for completion in 2002 in Taipei, Taiwan, will measure 1,667 feet.

the financial demands being placed on them. Hoover was unwilling to commit the federal government to footing the bill during this national emergency. Moreover, he refused to allow federal funds to be spent directly on relief for individuals, believing that to do so would undermine the spirit of individual initiative. He appealed to private charities and city agencies to pick up the slack. But, of course, they had no money.

Symbols of America during the 1920s had included, on the one hand, wild flappers and carefree flagpole sitters, but, on the other hand, the assembly lines and puffing smokestacks of industry. By the early 1930s, these icons had been replaced by ubiquitous images of bread lines, soup kitchens, and men selling apples on street corners. The phrase "brother, can you spare a dime" became so familiar that songwriters E.Y. Harburg and Harold Arlen turned it into a Depression-era anthem that portrayed the lot of the worker and war veteran now unemployed, reduced to begging:

> *Once I built a railroad,*
> *Made it run,*
> *Made it race against time.*
> *Once I built a railroad.*
> *Now it's done.*
> *Brother, can you spare a dime?*

People did not merely leave pleasant homes for slum flats; they left the slums to shelter themselves in jerry-built shanty towns christened *Hoovervilles*.

In contrast to the squat Hoovervilles spreading like creeping vines across the American landscape was the skyscraper ballyhooed as the world's greatest building in the world's greatest city. Begun at the end of the Roaring Twenties, the Empire State Building was opened to the public on May 1, 1931. At more than 100 stories, 1,250 feet in height, it was the tallest skyscraper ever built. Built in just over a year, it incorporated the most advanced prefabricated technology, expressing in beautiful art moderne style the might and optimism of an era that would be dead and gone before the building was completed.

Hailed by some as the Eighth Wonder of the World, it was viewed by others as a sadly ironic monument to lost prosperity. When New York's lame-duck governor cut the ceremonial ribbon at the dedication of the building, a local wag was quick to christen the structure "Al Smith's Last Erection." For some time after the building's opening, acres of office space sat empty, waiting for an economic recovery that would fill it with commerce.

The Empire State Building, begun during economic boom and opened during deep depression. This photograph shows the building in 1931, long before it acquired its familiar television broadcast mast.
(Image from arttoday.com)

The Bonus Army on the March

In 1924, flushed with prosperity, Congress had voted to pay veterans of the world war Adjusted Compensation certificates—popularly called "bonuses"—over a period of time through 1945. In the summer of 1932, a band of some 12,000 to 15,000 unemployed veterans marched on Washington to demand immediate lump-sum payment of benefits now urgently needed. They called themselves the Bonus Army, and some 2,000 to 5,000 remained in the nation's capital after the initial demonstration, settling into a Hooverville cobbled together on the "flats" along the Anacostia River.

Hoover, by nature and inclination a humanitarian, declared that this so-called Bonus Army was nothing more than a collection of criminals. He authorized a force of federal troops to clear out the squatters with bayonets, tear gas, and tanks. In the resulting melee, miraculously, only a single protestor was killed. The image of the United States Army turning against United States citizens—veterans, no less—was too much for most voters to bear. Herbert Hoover was handed an overwhelming defeat in the 1932 elections, and, unjustly, was also handed most of the blame for the Depression.

20th-Century Life

After the bonus bill was defeated in Congress, most of the Bonus Army left for home, except for some 2,000 to 5,000 men (some with wives and children), who remained in the Anacostia encampment. President Hoover explicitly directed that no troops were to advance against the protesters, but General Douglas MacArthur, at the time the U.S. Army chief of staff, claimed that he would not be bothered by "people coming down and pretending to bring orders." Directly disobeying Hoover's instructions, and arrayed in a full-dress uniform, he took personal charge of the troops he ordered to "clear out the [Anacostia] Flats." The soldiers leveled or burned the protesters' shanties and tents and used tear gas to disperse the mob. The mounted troops used the flats of their cavalry sabers to move the protesters along. One veteran was killed in the assault. A young Dwight David Eisenhower, at the time an assistant to MacArthur, recoiled in disgust.

Europe: A Gathering Darkness

As bad as things were in the United States—and they were very bad indeed—they were far worse overseas. The world war had bled the nations of Europe and had also drained their treasuries. Not only were the direct costs of the war great, but also the damage to trade and to infrastructure were staggering. Moreover, much of an entire new generation of industrial and business leaders had perished in the trenches. The economic recovery of Europe would have been extremely difficult under the best of economic conditions. Under the worst, it was impossible.

Legacy of Versailles

In many ways, Germany, the "loser" in World War I, suffered the least material damage. Most of the war had been fought in France. The defeated German armies marched back to a country that was at least physically intact. Economics was another matter. The Treaty of Versailles had levied severe financial penalties on Germany and had also mandated the disarmament of the nation. The Depression drove unemployment in Germany well above 25 percent.

The Allies' desire for vengeance against "the Hun" was understandable, but tragic. Punishment might force compliance in the short term, but, over time, it generally produces defiance or outright rebellion.

Immediately after the war, Germany was devastated by the influenza pandemic (see Chapter 12, "Victims and Heroes") and was on the verge of a communist revolution led by the left-wing Spartacus League. The communist threat was met by right-wing extremists, whose military arm was the Freikorps, a collection of private paramilitary groups composed of veterans, unemployed men, and just plain malcontents, all led by former military officers. The Freikorps put down left-wing revolts in Berlin, Bremen, Brunswick, Hamburg, Halle, Leipzig, Silesia, Thuringia, and the Ruhr, and Freikorps members murdered Karl Liebknecht and Rosa Luxemburg, the nation's most prominent communist leaders.

By suppressing communist revolution, the Freikorps enabled the survival of the struggling *Weimar Republic*, the ostensibly democratic government of Germany after the world war. For many of the jobless men who were its members, the Freikorps was the only meaningful order in their ravaged country, and neither the rank and file of the Freikorps nor its leaders were friends of the democracy they had saved. The Freikorps would evolve into the SA or Brownshirts, the paramilitary arm of the Nazi Party, which would crush the Weimar Republic and would rearm Germany in open defiance of the Treaty of Versailles.

Talk of the Times

The **Weimar Republic**, so called because it was established by a constitution drawn up in the city of Weimar in 1919, governed Germany from 1919 to 1933.

The League Stumbles

With hunger and desperation seething in Germany and elsewhere, the League of Nations, established by the Treaty of Versailles, struggled feebly to stave off international conflict. The deliberative body, headquartered in Geneva, Switzerland, had successfully settled a number of minor disputes during the 1920s, but it was fatally weakened by the failure of the United States to join when the Senate refused to ratify the Treaty of Versailles.

20th-Century Life

Born Tafari Makonnen on July 23, 1892, Haile Selassie came to power in 1916 when King Lij Yasu unwisely attempted to change Ethiopia's state religion from Coptic Christianity to Islam. He aggressively centralized Ethiopian government and instituted various reforms, most significantly the abolition of slavery. Regarded as an early anti-fascist hero, Haile Selassie was forced into exile after Italy annexed Ethiopia; however, because Ethiopia was liberated early in World War II, Haile Selassie was restored to his throne by 1941. His record after the war can best be characterized as enlightened despotism. He weathered a number of attempted coups d'etat before he was finally deposed by the army in 1974. He died in the Ethiopian capital of Addis Ababa the following year.

When Japan invaded Manchuria in the 1930s, the League was powerless to intervene. In 1935–36, Mussolini's Italy invaded Ethiopia, and, once again, despite the eloquent appeal of Ethiopian emperor Haile Selassie I, the League was unable to prevent, resolve, or redress the aggression. The League of Nations was not formally dissolved, but, by the mid-1930s, it had become a empty shell and a forlorn hope.

Ethiopian emperor Haile Selassie impressed the world when he addressed the League of Nations when Italy invaded his nation. He is seen here, at lower left, in 1943, on the USS Quincy, *Great Bitter Lake, Egypt.*
(Image from the National Archives)

Man of Steel

While Germany smoldered with revolution and reaction, and while the League of Nations faltered and failed, the reins of government in Communist Russia had passed from Vladimir Lenin, who died in 1924, to Josef Stalin.

Born Josef Vissarionovich Djugashvili in the czarist state of Georgia in 1879, Stalin was initially destined for the Orthodox priesthood, enrolling in the Tiflis Theological Seminary at the age of 14. His rebellious ways, however, had by this time earned him the nickname "Koba," after a famous Georgian rebel bandit. Before the 19th century ended, the seminary student was deeply involved in covert anti-czarist activity. Repeatedly arrested, he always managed to escape, and in 1912, Lenin elevated him to membership on the Bolshevik Central Committee and made him editor of the Communist Party's newspaper, *Pravda* ("Truth"). It was at this time that he took the name by which history would come to know him: Stalin—"Man of Steel."

Through the revolutionary period, Stalin rose to power, becoming general secretary of the Central Committee of the Communist Party. Lenin, debilitated by wounds sustained in a botched assassination attempt, began to become wary of Stalin's ruthlessness and, upon his death in 1924, left behind a letter warning against allowing Stalin to assume control of the government.

The warning came too late. Lenin's death left a power vacuum that Stalin rushed to fill. He eliminated all opposition by first attacking party leftists, and then, in an about-face, the rightists as well. By 1930, Stalin had eliminated opposition on both sides of the Communist Party.

Like the rest of the world, the Soviet Union was in the grip of economic depression. Unlike the nations of the West, however, the Soviet economy was under direct central control. Stalin decided to transform his agricultural nation into an industrial power. To do so, he seized the lands of the *kulaks*, the middle-class farmers, killing any who resisted. In this way, he *collectivized* the farms so that their production of grain and other staples could be centrally controlled and distributed.

But distributed to whom? The Soviet Union was suffering a devastating famine. Its people badly needed the produce from these collectivized farms. Yet, in his zeal to finance the building of an industrial economy, Stalin ordered most of the crops exported. Millions who resisted this policy were killed outright or sent into internal exile in Siberia—often the equivalent of a death sentence. Others simply starved.

Voice of the Century

"He who wishes to lead a movement must conduct a fight on two fronts—against those who lag behind and those who rush ahead."

—Josef Stalin, 1937

Talk of the Times

Collectivization was the policy and process by which Lenin and, later, Stalin forcibly nationalized agriculture in the Soviet Union. A 1988 estimate put the number of deaths directly resulting from Stalin's collectivization program of 1928–1933 at more than 25 million.

Josef Stalin in the early 1930s.
(Image from the Library of Congress)

Savage Men with Long Knives

In Chapter 12, we left Adolf Hitler, having been released from prison after serving part of a brief sentence for treason, having written *Mein Kampf*, and having risen to power as chancellor of Germany (appointed January 30, 1933), second in position only to Paul von Hindenberg.

Adolf Hitler with President Paul von Hindenburg on the occasion of Hitler's appointment as German's chancellor. (Image from arttoday.com)

Hindenberg, aging and infirm, was powerless to prevent Hitler from building a power base and acquiring for himself dictatorial power. When a fire (probably set by Nazi agitators) destroyed the Reichstag, the German parliament building, on February 27, 1933, Hitler pinned the blame on the communists, readily secured the authority to abolish the Communist Party, and imprisoned the party's leaders. The next month, he gained passage of the Enabling Act, which granted him dictatorial authority for four years.

Thus empowered, Hitler wasted no time. He outlawed all political parties in Germany, save the Nazi Party. He purged all Jews and other "undesirables" from government and from government-controlled institutions. He then turned on his own party. Ernst Röhm, the former Freikorps leader who had organized the Brownshirts (the SA) and whose strong-arm tactics had been essential to the elevation of Hitler, was now perceived as a threat to

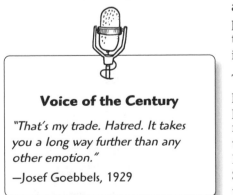

Voice of the Century

"That's my trade. Hatred. It takes you a long way further than any other emotion."

—Josef Goebbels, 1929

Hitler's absolute rule. On June 30, 1934, Hitler unleashed the "Night of the Long Knives," a violent purge of Röhm and the SA. Röhm and hundreds of potential challengers to Hitler were massacred. Hitler summarily replaced the SA with the SS, the *schutzstaffel*, or Blackshirts.

Under the command of Hitler henchman Heinrich Himmler, the SS worked with a secret police force, the *Gestapo*, to begin the round-up and elimination of Jews and political adversaries. While this was under way, Hitler assigned Josef Goebbels, his propaganda minister, to bring the nation into line behind him as he led it to an economic recovery based on massive, immediate, and total rearmament—the Treaty of Versailles and the League of Nations be damned.

America Gets a New Deal

In a starving, dazed, and demoralized Europe, the tactics of terror and brutality proved devastatingly effective in securing power. In the United States, however, the vision of the army pursuing unarmed Americans, coupled with dire economic and social conditions, spelled defeat for Herbert Hoover and brought into the White House the buoyant and effervescently optimistic Franklin Delano Roosevelt.

Knight in a Wheelchair

Born to a life of wealth and privilege in Hyde Park, New York, in 1882, Franklin Delano Roosevelt attended Groton School, followed by Harvard University and Columbia University Law School. The young patrician became a Wall Street lawyer and seemed destined to continue the life of privilege and affluence he had known. But he began to dedicate some of his time to free legal work for the poor and, in so doing, came to know and understand the life of the so-called common man.

Roosevelt left his lucrative law practice for local Dutchess County (New York) politics and then entered the federal arena when he was appointed assistant secretary of the Navy in the Wilson administration. In 1920, he was running mate to James M. Cox, the Democratic presidential hopeful who lost to Republican Warren G. Harding.

Defeat may have stung, but Roosevelt was to face a much graver challenge. In the summer of 1921, he was vacationing at his summer home on Campobello Island (New Brunswick, Canada) when he was stricken with polio. He fell desperately ill, fought his way to recovery, but was left paralyzed from the waist down. Always protective of him, Roosevelt's mother urged him to retire to the family's Hyde Park estate. But FDR's wife, the remarkable Eleanor Roosevelt—FDR's distant cousin and the niece of Theodore Roosevelt—persuaded her husband to return to public life. He took up Eleanor's challenge and embarked on a

Voice of the Century

"I pledge you, I pledge myself, to a new deal for the American people."

—Franklin D. Roosevelt, at the 1932 Democratic National Convention course of intensive physical therapy, learning to stand using iron leg braces and to walk with the aid of crutches. He had an automobile modified with hand controls, and he took great pleasure and pride in driving himself.

Roosevelt ran for governor of New York, won, and brought to the state a roster of progressive reforms that included the development of public power utilities, revision of the civil-service system, and social-welfare programs. Despite his success in Albany, few thought his run for the White House would be taken seriously. FDR proved the doubters wrong. At the 1932 Democratic National Convention, he pledged to deliver to the American people a "New Deal": a *federally* funded, *federally* administered program of relief and recovery.

The "Hundred Days"

Roosevelt was inaugurated in 1933, and, perhaps because he did not have the use of his legs, he made moving with astonishing speed his top priority. Within the first three months of the new administration—dubbed the "Hundred Days" by the press, with Napoleonic grandeur—FDR introduced to Congress reams of legislation to stimulate industrial recovery, assist individual victims of the Depression (something Hoover and all previous presidents had refused to do), guarantee minimum living standards, and help avert future crises. Above all, the rapidly enacted legislation was aimed at improving the immediate situation.

The Federal Deposit Insurance Corporation (FDIC) was established to protect depositors from losing their savings in the event of bank failure. The measure did much to restore confidence in the nation's faltering banking system. The Federal Reserve Board, which regulates the nation's money supply, was strengthened. The Home Owners Loan Corporation was established to supply funds to help beleaguered home owners avoid foreclosure. A Federal Securities Act reformed the regulation of stock offering and trading—an effort to avert the kind of wild speculation that helped bring about the crash of 1929.

FDR formed the Civilian Conservation Corps—the CCC—a military-style civilian organization that put thousands of men to work on projects in national forests, parks, and public lands. The National Recovery Act (NRA), the early New Deal's most sweeping and controversial legislation, established the Public Works Administration (PWA) and imposed upon industry a strict code of fair practice, setting minimum wages and maximum working hours and giving employees the right to collective bargaining.

Private industry fought FDR savagely over the NRA, accusing the new administration of resorting to communism. But the Depression was so severe, and FDR's personal charisma so persuasive, that he prevailed. Indeed, most Americans saw the radical measures of the Hundred Days not as a threat to democracy, but as its salvation—nothing less than a means of averting starvation, revolution, or both.

There is no doubt that FDR used his personal presence to lead the nation. He made masterful use of the medium of radio in a series of "Fireside Chats," informal addresses to the nation by which he sought to explain the steps being taken to recover from economic disaster. Although dictators such as Mussolini, Hitler, and Stalin created cults of personality, elevating themselves to godlike stature, Roosevelt used his considerable power of persuasion to help the American people realize the resilience, strength, and greatness within themselves.

In contrast to Stalin in particular, the Roosevelt administration showed equal concern for the industrial worker and the farmer. In May 1933, FDR prevailed on Congress to create the Agricultural Adjustment Administration, a program of production limits and federal subsidies. In effect, the government would pay farmers *not* to produce certain crops beyond specific limits, thereby stimulating the demand side of the supply-and-demand equation and increasing prices paid to farmers for their crops. Perhaps the single most visible manifestation of the New Deal program of agricultural reform was the establishment of the Tennessee Valley Authority (TVA), which built roads, great dams, and hydroelectric plants in seven of the nation's poorest states.

We will see some more aspects of the New Deal in the next chapter. To be sure, they were controversial when they were introduced, and, even in retrospect, the entire program still evokes debate. Critics were and remain quick to point out that none of the costly programs brought full economic recovery. (That would not come until a new war created a new demand for goods.) But few deny that the New Deal did help to restore confidence in the American government at a time when democracy in the rest of the world was being challenged, was being beaten, or had already been defeated.

The Least You Need to Know

➤ Unwise investment, unregulated banking practices, and overproduction were the main causes of the Great Depression; the 1929 stock-market crash merely signaled its beginning.

➤ Herbert Hoover was (and sometimes still is) unjustly blamed for the Depression; in fact, he initiated steps to combat it but refused to commit federal funds to the direct aid of individuals.

➤ The League of Nations proved ineffectual in coping with international crisis.

➤ Economic hardship created the social conditions that enabled Stalin to consolidate his power and Hitler to build his.

Chapter 14

"Happy Days Are Here Again" (1934–1938)

In This Chapter

➤ The Dust Bowl

➤ Keynesian economics and the New Deal

➤ Gangster culture

➤ The Spanish Civil War

➤ The power of the media

Talk to people who lived through the Depression, and their stories are remarkably similar. They talk about the little things: How folks would hang used tea bags from the wash line with clothes pins so they could be reused; how they would cut cardboard to fit inside their shoes, temporarily sealing holes in the sole; how they would walk to save a nickel streetcar fare. There were also the big things: The neighbors who "ate the car"—selling the family automobile for money to pay rent and buy groceries. The midwinter evictions, the dispossessions, and sheriff's sales. The loss of investment money in the stock-market crash or life savings in a bank failure. (About 4,000 banks collapsed during 1930–1932.)

Yet most of these Depression survivors will also tell you that economic hardship focused life, made it simpler, clearer. The object for most was simply to stay afloat in anticipation of better times. Franklin Delano Roosevelt was determined that his countrymen would never doubt that those better times were coming. His 1932 presidential campaign was propelled by the popular tune "Happy Days Are Here Again," and he declared in his first inaugural address "that the only thing we have to fear is fear itself."

Most people believed him—even though economics, politics, and even nature made believing a very hard thing to do.

Dust Bowl Disaster

If the stock-market crash of 1929 came as a shock to American urban dwellers, it struck most farmers as just one more tough break. In contrast to industrial and white-collar America, farmers had enjoyed little prosperity during the 1920s. They had been urged and driven to overproduce during World War I, and, after the war, the oversupply they had created caused food prices to plummet. Farmers just never cashed in.

Hardest hit were the farmers and ranchers of the Great Plains. The 150,000-square-mile area encompassing the Oklahoma and Texas panhandles as well as portions of Kansas, Colorado, and New Mexico offered poor, light soil, scant rainfall, and high prevailing winds that regularly took off vast quantities of precious topsoil. During the agricultural boom years of the war, Plains farmers had plowed up thousands of acres of natural grass cover in order to plant more and more wheat. To fulfill big government beef contracts, ranchers turned out huge herds, which grazed the land bald.

What holds the arid Plains together? Grass roots. Tear these up, by too much cultivation or too much grazing, and the soil becomes just so much dust in the wind. In 1934, drought visited the Plains and did not depart until three years later. The topsoil—it seemed the Earth itself—blew away in a series of dust storms and "black blizzards."

The crops that somehow managed to take hold were swept up by the wind. The cattle that somehow managed not to starve were choked to death on the driving dust.

Like their crops and cattle, the people of the Plains starved, choked, were uprooted, and took flight. More than 60 percent of the region's population—collectively dubbed *Okies*, whether or not they actually came from Oklahoma—embarked on an exodus of biblical proportions, pressing westward to the land that had held the promise of wealth and salvation since the Gold Rush of 1849. California, they were told, still had rich soil, and its towns and cities offered the promise of jobs.

In fact, California in the 1930s was no El Dorado. True, the soil was better, but farming was still a hard way to make a living. Those who sought work in cities and towns were met by billboards along the state's highways warning them that the community they were approaching had no jobs to offer.

Europe and Asia were all too familiar with such human/ecological disasters. The history of the Old World was punctuated by famine and drought. Not so in America. Here, people were used to plenty, and the panic now was barely contained.

Talk of the Times

Okies was the popular (and often derisive) term for victims of the Dust Bowl who traveled—mostly to California—in search of a better life or even better prospects for survival.

Franklin Delano Roosevelt: No American president since Abraham Lincoln faced so much crisis, including the Great Depression and World War II.
(Image from the author's collection)

Roosevelt's New Deal government acted quickly to stem the fear and deal with the crisis through a spectrum of aid agencies and relief programs. The most prominent of the Dust Bowl agencies was the Soil Conservation Service, founded in 1935. Not only did the service give farmers direct financial aid, but also it instructed them in the practical science of soil conservation, including such practices such as planting trees and grass to anchor the soil, contouring furrows in terrace fashion to hold precious rainwater and prevent erosion, and rotating crops to allow the soil to regenerate.

The government also aided the land itself. In a massive subsidy program, federal authorities purchased 11.3 million acres in order to take it out of production and give its root systems time to regenerate.

Nor was the spiritual and human face of the Dust Bowl neglected. Remarkably, the Farm Security Agency commissioned a group of the nation's most promising young photographers, including such artists as Dorothea Lange and Walker Evans, to document conditions in the Dust Bowl. Not only did this coverage result in some of the century's greatest photography, but also it supplied images that raised the consciousness of the nation—which was further heightened by John Steinbeck's 1939 novel *The Grapes of Wrath*, which narrated the saga of the Joads, a family of "Okies" on an epic trek to California. The novel was filmed by director John Ford in 1940.

Even critics of the New Deal admit that the FDR administration's response to the Dust Bowl was highly successful. Most of the land had been

Voice of the Century

"Well, by God, I'm hungry.... My guts is yellin' bloody murder."

—John Steinbeck, *The Grapes of Wrath*, 1939

reclaimed by the beginning of World War II—just in time for farmers, once more, to begin overworking the land. When drought struck again after the war, in the 1950s, the government, recalling the lessons of the Dust Bowl, responded quickly with large subsidies paid to farmers to take land out of production. The idea of paying for non-production appalled many Americans, but the program succeeded in averting a second Dust Bowl by returning millions of acres to grassland.

A Tale of Two Nations

That most Americans embraced the New Deal is a measure both of the nation's desperation and of the persuasive power of FDR. The idea of so much direct federal intervention in private lives and private enterprise ran contrary to deeply held American values. Indeed, some conservative voices were raised in protest, accusing Roosevelt of leaning toward communism, by which they really meant the kind of autocratic, central control Stalin was exercising over the Soviet economy.

Economics According to Keynes

Franklin Delano Roosevelt was far from being a Stalin. He certainly did not take his cue from the Soviet leader, but, rather, from the work of a British economist, the single most influential economist of the 20th century, John Maynard Keynes.

Born in 1883, the son of a celebrated economics scholar, Keynes graduated from Cambridge, hobnobbed with the brilliant intellectuals of London's "Bloomsbury Group"—including the novelists Virginia Woolf and E.M. Forster, the philosopher Alfred North Whitehead, the literary critic Lytton Strachey, the painter Duncan Grant, and the art historian Clive Bell—and then entered the British civil service as an economist with the India Office.

Although Keynes left the India office for a time to teach at his alma mater, he was pressed into government service again during the Great War, managing the nation's treasury and then serving as economic adviser to Prime Minister David Lloyd George at the Versailles Peace Conference. Keynes resigned in disgust at the punitive measures imposed on Germany, writing a book titled *The Economic Consequences of Peace*, in which he demonstrated that the Treaty of Versailles imposed war indemnities that could never be paid and that would ruin the German economy, creating the conditions in which revolution and war were likely to develop.

With his book, Keynes had shown himself to be a maverick, an iconoclast in a profession typically dominated by conservative defenders of the status quo. The truth was that he had begun to have doubts not only about the economics of the Treaty of Versailles, but also about *laissez-faire capitalism* itself: the idea, first fully presented by the economic philosopher Adam Smith in *The Wealth of Nations* (1776), which held that economies functioned most efficiently, "naturally" and "inevitably" reaching the optimum level of health, if they were left alone by government. Business cycles, Adams argued, the inevitable ups and downs of an economy, ultimately corrected themselves. He believed that, in sum, the selfish actions of individuals and firms ultimately move the economy—as by an "invisible hand"—toward the best possible state; therefore, the free market should be left precisely that way: free.

Keynes held his tongue—and his pen—until the 1929 stock-market crash. Then, in 1930, he wrote *Treatise on Money* and, in 1935–36, *General Theory of Employment, Interest, and Money*. In these works, Keynes directly challenged the gospel according to Adam Smith, arguing that excessive unemployment and economic depression were not necessarily temporary and self-correcting. He held that no wage was so low that it could eliminate unemployment and that prosperity depended ultimately on demand. Keynes argued that, because consumers could not spend more than they earned, the source of the business cycle's ups and downs was business investors and government, the entities that ultimately controlled income, enabling demand. In a depression, it was essential to increase investment, and if investors proved timid (which they inevitably did during depressions), it was up to the government to create public substitutes for the missing investment funds (which the timorous rich hoarded instead of circulated).

FDR and his New Deal administration seized on these Keynesian principles. The government would make up for the loss of investment. The government would assist the people—consumers—in order to create demand, which would, in turn, drive supply and thereby revive languishing industry. Thus jump-started, the economy should once again invite investment, and the world would be made safe for the free market.

The price? In addition to relinquishing absolute adherence to capitalist ideals, government would have to engage in deficit spending to finance public works projects as well as direct subsidies to victims of the Depression. American government and the American economy would never be the same.

Talk of the Times

Laissez-faire capitalism is an economic system in which the marketplace is left to balance and correct itself, regardless of "temporary" consequences and without government intervention.

Voice of the Century

"[The Depression] is not a crisis of poverty, but a crisis of abundance. It is not the harshness and the niggardliness of nature which are oppressing us, but our own incompetence and wrongheadedness which hinder us from making use of the bountifulness of inventive science and cause us to be overwhelmed by its generous fruits."

—John Maynard Keynes, 1932

Politics According to Stalin

As we saw in Chapter 13, "The Party Ends," Russia's Josef Stalin had no compunctions about imposing government into the economic lives of his people, even if it killed them. We saw how he dealt with the devastation of the Depression—by sacrificing Russian farmers and others to the cause of forced industrialization.

Stalin took a similarly ruthless view of politics. Whereas Roosevelt, the master politician, used emotional and moral appeals to persuade ordinary citizens as well as fellow political leaders to climb aboard the New Deal bandwagon, Stalin resorted to the more direct expedient—murder—in order to get his way.

In 1934, when the 17th Communist Party Congress, reacting to the nationwide famine that had been exacerbated by Stalin's program of forced collectivization, supported Sergei Kirov, a moderate rival to Stalin, the "Man of Steel" responded by having Kirov killed. Then, feigning outrage at the killing, Stalin ordered the arrest of most of the party's top officials on suspicion of counterrevolutionary conspiracy.

Beginning in 1936, Stalin staged public "show trials" of these officials as well as senior military officers. Through 1939, these *purges* resulted in the execution of 98 of the 139 Central Committee members who had been elected in 1934. Of the 1,966 delegates to the rebellious 17th Party Congress, 1,108 were arrested—some condemned to death, others to exile.

Even this was not enough. Through Lavrenti Beria, head of the secret police force known as the KGB, Stalin effected the arrest, execution, or exile of millions of ordinary Soviet citizens who were suspected of something less than absolute loyalty to Stalin.

20th-Century Life

In an era with no shortage of evil men, Lavrenti Beria (1899–1953) was among the most sinister. Joining the Communist Party in 1917, he became active in intelligence and counterintelligence operations for the Bolsheviks in 1921 and was made head of the secret police in Georgia. During the 1930s, he took personal charge of Stalin's purges. Summoned to Moscow in 1938 to serve as deputy to Nikolay Yezhov, head of the Soviet secret police, he replaced Yezhov when Stalin ordered Yezhov's execution.

Beria ruthlessly purged the secret police and set up a network of labor camps to receive the hundreds of thousands being sent into internal exile. During World War II, Beria would be hailed as a hero for creating labor camps to increase the production of war materiel. In March 1953, after Stalin's death, Beria tried to leverage his position as head of the secret police to become sole dictator of the nation, but he was checkmated by a coalition led by Georgy M. Malenkov, Vyacheslav M. Molotov, and Nikita S. Khrushchev. Beria was accused of being an "imperialist agent" and of conducting "criminal antiparty and antistate activities," speedily convicted, and executed in December 1953.

America Pulls Together

Stalin conducted his trials and purges with a mixture of public display and utmost secrecy, but, really, in the world of the 1930s, it was difficult to keep anything secret for long. The mass media, including large-circulation newspapers, radio, and the newsreels (short news films shown in movie theaters, usually before the main feature), provided broad and rapid coverage of the world's events. For most Americans, the show trials and purges of Stalin's Russia were ample evidence that communism was no answer to the nation's economic woes.

During the 1920s and '30s, it is true, numbers of American intellectuals flirted with and even embraced communism. In the face of Stalin's outrageous purges, some persisted in their loyalty, but others were driven to abandon the ideology altogether. Leaving the communist fold was a difficult choice. During the 1930s, significant numbers of American political activists retained ties to the Communist Party in part because they saw it as an alternative to the Depression-era failings of capitalism, but, even more important, because they believed it presented the only viable means of resisting the increasingly menacing fascism of Mussolini's Italy and Hitler's Germany.

Still, for the vast majority of Americans, revolution, whether communist or fascist, seemed less and less an answer to the Depression. The New Deal, by circumventing some of the shortcomings of capitalist democracy, succeeded in restoring the faith of most Americans in capitalism and democracy. As harsh and terrifying as the Depression was, it ultimately served to unite Americans rather than pull them apart. People felt that they were "in it" together, and they drew strength from one another.

Depression Culture

It is a measure of the spirit of the American people that, in a time of want and austerity, the arts not only didn't suffer, but they actually flourished. The 1930s saw the maturation of jazz, with the ascendancy of the exuberant swing style of Duke Ellington, Count Basie, Benny Goodman, and many others. Writers such as Hemingway, Fitzgerald, and Faulkner, whose careers had been launched in the 1920s, rose to new heights of maturity, while new voices, including John Steinbeck and the African-American novelist Richard Wright, emerged. As for painting, a school of new realists, including Edward Hopper, Grant Wood, and Thomas Hart Benton, among others, were achieving international renown.

Eugene O'Neill, who revolutionized American theater in the 1920s with such plays as *The Emperor Jones, The Iceman Cometh,* and *Desire Under the Elms*, was recognized in 1936 with a Nobel Prize for Literature. His work paved the way for the likes of Clifford Odets (*Waiting for Lefty*, 1935; *Awake and*

Talk of the Times

Musical comedy (also called the **musical**) is a form of popular theater in which the dialogue and action are interspersed with song. More colloquial and popular in tone than either opera or operetta, musical comedy developed to maturity on the American stage during the 1920s to 1950s.

Sing, 1935; and *Golden Boy*, 1937) and, in subsequent decades, Tennessee Williams, Arthur Miller, and Edward Albee.

On the popular stage, the musical came of age. Composer-lyricist teams, including brothers George and Ira Gershwin, Jerome Kern and Oscar Hammerstein II, Richard Rodgers and Lorenz Hart, and Cole Porter (who wrote both music and lyrics), transformed the musical stage revue of the 1920s into genuine *musical comedy*—musical theater that tells a story.

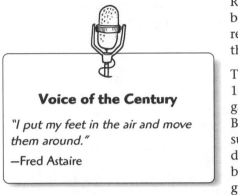

Voice of the Century

"I put my feet in the air and move them around."

—Fred Astaire

The musical translated readily from stage to film in the 1930s, as Depression audiences warmly greeted extravagant, lavish, and elegant productions directed by Busby Berkeley (featuring bevies of chorus girls in elaborately suggestive precision dance routines) or starring the dance team of Fred Astaire and Ginger Rogers, who brought lighthearted romance and incredible ballroom grace and tap acrobatics to screens across the country.

The Ride of Bonnie and Clyde

Offering elegant escape and carefree romance, the musical was the most popular film genre of the Depression-burdened 1930s. Not far behind in popularity, however, was the gangster film. In the 1920s, the American public had been amused, indifferent, and even grateful to gangsters, who, after all, supplied them with liquor during Prohibition and seemed intent on doing harm only to their own kind. These benign sentiments turned to outrage after Al Capone's brutal St. Valentine's Day Massacre of 1929, but then, the public attitude shifted yet again with the onset of the Depression.

Prohibition was repealed in 1933, so the bootlegger's trade vanished, but, trapped in hard times, at the mercy of the economy, an employer (if one was lucky enough to have a job), a landlord, and, perhaps most of all, the banks, people now became fascinated by the doings of gangsters. If the movies were full of them—portrayed by such character actors as Edward G. Robinson, George Raft, Humphrey Bogart, and Jimmy Cagney—so were the streets of America.

The gangsters of the 1930s are some of the most familiar names in American history. There were the kingpins of organized crime: Albert Anastasia (1907–1957), who headed up the Mafia's strong-arm division, "Murder, Inc."; Lucky Luciano (1897–1962) and Meyer Lansky (1902–1983), who had virtually created organized crime; and Frank Costello (1891–1973), who was dubbed Prime Minister of the Underworld. Men such as these had gotten their start in the heady days of 1920s Prohibition and found new outlets for organized crime in drugs, gambling, and corrupt labor unions after repeal.

Another class of criminal also flourished in the 1930s. They were the bank robbers, such as the criminal gang led by Kate "Ma" Barker (ca. 1871–1935), or the "lone wolf" types, such as John Dillinger (1903–1934). The public was both appalled and transfixed by Barker, Dillinger, and their ilk. Many decried their brutality, but even more were willing to overlook this because they didn't prey upon the "little guy," but targeted the banks—those heartless institutions that destroyed peoples' lives by going belly up, denying loans, or foreclosing on defaulted mortgages. Banks commanded precious little sympathy in the 1930s, but many of those enrolled on the FBI's "Most Wanted" lists were admired as latter-day Robin Hoods (not that there was any evidence that they shared their spoils).

20th-Century Life

John Dillinger (1903-1934) was the first felon to be branded "Public Enemy Number One" by the FBI. The Indianapolis-born petty thief graduated to bank robbery after spending nine years in prison for having robbed a grocery store. His spectacular escape from a combined ambush by Chicago police officers and FBI agents at the Little Bohemia Lodge, just north of Chicago, in Wisconsin, resulted in a bloodbath that disgraced the FBI when agents' bullets killed three innocent bystanders.

After Little Bohemia, J. Edgar Hoover made the capture of Dillinger a personal crusade. On July 24, 1934, with the aid of a "confidential informant," Dillinger girlfriend Anna Sage, agents led by Hoover's right-hand man, Melvin Purvis, ambushed Dillinger as he exited the Biograph Theater on Chicago's Near North Side. Dillinger was slain in a hail of bullets—and two female bystanders were wounded.

Most appealing of all the Depression-era criminals were Bonnie Parker (1911–1934) and Clyde Barrow (1909–1934). When the two met in Texas in January 1930, Clyde was already a bank robber and Bonnie, age 19, was the wife of an imprisoned murderer. Shortly after they became a couple, Clyde was arrested for a burglary, sent to jail, and managed to escape using a gun Bonnie had smuggled to him. Recaptured, he was returned to prison but paroled in February 1932. He immediately rejoined Bonnie, and the pair took up a life of crime together. They worked briefly with Raymond Hamilton, a young gunman who was replaced by William Daniel Jones in November 1932. When Ivan M. "Buck" Barrow, brother of Clyde, was released from the Texas State Prison on March 23, 1933, he and his wife, Blanche, joined Bonnie, Clyde, and Jones.

The five embarked upon a series of bank robberies throughout the Dust Bowl region so bold that they captured headlines across the country. The public hungrily followed the exploits of this "romantic" gang, who handily evaded all attempts at capture until a shootout with police in Iowa on July 29, 1933, resulted in the death of Buck Barrow and the wounding and capture of Blanche. A short time later, in Texas, Jones, frequently mistaken for another 1930s gangster icon, "Pretty Boy" Floyd, was apprehended.

This left Bonnie and Clyde to continue on their own. On the run, they held up an attorney encountered along a highway and made off with his car. They next robbed a citizen in Shreveport, Louisiana, and, then, on January 16, 1934, they liberated five prisoners (serving sentences totaling more than 200 years) from the Eastham State Prison Farm at Waldo, Texas. Two guards were shot in the process. Indeed, Bonnie and Clyde were not so much the Maid Marion and Robin Hood of the Dust Bowl as they were sociopathic killers, suspected of 13 murders (mostly of police officers) and numerous robberies, burglaries, and auto thefts.

By the early spring of 1934, the man hunt for the pair was intensive. On April 1, 1934, Bonnie and Clyde encountered and shot two young highway patrolmen near Grapevine, Texas. On April 6, they fatally wounded a constable at Miami, Oklahoma, and wounded and kidnapped the local police chief. At last, on April 13, 1934, the FBI determined their whereabouts in Louisiana. Before dawn on May 23, 1934, a posse of officers from Louisiana and Texas set up an ambush near Sailes, Louisiana. When their automobile drove by, the police opened fire, riddling the car—and Bonnie and Clyde—with a hail of bullets.

From Folksongs to Dams

In truth, the saga of Bonnie and Clyde was brief, brutal, and sordid. But a generation of victimized Americans transformed it into the stuff of legend, as an earlier generation had celebrated the lives of such cold-blooded killers as Billy the Kid and Frank and Jesse James.

The people of the '30s were hungry for heroes, antiheroes, and myths to cling to. They sought these in the activities of Bonnie and Clyde and others of their ilk. But the federal government was eager to supply more wholesome material. Among the many remarkable projects funded by the New Deal were the Federal Theater Project, the Federal Art Project, and the Federal Writers' Program.

The Federal Theater Project sponsored and supported productions by new playwrights and directors, launching the careers of John Houseman and Orson Welles, among many others. The Federal Art Project fostered the creation of art in public places, including murals in many post offices, schools, and public buildings. The Federal Writers' Programs commissioned an impressive series of local guidebooks and local histories and also funded teams of folklorists to collect and record the folk heritage of the nation, especially in rural areas where the "old ways" were rapidly disappearing. In the depths of the Depression, field workers collected and classified a rich treasury of folktales and folksongs that celebrate American heritage.

Yet it is for the great public works of concrete and steel that the WPA and other New Deal programs are most remembered. Greatest of all the federally funded projects was Boulder Dam (since 1947, called Hoover Dam). By the late 1920s, westerners, especially those who were developing a rather sleepy Southern California city called Los Angeles, were agitating for a scheme to bring the mighty Colorado River under human control by building a great dam and reservoir, which would irrigate tens of thousands of acres of farmland and, not incidentally, ensure a supply of water for Los Angeles and other growing desert communities.

The project to dam the Colorado at Black Canyon, on the Arizona-Nevada border, began in 1930. It would have been a gargantuan undertaking in the best of times, America's answer to the pyramids of Egypt or the Colossus of Rhodes, an attempt to wrestle into submission one of the mightiest rivers in the world. In the midst of an economic depression of unprecedented magnitude, the project was nothing less than a collective national leap of faith.

The nation believed it *could* be done. Franklin Roosevelt, who inherited the project from the Hoover administration, believed it *had* to be done, not just because it would provide work for several thousand men and women, and not just because it would irrigate many acres, provide water for many people, and generate electricity for a region, but because the nation, especially at this time, *had* to do it.

The work consumed six years—a remarkably short time, considering all that had to be accomplished. A reinforced concrete structure 726 feet high and 1,244 feet long (across its crest) was built, along with massive pumping towers and other support structures, including a huge electrical generating plant. To build the dam, the Colorado River had to be temporarily diverted—a feat that had never before been contemplated, let alone attempted, with so powerful a river.

Century Stats

Hoover Dam has a volume of 4,400,000 cubic yards and can generate 1,345 megawatts of electricity.

Called Boulder Dam when it was completed in 1936, it was renamed Hoover Dam in 1947 to honor the president who had authorized its construction.
(Image from arttoday.com)

All was accomplished ahead of schedule. Moreover, the dam was designed to be beautiful, a monument in the 1930s art moderne style, erected to honor the government and the people who had built it.

America justly took pride in Boulder Dam. Collectively, it made people feel less like victims and more like masters. It was a heady feeling—and a dangerous one, perhaps all too typical of the 20th century. Over succeeding years, 25 more dams would follow Boulder Dam along the Colorado River, until it was blocked and bled on every side.

Today, the mighty Colorado no longer flows to the Pacific; strangled, it peters out in a salty waste in Baja, California.

Rehearsal for Armageddon

The show trials and purges of Stalinist Russia had put the world's communists, including those in the United States, in a difficult position. How could one reconcile so much apparently arbitrary bloodshed with—well, with *anything* decent and good?

For many, the answer came in 1936. Spain had been coming apart at the seams. It was a deeply divided nation, with, on one side, the Roman Catholic Church, the military, the landowners, and the prosperous business interests, and on the other side, urban blue-collar workers, agricultural workers, and many of the educated middle class. The extremes of each of these classes were represented on the far right by the Fascist-inspired and aligned *Falange* and on the far left by anarchists. Between the extremes was a spectrum of political parties, encompassing monarchism, liberalism, socialism, and communism.

By the 1930s, debate and dissension had escalated to assassinations and random acts of terrorist violence and reprisal. In 1934, general strikes were called in Valencia and Zaragoza, and street fighting broke out in Madrid and Barcelona. A bloody uprising by miners in Asturias was suppressed by troops under Gen. Francisco Paulino Hermengildo Teodulo Franco-Bahamonde—Francisco Franco—who thereby earned respect from the Spanish right wing and hatred from the left.

From this point, the Republican government suffered a series of crises, culminating in the elections of February 16, 1936, which brought to power leaders of the Popular Front, a left-wing party opposed by the various parties of the right as well as those few parties that identified themselves as centrists.

With the ascension of the left wing, General Franco was exiled to a remote military post in the Canary Islands. Here, he organized a military-conservative conspiracy that erupted on July 18, 1936, into the Spanish Civil War when military garrisons throughout Spain suddenly took over the garrison towns. Within a few days, the right-wing rebels were in control of Spanish Morocco, the Canary Islands, and the Balearic Islands (except Minorca), as well as parts of the Spanish mainland.

The Republican forces set about crushing uprisings wherever they could, and soon, the nation was divided roughly north and south. Thousands were killed in fighting, but many more—perhaps 50,000 on each side, were executed, murdered, or assassinated.

Battle on the outskirts of the beautiful medieval town of Toledo. (Image from arttoday.com)

Franco assumed overall command of the right-wing, or Nationalist, forces and was named head of state of a government set up in Burgos. The Republican government was headed by a succession of socialists. Both the Nationalists and the Republicans believed that they possessed insufficient strength to win a decisive victory, so they transformed their civil war into an international conflict: an ideological contest between fascism and communism.

Franco enlisted the aid of fascist Germany and Italy, which sent troops, tanks, and planes. The Nationalists turned to the Soviet Union and also to France and Mexico. The United States remained officially neutral in the struggle, but many young American idealists enlisted in the Abraham Lincoln Brigade, one of many International Brigades formed by the Republicans to accept foreign troops. Some 40,000 foreigners served in military units, and about half that number enlisted in ambulance corps and other non-combatant support units. Most famous of all the American volunteers was Ernest Hemingway, whose 1940 novel *For Whom the Bell Tolls* draws on his experience in the Lincoln Brigade.

By the end of 1936, the struggle between the Nationalists and the Republicans had become a grinding war of attrition. For the Italian and German troops involved, it was something more: a full-dress rehearsal for the next European war they already planned. German pilots, in particular, practiced dive-bombing techniques on such towns as Guernica, in the northern Basque region of Spain. The bombing inspired the creation of perhaps the most powerful modern artistic evocation of the horrors of war, the 1937 mural *Guernica* by Pablo Picasso.

Voice of the Century

"They wrote in the old days that it is sweet and fitting to die for one's country. But in modern war, there is nothing sweet nor fitting in your dying. You will die like a dog for no good reason."

—Ernest Hemingway, 1935

By early 1939, the Republicans were on the run, and on March 5, the Republican government flew to exile in France. On March 7, combat took place in Madrid between communist and anti-communist factions, but by March 28, all Republican armies had either disbanded or surrendered. Spain was a fascist nation under the military dictatorship of Francisco Franco.

Spain's Franco shakes hands with the man who aided his cause in the Spanish Civil War, Adolf Hitler.
(Image from arttoday.com)

Aliens Land in New Jersey

The Spanish Civil War rallied a small but determined band of Americans to a fight against Fascism, but, as late as the end of the 1930s, few in this country had their eyes open to the meaning of Fascism. Few could see—or wanted to see—the new war that was brewing in Europe. Even fewer suspected that this European war would be wedded to a war in Asia and the Pacific. The news out of northern Europe as well as Spain was all over the radio. Many Americans *listened*, but they did not *hear*.

What did come through loud and clear, on the evening of Halloween 1938, was a broadcast of the *Mercury Theatre on the Air*, the radio spinoff of a theatrical troupe partly financed by the WPA and led by a young actor-director with the face of a cherub named Orson Welles.

Welles's program was in trouble. The network had slotted it opposite the most popular show on radio, *The Chase and Sanborn Hour*, starring ventriloquist Edgar Bergen and his smart-aleck dummy Charlie McCarthy. To win back an audience, Welles knew he had to do something outrageous. He decided to modify and update H.G. Wells's *War of the Worlds*, an 1898 novel about what happens when the Martians invade earth, and present it as if it were a live, real-time radio news story.

Welles was careful to begin the program by having the announcer explain that it was a dramatization of *The War of the Worlds*, but many listeners seem not to have paid attention. Instead, they were utterly taken in by a program of dance music broadcast from the "Meridien Room of the Hotel Plaza Park," which is suddenly interrupted by a "special bulletin": A "huge flaming object" had landed on a farm near a place called Grover's Mill, New Jersey.

The bulletin concluded, listeners were returned to the Meridien Room and the music of "Ramon Raquello"—until newsman "Carl Philips" broke in with an announcement:

> *Ladies and gentlemen, this is the most terrifying thing I have ever witnessed....Wait a minute; someone's crawling. Someone or...some thing. I can see peering out of that black hole two luminous disks...are they eyes? It might be a face. It might be...good heavens, something's wriggling out of the shadow like a gray snake. Now it's another one, and another one, and another one....*

Then, incredibly, it was back to the Meridien Room, the insipid dance music punctuated by a series of increasingly alarming bulletins:

> *Incredible as it may seem, both the observation of science and the evidence of our eyes lead to the inescapable assumption that those strange beings who landed in the Jersey farmlands tonight are the vanguard of an invading army from the planet Mars!*

Welles's program was indeed outdrawing Edgar Bergen and his dummy, but it was also igniting a nationwide panic. Police departments across the country were inundated by terrified calls, many vividly describing Martian sightings. In some places, people instinctively poured into the streets. There were even suicide threats.

Local announcers broke into the network feed to assure listeners that they what they were hearing was only fiction, and, at last, the panic was quelled. But the ripples that panic had created are felt still. Welles had inadvertently demonstrated the overwhelming power of the mass media to *create* reality—something Hitler and his propaganda minister Josef Goebbels had already discovered and were exploiting daily.

He had also demonstrated something else. Almost willfully blind to the gathering storm in Europe and Asia, the American people, on a deeper level of consciousness, were becoming aware of their dangerous world. Did the broadcast prove that Americans in 1938 were simply a gullible lot? Maybe. More important, it suggested that they were also primed to believe not so much in a war of the worlds, but in a world at war.

The Least You Need to Know

➤ The Dust Bowl, caused by a combination of drought and poor farming practice, devastated American agriculture and drove thousands out of the Midwest and Southwest.

➤ The Roosevelt administration used the new economic theories of John Maynard Keynes to justify government intervention in the free market system. Doing so permanently changed the relation of government and commerce.

➤ While Stalin violently reshaped Soviet government, the Spanish Civil War became an international arena in which the forces of communism vied with those of fascism.

➤ Orson Welles's infamous *War of the Worlds* radio broadcast not only demonstrated the power of mass media, but also revealed the level of anxiety of a world suffering through a Depression and on the brink of all-out war.

Part 4
To Hell and Back: 1939–1949

The great catastrophe that had been the first world war was scarcely a generation old when the world rushed headlong into a second. There are, we will see, political and economic reasons for World War II, and, as the 1930s exploded into the 1940s, there were plenty of sophisticated people willing to offer sophisticated analysis of how this second worldwide cataclysm had come about. But, in truth, whatever its many causes, the war was begun by a little man with an absurd Charlie Chaplin "cookie duster" moustache. In a century grown too sophisticated to put such stock in words like good and evil, Adolf Hitler was the incarnation of evil.

The chapters in this section speak of the causes, conduct, and conclusion of World War II. If the war changed the world in so many ways, the manner in which the war was ended, with two nuclear detonations over cities of Japan, changed it even more profoundly. The rest of the century would be lived in the knowledge that all we were, all we knew, all we had could vanish in a flash and a mushroom cloud.

Chapter 15

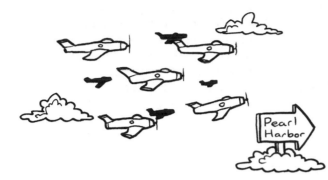

"Peace in Our Time" (1939–1941)

In This Chapter

➤ Germany defies the Treaty of Versailles

➤ France and Britain give Hitler what he wants

➤ Hitler and Stalin sign a non-aggression pact

➤ Hitler invades Poland, igniting World War II

➤ Lend-lease and Pearl Harbor: the U.S. enters the war

At its signing, the Treaty of Versailles was sweet revenge for the Allies. Oh, there had been dissenting voices; Woodrow Wilson argued endlessly with the prime ministers of France, Britain, and Italy that to leave a defeated foe without dignity, hope, and the economic means to carry on as a stable national entity was a dangerous policy. But Wilson's head was filled with the League of Nations, and if getting the League meant letting America's allies have their way, at least for now, so be it.

Woodrow Wilson and the United States were clear across the ocean. As for policy makers in Britain, France, and Italy, *they* had to occupy the same continent as Germany. For Britons, Frenchmen, and Italians, containing German aggression was just as important as exacting revenge. The Treaty of Versailles was aimed at keeping Germany a beaten nation—financially and militarily. What could possibly go wrong?

Tomorrow...the World

Even before the 1930s were out, the world would learn just how tragic a document the Versailles treaty was. It had all seemed so absolute, so ironclad: Not only did it saddle Germany with a war debt equivalent to a convict's ball and chain, but also it limited the German army to a mere 100,000 men, of which only 4,000 were to be officers. Heavy weapons, aircraft included, were prohibited. As for the navy, the limit was set at only 15,000 sailors, and it was barred from building any new submarines.

What the Treaty of Versailles failed to contemplate was a man like Adolf Hitler.

Germany Arms Itself

Abused by a brutal father, thwarted in his ambition to become a great artist, friendless, and shiftless, Hitler understood well what it meant to be an underdog. When the Munich beer hall *Putsch* failed in 1923, and he was imprisoned, he used that time to think, to plan, and to create his persuasive political autobiography, *Mein Kampf* (as we saw in Chapter 12, "Victims and Heroes"). His rise to power had come thanks to the financial hardships imposed by the Treaty of Versailles. A broken, desperate nation was hungry for a leader who made extraordinary promises.

Talk of the Times

Fuhrerheer is a German word roughly translated as "army of leaders." It refers to the small, highly professional army Germany developed in accordance with the restrictions of the Treaty of Versailles.

Even before Hitler's rise, the German military was finding ways to turn the treaty to their advantage, too. Under General Hans von Seeckt, an officer of the old Prussian school, the skeleton army left by Versailles became a *Fuhrerheer*—an army of leaders, of the military elite. Although it was small, it was an all-volunteer force, selective, the highly polished core around which a new army could be quickly, efficiently, and effectively formed—when the time came. Few in Germany doubted the time would come.

As for the treaty restrictions on military hardware, Germany found various ways around those. One of the most ingenious of these was the Treaty of Rapallo with the Soviet Union (1922), which established a program of military cooperation between Germany and the USSR. The Treaty of Versailles restricted development of weapons *in Germany*; the Treaty of Rapallo provided facilities *in Russia* where Germany could develop advanced ground weapons and aircraft. Another agreement, the London Naval Treaty, concluded in 1935 with Britain, allowed Germany increased tonnage in warships—and gave Hitler hope that Britain and Germany might actually become allies.

Talk of the Times

Blitzkrieg, literally "lightning war," was the doctrine of strategy and tactics developed by German military planners designed to attack an enemy with great speed and violence, penetrating his front lines while encircling and destroying him.

Important as these treaties were to Germany, they weren't absolutely necessary to that nation's rearmament. With or without treaties, Germany rearmed, secretly at first, and then quite boldly, after it became increasingly apparent that the other nations of Europe, either acting on their own or through the League of Nations, lacked the will to take action in response to violations of the Treaty of Versailles.

While Germany honed the *Fuhrerheer* and rearmed, its military planners also developed a revolutionary new approach to war. It was christened *Blitzkrieg*—lightning war—a combination of tactics and weapons designed to move against an enemy with overwhelming force and great speed, penetrating its front-line defenses while encircling and destroying it. The Spanish Civil War (as we saw in Chapter 14, "Happy Days Are Here Again") provided a dress rehearsal for the new doctrine of German warfare.

France Bars the Door

While Germany prepared to take the offensive, the French took other action, which all too aptly symbolized the hunkered-down, defensive attitude of non-Fascist Europe. Andrè Maginot (1877–1932) had been elected to the French Chamber of Deputies in 1910 and became undersecretary of war three years later. A patriot, he left the war department to join the army as a private at the start of World War I and received a crippling wound. Discharged, he returned to political life, and, after the war, agitated for the construction of a line of defensive fortifications on the eastern frontiers of France.

At last, in 1929, while Maginot was serving as minister of war, construction began. Maginot died in early 1932 and did not live to see the 1938 completion of the system of fortifications that would bear his name. The Maginot Line was a wonder of 20th-century military engineering. It was essentially a string of fortresses connected by a network of tunnels through which troops and supplies could be transported by rail. Exposed structures were built of thick concrete designed to withstand bombardment by any artillery then known. Troop quarters were air-conditioned, and it was said that life "on the Line" was more comfortable than in most modern cities.

The comfort of the troops was nothing compared to the comfort the Maginot Line gave the people of France. It covered the entire French-German frontier, from the southern tip of Belgium down to the top of Switzerland. It was like barring the doors and shutting the windows of one's house. What could be safer?

War is supposed to whet the martial appetite of the victors. In the 1930s, the victors of the Great War wanted no more fighting. They barred the doors and closed the windows—with new treaties, new agreements, new promises, and, in the case of the French, an air-conditioned, concrete-reinforced, state-of-the-art ditch. In the meantime, Germany, the loser, eagerly sharpened its many swords.

Living Room

Friedrich Ratzel (1844–1904) was a German geographer and ethnographer who, in 1901, wrote an essay called "*Lebensraum*"—literally, living room or living space. He pointed out that states tended to expand or contract their boundaries according to their ability to do so. Years later, during the early 1930s, Adolf Hitler twisted the concept of *Lebensraum* in somewhat the same way that Americans had seized on the phrase "manifest destiny" back in the mid-19th century (Chapter 3, "Century of Iron"): to justify expansion.

Hitler declared it only right and natural—and inevitable—that the German people should have the living space the might of the German state could obtain for them. By the mid 1930s, Hitler's talk of *Lebensraum* prompted Britain, France, and even Italy to issue a joint statement of opposition to German expansion. The French also entered into a defensive alliance with the Soviets in 1935, and the Soviets concluded a similar pact with the Czechs.

This schematic of the Maginot Line appeared in a publication of an American veterans' organization in the early 1930s.
(Image from arttoday.com)

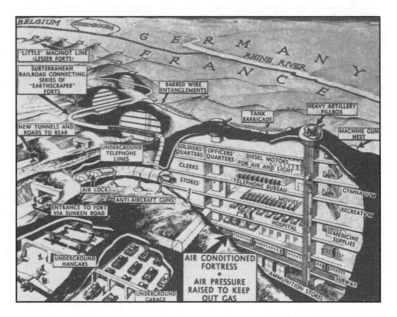

Peace or Appeasement?

It was Italy, not Germany, that made the first expansionist move by invading Ethiopia (as we saw in Chapter 14), and, in response, the British foreign secretary, Sir Samuel Hoare, sought to "appease" Mussolini by offering him most of Ethiopia in return for a truce that would preserve the defensive alliance against Germany. Hoare's plan not only was aborted, but also created a scandal that caused Hoare to resign his cabinet post. Mussolini waged his war against Ethiopia, bombing and even gassing the all but defenseless nation into submission. However, the concept of *appeasement* had been introduced into European politics.

Having seen how Britain and France reacted to the aggression of Italy against Ethiopia, Hitler was emboldened to take the first step in his program of expansion. The Treaty of Versailles had ordered the evacuation of all German forces from the Rhineland. On March 7, 1936, Hitler ordered 22,000 soldiers back across the bridges of the Rhine. It was a token force—a testing of the waters—and Hitler was prepared to retreat if the French intervened.

Neither France, nor Britain, nor Italy resisted or even protested this violation of the Treaty of Versailles. An editorial in the *Times* of London spoke for the Allied position: "It's none of our business, is it? It's their [Germany's] own back-garden they're walking into."

The weakness of France and Britain persuaded Mussolini to conclude a pact with Hitler. On July 11, 1936, Italy agreed that Austria should be deemed "a German state," and on November 1, Italy and Germany concluded the Rome-Berlin Axis, which was followed on November 25 by the German-Japanese Anti-Comintern Pact—an alliance ostensibly against communism, but, in fact, an alliance of general military cooperation.

In May 1937, Neville Chamberlain replaced the retiring Stanley Baldwin as prime minister of Britain. The policy he proposed with regard to Germany was one of "active appeasement": Find out what Hitler wanted and then give it to him, in order to conserve military resources to fight what Chamberlain saw as the more serious threats from Italy and Japan.

What Hitler wanted he had expressed unambiguously shortly after gaining the chancellorship: "Today, Germany; tomorrow, the world." Chamberlain believed and hoped "Herr Hitler" (as he called him) would settle for considerably less.

Talk of the Times

Appeasement was a term used by British prime minister Neville Chamberlain to describe British policy toward German expansionism in the late 1930s. By "appeasing" Hitler—making certain territorial concessions to Germany—Chamberlain hoped to secure "peace in our time." The policy helped create World War II.

Talk of the Times

The **Anschluss** was the "union" of Germany and Austria in March 1938. It was, in fact, the German annexation of Austria, which was unopposed by any European power.

On March 13, 1938, Hitler invaded Austria. Unopposed by Austria or by Italy, he declared Austria a province of the German Reich. Called the *Anschluss*, the annexation of Austria put Germany in position to make its next move—into Czechoslovakia.

British prime minister Chamberlain, while intent on appeasing Hitler, began by warning him to negotiate with the Czechs. When Hitler stood firm, Chamberlain caved. He traveled to Berchtesgaden, Hitler's Bavarian chalet, and baldly proposed to give Hitler all that he demanded. Stunned and delighted by his good fortune, Hitler demanded cession of the Sudetenland, the German-speaking region of Czechoslovakia. Chamberlain agreed, asking Hitler to hold off the invasion until he could persuade Paris and Prague to go along with the plan.

The French appealed to Roosevelt but failed to shake the U.S. out of its renewed attitude of isolationism. The French agreed to hand the Sudetenland to Hitler.

Voice of the Century

"My good friends, this is the second time in our history that there has come back from Germany to Downing Street peace with honor. I believe it is peace in our time. I thank you from the bottom of our hearts. And now I recommend you go home and sleep quietly in your beds."

—Neville Chamberlain, speech at 10 Downing Street after returning from the Munich Conference, September 30, 1939

A Piece of Paper from Munich

At first, the Czechs proposed to fight. "How horrible, fantastic, incredible it is that we should be digging trenches and trying on gas masks here because of a quarrel in a far-away country between people of whom we know nothing," a disconsolate Chamberlain observed. What he failed to grasp is that Czechoslovakia was the strategic keystone of Europe. Its geographical location was critical, and it already contained a major arms works as well as 30 army divisions.

Chamberlain organized the Munich Conference on September 29–30, which summarily sold out the Czechs to Germany, in return for Hitler's pledge that he make no more territorial demands in Europe. Chamberlain flew back to London, stepping off the plane, waving a scrap of paper, and declaring that he had returned with "peace in our time."

All of Europe cheered—save for the Czechs, who wept in the streets, and for Winston Churchill (who held no office at the time), who declared that Britain had just suffered its worst military defeat—without a shot having been fired.

British prime minister Neville Chamberlain walks to the conference with Adolf Hitler at Munich.
(Image from arttoday.com)

Hitler Makes Another Pact

Chamberlain and the world soon reaped the folly of "appeasing" Hitler. The ink was scarcely dry on the Munich pact before Hitler maneuvered to take all of Czechoslovakia, not just the Sudetenland. On March 16, 1939, German army units occupied Prague, and the Czech nation ceased to exist.

As leader of world communism, Josef Stalin was by definition the arch foe of Adolf Hitler, who had already eclipsed Mussolini as leader of world fascism. Nevertheless, as Nazi Germany came to dominate more and more of Europe, Stalin proposed to Hitler a "Non-Aggression Pact." Signed on August 23, 1939, the pact gave Hitler Stalin's permission to invade Poland (the Soviets would even help!), and Hitler agreed not to interfere with Stalin's plan to invade Finland.

The Non-Aggression Pact stunned the communist world, especially those in the United States who saw the Soviet Union as the world's hope against fascism.

Betrayal

Stalin's betrayal of world communism was nothing compared to Hitler's betrayal of the Non-Aggression Pact. As planned, Stalin aided Hitler's invasion of Poland on September 1, 1939, by attacking from the east as Hitler invaded from the west. Also as planned, Stalin invaded Finland, annexing that nation on March 12, 1940, after a short but costly war.

What Stalin had failed to plan for was the magnitude of Adolf Hitler's treachery. On June 22, 1941, without warning, the German armies invaded the Soviet Union. Stalin's political purges of 1936–1938 had stripped the Red Army of most of its senior officer corps, and Stalin himself was thunderstuck into inaction. As a result, the German forces simply rolled over the Red Army in the opening weeks of the invasion. This—and what happened in Poland months before—was blitzkrieg: war conducted with the speed and force of lightning, leaving the enemy no time to react, no time to regroup, and barely time to die.

The invasion, which exploited the consequences of Stalin at his worst, would also reveal Stalin at his best. Within a short time, the dictator was able to shake off his panicked stupor and taking personal command of the Red Army, he mounted an increasingly effective defense. Grasping the strategic situation the invasion presented, he moved immediately to evacuate vital war industries east, into Siberia and Central Asia, just ahead of the advancing German armies. He then rallied the Soviet people, not in the name of Communism, but for the sake of Mother Russia. He even officially rehabilitated the Russian Orthodox Church.

The Stain Spreads

Although the war began for the Soviets on June 22, 1941, it had, for the rest of Europe, started many months before, at 4:30 on the morning of September 1, 1939, when, without a declaration of any kind, Hitler's *Luftwaffe* (air force) bombed airfields all across Poland. Simultaneously with this operation, a German battleship "visiting" the Polish port of Danzig opened fire on Polish fortifications, and the *Wehrmacht* (army) surged across the Polish frontier.

The German army, superbly trained and equipped with the latest weaponry, made quick work of the valiant but hopelessly outgunned Polish forces, which met machine-gun fire and *Panzer* (Panther) tanks with horse cavalry and lances.

Voice of the Century

"In spite of the hardness and ruthlessness I thought I saw in [Hitler's] face, I got the impression that here was a man who could be relied upon when he had given his word."

—Neville Chamberlain, after the Munich Conference, 1938

Hitler's Polish campaign was over in little more than a month. On September 27, Warsaw fell, and, the next day, the town of Modlin surrendered. In a single action, 164,000 Polish soldiers became prisoners of war. By early October, the last organized Polish force, at Kock, had been crushed.

Against a background of newsreel images showing gull-winged Stuka dive bombers swooping in for the kill, great lumbering tanks rolling over entrenchments, and the inexorable advance of German troops, Hitler, on September 27, 1939, announced his intention to launch an attack in the West at the earliest possible moment. With a sense of hopeless *déjà vu*, Britain and France, bound by treaties with Poland, declared war on Germany.

The Phony War and the Fall of France

Following the invasion of Poland, no major fighting broke out in the West. France and Britain had declared war on Germany but did little about it. In its first months, for them, the war become nothing more than a "Sitzkrieg," or "Phony War."

The French and British did ponder taking the offensive in Finland but delayed, and the Soviets—at the time still allied with the Germans—successfully invaded. This toppled the government of French premier Edouard Daladier, which was replaced by one under Paul Reynaud, who cooperated with Chamberlain in an attempt to mine and occupy Norwegian ports in order to close them to German U-boats. The German navy and Luftwaffe quickly occupied Denmark and then, with the help of Norwegian turncoat Vidkun Quisling, took over Norway as well. The British evacuated Norway on June 6, 1940, and, at the urging of Parliament, Neville Chamberlain was compelled to appoint his harshest critic, Winston Churchill, to head the War Cabinet.

On May 10, 1940, the Germans swept through Holland, the Luftwaffe bombing Rotterdam into oblivion. They marched through, simply going around the much-vaunted Maginot Line, which only extended as far north as the southern tip of Belgium, and within 10 days had reached Abbeville, on the French coast, just below the Strait of Dover. In the process, the Germans had cut the Allied armies in two.

Belgium, in a hopeless position, surrendered on May 28, while the British Expeditionary Force, which had been dispatched to the continent, now in imminent danger of annihilation or capture, made for the coastal town of Dunkirk to await evacuation by sea.

French premier Reynaud wanted to continue the war, but he was outvoted and so resigned rather than accept an armistice. His vice premiere, Marshal Henri Phillipe Pétain, hero of Verdun in World War I, asked for an armistice. Pétain's World War I subordinate, General Charles de Gaulle, in exile in London, broadcast to the French people a plea to fight on.

Vidkun Quisling was the Norwegian fascist who cooperated with Hitler in his invasion and occupation of Norway. Quisling was tried and executed for treason in 1945, but his name lives on as a word to describe a traitor who serves as a puppet for an occupying power.
(Image from arttoday.com)

20th-Century Life

The German blitzkrieg through France cut communication between the Allied armies, trapping the British Expeditionary Force in the north of France. German General Heinz Guderian was closing in for the kill on May 24, 1940, when Hitler ordered him to pull back. The German blunder gave the BEF its chance to evacuate the continent via the port of Dunkirk. The British Admiralty had scurried to collect a motley assortment of small craft—civilian and military—to carry the troops back to England before the Germans entered Dunkirk.

The evacuation began on May 26. The next day, the Belgians surrendered, and the Luftwaffe began an intensive bombing of the harbor of Dunkirk. Thousands of soldiers thronged the beach, clambering into light craft—fishing and pleasure yachts, mostly manned by amateur civilian sailors—to be ferried to larger vessels waiting to carry them to Britain. In this manner, by June 4, 198,000 British and 140,000 French and Belgian troops had been rescued. Although all of the Allied heavy equipment had to be abandoned (six destroyers were sunk, and another 19 were badly damaged), the escape of the British army was miraculous and certainly saved Britain from immediate invasion.

It was to no avail. On June 22, 1940, the French signed an armistice at Compiègne, in the very railway car in which the Germans had signed the 1918 armistice ending World War I. The Germans occupied all of northern France and the west coast—about two thirds of the country—and the rest was administered by Pètain as essentially a German puppet.

General Charles de Gaulle (left) emerged as the leader-in-exile of the Free French Forces in World War II. Henri Giraud, another Free French leader, is pictured to the right.
(Image from the National Archives)

Marshal Phillipe Henri Pétain, (left) hero of Verdun in World War I, concluded an ignominious armistice with Hitler (right), which relinquished two thirds of France to German occupation.
(Image from author's collection)

Arsenal of Democracy

The actions of Adolf Hitler were so outrageous that, with the invasion of Poland and the threat to Britain, isolationism rapidly dissolved in the United States. Whereas Woodrow Wilson had preached to his fellow Americans neutrality in "thought as well as deed" prior to 1917, FDR successfully sought to lead public opinion in favor of the Allies.

On November 4, 1939, FDR secured repeal of the arms embargo on belligerent nations. However, Britain and France were to be permitted to purchase war materiel from the United States on a "cash and carry" basis only. Winston Churchill, who had replaced Chamberlain as Britain's prime minister on May 13, 1940, boldly interpreted Roosevelt's sentiments, declaring to the House of Commons that Britain would fight on "until, in God's good time, the New World, with all its power and might, steps forth to the rescue and liberation of the Old."

Voice of the Century

"I have nothing to offer but blood, toil, tears, and sweat."

—Winston Churchill's first speech to Parliament after becoming prime minister, May 13, 1940. Popularly misquoted as "blood, sweat, and tears."

Lend-Lease Politics

With the fall of France, America's participation in the war became more direct. Defense appropriations shot up, and Americans now favored a policy of all aid to Britain—short of war.

In the summer of 1940, Churchill advised Roosevelt that his country was running out of cash. The president responded on December 8, 1940, with the concept of lend-lease, which was passed into law in March 1941. Now, FDR had the authority to aid any nation whose defense he believed vital to the United States and to accept repayment for such aid "in kind or property, or any other direct or indirect benefit which the President deems satisfactory."

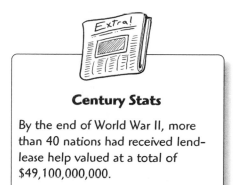

Century Stats

By the end of World War II, more than 40 nations had received lend-lease help valued at a total of $49,100,000,000.

Soon, lend-lease was extended beyond aid to Great Britain. In April 1941, China was included, and, in September, the Soviet Union.

Greetings from the President

The American public was unaware that FDR was doing much more than lending money and material to the British. He had secretly ordered the U.S. Navy to cooperate with the British in curbing the German U-boat menace, and, in a secret conference with Churchill, he developed the Atlantic Charter: a statement of shared war aims.

Voice of the Century

"If Great Britain goes down, all of us in the Americas would be living at the point of a gun.... We must be the great arsenal of democracy."

—Franklin D. Roosevelt, speech in support of the Lend-Lease Act

The charter was made public on August 14, 1941; privately, FDR assured Churchill that he would "wage war but not declare it." In August and September, U.S. merchant ships were armed for self-defense.

For most Americans, lend-lease did not represent the most dramatic step toward U.S. involvement in the war. That had come in September 1940, when Congress passed the first peacetime draft in U.S. history. Some 17 million young men began receiving telegrams that began "Greetings from the President of the United States."

Lives, it is true, were disrupted. But the war production and the draft accomplished in a matter of months what the New Deal had never fully achieved after almost a decade. Prosperity returned.

Day of Infamy

Although the Depression was at an end, there would be little time for rejoicing. The attack on a territory of the United States, when it came, at 7:55 a.m., December 7, 1941, should have surprised no one. While the eyes of most Americans were turned toward Europe, tension between the United States and Japan was running high. In Washington, negotiations with Japanese diplomats were so close to breaking down that, on November 24, Admiral Harold Stark sent a telegram to Admiral Husband E. Kimmel, commander of naval forces at Pearl Harbor, Hawaii, headquarters of the U.S. Pacific Fleet: "Chances of favorable outcome of negotiations with Japan very doubtful...a surprise aggressive movement in any direction" is anticipated.

The next day, Stark was even more blunt, telling Kimmel that FDR and Secretary of State Cordell Hull expected Japan to launch a surprise attack. On November 26, just before he issued war-alert messages to the military, Secretary of War Henry Stimson spoke openly about the strategic *desirability* of maneuvering the Japanese into war. U.S. intelligence had broken the diplomatic ciphers Japan used to encode messages sent to its ambassadors. Increasingly, these indicated that an attack was imminent.

Century Stats

Considering the devastation created at Pearl Harbor, Japanese losses were slight: 29 to 60 planes shot down, 5 midget submarines, possibly 1 or 2 fleet submarines lost. Total deaths were fewer than 100 Japanese sailors and airmen.

But the attack on Pearl Harbor, that Sunday morning, caught Navy and Army personnel sleeping—literally. Through a combination of bureaucratic inertia, poor communication between Army and Navy commanders on Hawaii, and just plain blundering, the ships of the Pacific fleet (all but the aircraft carriers, which, fortunately, were out to sea) and an array of B-17 bombers and fighter aircraft were left exposed to attack.

The battleship Arizona, *attacked by Japanese torpedo bombers, sinks at Pearl Harbor, December 7, 1941.*
(Image from the National Archives)

The ships were securely moored, many docked side by side. The aircraft had been grouped together, wingtip to wingtip, to make it easier to guard them against sabotage from the ground. From the air, the ships and planes made obligingly easy targets.

The attack was an unqualified success. Some 200 Japanese aircraft bombed and sank the battleships *Arizona, Oklahoma, California, Nevada,* and *West Virginia* and severely damaged three other battleships, three cruisers, three destroyers, and other vessels. On the ground, 180 U.S. aircraft were destroyed. Casualties totaled more than 3,400 men, including more than 2,403 killed.

Admiral Isoroku Yamamoto, who had masterminded the Pearl Harbor attack, was one of few Japanese military men who saw no reason to celebrate the great victory. Although he had carried out his orders—brilliantly—he had, in fact, strongly advised against the attack, arguing that far from dealing a death blow to American power in the Pacific, it would serve only to bring America into the war with a vengeance. Yamamoto had studied in the United States at Harvard University during 1919–1921 and had been naval attaché in Washington from 1925 to 1928. He warned that Japan was waking a sleeping tiger, whose industrial and military resources would make Japan's defeat inevitable.

Voice of the Century

"Yesterday, December 7, 1941—a day which will live in infamy—the United States of America was suddenly and deliberately attacked by naval and air forces of the Empire of Japan."

—Franklin D. Roosevelt, speech to Congress requesting a declaration of war, December 8, 1941

Admiral Isoroku Yamamoto, who planned the Pearl Harbor attack, counseled against going to war with America. (Image from the National Archives)

On December 8, 1941, President Roosevelt spoke to a joint session of Congress to ask for a declaration of war. Thus, America entered its second world war and would fight not just across the Atlantic, but on, over, under, and across the Pacific as well.

The Least You Need to Know

➤ The unwillingness of the Allied nations of Europe to resist Hitler's violations of the Treaty of Versailles made World War II inevitable.

➤ Germany's early victories in World War II were the result of *blitzkrieg,* a strategy of "lightning war," by which the enemy was attacked so quickly and violently that effective response was virtually impossible.

➤ America's growing involvement in the war in Europe had one major dividend; it created employment, bringing the Great Depression to an end.

➤ The United States became involved in World War II first by supplying material aid to the Allies (especially Great Britain) and then, directly, in response to the devastating Japanese attack on Pearl Harbor, December 7, 1941.

Total War (1941–1945)

From June 1940 to April 1941, the German Luftwaffe rained bombs on England in preparation for an invasion Germany and most of the world believed was inevitable. At first, the air raids were directed against military targets—mainly British ports and Royal Air Force facilities—but in September Hitler ordered the bombing of London and other cities. London was attacked on 57 consecutive nights, beginning September 7, 1940, and the raids continued sporadically through the spring of 1941.

All that stood between Britain and invasion was the Royal Air Force, which, although greatly outnumbered, blocked the Luftwaffe in what came to be called the Battle of Britain. Prime Minister Churchill praised the RAF in a speech to the House of Commons on August 20th: "Never in the field of human conflict was so much owed by so many to so few."

Yet despite his vow that "we shall fight on the beaches, we shall fight on the landing grounds, we shall fight in the fields and in the streets, we shall fight in the hills, we shall never surrender," Churchill knew that England, standing alone in 1941, could not, alone, resist Hitler forever. Once the United States was in the war, after Japan's raid on Pearl Harbor, Churchill tried to persuade the Americans to sacrifice the Pacific front—temporarily—and concentrate on fighting shoulder to shoulder with Britain. Officially, the United States did assign top priority to rescuing Europe from Nazi Germany, but the American public was more interested in exacting revenge against Japan, and, indeed, the most dramatic first American counterstrikes took place in the Pacific theater.

The Relentless Empire

Before Pearl Harbor, few Americans gave much thought to Japan as a world power. As we saw in Chapter 7, "Rising and Sinking," Japan stunned the West by defeating Russian forces in the Russo-Japanese War of 1905, and, in the years following this victory, it had extended its influence in China by converting Manchuria (northeast China) into a Japanese puppet state called Manchoukuo. Yet, to most Americans, the Japanese were the doll-like people composer Giacomo Puccini depicted in his 1901 operatic masterpiece *Madama Butterfly*.

20th-Century Life

Between December 1937 and January 1938, Japanese invaders massacred Chinese citizens and prisoners of war in what has come to be called the Rape of Nanking. Estimates of the number of Chinese killed in the massacre varies between 100,000 to more than 300,000. Executions, ordered by Matsui Iwane, commanding general of the (Japanese) Central China Front Army, were done in masses. In addition, tens of thousands of women were raped by Japanese soldiers. What was left of Nanking became capital of a puppet government.

Matsui and Tani Hisao, another general who had personally participated in murder and rape, were found guilty of war crimes by the International Military Tribunal for the Far East and executed.

Then, in 1937, Chinese and Japanese troops exchanged fire at the Marco Polo Bridge north of Beijing. Soon, an undeclared war began, and the Japanese bombed the cities of northern China, hitting Shanghai the hardest. Except for the fascist nations, the world denounced Japan's aggression, and the United States at last took notice. In the months before Pearl Harbor, anticipating eventual war with Japan, the United States covertly authorized the creation of the American Volunteer Group, a unit of Chinese Air Force volunteer pilots recruited by Colonel Claire L. Chennault to fight the Japanese in Burma (present-day Myanmar) and China. To maintain America's neutrality, the pilots had to resign from the U.S. military and fly as civilians. After they painted saber-toothed tiger-shark jaws on the noses of their Curtiss P-40 fighter planes, the AVG was unofficially called the Flying Tigers, and, as such, earned legendary renown defending the strategically vital Burma Road and the Chinese capital of Chungking. (On July 4, 1942, the Flying Tigers were absorbed into the U.S. 10th Air Force.)

Desperate Stand at Corregidor

The triumphs of the Flying Tigers were among the precious few bright spots for the Allies in the early months of the Pacific war. Each day after Pearl Harbor brought news of fresh disaster. Within two hours of the attack in Hawaii, Clark Field, principal U.S. air base in the Philippines, was bombed. Half the United States Far East air force was wiped out on the ground. Japanese troops then invaded the islands, landing on Luzon on December 10 and taking Manila on January 2, 1942. Those U.S. and Filipino troops who weren't captured or killed were driven into strongholds on the Bataan Peninsula and Corregidor Island.

In the meantime, Hong Kong was bombed on December 8 and fell to the Japanese on Christmas day. Another British outpost, Bangkok, was occupied on December 9, with southern Burma following on the 16th. Worst of all, after landing in Malaya during December, the Japanese overran Singapore, keystone of the British defenses in Asia. Ninety thousand troops were captured.

At the same time, the Japanese bombed U.S.-held Wake Island on December 8 and overran it by December 23. Early on February 10, Guam and Tarawa in the Gilbert Islands and Rabaul and Gasmata on New Britain were occupied.

In the Philippines, the remainder of U.S. and Filipino forces hunkered down on Corregidor, a rocky island—a kind of natural fortress—at the entrance of Manila Bay, just south of Bataan province. After Bataan fell to the Japanese on April 9, 1942, Corregidor stood as the last Allied outpost in the islands. For 27 days, Lieut. Gen. Jonathan Wainwright held fast against the invaders, finally surrendering on May 6, 1942.

March to Bataan

A number of international conferences, beginning in the 19th century, but gaining in importance and scope during the years following World War I, focused on creating rules intended to make war more humane. The Japanese flouted these agreements, subjecting civilians as well as prisoners of war to great brutality.

Century Stats

Of the original 70,000 prisoners who began the march to Bataan, only 54,000 reached the camp. Seven to 10,000 died along the march, of starvation, exhaustion, and merciless beatings. Those who fell by the wayside were quickly dispatched with a bayonet thrust. Perhaps as many as 4,000 prisoners fled into the jungle.

Americans quickly learned what kind of enemy they were dealing with when, following the Japanese capture of Bataan, 70,000 American and Filipino POWs were force-marched from Mariveles, on the southern end of the Bataan Peninsula, on April 9, 1942, 55 miles to San Fernando, then loaded onto trains to Capas, from which they marched eight miles to the captured Camp O'Donnell.

The "Bataan Death March" became an infamous episode of World War II—the first of many. After the war, Lieutenant General Homma Masaharu, in command of the Japanese invasion force, was tried for war crimes and executed.

"I Shall Return"

General Douglas MacArthur (1880–1964), one of the U.S. Army's most distinguished commanders, was field marshal of the Philippine military planning defenses. He directed the valiant defense of the islands against hopeless odds and in the absence of reinforcements. At last, on February 23, 1942, President Roosevelt personally ordered MacArthur to evacuate the Philippines and report to Australia. On March 12, he, his wife, son, and a small staff boarded PT boats for Mindanao. There, the party embarked on B-17 bombers and flew to Australia.

On March 17, the general issued a brief statement to the press, "I have come through" and concluded with a three-word promise: "I shall return."

MacArthur's character and reputation were so strong that these words were believed and served to buoy Allied spirits during the darkest hours of the Pacific war.

30 Seconds Over Tokyo

The United States was in full mobilization. Men were being drafted into the army with headlong speed. Soon, 16 million young Americans were in uniform. Factories, too, were gearing up for war production. And, as in World War I, every man, woman, and child was exhorted to "do their bit." People in war-related industries worked harder and longer than they ever had before. Children and their parents planted and tended backyard "victory gardens" in order to conserve food. People learned to accept rationing of food, clothing, gasoline—almost every consumer item.

Perhaps the enemy said it best. Admiral Yamamoto, mastermind of the Pearl Harbor attack, remarked to those who congratulated him, "I fear we have only awakened a sleeping giant, and his reaction will be terrible."

But preparing that reaction would take time. Men had to be trained. War materiel had to be produced. What could be done *now*—other than endure one humiliating defeat after another?

Counterstrike

Lieutenant Colonel James Doolittle, United States Army Air Force, proposed something very close to a suicide mission. Desperate for results, the U.S. high command bought in. On April 18, 1942, Doolittle led 16 B-25 twin-engine bombers off the deck of the aircraft carrier *Hornet.* That he was able to launch these planes in such an unorthodox manner—aircraft carriers were never intended to accommodate army air force bombers!—was a feat in itself. What he did next was nothing less than spectacular.

He led the planes on a low-altitude bombing raid against Japan's capital city, Tokyo, as well as Yokohama and some lesser targets. While the physical damage caused by these medium bombers carrying relatively modest payloads was minimal, the effect on Japanese morale was devastating. In America, the effect on morale was downright delirious.

Doolittle and his aircrews had taken off with the knowledge that it would be a one-way ride. Not only was it impossible for a B-25 to carry sufficient fuel for a round trip, it was also impossible to land one of the planes on a flattop. Instead, the plan was to land in China, evade the Japanese occupying the country, and—somehow—get back to U.S. military control.

If the raid itself was incredible, the fact that most of the aircrews did indeed find their way back was miraculous. After the raid, Doolittle was promoted to brigadier general and given the Medal of Honor.

Voice of the Century

I Could Never Be So Lucky Again
—Title of Jimmy Doolittle's 1991 autobiography

Miracle at Midway

Nor were the miracles at an end. Seeking to strike a decisive blow against the numerically inferior U.S. fleet, Admiral Yamamoto sent out most of the Japanese fleet, including four heavy and three light aircraft carriers, to defeat the Americans and invade Midway Island, location of a key naval base. Having broken the Japanese naval code and intercepted Yamamoto's order, U.S. Admiral Chester A. Nimitz was ready. He strategically positioned three heavy aircraft carriers, which would coordinate flights with those of land-based planes from Midway. Yamamoto was anticipating a naval battle. Nimitz would fight from the air.

Initial results after the battle began on June 3, 1942, were disappointing, but the next day U.S. planes sank three heavy Japanese carriers and one heavy cruiser. Late that afternoon, they disabled a fourth heavy carrier, which was subsequently scuttled. On June 6, a Japanese submarine sank the U.S. carrier *Yorktown,* as well as its escorting destroyer, but the Japanese navy lost a heavy cruiser that day. Crushed by their grave losses, the Japanese attempted no invasion of Midway and withdrew.

The hard-fought Battle of Midway was not only the first major defeat Japan suffered, it marked the turning point of the war in the Pacific. It brought the relative strengths of the American and Japanese navies to parity, and it was a first step in America's fight to regain control of the Pacific.

*Admiral Chester A.
Nimitz.*
(Image from
arttoday.com)

"Relocation"

The Doolittle Raid and the naval triumph at Midway hardly meant that victory was at hand, but it gave Americans ample reason to believe that their nation would ultimately prevail. Indeed, while wartime anxieties were always high, many who lived through World War II remember the period fondly as years of common purpose and intense emotion—all played out to the hot and mellow swing of Benny Goodman, Harry James, and Glenn Miller.

But American solidarity during the war years was not universal. Whereas during World War I, German-Americans were subjected to harassment and discrimination, now popular wrath was turned against Americans of Japanese descent.

As of December 7, 1941, some 127,000 Japanese were living in the United States, of whom about 80,000 were "Nisei"—born in the United States—and therefore United States citizens. On February 19, 1942, President Roosevelt signed Executive Order 9066, directing that all Japanese Americans—whether resident aliens or citizens—living within 200 miles of the Pacific coast be "relocated" from their homes to special "relocation camps."

To be sure, the West Coast farmers and politicians who clamored for "relocation" had concerns about sabotage and espionage—but they were also interested in conveniently ridding themselves of competition from the highly successful Japanese farmers.

Whatever the motives, about 110,000 Japanese-Americans were forced to leave their homes and take up residence in camps located in California, Idaho, Utah, Arizona, Wyoming, Colorado, and Arkansas. About 1,200 young men left the camps to join the

U.S. Army, many serving with great distinction in the European theater. Most of the 110,000, however, remained in the camps until President Roosevelt ended the program of relocation on January 2, 1945.

By the standards of the time—which included the Holocaust and other acts of genocide and barbarism by the Germans and the Japanese—the relocation was a mild "war crime"; yet those relocated lost money, property, dignity, and their rights. The Supreme Court twice upheld the constitutionality of the government's actions, but in 1968, long after the passions of war had cooled, reimbursement was made to many victims, and in 1988 Congress appropriated funds to pay $20,000 to each of the 60,000 surviving internees.

Thrust into the Soft Underbelly

An ocean away, Adolf Hitler had transformed the continent of Europe into "Fortress Europa." While the tide was slowly being turned in the Pacific, Roosevelt sent Army Chief of Staff George C. Marshall to London to argue for invading across the English Channel by April 1943. But as far as Churchill was concerned, the hair's-breadth escape from Dunkirk (Chapter 15, "'Peace in Our Time'") proved the folly of such a direct and "premature" invasion. Instead, the prime minister proposed to enter Fortress Europa through the side door—or, as Churchill put it, the Allies would thrust into the "soft underbelly of Europe," via Italy. Over the objections of American generals, who felt this would prolong the war, and the protests of Stalin (since the Soviets, betrayed by Hitler, were now among the Allies), who felt that this strategy would delay aid to his battered nation, Churchill prevailed.

In Pursuit of the Desert Fox

In September 1940, an Italian army had invaded Egypt, but was driven back by the British, who advanced into Libya. In response, the Germans sent to North Africa one of their best commanders, Field Marshal Erwin Rommel (1891–1944), who created the Afrika Korps, a crack tank unit especially trained for desert warfare. In March 1941, Rommel—called the "Desert Fox"—forced the British out of Libya and back into Egypt. The British Eighth Army counterattacked in November, driving Rommel westward. In May 1942, however, Rommel once again took the offensive and scored victories that pushed the British some 250 miles into Egypt. The British then established a battle line from El Alamein on the coast to a forbidding badlands called the Qattara Depression. Rommel was unable to break through, and, on October 23, 1942, General Bernard L. Montgomery (1887–1976) proved himself a match for the Desert Fox by defeating Rommel at the Battle of El Alamein.

El Alamein did not eliminate the German threat in North Africa, but it did prevent Rommel from capturing Cairo and the Suez Canal and was a great boost to Allied morale. For at stake in North Africa was not only control of the strategically key Suez Canal, but possession of a staging area for the invasion of Italy.

Erwin Rommel, the Desert Fox.
(Image from the National Archives)

Field Marshal Bernard L. Montgomery, who finally defeated Rommel.
(Image from the National Archives)

Montgomery's triumph was followed, in the closing months of 1942, by Operation Torch, the combined U.S. and British invasion of North Africa. Torch introduced into combat the great American commanders: Dwight D. Eisenhower (1890–1969), who was appointed Supreme Allied Commander, charged with coordinating the entire Allied war effort in Africa and Europe; George S. Patton (1885–1945), a controversial and difficult personality, who would nevertheless prove to be perhaps the greatest field commander of the war; and Omar Bradley (1893–1981), modest and plain-spoken, who would emerge not only as a brilliant field commander, but as the "G.I. general," a commander the public and the ordinary soldier readily rallied behind.

General Omar Nelson Bradley, the "G.I. general." (Image from the National Archives)

On May 12, 1943, the Axis forces in North Africa surrendered after defeat by the British and American armies in Tunisia. The Desert Fox had been beaten. During January 1943, Roosevelt and Churchill met in Casablanca, Morocco, and, after much debate, decided to jump off from Africa to an invasion of Sicily and thence on to the Italian mainland.

By Air and Sea

While the ground war was fought in North Africa through the spring of 1943, combat in western Europe raged in the skies, and, in the Atlantic, U-boats preyed upon supply convoys.

Early in 1942 the British Royal Air Force began intensive *strategic bombing* of German and German-held French factories, rail depots, dockyards, bridges, dams, and German cities. Beginning in January 1943, the U.S. 8th Air Force, flying from

Talk of the Times

Strategic bombing is the practice of massive bombing of civilian and industrial targets in order to diminish the enemy's overall capacity for war. Contrast **tactical bombing**, which is the smaller-scale bombing of specific military targets directly involved in combat.

bases in Great Britain, joined in the campaign. The British bombed by night, while the Americans bombed by day—which made American operations both more accurate and far more risky. Pursued by Messerschmidt and Focke-Wulf fighters and barraged by antiaircraft *flak*, the average life expectancy of a B-17 "Flying Fortress" bomber crew was 15 missions. Trouble was that the prescribed tour of duty was 25 missions. "Skipper," one navigator remarked to his pilot, "mathematically there just ain't any way we're gonna live through this thing."

A B-24 Liberator bomber gets the finishing touches at the factory. Given the high cost of strategic bombing, many of these —and many of the more famous B-17s—were needed throughout the war.
(Image from the author's collection)

On the Atlantic, throughout 1942, German U-boats sank more than 6,266,000 tons of Allied shipping, but beginning in the spring of 1943, the Allies introduced the escorted convoy system. Now cargo and other vessels, grouped into large convoys, were guarded by "support groups" that included aircraft carriers and other warships, as well as long-range Liberator bombers. Losses from U-boat attacks steadily decreased.

Talk of the Times

Flak is an acronym for the German *Fliegeraabwherkanone,* "antiaircraft gun"; it describes ground-based antiaircraft fire.

Until late in 1944, when German U-boats were equipped with snorkels, which furnished the oxygen necessary to recharge the batteries that drove the electric engines used underwater, submarines were not so much underwater craft as they were submersible boats. That is, they spent much of their time on the surface and were, therefore, vulnerable to detection by one of the war's most important technological developments: radar. "Radio detecting and ranging"—*radar*—broadcasts radio signals, then receives and interprets the echoes of those signals as they reflect off distant objects—ships, aircraft, and so on.

The principles of radar may be traced to the work of a German engineer, Christian Hülsmeyer, in 1904, and to that of radio pioneer Guglielmo Marconi and of American physicists in the 1920s. However, it was during the 1930s that Great Britain, France, the United States, Germany, and Japan began serious research into the military applications of the technology. Britain took the lead, constructing before World War II a network of radar stations to provide early warning of the approach of enemy aircraft. British and American scientists cooperatively developed aircraft-intercept radar, equipment small enough to be installed in fighters, enabling them to find their targets—typically enemy bombers—much more effectively.

Century Stats

How dangerous were U.S. bombing missions? The raid against the key ball-bearing factory at Schweinfurt, Germany, on October 14, 1943, was all too typical: 60 out of the 291 bombers participating were lost, and 138 of those that returned were severely damaged.

20th-Century Life

The Allies' lead in radar development gave them a crucial edge in World War II and created a technology that would find many applications after the war. Military radar would achieve extreme levels of sophistication, enabling the guidance of long-range missiles and "smart" weapons, capable of hitting distant targets with pinpoint precision. Civilian applications of radar made high-volume commercial aviation possible, serving not only to manage air traffic, but to enable flight even under conditions of poor visibility. Similar systems installed on ships make navigation far safer, even in bad weather.

Astronomers use radar to measure planetary distances and to map the surface features of planets, and meteorologists make extensive use of radar to predict the weather and to track dangerous storms. Many motorists are all too familiar with the portable radar units police officers use to "clock" speeders.

To Italy

On July 10, 1943, U.S. and British soldiers embarked from North Africa to a stealthy nighttime amphibious landing on the shores of southern Sicily. Surprise was total, and the Allies gained control of 150 miles of Sicilian coast within hours. Palermo, chief city of Sicily, quickly fell to the Allies, and, by August 17, 1943, all of Sicily was in British and American hands.

During the invasion, on July 24, Benito Mussolini was overthrown, arrested, and then imprisoned on a supposedly impregnable island fortress. On September 12, 1943, however, German commandos rescued the Italian dictator, who was flown to Munich, from which he agreed to govern a puppet Fascist government in northern Italy. In the meantime, however, Pietro Badoglio, who had replaced Mussolini as head of state in the south, concluded an armistice with the Allies. (As for Mussolini, he and his mistress, Claretta Petacci, were captured by Italian partisans in April 1945. They were executed by firing squad on April 28 and their bodies strung up by the heels in a public square at Milan.)

Despite the armistice, fighting on the Italian mainland was extraordinarily difficult, as Hitler, determined to hold Italy, continually reinforced strategic positions there. Not until May 1944 was major German resistance at Anzio and Monte Cassino overcome. Rome was liberated on June 4, 1944, and Florence two months later. But the Allies were once again stalled at the so-called "Gothic Line," extending across the Alps in northern Italy. It was April 1945 before the Allies crossed the Po River and Italian partisans captured Milan, Genoa, and Venice. On April 29, 1945, German forces in Italy finally surrendered.

A Soldier's Battle

In 1998, acclaimed director Steven Spielberg released *Saving Private Ryan*, a movie depicting an incident during the frontal assault on Fortress Europa, the cross-Channel invasion at Normandy popularly known as *D-Day*. The film was a commercial triumph and profoundly moving. While some historians have carped about various details in the movie, all agree that few popular depictions of war more effectively convey the visceral realities of combat. But perhaps most important of all, Spielberg succeeded in communicating the essence of the D-Day invasion as what military men call a "soldier's battle."

Talk of the Times

While **D-Day** has come to be identified exclusively with the Normandy invasion, it is general military jargon for the day on which an operation commences. **H-hour** is the specific hour of that day appointed for commencement of the operation.

What is a soldier's battle? It is one in which the outcome is determined more by the enlisted men and junior officers than by the leadership of principal commanders. The Union victories at Gettysburg and at Lookout Mountain (outside Chattanooga) were celebrated soldier's battles of the Civil War. The D-Day landing, although planned at the very highest levels, was the great soldier's battle of World War II. For all the planning and preparation, the actions of individual soldiers and junior officers commanding small combat units made the war's greatest operation a success.

The D-Day Armada

Born in Texas and raised in Abilene, Kansas, Dwight David Eisenhower (1890–1969)—universally called "Ike"—graduated below the middle of the West Point Class of 1915.

Put in charge of a tank training unit during World War I, he didn't enter a combat zone until World War II. But Eisenhower clearly excelled as an administrator and strategist. He also had a way of getting along with everybody and coaxing cooperation even out of the notoriously uncooperative.

Ike Eisenhower caught the attention of General George C. Marshall, U.S. Army chief of staff. At the outbreak of World War II, Eisenhower was a brigadier general. Marshall put him in charge of preparing plans for the Allied invasion of Europe, then, promoting him over the heads of 366 senior officers in March 1942, Marshall appointed him commander of all U.S. troops in Europe. Later, Eisenhower was named supreme commander of all the Allied forces and, in this capacity, took charge of coordinating a plan code named Operation Overlord.

General Dwight D. Eisenhower (right), Supreme Allied Commander. (Image from the National Archives)

Overlord called for an invasion of the coast of France originating from England via the English Channel. The most logical place to invade was at the Pas de Calais, at the narrowest point of the Channel. For this very reason, Eisenhower and the other planners decided to attack at Normandy instead. Furthermore, they employed an elaborate scheme of transmitting "disinformation" through double agents and compromised spies bolstered by decoy forces (plywood planes and inflatable tanks) deployed at supposed staging areas along the British coast to deceive the Germans into thinking that Calais was indeed the target. The boldest step of all was to keep George S. Patton, the most visible—and perhaps most able—Allied general out of the fighting, in England, as commander of the phantom army waiting to invade at Calais.

In this way, preparations for the real invasion, involving a million troops, together with unprecedented numbers of ships, landing and assault craft, tanks, artillery, and planes, were kept under wraps, and the Germans were tricked into spreading out their

243

defensive forces all along the coast. To ensure that these dispersed forces could not readily be concentrated, British-based bombers hit rail lines, bridges, and air fields throughout France for two months preceding the assault.

Hit the Beach

On June 5, the night before the Normandy landings, paratroopers were dropped inland to disrupt communications. Next, naval artillery began to pound the reinforced shore batteries.

At the last minute, the weather turned bad: If conditions were calm enough to land a few units of troops, then suddenly kicked up waves too high to land more, those caught on the beach would be slaughtered. But to wait for more favorable weather would sacrifice the element of surprise and thus certainly doom the mission.

Talk of the Times

Battle fatigue is an emotional breakdown caused by the unrelieved stress of combat. In World War I, it was called **shell shock**. Today, it is often called **post-traumatic stress syndrome**. An intolerant General Patton called it cowardice.

Voice of the Century

"I want you men to remember that no bastard ever won a war by dying for his country. He won it by making the other dumb bastard die for his country."

—George S. Patton, speech to the Third Army, 1943 (often repeated, with variations)

Eisenhower pondered. Then decided. "OK. Let's go," was all he said.

At low tide, in the early morning gloom of June 6, 1944, the greatest amphibious invasion in the history of the world began. Five thousand Allied ships approached the Normandy coastline, which the invaders—British, Canadian, and American—had divided into beaches code-named Gold, Juno, Sword, Utah, and Omaha. The landings on all but Omaha Beach went smoothly, and the troops encountered surprisingly light resistance.

But at Omaha Beach, key position for securing the landing, American soldiers were met by withering German fire. Some landing craft sunk, drowning the invaders before they even reached the shore. Those that made it to the beach were raked by machine gun, artillery, and mortar fire. Yet, largely through individual acts of heroism and leadership, even the sharply contested Omaha Beach was secured.

Over the next five days, 16 Allied divisions landed at Normandy, and, at long last, Fortress Europa had been breached.

Real Estate Bought Dear

Germany was now being squeezed from the west—the landings at Normandy—from the south—the campaign in Italy—and from the east—the Russian Front.

While the Italian campaign proceeded at an agonizingly slow and costly pace, the breakout from Normandy eastward, thanks in large part to the leadership of George S. Patton, was astoundingly swift.

Patton—popularly called Old Blood and Guts—was both a stickler for discipline (insisting, for example, that soldiers not directly engaged in combat wear full, proper, and immaculate uniforms, complete with the prescribed neckties and leggings) and a savage warrior. He fell into disrepute after publicly slapping two G.I.s, hospitalized for *battle fatigue,* calling them cowards and threatening one with execution before a firing squad.

George Smith Patton, Jr.— Old Blood and Guts, typically immaculate in uniform.
(Image from the Patton Museum of Cavalry and Armor, Fort Knox, Kentucky)

But, pleasant or not, Patton was a military genius. Given command of the newly formed Third Army in January 1944, he arrived in France on July 6. Over the next nine months and eight days, the Third Army liberated or gained 81,522 square miles in France, 1,010 in Luxembourg, 156 in Belgium, 29,940 square miles in Germany, 3,485 in Czechoslovakia, and 2,103 in Austria. An estimated 12,000 cites, towns, and villages were liberated or captured, 27 of which contained more than 50,000 people. The Third Army captured 1,280,688 prisoners of war from August 1, 1944 to May 13, 1945. The enemy lost 47,500 killed and 115,700 wounded—a total of 1,443,888 casualties—to the Third Army, which incurred 160,692 casualties, including 27,104 killed, 86,267 wounded, 18,957 injured, and 28,237 missing—of whom many were later reported captured.

Century Stats

The Battle of the Bulge was the costliest single battle in U.S. military history, resulting in more than 75,000 casualties and the loss of 730 tanks and tank destroyers. German losses, however, were 120,000 casualties, 600 tanks, 6,000 other vehicles, and some 1,600 aircraft.

The Third Army embodied the Allied war effort at its best, going farther and faster than had any other force in the history of warfare.

The Bulge

Pushed to desperation, Adolf Hitler ordered an all-out offensive against the Allied advance in the Ardennes Forest of Luxembourg and southern Belgium. On December 16, 1944, three entire German armies were hurled against four fairly inexperienced U.S. divisions, pushing them back and creating a bulge in the Allied lines.

Voice of the Century

"Nuts!"

—General Anthony McAuliffe, commanding the 101st Airborne Division, responding to a German demand for surrender during the Battle of the Bulge

Despite the string of Allied victories that had preceded it, the Battle of the Bulge looked hopeless. The entire 101st U.S. Airborne Division was cut off and threatened with imminent capture. The entire Allied push was stalled.

Patton then performed another military miracle. He wheeled his entire half-million-man weary army 90 degrees to the north and launched a devastatingly successful counterattack in record time, driving the enemy back to its starting line by January 28, 1945.

Victory in the Battle of the Bulge, while achieved at terrible cost, was the death knell for Nazi Germany. The war in Europe was winding down. But the *world* war was far from over—and of dying there would be much, much more.

The Least You Need to Know

➤ Jimmy Doolittle's bombing raid on Tokyo (April 18, 1942) was an important symbolic counterstrike against Japan, but the U.S. naval victory at the Battle of Midway (June 3–6, 1942) actually turned the tide of war against the Japanese.

➤ Early in the war, President Roosevelt ordered the "relocation," into special camps, of Japanese-Americans living within 200 miles of the Pacific Coast.

➤ At the insistence of Winston Churchill, the Allies attacked on the European front first by taking North Africa and then invading Sicily and Italy—the "soft underbelly" of Europe.

➤ The main invasion of Europe began at Normandy on "D-Day," June 6, 1944; from here, U.S. and British forces raced across France and into Germany, bringing the war home to the German heartland.

Chapter 17

"Now I Am Become Death" (1941–1945)

In This Chapter

➤ Stalin takes the offensive

➤ The defeat of Germany

➤ Soviet land grab

➤ The Holocaust

➤ Hitler's suicide

➤ The atomic bomb ends the war with Japan

It's very easy, more than half a century later, to look back at World War II and identify the Battle of Midway and the Normandy landings as "turning points" in the conflict. It sounds neat and simple, like a game of chess. But this was no game of chess. These battles were turning points, but much more war and much more killing followed them.

On the eastern front, the great turning point was the Battle of Stalingrad, and, surely, no turning point was more costly or more horrific. This chapter begins on the Russian front.

Russian Front

Adolf Hitler christened the German invasion of the Soviet Union Operation Barbarossa, in tribute to Frederick I—called Frederick Barbarossa, Red Beard—the 12th-century German emperor who challenged papal authority in order to unite a fractious medieval collection of dukedoms and principalities into a single German state that (Barbarossa hoped) would dominate all Europe. At first, it looked as if Hitler might well make good on Barbarossa's ancient, unfulfilled dream of domination.

Scorched Earth and Frozen Bodies

Using the tactics of blitzkrieg, Hitler planned to overrun Russia in four to six weeks. On June 22, 1941, the Germans invaded along a 2,000-mile-front.

Century Stats

The force Hitler assembled to invade the Soviet Union consisted of some 4 million men, the largest invasion force in history. It included 50 Finnish and Romanian divisions in addition to 207 German divisions armed with 3,300 tanks. The Soviet Red Army numbered about 4,500,000 men, and the Soviets had about 15,000 tanks.

Talk of the Times

A **scorched-earth policy** is the practice of destroying crops and other resources in order to keep them from falling to an invading enemy or done by invaders to destroy sustenance for locals.

They seemed unstoppable, sweeping relentlessly eastward against the retreating Russians. Leningrad was surrounded and besieged—besieged for two years by artillery and aerial pounding, starvation, and disease—but never taken. Kiev did fall; half a million of its defenders were killed or taken prisoner. With the loss of Kiev, the Ukranian breadbasket and industrial region was occupied and exploited by the invaders.

And then the Germans closed in on the Soviet capital, Moscow itself—but then the winter set in, and the German advance ground to a frozen halt. Like Napoleon before him, Hitler now learned that a would-be conqueror of Russia faced three great obstacles.

First, there was the valor and determination of the Russian people: soldiers who seemed to fear no sacrifice, and civilians who were willing to destroy all that they had—shelter, factories, crops—rather than let them fall into enemy hands. Stalin decreed a *scorched earth policy*; the invaders were to be left nothing. And to be left without food or supplies in the vastness of Russia was to be sentenced to death.

These vast distances—the second obstacle to invasion—made supply from outside almost impossible, while the scorched-earth policy made it impossible to live off the land.

Finally, if the Russian people and the Russian distances weren't enemy enough, there was the third obstacle: the Russian winter. It had doomed Napoleon's Russian campaign in 1812, and now it stalled the Germans.

Turning Point at Stalingrad

With the spring thaw of 1942, the Germans resumed the offensive, with the primary objective of conquering the Caucasus region, rich in oil. But they were stopped again, at a city formerly called Volgograd and recently renamed Stalingrad. No Soviet citizen wanted the city named in honor of the nation's leader to fall to the Germans.

Although the Germans bombed Stalingrad to dust, the Red Army fought house to house and rubble heap to rubble heap. While holding the Germans at Stalingrad, Stalin decided on a desperate gamble. He assembled virtually all that remained of the Red

Army and ordered it to advance on Stalingrad from the north and south. In a brilliant strategic stroke, the two Russian forces met *behind* the German lines, thereby trapping the enemy within the ruined city. The invaders now found themselves besieged. After many bloody attempts to break out, the Germans surrendered to the Red Army on February 2, 1943.

After Stalingrad, the Red Army took the offensive and never relinquished it, driving the Nazis, in full retreat, out of Russia. The retreat was costly to the Russian people as well as to the Wehrmacht, however; the Germans left a path of destruction and slaughter as they made their way to the borders. Still, by 1944, not only were the Nazi armies out of Russia, but Soviet troops were in control of the Baltic states, eastern Poland, the Ukraine, Rumania, Bulgaria, and Finland, a situation that foreshadowed the Cold War that would follow the world war (Chapter 18, "A War Served Cold").

Field Marshal Friedrich von Paulus commanded the German forces against Stalingrad. Made a POW after his surrender, he was not released until 1953— and then only permitted to live in Soviet-controlled East Germany.
(Image from the National Archives)

Germany had fielded 330,000 troops against Stalingrad. After that force had been reduced to fewer than a quarter million, the German high command asked Hitler for permission to withdraw. Hitler ordered that they "stand and fight." When General Friedrich Paulus at last surrendered, his army consisted of no more than 91,000 frozen, starving men. As for the victorious Soviets, their losses had been almost as great.

In the Jaws of the Vise

The collapse of the Russian front doomed the German cause. The Soviets, having taken the offensive, pushed from the east. The Americans and British advanced from the west and, slowly, from the south as well. Hitler, who had once spoken boldly of claiming for the German people their rightful *Lebensraum*—living space—found his world growing smaller and smaller with each passing day.

The Enemies Within

Before Stalingrad, Adolf Hitler had been accustomed to success. After defeat in Russia, he, like his armies, retreated, not from battle, however, but from reality itself. He holed up in his headquarters, refusing to tour his nation's bombed-out cities and taking his news only from his secretary, Martin Bormann, and a small circle of close associates— men who endeavored to give him nothing but good news when, in fact, all the news was bad.

By 1943, a growing cadre of soldiers and influential civilians began plotting the removal of Hitler. It was a short step from the idea of removal to the necessity of assassination.

The leaders of the assassination plot included Col. Gen. Ludwig Beck (formerly chief of the General Staff), and other highly placed officers, the most prominent of whom was none other than Field Marshal Erwin Rommel. Claus Philipp Schenk, Graf (Count) von Stauffenberg, personally carried out the attempt on Hitler's life. On July 20, shortly before a meeting Hitler was to attend at Wolf's Lair, his field headquarters at Rastenburg, East Prussia, Stauffenberg placed a briefcase containing a bomb in the conference room. He slipped out of the room, paused to witness the explosion at 12:42 P.M., and, confident that Hitler had been blown to bits, flew to Berlin, where he was to join the other conspirators in a takeover of the Supreme Command Headquarters.

But Hitler survived. An officer in the conference room nearly tripped over the briefcase, so he kicked it under the heavy oak support of the conference table. This shielded Hitler from the full force of the blast. Although a stenographer and three officers were killed, Hitler escaped with relatively minor injuries.

In the meantime, Stauffenberg's co-conspirators had failed to move against the Supreme Command Headquarters. They had decided to await confirmation of Hitler's death. This delay afforded time for the development of a countercoup, and General Friedrich Fromm, who had known about the plot and had tacitly approved it, now scrambled to prove his loyalty. He ordered the immediate arrest of Stauffenberg and other officers, all of whom were summarily shot. Rommel and another officer were given the alternative of "honorable" suicide. Over the succeeding days and weeks, almost 200 plotters were rounded up, tortured, tried, then shot or hanged—in some cases, using piano wire or meat hooks. As for General Fromm, his complicity was discovered in due course, and he, too, was executed.

On Hitler's orders, some of the executions were filmed and subsequently screened for the Fuhrer.

The Allies Meet

Hitler and the Germans were not the only people concerned about Stalin's rapid advance through eastern Europe. The United States and Great Britain saw Poland,

250

Hungary, Czechoslovakia, Yugoslavia, and the other nations of the region gain liberation from Hitler only to fall under the dominion of Stalin.

Winston Churchill traveled to Moscow on October 9, 1944, in an effort to reach an agreement with Stalin that would at least confine communism to eastern Europe, preserving central Europe for the Western powers. Perhaps a bit absurdly, Churchill proposed a series of formulas for postwar *"spheres of influence"*: Romania, for example, would be 90 percent Soviet, whereas Greece would be 90 percent British. Yugoslavia and Hungary would be divided 50-50. The Soviet presence in Bulgaria would be 75 percent, with 25 percent reserved for the British. And so on. The formulas had the air of being specific, yet were ultimately meaningless, and, in any case, unenforceable. (Just what *is* a 25 percent sphere of influence?)

Only somewhat more productive was the February 1945 conference among Churchill, Roosevelt, and Stalin at the Crimean resort town of Yalta. In the face of Soviet expansion, Churchill and Roosevelt came to the conference with two goals. The first was to preserve the alliance with Stalin. Roosevelt in particular was anxious to secure Soviet aid in prosecuting the war against Japan. The second, goal, however, was to contain the spread of communism.

Talk of the Times

A **sphere of influence** is a territorial area over which political or economic influence is wielded by a nation.

While the first goal was achieved—Stalin promised to declare war on Japan within 90 days of Germany's surrender—the second was more or less postponed. It was decided that a joint European Advisory Commission would divide Germany into U.S.-British, French, and Soviet occupation zones, and that Berlin, although within the Soviet zone, would itself be similarly divided. Another major issue, the government of Poland, was largely left unresolved; however, Stalin did agree to the idea of a permanent United Nations—a more powerful reincarnation of the old League of Nations.

Despite the nominal good feelings of Yalta, the final advances into Germany during the concluding weeks of the war amounted to a land grab. Although many Western military leaders advocated racing the Soviets to obtain as much German territory as possible, the Western civilian leadership was determined to show support for the Soviet alliance and the Soviet advance. In the name of this support, British and American armies were restrained from racing the Red Army to Berlin. When they happened to exceed the limits of occupation zones created at Yalta, Eisenhower called them back.

Also, in the name of support for the Russian advance, U.S. bombers perpetrated one of the saddest and most destructive raids of the war, intensively bombing Dresden, Germany, with incendiary bombs, killing perhaps 135,000 civilians and destroying the beautiful medieval city during February 13–14, 1945. The rationale for the bombing was the destruction of a communications center for Germans facing the Red Army. In reality, the raid served no military purpose.

The "Big Three"—Stalin, Roosevelt, and Churchill— at the Yalta Conference, February 1945.
(Image from the National Archives)

20th-Century Life

Born in 1874, the son of Lord Randolph Churchill and an American woman, Jennie Jerome, Churchill served heroically in the Sudan (1898) and wrote a best-selling account of his experience. After covering the Great Boer War as a journalist, Churchill entered politics, becoming a member of Parliament and then serving in various cabinet-level posts. As first lord of the Admiralty, Churchill backed the disastrous attack on Gallipoli during World War I. He was removed, but returned to government later in the war.

Churchill held no government post from 1929 to 1939, when he returned as first lord of the Admiralty and, a short time later, replaced Neville Chamberlain as prime minister. As a war leader, Churchill achieved true greatness, holding British defenses together single-handedly, it seemed. Defeated in a reelection bid in July 1945, Churchill refused to be bitter. He heard the news of his defeat while taking a bath. "They have a perfect right to kick us out. That is democracy. That is what we have been fighting for. Hand me my towel."

Churchill returned to office during 1953–1955, when he suffered a stroke. He spent the last decade of his life writing historical masterpieces, including *History of the English-speaking Peoples* and a six-volume history of World War II.

Holocaust

In the final weeks of the war, British, U.S., and Soviet soldiers, accustomed to seeing the hardships and horrors of the bombed-out, war ravaged villages and cities they marched through, began encountering a new horror—one beyond imagining.

Outside obscure towns in Germany, Poland, and elsewhere—places with names like Bergen-Belsen, Auschwitz, Buchenwald, Dachau, Sobibor, and Treblinka—Allied troops began liberating camps populated by the living dead: emaciated and diseased prisoners, most of them Jews. These, it turned out, were the lucky ones. For the troops soon discovered mass graves, crematoria, and piles of unburied corpses—in Bergen-Belsen, for example, some 13,000 corpses. A world that thought it had seen all that could be seen of human cruelty now began to learn about Hitler's "final solution to the Jewish problem."

A System for Genocide

The persecution of Jews was not a 20th-century innovation. Records of organized anti-Semitism go back some 1,800 years. But between 1933 and 1945, Adolf Hitler ordered and directed the murder of more Jews than had been killed in 18 centuries of persecution—almost six million, roughly two-thirds of Europe's Jewish population.

Beginning in 1933, the Nazis organized boycotts of Jewish businesses. They also established Jewish quotas for Germany's professions and schools, and, in 1935, they enacted the Nuremberg Laws, banning intermarriage between Jews and gentiles.

In 1933, Dachau was established near Munich. It was a *concentration camp*, intended for the incarceration of communists and other political "undesirables." Dachau became the prototype for many more concentration camps, which, beginning in 1938, began receiving Jewish "deportees"—Jews removed from their homes and sent to the camps as a form of internal exile.

After a Nazi official was assassinated, Hitler unleashed his stormtroopers on November 9–10, 1938, to burn synagogues (267 were destroyed) and to arrest Jews (20,000 were taken into custody). In addition, Jewish homes and businesses were destroyed, and so much smashed glass littered the streets that the night of destruction was dubbed *Kristallnacht*—crystal night, "the night of broken glass."

Two years later, after Poland had been overrun, the German invaders rounded up Warsaw's nearly

Talk of the Times

The term **concentration camp** was apparently first used during the period immediately preceding the Spanish-American War to describe camps in Cuba to which Spanish authorities consigned those active in the Cuban independence movement. The term resurfaced in World War II to describe the deportation and death camps of the Nazi regime.

half-million Jews and confined them to the ancient Jewish ghetto, which they cut off from the rest of the city. In crowded conditions, many died from starvation and disease. Another 300,000 were deported to the concentration camps.

On April 19, 1943, 2,000 German regulars and a force of Lithuanian militiamen and Polish policemen and firefighters attacked the Warsaw ghetto, expecting to slaughter the Jews remaining there. They were stunned when some 60,000 Jews—all who remained in the ghetto—met their attack with homemade weapons and a few rifles, pistols, and machine guns.

Before the Nazis, the Warsaw Ghetto was a vibrant place.
(Image from arttoday.com)

The valiant resistance was ultimately futile. On May 16, 1943, General Juergen Stroop reported: "The former Jewish quarter of Warsaw is no longer in existence."

The Final Solution

About 20,000 Jews were killed in the streets of the Warsaw ghetto. The rest were sent to the camps—which were no longer work camps or detention camps, but death camps. Pursuant to a conference chaired in January 1942 by Heinrich Himmler's aide Reinhard Heydrich, it was decided to apply what Hitler called the "final solution" to the Jewish problem: genocide—the "liquidation" of an entire people.

Auschwitz, in southern Poland, was the camp chosen as the center of annihilation. Here, one to three million human beings—the slaughter was so prodigious that no one knows exactly how many died in this place—were routinely stripped naked and herded into what they were told were delousing showers. In reality, they were chambers of mass execution, into which lethal "Zyklon B," hydrocyanic gas, was introduced.

The Nazis had arrived at this method of killing after trying many others, including carbon monoxide asphyxiation, electrocution, phenol injections, immolation by flame-thrower, death by hand grenade, gunshot, beating, torture, and "medical experimentation." None was more efficient than the use of poison gas.

And the Nazi executioners were nothing if not efficient. The clothing and valuables (including gold dental fillings extracted from teeth) of the condemned were systematically collected and sorted. The bodies were burned in massive crematoria constructed expressly for the purpose—although the pace of the killing usually outran the capacity of the ovens.

While Jews were the principal victims of Nazi genocide, large numbers of Poles, Russians, Gypsies, and homosexuals were also murdered. When the demand for death exceeded the capacity of Auschwitz, facilities at Oranienburg, Buchenwald, Dachau, Bergen-Belsen, and elsewhere became death camps as well.

In 17 concentration camps, most notably at Sobibor and Treblinka, inmates mounted resistance, but it was always hopeless. The Allies, who were certainly aware of the persecution and murder of Jews—though, doubtless, unaware of the vast extent of the program—did nothing to stop it. Perhaps there was nothing they could have done. The full horror of the "final solution" remained unknown outside of Germany and occupied eastern Europe until the liberation of the camps.

Voice of the Century

"It took from 3 to 15 minutes to kill the people in the death chamber, depending on climatic conditions. We knew when the people were dead because the screaming stopped."

—Rudolf Hoess, commandant of Auschwitz, Nuremburg trial affidavit, April 5, 1946

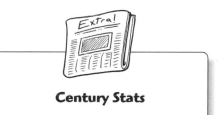

Century Stats

The German death system eventually built 300 concentration camps.

Buchenwald—at the time of its liberation in 1945. (Image from arttoday.com)

Retreat to the Bunker

As the Western armies held back, Soviet forces captured Vienna and Königsberg on April 9, 1945, then encircled Berlin on the 25th. During this period, Adolf Hitler, refusing to surrender, had pressed children and old men into the army in an effort to swell its dwindling ranks. Leaving his people to suffer air raids and street fighting, he retreated to a hardened command bunker beneath the streets of Berlin.

About midnight of April 28–29, he married his mistress, Eva Braun. He then appointed Admiral Karl Dönitz as head of state and Josef Goebbels as chancellor. On April 30, Hitler bade farewell to Goebbels and the few others who had remained with him in the bunker. He then retired to his suite. Eva Braun took poison, and Hitler either poisoned or shot himself—or did both. It is impossible to say exactly how Hitler died, because he had ordered that his body and that of Eva Braun be cremated. When the Soviets overran the bunker, they found the charred remains of two people, which they identified as Hitler and Braun—although, for many years, rumors that Hitler had escaped and was at large persisted. Like a vampire or a werewolf, the mythic Hitler was hard to kill.

Hitler named Admiral Karl Dönitz, the brilliant chief of the German navy, to succeed him as head of state. No sooner was Hitler dead than Dönitz sued for peace with the Western Allies.
(Image from the National Archives)

Dönitz immediately opened negotiations with the Western powers, hoping to save as many troops and refugees as possible from the reprisals he knew the Soviets would bring down upon them. The Soviets refused to recognize a surrender ceremony held at Eisenhower's headquarters on May 7, but accepted a separate surrender the next day, in Berlin.

Atomic Dawn

V-E Day—Victory-in-Europe Day—was celebrated in England, France, and the United States, but no one knew better than the Americans that the war was not yet over.

256

Militarily, the Japanese were defeated. Yet they refused to surrender. A tenacious enemy driven by an ancient warrior code, they regarded surrender as a dishonor to which death was far preferable. Ever since the naval victory at Midway, the American strategy for prosecuting the war in the Pacific had been one of *island hopping*, retaking each Japanese-held island one by one, steadily closing in on the Japanese mainland itself.

Each of these battles was grimly fought, almost literally to the last surviving Japanese soldier. The cost in lives, on both sides, was staggering.

Talk of the Times

Island hopping is the term U.S. military commanders used to describe the strategy for regaining the initiative in the Pacific and ultimately achieving victory. The idea was to retake one Japanese-held island after another, always closing in on the Japanese mainland.

Loss of a Leader

If the prospect of finishing the war in the Pacific dampened the joy of V-E day, worse news was to come. It broke over the nation's radios at 5:47 p.m., Eastern War Time, on April 12, 1945. Less than an hour earlier, Franklin Delano Roosevelt had died of a cerebral hemorrhage at the "Little White House" in Warm Springs, Georgia. The only president ever to serve more than two terms (FDR was elected to *four*), the president who had led the nation through the Depression and, now, to the verge of victory in the most catastrophic war humankind had ever visited upon itself, was gone.

Harry S Truman, FDR's vice president, took the oath of office two hours and 24 minutes after the president's death. The next day, Truman addressed a group of reporters. "Boys," the unassuming man from Independence, Missouri, began, "if you ever pray, pray for me now. I don't know whether you fellows ever had a load of hay fall on you, but when they told me yesterday what had happened, I felt like the moon, the stars, and all the planets had fallen on me."

Manhattan Project

With a war yet to be won and the Soviet presence looming for the postwar world, it is no wonder that Truman felt the way he did. And he was about to learn that the responsibility that had fallen on him was even heavier than he had imagined. On April 25, Secretary of War Henry L. Stimson handed Truman a typewritten memorandum. It began:

> *Within four months we shall in all probability have completed the most terrible weapon ever known in human history, one bomb of which could destroy a whole city.*

Franklin Roosevelt had confided little in his vice president, and this note was the first Truman heard about the "Manhattan Project," code name for an enormous undertaking—the biggest scientific and technological project ever undertaken by any nation in history—the object of which was to liberate the tremendous energy that holds together atomic nuclei, all at once, in an explosion more terrible than humankind had ever before created.

In the opening years of the century, as Chapter 7, "Rising and Sinking," mentioned, Albert Einstein—an obscure German-born Swiss patent clerk—transformed the way we look at reality. In a simple, elegant equation, he showed how mass and energy were equivalent, how, in effect, mass was a highly concentrated form of energy.

How concentrated? Energy *(e)*, measured in joules, is equal to mass *(m)*, measured in kilograms, times the square of the speed of light *(c)*—an enormous number: a billion times more energy per atom than is released in "ordinary" chemical reactions.

This energy could be liberated through *fission* of the atomic nucleus. If the particles that make up the nucleus could be split apart, prodigious amounts of energy would be released.

Of course, an atom is a very small thing. Its mass is tiny. Split one atom, and even if $e = mc^2$, *e* will not be a large force. But, in 1939, the Hungarian-born physicist Leo Szilard theorized that, under the right circumstances, the fission of a single atom could induce a *chain reaction* in other atoms, which would yield unprecedented amounts of energy; that is, the particles split off from one atom would possess sufficient energy to split off particles in more atoms, which, in turn, would do the same to yet more.

As Europe fell under Nazi domination, scientists who had found refuge in America worried that those who remained in Germany would pursue the power of fission and create a weapon of unprecedented destructiveness. In 1939, the scientists prevailed on Albert Einstein—the most famous among them—to write a secret letter to President Roosevelt, apprising him of the danger and urging him to commence a project to develop an atomic bomb. In February 1940, $6,000 was appropriated to start research; on December 6, 1941, just one day before the Japanese attack on Pearl Harbor, the project was fully authorized and put under the direction of Vannevar Bush, one of the nation's most prominent scientists. In September 1942, the work, now generally referred to as the Manhattan Project, was assigned to the overall direction of General Leslie R. Groves, an Army engineer who was not a scientist, but who, after directing construction of the Pentagon, had earned a reputation for getting big things done.

Talk of the Times

Fission is a nuclear reaction in which an atomic unit splits into fragments, thereby releasing energy. Given a sufficient amount of fissionable material, the split-off fragments collide with other nuclei, causing them to fragment as well, until a self-sustaining **chain reaction** is under way.

Fermi's Gamble

The first step toward creating a weapon, the Manhattan Project scientists determined, was to produce the kind of chain reaction Szilard had theorized. The assignment was given to Enrico Fermi. Born in Rome in 1901, Fermi became absorbed in physics as a teenager and, as an adult, was regarded as Italy's leading physicist. One of the small mercies of the Nazi reign was that its hatred and brutality drove out of the Axis nations many of its best minds—the very people Hitler needed to create weapons of mass destruction. Despite his fame, Fermi, in 1938, was subject to the anti-Semitic decree Mussolini had promulgated in obedience to Hitler. Fermi wasn't Jewish, but his wife was. That year, he secured a professorship at Columbia University in New York City and, with his wife and children, left Italy.

The reactor was built in a squash court under the stands of the University of Chicago's Stagg Field. Uranium and uranium oxide were piled up in combination with graphite blocks. Neutrons colliding with the carbon atoms in the graphite would not affect the carbon nuclei, but would bounce off them, giving up energy and moving slowly as a result, thereby increasing the chance that they would react with the uranium 235. By making the atomic pile large, the chances that neutrons would strike the uranium 235 were increased. But the pile had to be just large enough—that is, it had to reach what the scientists called *critical mass*—to start and sustain the chain reaction.

To control the reaction, cadmium rods were inserted into the pile. When the pile approached critical mass, the rods would be slowly withdrawn, and the number of neutrons produced would increase. At some point during the process, more neutrons would be produced than were being consumed by the cadmium. At this juncture, the pile would "go critical," and the nuclear chain reaction would begin. If allowed to proceed un-checked, the reaction would create an atomic explosion.

Talk of the Times

Critical mass is the smallest mass of fissionable material that will sustain a nuclear chain reaction.

What would that be like? No one was sure. Certainly, it would destroy a good part of Chicago—and those people the explosion didn't kill would be subject to potentially lethal doses of radiation. The harmful effects of radiation were apparent very early in the century: Wilhelm Roentgen died from too many x-rays, and Madame Curie knew that exposure to radium was making her ill. Diseases afflicting women who painted radium watch dials in the 1910s were well documented. It was certainly understood that gamma and beta radiation easily penetrated body tissue, destroying or damaging it. Perhaps an atomic explosion would be even more terrible. Some scientists theorized that an out-of-control chain reaction might set off a chain reaction in the very atoms of the atmosphere, effectively bringing the world to an end.

But 1942 was a desperate year, desperate enough that scientists, military men, politi-cians, and Enrico Fermi were willing to gamble with Chicago and even with the world. And, in any event, those cadmium rods could be reinserted to put an instant halt to any chain reaction. At least, that was the theory.

Just before 3:45 on the afternoon of December 2, 1942, Enrico Fermi gave the order to withdraw the cadmium control rods. Geiger counters sprang to life, indicating a large release of energy. It was apparent that a nuclear chain reaction was under way. At 3:45 exactly, the reaction became self-sustaining, at which point Fermi ordered that the rods be shoved back into place.

The Geiger counters became quiet once again. Chicago was safe, and—for the present—so was the world.

A New Sun in the Desert

The Manhattan Project was perhaps the greatest intellectual endeavor humankind had ever embarked on. Its scientific dimension was directed by J. Robert Oppenheimer, a charismatic American physicist, who coordinated the efforts of a small army of the most prominent physicists, chemists, and mathematicians in the world.

But the Manhattan Project was also a vast manufacturing enterprise. Two radioactive isotopes, uranium 235 and plutonium 239, undergo fission most readily—if present in sufficient quantity to constitute critical mass. Vast processing facilities are required to produce enough of these isotopes to build bombs. General Groves oversaw construction of giant, secret plants at Oak Ridge, Tennessee, for the separation of uranium 235 from its natural companion isotope, uranium 238, and at Hanford, Washington, for the production of plutonium 239.

In 1943, Oppenheimer supervised creation of a laboratory on a remote mesa at Los Alamos, New Mexico. Here, theoretical physics would be transformed into the mechanics of creating a bomb. First, methods had to be found to reduce the fissionable products produced at Oak Ridge and Hanford to pure metal and then fabricating that metal to shapes suitable for bringing the chain reaction to an explosive level. The scientists also had to find a way of instantly bringing together sufficient amounts of the fissionable material to achieve a *supercritical mass*—and thus a nuclear explosion.

And there was one more problem. In his 1939 letter to Franklin Roosevelt, Albert Einstein had observed that "A single [atomic] bomb ... might very well destroy [a] whole port together with some of the surrounding territory." But he continued: "However, such bombs might very well prove to be too heavy for transportation by air." The scientists had to make a bomb that could be dropped from an airplane.

The theoreticians and the technicians worked in parallel. By the summer of 1945, when sufficient amounts of plutonium 239 had become available from the Hanford Works, the physicists at Los Alamos were ready.

The first test of the bomb, code named Trinity, took place in the Almagordo desert at Los Alamos at 0529:45 on July 16, 1945. All who witnessed it described it as something very like the creation of a sun on earth. A blinding flash, followed by a tremendous shock wave that hit like a body blow.

Century Stats

In 1940, $6,000 was appropriated for nuclear weapons research. By the early summer of 1945, $2,000,000,000 had been spent on the Manhattan Project.

The "gadget," as the Los Alamos scientists called it, had worked beyond all expectation. Instantly, the austere New Mexico laboratory erupted into shouts and cries of celebration. Then, just as quickly, the scientists began to realize what they had created. As Oppenheimer recalled in 1965,

> We waited until the blast had passed, walked out of the shelter, and then it was extremely solemn. We knew the world would not be the same. A few people laughed, a few people cried. Most people were silent. I remembered the line from the Hindu scripture, the Bhagavad Gita: Vishnu is trying to persuade the Prince that he should do his duty ... and says, "Now I am become death, destroyer of worlds." I suppose we all thought that one way or another.

Hiroshima and Nagasaki

With Franklin Roosevelt dead, it now fell to Harry Truman to decide whether to use the new weapon against the nation's remaining enemy, the empire of Japan.

"The atom bomb was no 'great decision,'" Truman told a Columbia University student during a seminar on statecraft in 1959. "It was merely another powerful weapon in the arsenal of righteousness. The dropping of the bombs stopped the war, saved millions of lives."

When he authorized the use of the bomb, Truman did so with the knowledge that, although defeated—its navy neutralized, its army depleted, most of its cities reduced to rubble—Japan refused to surrender. Invading the islands, it was estimated, would cost many tens of thousands of Allied lives as well as those of untold numbers of Japanese. And there was another consideration. Churchill and Roosevelt had begged Stalin to enter the war against Japan. Now Truman feared that, if Japan delayed surrender, Stalin would enter the Pacific war with a vengeance and grab Japan as he had eastern Europe.

On August 6, 1945, a lone B-29 Superfortress prepared for take-off from an airfield on Tinian Island. Like most U.S. bombers in World War II, it sported a touch of artwork on its nose, the name Enola Gay written in script. It was the name of the pilot Paul Tibbets's mother.

At 8:15 in the morning, local time, the uranium-235 bomb, nicknamed "Little Boy," was dropped and detonated in the air 1,900 feet above the city of Hiroshima.

Within an instant, two-thirds of the city area was flattened. The population at the time was about 350,000 human beings. Many died instantly. Others, horribly burned, lingered for hours or days. Still others, apparently uninjured, sickened and died. (The world would soon learn to fear radioactive fallout.) By the end of 1945, 140,000 were dead.

Voice of the Century

Sublime is the moment
When the world is at peace
And the limitless deep
Lies bathed in the morning sun.

—Untitled poem by Hirohito, emperor of Japan

Emperor Hirohito poses with General Douglas MacArthur after the war, when MacArthur served as head of a U.S.-administered government of occupation in Japan.
(Image from arttoday.com)

On August 11, a plutonium-239 bomb, called "Fat Man," was loaded aboard another B-29, *Bock's Car*, bound for Kokura. When the cloud cover over that city proved unfavorable, the aircraft flew to the secondary target, Nagasaki. At 11:02 A.M. local time, Fat Man was air-burst at 1,650 feet, leveling half the city. Of 270,000 people present at the time, some 70,000 would be dead by the end of the year.

At noon on August 15, 1945, the people of Japan heard the voice of their emperor, Hirohito, for the first time. No Japanese emperor had ever deigned to speak to his people before. But no occasion like this had ever occurred before.

Hirohito broadcast his acceptance of the Allied surrender terms, citing the explosion of a "cruel new bomb." World War II was over. In America and among the Allied nations, there would be celebration, to be sure, yet no one spoke now, as they had after World War I, of a "world made safe for democracy." Indeed, no one spoke now of a world made safe.

The Least You Need to Know

➤ The Battle of Stalingrad, November 1942–February 1943, turned the tide against the German invaders of the Soviet Union.

➤ By 1943, the German army was being pressed by the British and Americans from the west and south, and by the Russians from the east.

➤ The closing months of the war put a great strain on the Western alliance with the Soviets, who were intent on occupying vast tracts of eastern Europe, bringing it under communist domination.

➤ Only at the end of the war, when Allied forces liberated the Nazi death camps, were the genocidal horrors of the Holocaust fully understood.

➤ The war in Japan was ended suddenly by the use of the world's first nuclear weapons, against Hiroshima (August 6, 1945) and Nagasaki (August 11).

Chapter 18

A War Served Cold (1946–1949)

In This Chapter

➤ The Iron Curtain descends

➤ Formation of the United Nations

➤ The nation of Israel becomes the first Jewish homeland since biblical times

➤ Cold War politics

➤ Showdown in Berlin

➤ China becomes communist

The Treaty of Versailles that formally ended World War I was ceremoniously concluded in the Hall of Mirrors at the great Palace of Versailles. The setting was a symbol of old Europe, expressing the world's desire, after the "Great War," to return to the golden age the war had obliterated. In contrast, the acceptance of Japan's surrender, ending World War II, took place not in an Old World palace, but on a modern warship, the USS *Missouri*. General MacArthur, presiding, was arrayed not in an elegant dress uniform, but in his work clothes, the rumpled khaki of the Pacific campaign.

Peace concluded on a battleship. It was a fitting a symbol of the postwar world—and an admission that, after *this* war, a war of genocide and the fires of nuclear fission, the world would never, *could* never, be the same again.

The World Unites—and Divides

Perhaps you've seen the grainy black-and-white photographs and newsreel footage of the delirious rejoicing on V-J Day, Victory Over Japan Day, the day the war ended.

Those celebrations were intense, but all too brief. The Soviet Union, portrayed by U.S. politicians and the popular press throughout the war as a valiant ally, suddenly loomed as the ideological and political enemy it had been after World War I.

But with a terrible difference. After the Bolshevik Revolution and ignominious surrender in World War I, Soviet Russia was torn by a debilitating civil war. True, Lenin had created cominterns in an effort to convert the world to communism. But he didn't have the economic or military power, let alone the national unity, to spread the communist ideology by force. Now, after World War II, Soviet armies were already occupying Eastern Europe, and Stalin was not about to lose his grip on those nations.

Justice at Nuremberg

Although Germany was divided after World War II, the Western and Soviet allies were agreed on creating an orderly process to bring to justice the major German war criminals, those guilty of "crimes against humanity," ranging from torture to genocide.

The Nuremberg Trials, which took place in that German city from November 1945 to October 1946, were presided over by jurists from all the Allied nations. The principal proceeding tried 22 Nazi leaders, of whom 12 were sentenced to death, including Wilhelm Keitel (Hitler's closest military adviser), Joachim von Ribbentrop (German foreign minister), Alfred Rosenberg (a principal architect of Nazi genocide programs), and Martin Bormann (Hitler's secretary). Bormann vanished after Hitler's suicide on April 30, 1945, and was tried in absentia; in 1972, a skeleton identified as his was discovered in West Berlin. Hermann Goering, second only to Hitler in authority, committed suicide before he could be executed. Three other war criminals were given life sentences, and four received 20-year terms. Three of the first 22 tried were acquitted. Over the succeeding months, lesser criminals were tried in a series of 12 proceedings.

In the Pacific, war crimes trials were authorized by General Douglas MacArthur, head of the military government the Allies installed in Japan immediately following the war. Modeled on the London Agreement, which had established the rules for the Nuremburg Trials, MacArthur's charter differed significantly from that document by allowing defendants to argue that their actions were taken on orders of their government. Eleven nations were represented at the tribunal, which began in Tokyo on May 3, 1946, and continued for two years. Of 25 Japanese defendants, 7 were sentenced to hang, 16 to life imprisonment, and 2 to lesser prison terms.

"We the Peoples..."

Having defeated one system of totalitarian tyranny, the United States and the Western powers were confronted by another system, ideologically opposed to fascism, it is true, yet even more totalitarian and, apparently, every bit as militaristic.

In an address at Westminster College, in Fulton, Missouri, on March 5, 1946, Winston Churchill summed up the situation of postwar Europe: "From Stettin on the Baltic to Trieste in the Adriatic, an *iron curtain* has descended across the Continent."

It was a scary world.

Two things made the world a little less scary. The first was the fact that the United States had a monopoly on "the Bomb"—nuclear weapons—and American scientists and politicians believed that the Soviets were years away from developing a bomb of their own.

The second reason for hope was the United Nations. The name came from what the powers allied against the Axis had called themselves: the "United Nations." The hope of Roosevelt and Churchill—and, to a far lesser extent, even Stalin—was to perpetuate, if not an outright alliance, at least cooperation after the war. So, from August to October 1944, representatives of the United States, Great Britain, the USSR, and China met at a Washington, D.C. estate called Dumbarton Oaks to sketch out plans for a new world body. The wartime allies—plus France—would constitute a peacekeeping ("security") council, while the other nations of the world, though fully represented, would play secondary roles.

The atmosphere of the Dumbarton Oaks Conference was much more promising than that which had surrounded the creation of the League of Nations. Even so, two major issues were vexing: Should United Nations action require the unanimous agreement of the Security Council members? And should the Western powers agree to the Soviet demand for separate membership for each of the 16 "republics" that made up the USSR?

Talk of the Times

Iron Curtain was the term Winston Churchill used to describe the extent of the Soviet sphere of influence and domination in the postwar period. The term was popularized in a March 5, 1946, speech at Westminster College in Fulton, Missouri, but it was first used by Churchill in a May 12, 1945 telegram to Harry Truman.

Century Stats

Fifty nations signed the U.N. Charter in 1945; today, the United Nations hosts representatives of 185 nations.

These differences were resolved at the Yalta conference in February 1945 (Chapter 17, "'Now I Am Become Death'"). Roosevelt, Stalin, and Churchill agreed to uphold the principle of unanimity: Any permanent member of the Security Council could veto enforcement actions, but no member could veto discussion and debate. For his part, Stalin reduced his demand for separate memberships from a whopping 16 to a more reasonable 3: Russia, Ukraine, and Byelorussia.

Later in the year, a formal United Nations Charter was drawn up and adopted by 50 nations at the San Francisco Conference. The Preamble to the Charter reflected the example of the United States Constitution. Whereas that document begins, "We the people of the United States," the U.N. Charter starts with the words, "We the peoples of the United Nations determined to save succeeding generations from the scourge of war, which twice in our lifetime has brought untold sorrow to mankind ...."

After a majority of the signatory nations ratified the Charter on October 24, 1945, the United Nations, the most significant deliberative body in world history, became a reality.

Stalin's Grasp

"Untold sorrow"? No nation knew the significance of that phrase more fully and more bitterly than the Soviet Union. Stalin, determined never again to leave his nation vulnerable to invasion, simply swallowed up his neighbors.

In 1946, the Iron Curtain sliced Germany in two, dividing it into a Soviet Zone and Western Zones (controlled by the United States, Britain, and France), and it cut off from the West Poland, Hungary (as well as part of Austria), Romania, Bulgaria, and Albania. Yugoslavia was also behind the iron curtain, but its dynamic leader, Josep Broz Tito (1892–1980), although a staunch communist, retained a high degree of independence, refusing to become Stalin's puppet. Czechoslovakia, created as a democracy after World War I, dismembered by Hitler, then reborn after World War II, would fall under Soviet domination by 1948.

Josep Broz Tito, pictured as an anti-Nazi partisan leader during World War II.
(Image from the National Archives)

Nations bordering the Iron Curtain, especially Italy, Greece, and Turkey, were also in peril of Soviet domination, and the communist threat was not confined to Europe. In Asia, at war's end, China, Korea, and Vietnam tottered on the brink of communist domination.

Science Ascendant

The bombing of Hiroshima and Nagasaki conferred on scientists unprecedented prestige and power. Men like Albert Einstein, J. Robert Oppenheimer, Enrico Fermi, and Edward Teller, all of whom had had a hand in creating "the Bomb," were regarded as superhuman. Having achieved victory in a terrible war, Americans were fearful that they had won the war only to lose the peace. Communism was spreading like an evil stain across the face of Europe and elsewhere. But at least *American* scientists seemed to be supreme, step by step gaining ever greater control of the physical world, if not the political one.

Electronic Brains

It is tempting to think of war as the most mindless of human activities, but, as we saw in the last chapter, the needs of World War II drew upon the intellect of the world's greatest scientists to create the world's most terrible weapon. The fact is, the war greatly accelerated the development of science and technology.

One thing modern warriors require is the ability to make rapid and complex calculations for at least two purposes: the encryption and decryption of communication, and the direction of artillery fire and aerial bombardment.

The British mathematician Alan Turing served during the war as part of a team that broke the German master military code, the so-called Enigma cipher, using, in part, the concept of the *Turing machine*, which Turing had developed shortly before the war.

The Turing machine wasn't a machine, it was a concept or idealized model. In 1936, Turing imagined a machine consisting of an infinitely extensible paper tape on which a tape head could read and write information. The tape head included a modifiable control mechanism, which could store directions from a finite set of instructions (a "program"). As Turing envisaged it, the tape was divided into squares, each of which was either blank or bore one of a finite number of symbols. The tape head could move to, read, write, and erase any single square and could change from one internal state to another between one moment and the next, depending on both the internal state of the machine and the condition of the scanned square at a given moment. Once the machine stopped the process of scanning, writing, and erasing, the result would be a solution to the mathematical query that had been presented to it.

Turing had outlined the theoretical basis of computer science. Back in the United States, in 1939, IBM joined a development team at Harvard University to give computer-science theory physical form. They created Mark I, an advanced electromechanical device that is generally acknowledged to be the first truly modern *programmable computer*.

Talk of the Times

The **Turing machine** was not a physical machine at all, but a theoretical construct proposed in 1936 by British mathematician Alan Turing (1912–1954), which forms the basis of modern computer theory and technique.

Talk of the Times

A **programmable computer** is a "universal" device capable of performing a great many different calculational and logical operations, depending on the instructions (the program) presented to it. This is in contrast to simple calculators, for example, which can perform limited operations, such as addition, multiplication, and so on.

The company destined to become synonymous with computers through much of the 20th century was International Business Machines—IBM. It had its origin in the 19th century, in solving a problem for the U.S. Census Bureau. In 1888, bureau officials were alarmed. An army of clerks, working full shifts, had only that year finished counting the 1880 census. At that rate, the officials calculated, the upcoming 1890 census wouldn't be counted until 1902—two years after the 1900 census was under way! And, with the U.S. population growing, the lag between census and tabulation could only continue to increase. What to do?

The bureau's John Shaw Billings proposed using punch-hole cards to record and then process census information, and he hired Herman Hollerith to develop the cards as well as an electric machine to read them. The result was impressive. The census of 1890 was completed in less than three years, and Hollerith went on to join the company that, in 1924, would officially become IBM.

Of course, Hollerith's device was really a tabulating machine, and not a truly programmable computer, a general-purpose device that can be programmed to solve any specific solvable problem. Although it wasn't until 1936 that Alan Turing put together the theoretical foundation that enabled the creation of such a machine, there were far earlier breakthroughs in computer science. For example, the French mathematician and philosopher Blaise Pascal had developed a calculating machine in 1642, followed by a device that German philosopher Gottfried Wilhelm Leibniz produced in 1693. The "prehistory" of the modern computer culminated in the never-quite-completed "analytical engine" Englishman Charles Babbage and Lady Ada Lovelace cobbled together in 1835. In 1930, American electrical engineer Vannevar Bush produced a machine capable of solving differential equations—something no simple calculator could do.

The evolution from these early machines to Mark I was significant, but it is important to note that the IBM device was *electromechanical*, incorporating electronic elements as well as the mechanical components of traditional calculating machines.

The first fully *electronic* computer—the Electronic Numerical Integrator And Calculator, or "ENIAC," was unveiled in 1946, the work of two American engineers, John William Mauchly and John Prosper Eckert Jr.

Like the Mark I, ENIAC had been funded largely by the war effort. It was designed to calculate complex mathematical tables to determine the speed and trajectory of artillery shells directed at such targets as slow-moving warships and fast-moving aircraft. When it was first demonstrated at the University of Pennsylvania, ENIAC proved much faster and much more flexible than the partially mechanical Mark I.

ENIAC did share with Mark I a significant feature, however. It was monstrous in size. Mark I was 50 feet long and 8 feet high, while ENIAC displaced 3,000 cubic feet of volume, weighed 30 tons, and required 18,000 vacuum tubes—as well as a team of fleet-footed technicians to locate and replace the tubes as they burned out. Nevertheless, the era of the "electronic brain" had dawned, and people were amazed. Although the enormous ENIAC lacked the power and speed of even the most rudimentary of today's hand-held calculators—let alone a desktop or laptop computer—it ushered in an age increasingly dominated by computers, in science and engineering as well as in the creation and tracking of academic, government, and commercial records. Science was never the same, and neither were government or commerce. Nor could people ever regain a sense of absolute privacy and individuality. With each passing year, computers played a greater and greater role in everyone's life.

Voice of the Century

"Do not fold, bend, or mutilate."

—Warning message on IBM punch cards, universally used in the 1960s–'70s for bills and other records.

Faster Than Sound

What so impressed the public about the early "electronic brains" was the speed with which they performed even highly complex calculations. Speed was indeed an obsession of the 20th century. It was a large part of the fascination behind the automobile and the airplane. In the world of sport, people spoke reverently of the "four-minute mile," many doubting that any human being could ever hope to run so fast—until Sir Roger Bannister did just that, breaking the four-minute barrier at a meet in Oxford on May 6, 1954, with a time of 3 minutes, 59.4 seconds.

Another barrier, one even more awesome, was shattered seven years before the achievement of the four-minute mile. On October 14, 1947, Charles E. Yeager, an Air Force test pilot, flew a small, bright orange rocket plane, the Bell X-1, in excess of 740 miles per hour: faster than the speed of sound. He had "broken the sound barrier."

Just as aircraft had flown higher and higher since the Wright Brothers made their first flight in 1903, they also had been getting faster and faster. The demands of World War II brought propeller-driven flight to its maximum development, and such fighter aircraft as the North American P-51 Mustang could reach speeds faster than 500 miles per hour.

At the beginning of the war, the British aeronautical engineer Frank Whittle began working on aircraft driven by a new kind of engine, not one that moved air above the wing by means of a propeller, but that pushed the craft through the air with a high-speed jet of exhaust.

As early as 1921, engineers had theorized that an engine could be designed to burn fuel and eject such an exhaust jet, thereby producing enormous forward thrust. Nothing really new here. It was the basic principle of the rocket. But there was an important difference. Whereas a rocket engine carries fuel plus an oxidizing agent, a jet engine "breathes," scooping in the oxygen necessary for combustion from the surrounding air.

Whittle proved the practicality of the principle of *jet propulsion:* yet, despite the incentive of combat, neither the British nor the Americans did much to develop jets during World War II. The Germans, in contrast, actually created a small number of jet fighters and introduced them at the end of the war. By that time, however, they were too late to make a difference.

Talk of the Times

Jet propulsion is the principle behind modern jet aircraft. Oxygen is rapidly mixed with fuel and burned, producing a jet of hot exhaust gases, which provide tremendous forward thrust.

Century Stats

The speed of sound is generally placed at 1,088 feet per second at sea level at 32°F. This is called Mach 1, a unit of measure named after Ernst Mach (1838–1916), a Czech-born Austrian physicist, who contributed to the study of sound. Mach 2 is twice the speed of sound, Mach 3 three times the speed of sound, and so on.

But British and American pilots now realized that, had Hitler developed his jets earlier, the effect would have been devastating. In the postwar years, the Americans and British—as well as the Soviets—rapidly developed jet aircraft, and, always looming on the horizon, was the sound barrier.

In a way, this "barrier" was just another more-or-less arbitrary goal, like the four-minute mile. But it also posed a formidable challenge to pilot and machine. At speeds under 740 miles per hour, the air molecules an aircraft encounters slip smoothly over the surfaces of the plane, but, as the aircraft approaches the speed of sound, the molecules cannot move out of the way before they are overtaken. Therefore, they pile up in front of the aircraft, which, in effect, flies into a "wall" of compressed air. Some aeronautical engineers theorized that, in hitting this wall, an airplane would disintegrate, and it was terrifyingly true that experimental jet aircraft were buffeted by extreme vibration and turbulence as they approached the speed of sound.

Bell aircraft engineers expressly designed the X-1 to cope with these conditions, creating an ultrastreamlined profile and short, very thin wings, which, it was hoped, would minimize the effects of turbulence.

Yeager's flight through the sound barrier was highly dramatic, creating a thunderous "sonic boom," the result of air piling up, suddenly slipping to one side of the aircraft, then rapidly reexpanding with a loud crack—a much bigger version of the crack produced by a whip, as air is compressed, passes by, and reexpands past the tip of the fast-moving whip. Yet the "sound barrier" proved less formidable an object than had been imagined. The Bell X-1 readily passed through it—not that anyone, including the courageous Yeager, had known it would.

Big Bang

As anyone who has ever heard one can testify, a sonic boom is an impressive display of sound. In 1948, a colorful Russian-born American physicist started thinking about a much bigger bang.

George Gamow was born Georgi Antonovich Gamow in 1904, in Odessa, Russia, and immigrated to the United States in 1934 to become professor of physics at George Washington University in Washington, D.C. He became particularly interested in *cosmology*, the origin of the universe, and he carefully studied theories proposed by Dutch astronomer Willem de Sitter in 1917, Russian mathematician Alexander Alexandrovich Friedmann in 1922, and the Belgian astrophysicist Georges Henri Lemaitre in 1927.

De Sitter had followed through the implications of Albert Einstein's general theory of relativity (Chapter 7, "Rising and Sinking") to their most extreme conclusion: The universe is not static, but is expanding. De Sitter reached this conclusion by making calculations based on an idealized universe, one without mass. In 1922, Friedmann (who had been one of Gamow's teachers) worked out calculations for the "real" universe, one with mass. This confirmed de Sitter's picture of an expanding universe.

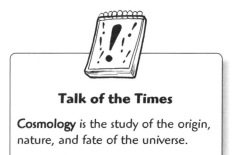

Talk of the Times

Cosmology is the study of the origin, nature, and fate of the universe.

Five years later, in 1927, Lemaitre reasoned that if the universe expands as time goes forward, it would contract if time were imagined to run in reverse. That is, the implication of an expanding universe is that it had developed from what must have been a relatively small, highly compressed body, which Lemaitre dubbed the "cosmic egg." He further reasoned that, at some point, this cosmic egg must have exploded, broadcasting the matter that is now the universe. As a result of this primordial explosion, the universe is still expanding, still traveling outward from the original egg.

Gamow set about weaving all of this speculation into a fully developed theory. He showed how the chemical elements were formed in the aftermath of the explosion and theorized that the primordial blast had wrought a vast surge of energy, but that the universe had necessarily cooled as it expanded, so that it was now, on average, barely above absolute zero (–217.15 degrees on the centigrade scale). Gamow reasoned that such a temperature would cause a background of microwave radiation at a certain wavelength. In 1948, when Gamow published his theory, there was no practical means of measuring such radiation. But, remarkably, the work of radio astronomers in 1964 revealed the existence of just such cosmic background radiation. It was physical proof of the validity of Gamow's theory.

Not everyone embraced the idea of an expanding universe. The prominent British astronomer Sir Fred Hoyle, for example, derided the whole theory as a "big bang."

Perhaps to Hoyle's chagrin, the name stuck—and even helped popularize what is now regarded as the most plausible theory of the origin of the universe.

TV Turns On

With the Big Bang theory, the year 1948 saw one of history's most profound acts of the human mind and imagination. The year also offered another act, somewhat less profound, to be sure, yet highly influential nonetheless.

Just how much less profound? Well, this act involved a former vaudeville comic who was fond of donning very homely drag and cavorting, not on a vaudeville stage, but within the eerily glowing confines of a television picture tube. His name was Milton Berle, and his show was something called the *Texaco Star Theater*. It premiered on September 21, 1948, and from then until it ended its run in 1956, the show gave Americans a reason to buy a television set.

The technology was not brand-new in 1948. Its origins may be traced to the work of many scientists and engineers, but the standout was Vladimir Zworykin. Born in Mourom, Russia, in 1889, Zworykin was trained as an electrical engineer, immigrated to the United States in 1916, and was naturalized in 1924. He went to work for Westinghouse, where, in 1925, he invented and patented something he called an "iconoscope." A specially treated vacuum tube, the iconoscope transformed light into electrical impulses and electrical impulses back into light, in the form of an image on a phosphor-coated screen. The iconoscope was the basis both for the television camera and the "picture tube," the heart of the television set.

Zworykin left Westinghouse to work at a high level for RCA and RCA Laboratories, refining and perfecting the iconoscope into a genuine television system. In 1933, he transmitted a television picture from New York to Philadelphia—the first TV broadcast.

Yet Zworykin's invention didn't set the world on fire. Six long years went by before the first *public* television broadcast was made, in 1939, when NBC aired live video of President Franklin D. Roosevelt at the New York World's Fair. This caused a stir, but World War II delayed commercial development of the medium. In 1944, regularly scheduled programs were broadcast to a handful of New York-area subscribers, most of whom were electrical engineers.

It seemed that the would-be pioneers of television were faced with a classic chicken-and-egg dilemma. Television sets were costly and very finicky. Few could afford to buy a set, especially when there was almost nothing to watch. Programming was desperately needed, but the radio-broadcast networks were reluctant to invest in TV programming for which an audience barely existed.

Vladimir Zworykin and others had solved the technical problems of television. Now the nation needed a

Voice of the Century

"Television is the first truly democratic culture—the first culture available to everyone and entirely governed by what the people want. The most terrifying thing is what people do want."

—Clive Barnes, critic, 1969

compelling reason to buy the device. Enter Milton Berlinger—Milton Berle. He had been born in New York City on July 12, 1908, and struggled to make a living as a vaudeville comic. In 1948, no major star would be caught dead on the fledgling medium of television. Berle, however, was by no definition a major star, and he had nothing to lose.

Dubbed "Uncle Miltie" and, more accurately, "Mr. Television," he quickly came to dominate the new medium. People dropped whatever they were doing every Tuesday evening to watch an hour-long program consisting mainly of the vaudeville antics of Berle, who was often attired in a cheap blonde wig and frumpy house dress.

At first, people congregated in the parlor of whatever neighbor happened to own a TV set. Soon, however, they began buying sets of their own. Families left the dinner table and brought their plates with them to watch. Berle made television a guest in the American home, so that it became a mass medium with an extraordinarily intimate appeal. By the mid 1950s, television had become more influential than books, movies, and radio—combined.

Behold the Transistor

Like radio before it, but to an even greater degree, television brought high technology into everyday life. Yet television also complicated everyday life. The chassis assemblies of early sets were camouflaged by wooden cabinets of various traditional furniture styles—even colonial and Chippendale! But the chassis itself was a mass of wires and vacuum tubes. Vacuum tubes, which we first encountered in Chapter 6, "First Years," are nothing more than electronic valves. Such controls are essential to doing anything useful with electronics, but the tubes were delicate and prone to burn out or operate erratically. What could take the place of the vacuum tube?

In 1948, Walter Houser Brattain, John Bardeen, and William B. Shockley, all scientists working for Bell Laboratories, created the *semiconductor*, a device that can control the electrical current that flows between two terminals by means of a low voltage applied to a third terminal. The heart of the semiconductor device, which the scientists dubbed the *transistor*, was a crystal grown from the element germanium. When silicon, an element much cheaper and more abundant than germanium, was discovered to possess suitable semiconductor

Century Stats

A week consists of 168 hours, of which an average of 40 are consumed by working one's daily job and another 56 in sleep. Of the remaining 72 hours in the week, Americans currently dedicate an average of 17.5 hours—almost a quarter—to television viewing.

Talk of the Times

The **transistor** is a **semiconductor** device that uses very low voltages to regulate higher voltages. It functions as both a control and amplification device in electronic circuits and is the heart of all modern electronic devices.

properties, the transistor emerged as a cheaper, far more reliable, and far more efficient alternative to the vacuum tube.

Most important of all, the transistor was also much smaller than the vacuum tube. This fact would help personalize technology just as surely as Milton Berle had.

From the 1950s onward, the century was marked by the emergence of *personal* electronic devices, beginning with portable transistor radios, but soon ranging to sophisticated medical applications and advanced computers, and to such devices as pocket calculators and tiny tape recorders. By the 1960s, it became possible to miniaturize the individual transistor to microscopic dimensions. Arrays of these tiny devices could be etched into thin wafers of silicon, *chips*, and electronic subassemblies as well as entire devices were reduced to areas of a few inches or centimeters. With this technology, the application of electronics became virtually unlimited. Soon, computers, which in 1948 weighed tons and occupied large rooms, were sitting on desktops and even laptops.

"Never Again"

Early television fare was, for the most part, pretty lightweight stuff. Among the great appeals of Milton Berle and those who immediately followed him was escape, escape from the realities of a world that, however rich with the wonders of science and technology, was also freighted with the horrors of the war so recently concluded.

Among the most terrible of those horrors was, of course, the Holocaust. As many Jews now saw it, a principle cause of the Holocaust was not Adolf Hitler or unreasoning hatred, but the fact that Jews were a people without a home country. "Never again," Jews said of the Holocaust. But, as long as Jews were without a home, "never again" was an empty vow.

The first tangible progress toward nationhood came on November 2, 1917, when Zionist leaders persuaded British Foreign Secretary Lord Balfour to endorse the establishment of "a national home" for the Jewish people in Palestine. Shortly after this "Balfour Declaration," during World War I, British General Sir Edmund Allenby invaded Palestine, capturing Jerusalem in December. In 1922, the League of Nations approved a British "mandate" over Palestine and neighboring Transjordan, and the provisions of the Balfour Declaration were written into the mandate document.

Transjordan became modern, independent Jordan, but Palestine, torn by violent dissension between Jews and Arabs, could not be granted sovereignty. Then, in 1939, came a devastating blow. The London Round Table Conference produced a "White Paper" promising the creation of an independent Palestine within a decade, but limiting Jewish immigration to 1,500 persons per month until 1944, after which Jews would no longer be admitted to Palestine.

Now the Zionists turned from Britain to the United States for support, demanding, in the May 1942 Biltmore Conference in New York, the formation of an independent Jewish state. It was a demand that attracted much American support. After World War

II, Jewish Holocaust survivors poured into Palestine. British administrators sought to block the immigration, but, in 1947, threw up their hands and turned the matter over to the United Nations. In November, the U.N. voted to divide Palestine into Arab and Jewish states, and on May 14, 1948, the state of Israel was created.

Immediately, the region was plunged into war. "Never again," declared the Jews, and, with great skill and courage, defeated the Arab armies that invaded Palestine in an effort to evict the Jews. Homeless since the diaspora, the Babylonian exile of the sixth century B.C., the Jews had a homeland once again.

A Policy of Containment

In 1823, President James Monroe issued his famous "Monroe Doctrine," a warning to the imperialist nations of Europe that the United States would act aggressively to halt any new attempts to colonize the Americas. In 1947, President Harry S Truman promulgated the "Truman Doctrine," warning the Soviet Union—which supported a threatened communist takeover of Greece and Turkey—that the United States would act to halt the spread of communism wherever in the world it threatened democracy.

The Truman Doctrine was based on a policy proposed by a State Department official, George F. Kennan. He believed that the most effective way of combating communism was to *contain* it, confronting the Soviet Union whenever and wherever it sought to expand its ideological influence.

George F. Kennan was the State Department official who proposed the policy of "containing" communism. (Image from the Wisconsin Historical Society Collection)

The *containment* policy was a dangerous game, which could have easily ignited a large-scale war. Yet the alternative to "playing" was to surrender much of the world to Soviet domination, and the recollection of President Truman burned with images of what it meant to "appease" a dictator, letting him have a piece of this nation or that.

With containment war did come—not an all-out shooting war, but a *Cold War*, a chronic state mobilization and hostility.

National Security

After World War I, the American armed forces rushed to demobilize, to stand down, to return (as presidential candidate Warren G. Harding had said) "to normalcy." While a return to civilian life likewise followed World War II, the armed forces remained large, and the peacetime draft remained in place. America was perpetually prepared for a new war.

In 1947, Congress passed a National Security Act, which reorganized the War Department into the Department of Defense. The new name sounded more pacific, yet it really reflected a perception that war preparedness was no longer an exceptional situation, but a full-time necessity.

Talk of the Times

Containment was the United States foreign policy during the *Cold War* years, calling for confronting the Soviet Union whenever and wherever it attempted to expand its ideological influence. Coined in 1947 by journalist Herbert Bayard Swope in a speech he wrote for financier Bernard Baruch, **Cold War** refers to the postwar strategic and political struggle between the United States (and its western European allies) and the Soviet Union (and communist countries).

The 1947 act also created the Central Intelligence Agency. Perhaps the most controversial federal agency ever established, the CIA's mission was covert intelligence gathering, which meant that it sometimes functioned with neither executive nor legislative knowledge, let alone approval. In the name of fighting communism, the National Security Act created the closest thing to a secret police force—hallmark of all oppressive eastern European regimes—this nation ever had.

Marshall's Plan

If the Cold War brought anxiety, the perpetual sharpening of sabers, and the creation of a shadowy intelligence agency, it also occasioned what Winston Churchill described as the "most unsordid political act in history."

In January 1947, President Truman appointed George C. Marshall, World War II chief of staff of the U.S. Army, as secretary of state. A brilliant military strategist and administrator, Marshall was also to prove himself farsighted in his humanity. In a commencement address delivered on June 5, 1947, at Harvard University, Marshall announced a plan to help Europe recover from the devastation of the war by restoring "normal economic health in the world, without which there can be no political stability and no assured peace."

The Marshall Plan, as it was soon dubbed, was humanitarian as well as political. Although Marshall attempted to assuage Soviet fears by stating that the policy was not aimed "against any country or doctrine but against hunger, poverty, desperation, and chaos," the Marshall Plan was a peaceful effort to contain communism, not only by enlarging the American sphere of influence in Europe, but by ameliorating the kind of desperate economic conditions in which totalitarian leaders thrive.

George C. Marshall, photographed during World War II, when he was Army chief of staff. (Image from the National Archives)

Great Britain and France oversaw the creation of a Committee for European Economic Cooperation, made up of delegates from 16 nations. The committee officially requested $22.4 billion from the United States. Congress appropriated more than $13 billion and also created a Displaced Persons Plan, through which nearly 300,000 Europeans, including many survivors of the Holocaust, became American citizens.

With the aid of the Marshall Plan, Western Europe struggled back to its feet, forming new alliances with the United States and laying the foundation for a grand military alliance, NATO, the North Atlantic Treaty Organization, created in April 1949.

Berlin Boxed In

With Eastern Europe fallen to the communists, on June 7, 1948, the Western nations announced their determination to save the Western-occupied zones of Germany. They would do nothing less than create a new nation, West Germany. Two weeks after this announcement, the Soviets blockaded West Berlin, arguing that Berlin, located deep within Soviet-occupied East Germany, could not serve as the capital of West Germany.

Believing that the loss of West Berlin would ultimately mean the loss of all of Germany, President Truman ordered an airlift. The Soviets could blockade roads and rails, but not the sky. So, over most of the next year, some 321 days, the Allies made more than 272,000 flights over Soviet-occupied territory to provide West Berlin with thousands of tons of supplies each day.

It was a bold gamble. Failure would have meant a Soviet triumph. And failure was a distinct possibility. The planes were flying round the clock in all weather, over potentially hostile territory. No city had ever been supplied exclusively from the air before. Yet, on May 12, 1949, the Soviets at last conceded that the blockade had failed, and they reopened Berlin to Western traffic. East and West Germany were formally created as separate nations later in the month.

The Soviet Bomb

The successful outcome of the Berlin Airlift was just about the only good international news for Americans. On September 23, 1949, President Truman came before the American people to announce that the Soviets had detonated their first atomic bomb, which U.S. intelligence designated "Joe 12." The shock was that the Soviet weapons breakthrough had come so soon. The mystery was explained in February 1950, when Washington learned that, for seven years, the Soviets had been receiving atomic secrets from Klaus Fuchs, one of the most trusted scientists on the Manhattan Project team.

Talk of the Times

Mutual deterrence describes the assumption that the possession of nuclear weapons by ideologically opposed states will prevent war, because each nation understands that such war would ultimately be self-destructive. This is related to the doctrine of **mutually assured destruction**, "MAD," the understanding that a nation's use of nuclear weapons will be met with nuclear retaliation, thereby assuring the destruction of both nations—and, presumably, most of civilization.

News of the Soviet bomb had at least three effects on America. First came fear. The prospect of a nuclear Third World War became all too real. The second effect was to spur development of another device, which American scientists such as the Hungarian-born Edward Teller referred to as "the Super," but which was soon known as the hydrogen bomb or "H-bomb."

Whereas an atomic explosion could be measured in *kilotons* (one kiloton is the equivalent of an explosion of 1,000 tons of TNT), the H-bomb bomb would yield forces measurable as megatons—millions of tons of TNT. The explosion of an atom bomb is created by nuclear fission, the splitting apart of an atomic nucleus. The far greater explosion of a hydrogen bomb is creation by nuclear fusion, the instantaneous joining together of subatomic particles.

While some scientists, including Manhattan Project director J. Robert Oppenheimer, objected to developing the H-bomb, President Truman announced, on January 31, 1950, that he favored developing the weapon. When Oppenheimer continued to voice reservations, he was subjected to government surveillance and was ultimately declared a security risk. The H-bomb program went on without him, and, on November 1, 1952, the first hydrogen bomb—code-named Mike—was detonated at remote Eniwetok atoll in the Pacific. The test was so secret that it wasn't announced to the public for almost two years.

But Americans had precious few months to savor their monopoly on thermonuclear—hydrogen—weapons. On November 23, 1955, the Soviets detonated *their* first H-bomb, igniting a thermonuclear arms race, which soon included France and China as well as the United States and USSR.

From the mid 1950s until the collapse of the Soviet Union in the early 1990s, the U.S. and the USSR spent untold billions on stockpiles of doomsday weaponry, devices capable of wiping out all life on earth many, many times over. It was all part of a kind of thermonuclear suicide pact called *mutual deterrence*. The idea is that if the world's two great ideological antagonists each possessed the capability of destroying civilization itself, neither side would be the first to use this capability. Sometimes the concept was referred to as *mutually assured destruction*, the all-too-telling acronym for which is MAD.

China Goes Red

People became accustomed to dividing the world between two *superpowers*, the Soviet Union and the United States. But another mighty power had entered the world stage. After a century of political turmoil (take a look at Chapter 8, "The World Reshaped"), China was finally unified under a single government. Mao Tse-tung, having defeated the forces of Western-allied Chiang Kai-shek, proclaimed the People's Republic of China in October 1949. The most populous nation on earth was now a communist force to be reckoned with.

The Least You Need to Know

➤ The spread of communism following World War II created a perpetual state of hostility between the Western powers and the Soviet bloc called the Cold War.

➤ The United Nations grew from the World War II anti–Nazi alliance into an organization designed to arbitrate disputes and maintain world peace.

➤ Driven by advances made during World War II, science and technology developed prodigiously and profoundly during the immediate postwar years.

➤ Two important "new" nations emerged shortly after World War II: Israel, the first Jewish homeland since biblical days, and the People's Republic of China, which made the world's most populous nation communist.

Part 5
American Dreams: 1950–1969

In Chapters 19 and 20, we enter the strange world of the 1950s. Americans lived under the cloud of nuclear weapons and under the shadow of an expanding communist bloc. Organized crime and the Korean War were early blights on the decade, then came the communist witch hunts of Senator Joseph McCarthy, but, for many white, middle-class Americans, it was the emergence of the black civil rights movement that was even more disturbing. And then there were the kids! Never before had parents felt so distant from their own children, these rebels without a cause.

At the same time, there were more jobs and more money than ever before, and it was very reassuring to come home each evening, open the gate of the white picket fence, and settle into a menu of wholesome television shows. With a benignly smiling Ike Eisenhower in the White House, most Americans felt richer, safer, and more self-satisfied than anyone could remember.

By way of interstate highways, Sputnik, Elvis Presley, Betty Friedan, and John Fitzgerald Kennedy, Chapters 21 through 23 take us out of the complacent '50s and into the turbulent '60s. There the journey continues through civil rights, Vietnam, the making of a counterculture, a trip to the moon, and a celebration called Woodstock.

Chapter 19

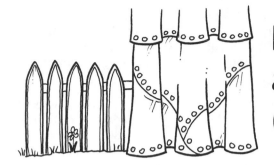

Picket Fence and Iron Curtain (1950–1954)

In This Chapter

➤ Anxiety and bliss in the 1950s

➤ A decade of prosperity, consumerism, and credit

➤ Religious revivalism

➤ Conspiracies: communism and organized crime

➤ The Korean War

➤ The Rosenberg affair

➤ Cold War battle lines harden

The 1950s are generally recalled as a time of prosperity, economic growth, and well-being—an age of innocence. That the 1950s summon up images of suburban bliss is no accident. The decade saw an explosion in the growth of tract housing just a car ride away from the big city. These new "suburbs" were an expression of the American dream, vintage 1950: snug little houses on clean, green, little plots of land, enclosed by white picket fences.

Never mind that the world beyond those fences was frightening and dangerous. Although the British poet W.H. Auden called the postwar decade the "Age of Anxiety," for most Americans it was more like an Age of Contentment. The white picket fence seemed stronger than the Iron Curtain—and, as for the Bomb, well, most people just tried not to think about it.

The Year 1950

Americans with an international perspective found plenty to be worried or depressed about in 1950. The Chinese had become communists, and communism was spreading throughout many of the nations Americans had fought, bled, and died to rescue from Nazi oppression. The Soviets had an atomic bomb, so that war, if it came again, might well destroy everything and everybody.

But few Americans took an international perspective. Instead, they confined their gaze to what immediately surrounded them. And what they saw was a high rate of employment, the expansion of business, and a general air of prosperity. Those tract houses springing up outside of the cities might have all looked pretty much the same, but they were shiny and new and clean, as were the postwar automobiles essential for getting to and from the new communities.

Charge It, Please

In fact, Americans didn't even have to look around to feel good: They could just look at themselves. With an end to wartime rationing came an outpouring of consumer goods of every description, and Americans had the money as well as the mobility to consume those goods.

One innovation that made it particularly easy to consume was introduced in February 1950 by Frank X. McNamara. He ran a modest New York loan company, and it one day occurred to him that department-store credit cards (*charge plates*, they were called), which virtually disappeared during the Depression, when a lot of people stopped paying their bills, had returned with a vengeance. McNamara then noticed something else. One of his regular loan customers had a great many department-store charge plates. This fellow would lend them to friends, whom he would charge for the privilege of using his cards. Then he would borrow from McNamara to pay off the outstanding debt. The profit was his to keep.

It was a dandy scheme—until one of the users proved to be a deadbeat, leaving McNamara's customer unable to pay for a loan. McNamara was lunching with his lawyer, Ralph Schneider, discussing debt-collection options, when it suddenly occurred to him: Why lend a bunch of credit cards to people? Why not create a *single* card that could be used in a bunch of places—then market that card to users for a fee?

Perhaps because the idea had been born over lunch, McNamara and Schneider decided to start by dealing exclusively with restaurants. The two pooled their personal nest eggs and opened an office in the Empire State Building. They called their new enterprise the

Talk of the Times

Charge plate was the term for what is now called a credit card. Early in the 20th century, many department stores issued metal plates stamped with the customer's name. These were used to imprint vouchers for items bought on credit. The name "charge plate" remained in common usage long after the metal plates had been replaced by plastic cards.

Diners Club, and that first year, they signed up 22 New York City restaurants and a hotel—and they took a $58,000 loss on their initial $40,000 investment. But the next year yielded a $60,000 profit on business of $6 million, and things only got better from then on.

By 1958, Diners Club was so successful that American Express entered the business, soon followed by Carte Blanche. By the mid 1960s, the idea of "master credit cards" caught on really big, as banks across the nation began first issuing their own cards, then pooling their credit resources into national networks, the first and best-known of which was Master Charge in 1967.

The availability of easy, instant credit not only fueled a business boom in the 1950s and 1960s, it changed forever certain core American values, which were at least as old as Benjamin Franklin's sage advice about a penny saved being a penny earned. To be sure, credit cards raised the general standard of living for most Americans, but they also tended to raise expectations beyond the economic ability of many to fulfill them.

There was never a shortage of moralists to issue dire warnings about materialism and about how universal credit created a dangerous live-for-today attitude. Yet, in reality, the credit card tended to fix our collective gaze on the future. Americans piled up debt in the faith that their future circumstances—a raise, a promotion, a new and better job—would enable them to pay it all off. It was an expression of the American dream stamped onto a plastic card.

Century Stats

Today, the average American household has eight credit cards, many charging interest rates only underworld loan sharks used to dream of, 22 percent and even more.

Religion Writ Larger

In the midst of a credit-borne upswelling of materialism, a new spiritualism emerged in 1950s, when William Franklin "Billy" Graham Jr., a Baptist preacher, founded the Billy Graham Evangelistic Association.

It is tempting to look back at the 20th century as a period of all-consuming industrial, technological, and scientific advancement punctuated by horrific seizures of all-consuming world violence. But this ignores an urge that has characterized the century just as surely as science and technology have. America has a strong tradition of emotional, individually focused religious inspiration. In 1734, for example, the fire-and-brimstone sermons of the great Jonathan Edwards sparked a religious fervor from Maine to Georgia known as the Great Awakening, and similar movements resurfaced throughout the 19th century. Then, at the beginning of the 20th century, William Ashley "Billy" Sunday, a onetime professional baseball player, made a sensation as an itinerant *evangelist*, preaching at tent-show "revivals" all across the nation and even via national radio broadcasts.

During the hard times of the 1930s, a host of Billy Sunday wanna-bes appeared, many of them no better than con men, preying upon the religious hunger of the masses to swindle tent-revival audiences out of hard-to-come-by money. With this new wave of bad preachers, evangelism fell into disrepute.

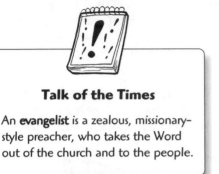

Talk of the Times

An **evangelist** is a zealous, missionary-style preacher, who takes the Word out of the church and to the people.

Then came Billy Graham. Born in Charlotte, North Carolina, on November 7, 1918, Graham was graduated from Wheaton College in Illinois in 1943 and became pastor of the First Baptist Church of Western Springs, Illinois, as well as a leader in the national Youth for Christ movement. In 1947, he put together a traveling revival team in the style of Billy Sunday. The break-through for Graham and this group came two years later, when several Hollywood celebrities came to him to convert to Christianity after Graham appeared in Los Angeles. With heightened visibility, Graham founded the Billy Graham Evangelistic Association in 1950.

Many religious leaders respected Graham, others were less certain; however, all marveled at Graham's genius in using the modern media, especially radio and television, to spread the Word. Graham became the best-known religious leader in the nation and was so universally admired that, in 1969, Richard M. Nixon asked him to offer a prayer at his inauguration. Subsequently, Graham served Nixon informally as a spiritual advisor and presided over the former president's funeral in 1994.

Witch Hunter from Wisconsin

However one may feel about Billy Graham, his methods, and his message, it cannot be denied that he fed a spiritual hunger in postwar America. To his great credit, he accomplished this without ever crossing the thin line separating spiritual appeal from an appeal to fear and prejudice, the emotions that are the stock in trade of the demagogue.

The same cannot be said for Joseph R. McCarthy. In 1950, he was a lackluster senator from Wisconsin in search of an issue that would put him in the spotlight. On February 9, 1950, he addressed the Women's Republican Club of Wheeling, West Virginia. He held up a sheet of paper and declared that he had in his hand a list of 205 card-carrying communists in the United States State Department. McCarthy had found his issue. The eyes of the nation turned suddenly upon him.

That no one actually saw the "list" McCarthy held up hardly mattered. In the anxious atmosphere of the Cold War, people were ready to believe that communists had infiltrated government—indeed, virtually all activities—at every level. For the next four years, McCarthy and a host of hangers-on, all looking to make political hay from the issue of communism, recklessly exploited the nation's fears.

The fact is that communist spies *were* present in various government and military agencies. But McCarthy didn't bother to undertake a serious investigation. Instead, he took every opportunity to make scatter-gun accusations, heedless of how many innocent lives his unproven accusations scarred. It was a *witch hunt*.

Typical targets of McCarthy were the likes of Owen Lattimore, a China expert and professor at Johns Hopkins University, and John S. Service of the State Department. At Senate hearings chaired by Millard Tydings of Maryland, no evidence was offered to support McCarthy's accusations that these men were communist spies, yet the accusations themselves were enough to destroy their careers and reputations as well as those of others.

Gaining the chairmanship of the Senate Subcommittee on Governmental Operations, McCarthy launched investigations of the Voice of America (an international radio service broadcasting especially to Iron Curtain countries) and the U.S. Army Signal Corps. McCarthy even accused George C. Marshall of being "soft on communism." It was, of course, the Marshall Plan that had done so much to counteract the spread of communism.

Talk of the Times

Witch hunt was the term derisively applied to the reckless investigation of communist infiltration in American government and industry led by Senator Joseph McCarthy from 1950 to 1954. In 1953, the playwright Arthur Miller wrote *The Crucible*, ostensibly about the witch trials in 17th-century Salem, Massachusetts, but really a devastatingly effective allegory criticizing the witch hunts of his own time.

Senator Joseph P. McCarthy (right). His young (and forever unrepentant) assistant Roy Cohn is in shirt sleeves, at the center of the picture. (Image from the Library of Congress)

Always in search of high-profile targets, McCarthy and his aides, most notably a young, ruthlessly opportunistic lawyer named Roy Cohn, launched investigations of prominent celebrities, including Hollywood stars, writers, and producers. The Hollywood witch hunt and similar campaigns against individuals in other industries were especially destructive. Accused individuals were *blacklisted*, which effectively put them off-limits to employers, investors, customers, clients, and business partners.

Talk of the Times

The word **blacklist** functioned both as a noun and a verb to describe the roster of those accused of Communist affiliation during the McCarthy era. Black-listed individuals were, in effect, off limits to employers—unemployable.

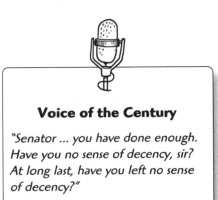

Voice of the Century

"Senator ... you have done enough. Have you no sense of decency, sir? At long last, have you left no sense of decency?"

—Joseph N. Welch, counsel for the U.S. Army, to Joseph McCarthy at the Army-McCarthy Hearings, 1954

Demagoguery is always a danger of democracy, but true democracy also is self-correcting. Given time, McCarthy took enough rope to hang himself. It was one thing to attack the government when the opposition party, the Democrats, were in control of the White House. But even after Republican Dwight D. Eisenhower was elected in 1952, along with a Republican majority in Congress, McCarthy continued the attacks. At last, in the spring of 1954, he accused the entire U.S. Army of being infested with communists. These wild accusations prompted Eisenhower, a man who had dedicated his life to the Army and served as supreme Allied commander during World War II, to launch his own investigation—of Joseph P. McCarthy.

Ike discovered that McCarthy had tried to coerce Army officials into granting preferred treatment for a former aide, Private G. David Schine. In light of this information, Eisenhower encouraged Congress to form a committee to investigate McCarthy's machinations. The so-called "Army-McCarthy" hearings were televised between April and June 1954, and they riveted the attention of the American public.

Here was television at its best, as a medium that could instantaneously transmit fact. For the first time, the mass of Americans saw McCarthy for what he was: a blowhard, a bully, and a very dangerous man.

Following the hearings, McCarthy was officially censured on December 2, 1954 by senatorial colleagues who no longer had any reason to fear a man publicly disgraced. Now largely ignored by Senate and public alike, McCarthy retreated into obscurity and heavy drinking. He died in 1957, at age 49.

Organized Crime

The Senate did not confine its hunting to expeditions targeting communists. In 1950 and 1951, Tennessee Democrat Estes Kefauver, chairman of the Senate Subcommittee to Investigate Crime in Interstate Commerce, began looking into the dealings of urban gangsters. As Senator McCarthy claimed to have uncovered a vast communist conspiracy in American government and industry, Senator Kefauver announced the discovery of a vast underworld conspiracy of organized criminals who cost the nation billions of dollars each year, corrupted government in almost every section of the country, and reached into the highest ranks of American society.

As Chapter 11, "Jazz Age," explained, large-scale criminal activity was loosely organized into a "syndicate" at a 1929 "conference" called by underworld kingpins Charles "Lucky" Luciano and Meyer Lansky. The underpinnings of the syndicate included elements of the old Mafia imported from Sicily, but Luciano and Lansky purposely designed the syndicate to be more businesslike, eschewing the intense "family" ties of the Mafia. Luciano and Lansky were vicious criminals, to be sure, but they wanted to avoid the kind of vendetta and vengeance that characterized the Mafia. Such mayhem, after all, added nothing to the bottom line.

Although the syndicate was never really run like a legitimate corporation, it did provide a forum for underworld bosses to get together and hammer out grievances before resorting to their guns. The gangsters were even bold enough to hold national conferences from time to time. The 1946 convocation in Havana included entertainment from no less than Frank Sinatra. In the wake of the Kefauver hearings, the syndicate couldn't afford to be quite so flamboyant. The so-called Appalachian Convention in 1956 was raided by New York State police.

Through the years, FBI director J. Edgar Hoover dismissed the notion of organized crime and directed the bureau's efforts to hunting down the bank robbers and deviant killers whose crimes were spectacular enough to merit their inclusion on Hoover's own "Public Enemies" list. But Kefauver was quickly convinced that organized crime was very real. The Senate hearings traveled from city to city, exposing local corruption from New York to New Orleans, from Chicago to Los Angeles. The hearings were widely reported and even televised, so that Americans saw not only minor hoods and major mobsters but crooked policemen, mayors, and even governors who had been bought by the mob.

Faced with an abundance of now very public evidence, Hoover, by the end of the decade, at last led the FBI into an all-out war against the organized underworld. The crime figures Kefauver brought before his committee repeatedly "took the Fifth," asserting the protection from self-incrimination guaranteed by the Fifth Amendment to the Constitution. By the 1960s, however, a federal witness-protection program was established, which shielded mob "snitches" from mob reprisals. The result was a growing body of testimony that revealed the hand of the Mob—sometimes called the Mafia or Cosa Nostra—in city governments, police forces, labor unions, and even in many "legitimate" industries.

"Police Action"

As the nation finally began to police organized crime, the phrase *police action* took on an entirely different meaning. It was the official description of United States military action in the divided nation of Korea. Official or not, however, it was wholly inadequate to describe what was actually under way there: a major war—barely five years after the conclusion of World War II.

The 38th Parallel

One of the many loose ends left by World War II was the "temporary" division of the nation of Korea along the 38th parallel into a communist North Korea and a democratic South Korea. This expedient enabled the Allies to proceed with disarming Korea's Japanese invaders. Following the war, the United Nations tried in vain to reunite the divided country. Then, on June 25, 1950, suddenly and without warning, North Korean troops crossed the 38th parallel and invaded South Korea. Within two months, the North Koreans had pushed south almost to the tip of the Korean peninsula, where South Korean defenses were established around Pusan.

Voice of the Century

"We shall land at Inchon, and I shall crush them."

—General Douglas MacArthur to the Joint Chiefs of Staff, August 29, 1950

Voice of the Century

"I still remember the refrain of one of the most popular barrack ballads [of the turn of the century], which proclaimed most proudly that 'Old soldiers never die, they just fade away.' And like the old soldier of that ballad, I now close my military career and just fade away—an old soldier who tried to do his duty as God gave him the light to see that duty. Goodbye."

—Douglas MacArthur, speech to Congress, April 19, 1951

Inchon Assault

The communist invasion of South Korea was a critical test of the Truman Doctrine and the policy of containment; however, the United States did not act alone, but worked through the United Nations, securing a resolution to enforce the 38th parallel. General Douglas MacArthur, architect of the campaign against Japan in World War II, was given command of U.N. forces (the bulk of which were American) in Korea and planned and executed perhaps the most brilliant amphibious landing in military history. U.N. troops landed *behind* enemy lines at the west-coast port of Inchon on September 15, 1950, and swiftly cut North Korean supply lines. This accomplished, MacArthur seized the offensive and drove the invaders not only out of South Korea, but, by November 24, 1950, all the way to the Yalu River, the border with China.

China Joins In

MacArthur's plan was to lead U.N. forces in two massive columns on either side of the mountains that run down the Korean peninsula like a spine. This assault would forcibly reunite Korea under southern—democratic—control.

What MacArthur had not counted on was the intervention of the Communist Chinese. On November 26, 1950, a large Chinese army invaded the north and, with the North Koreans, pushed U.N. forces south. By January 1, 1951, the North Korean-Chinese army of nearly half a million men had driven 365,000 U.N. troops back to the 38th parallel. The communist offensive continued, culminating in the capture of the South Korean capital of Seoul. A United Nations counteroffensive retook the city on March 14, 1951, and rancorous negotiations began as the fighting continued in a bloody stalemate.

In defiance of U.S. and U.N. orders, a frustrated MacArthur publicly advocated attacking and bombing Chinese bases in Manchuria, even at the risk of enlarging the war and possibly bringing China's ally, the nuclear-armed Soviet Union, into the fray.

Old Soldiers

President Harry S Truman responded uncompromisingly to MacArthur's insubordination. On April 11, 1951, he summarily relieved MacArthur of command of U.N. and U.S. forces. The president replaced MacArthur with the very able Matthew B. Ridgway, and MacArthur resigned from the Army with a moving, if grandiloquent, speech before Congress on April 19, 1951.

From the perspective of historical hindsight, this action has been called the most courageous of Truman's presidency. At the time, the dismissal of the popular war hero, hailed by many as the "American Caesar," seemed the most stunningly unpopular act of a president conspicuous for unpopular acts. More than one newspaper quipped, "to err is Truman."

Voice of the Century

"I fired [MacArthur] because he wouldn't respect the authority of the President.... I didn't fire him because he was a dumb son of a bitch, although he was, but that's not against the law for generals. If it was, half to three quarters of them would be in jail."

—Harry S Truman, quoted in Merle Miller's *Plain Speaking: An Oral Biography of Harry S Truman,* 1974

A 1944 photograph of Harry S Truman (right) with a tired, ailing Franklin Roosevelt. (Image from arttoday.com)

From Heartbreak Ridge to Pork Chop Hill

The fighting continued to be concentrated near the 38th parallel, especially in regions nicknamed the "Iron Triangle" and the "Punch Bowl," just north of the line.

The armies fought not over great cities, but for nondescript geographical features, on which the GIs bestowed such names as Bloody Ridge and Heartbreak Ridge. In September and October 1951, the U.N. secured Heartbreak Ridge at great cost, affording a strong defensive position.

Century Stats

The United States poured 1.8 million troops into Korea, of whom 54,200 were killed and 103,300 wounded. Another 8,200 were classified as missing in action.

From positions such as this, the United States and U.N. troops continued to fight, until Pork Chop Hill was won after a particularly bloody battle in April 1953. Once this objective was attained, the communists were driven back significantly, a fact that finally brought about an armistice on July 27, 1953.

The truce satisfied no one, but the shooting did stop. As for Korea, it was left divided at the 38th parallel, which remains a heavily armed borderland.

Soldiers of the U.S. Eighth Army at the Battle of Pork Chop Hill, 1953. (Image from arttoday.com)

In Korea, the Cold War had turned hot, but, like the Cold War itself, Korea had failed to prove decisive. The mission of "containing" communism had been accomplished insofar as the communists had been held above the 38th parallel. But there was no real victory. President Truman explained in his 1956 memoirs that "what we faced in Korea was the ominous threat of a third world war," and he did not want to drag China and possibly the Soviet Union into the conflict. Thus, he purposely limited the scope and objectives of the war.

Limited warfare would become a catchphrase of the 20th century in its second half, as the mission of containing communism became a matter of fighting wars in which full-scale victory was too risky, since it might trigger a nuclear Armageddon that would end life on earth.

Talk of the Times

Limited warfare is war strictly confined in order to avoid creating a larger (probably nuclear) conflict.

A World More Dangerous

Truman chose not to run for reelection in 1952. Illinois governor Adlai E. Stevenson was the nominee of the Democratic Party, which, made unpopular in large part because of the bitterness and frustration of the Korean War, lost the White House to Dwight David Eisenhower.

Eisenhower, who had been supreme Allied commander in Europe during World War II, a man whose good sense and winning personality had kept a very difficult coalition together through the war, projected a startlingly different image from Truman. Where Truman was contentious and outspoken, Eisenhower was smiling and conciliatory. Campaigning in support of Truman in 1948, people had cheered, "Give 'em hell, Harry." Eisenhower's leading campaign slogan in 1952 was "I Like Ike."

Some recent historians have criticized the Eisenhower administration as too easy-going, even complaisant. Yet, in a world of tenuous, frustrating conflict and terrifying politics always under the nuclear shadow, perhaps it was just such a benign president the nation needed. Certainly, Eisenhower was the president the nation wanted.

Mom and Pop Spies

Americans had been stunned in 1949 by the announcement that the Soviets had test fired an atomic bomb (Chapter 18, "A War Served Cold"). Loss of the U.S. nuclear monopoly spurred development of the much more powerful hydrogen (or thermo-nuclear) bomb, which was successfully tested at Eniwetok atoll in the Pacific on November 1, 1952. But less than a year later, on August 12, 1953, the USSR tested its own hydrogen bomb. Just as American scientists and politicians had puzzled over how the USSR could develop an atomic bomb as quickly as it had, so they now were left to wonder how the Soviet hydrogen bomb had been so soon in coming.

They did not have to wonder long. In 1950, the German-born British physicist Klaus Fuchs was arrested, tried, and convicted of having passed atomic bomb secrets to the Soviets. This led to investigations that uncovered espionage in both the U.S. atomic and hydrogen bomb programs.

Among the people Fuchs implicated during interrogation was Harry Gold, an American chemist who had been fed secrets by David Greenglass, a soldier stationed near the weapons laboratory at Los Alamos, New Mexico. Arrested and interrogated, Greenglass claimed that his brother-in-law, Julius Rosenberg, a machine-shop owner with ties to the Communist Party, had been the go-between who mediated the exchanges with Gold.

On July 17, 1950, federal agents arrested Rosenberg and his wife, Ethel. The Rosenbergs were a working-class Jewish couple, with two children. They were the "folks next door," and hardly fit anyone's image of a Soviet spy. The Rosenbergs did not deny their history of communist affiliation, but they pleaded not guilty to charges of espionage. Their trial deeply divided the nation. Some Americans were grateful that dangerous traitors were brought to justice. Others, however, believed that the prosecution of the Rosenbergs was motivated more by anti-Semitism and anti-communist hysteria than by genuine motives of national security.

Many believed that the Rosenbergs were being framed, and their cause became as central to American liberalism as that of Sacco and Vanzetti had been in the 1920s (Chapter 12, "Victims and Heroes"). Certainly, the testimony of David Greenglass was self-serving. His cooperation with government prosecutors bought him the comparatively light sentence of 15 years' imprisonment (of which he served 10); however, the evidence does point to Julius Rosenberg's involvement in at least some degree of espionage. Found guilty, the Rosenbergs heard the sentence of Judge Irving Kaufman: death, in the electric chair.

Century Stats

Following the United States and the Soviet Union, the United Kingdom successfully tested a hydrogen bomb in 1957, China in 1967, and France in 1968. By the late 1980s, some 40,000 thermonuclear devices were stockpiled in the arsenals of the world's nuclear–armed nations. Following the end of the Cold War in the 1990s, this number declined, but the nations of the world still possess enough nuclear and thermo–nuclear weaponry to destroy civilization many, many times over.

During an appeal process that stretched into 1953, newsreels followed the couple's children on their visits to prison, and even people who believed the Rosenbergs guilty protested the execution of two parents.

The Supreme Court refused to overturn the conviction, but, at the last minute, in June 1953, Justice William O. Douglas granted a stay of execution on the grounds that Judge Kaufman may have lacked the authority to impose a death sentence. In a special session, the Supreme Court decided, in a 6 to 3 vote, to permit the execution. The couple was put to death on June 19.

For many Americans, the fate of the Rosenbergs made the Cold War world seem that much bleaker. On the one hand, this humble, homely couple may have put the entire world in peril. On the other hand, the United States of America, in the name of liberty, democracy, and justice, had electrocuted the parents of two young boys.

NATO and SEATO

The execution of the Rosenbergs created a bitterness that went beyond the judicial orphaning of two children. Many Americans saw the trial and execution as an impotent gesture in a losing war against the forces of communist world domination. The fact is, however, that the United States was leading what the West liked to call the Free World in creating twin alliances against the spread of communism.

The first was the North Atlantic Treaty Organization, NATO, which was established pursuant to the North Atlantic Treaty, signed on April 4, 1949. It was a grand military alliance for the collective defense of Europe in opposition to Communist forces. Belgium, Canada, Denmark, France, West Germany, Greece, Iceland, Italy, Luxembourg, the Netherlands, Norway, Portugal, Spain, Turkey, the United Kingdom, and the United States were all charter or early members, and in 1999, Poland, the Czech Republic, and Hungary, all formerly Iron Curtain countries, joined what many have proclaimed the most successful military alliance in history.

The Soviet Union responded to NATO in 1955 with the Warsaw Treaty of Friendship, Cooperation, and Mutual Assistance, popularly called the Warsaw Pact, an alliance between the USSR and what must be called its puppet states, Albania (which would withdraw in 1968), Bulgaria, Czechoslovakia, East Germany (withdrew in 1990), Hungary, Poland, and Romania.

In Asia, SEATO, the Southeast Asia Treaty Organization, was formed in 1955 (pursuant to a treaty concluded the year before) on the model of NATO. It was an alliance of Australia, France (which partially suspended support in 1975), New Zealand, Pakistan (which would withdraw in 1968), the Philippines, Thailand, the United Kingdom, and the United States to counteract communist military aggression in Korea and Indochina, as well as communist-sponsored subversion in Malaysia and the Philippines. (SEATO disbanded in 1977.)

NATO and SEATO formally drew the military and ideological battle lines that would define world affairs through all but the final decade of the century. These organizations crystallized the great division between communism and democracy, and they made it difficult for any nation to see itself in isolation from one side or the other.

The Least You Need to Know

➤ Viewed from an international perspective, the early 1950s were a time of great peril, yet, from the perspective of most Americans, they were regarded as a time of prosperity and well-being.

➤ The early '50s—tense, war-torn, and driven by technology and consumerism— also spawned an era of religious revivalism led by the evangelist Billy Graham.

➤ During the early 1950s, the Senate publicly investigated two perceived national conspiracies: infiltration of government and industry by communists and by "organized crime."

➤ The Korean War was a costly, indecisive conflict born of the Truman Doctrine and the U.S. policy of "containing" communism.

Chapter 20

MarTin
LuTher
King
Jr.

The Back of the Bus (1954–1963)

In This Chapter

➤ Growth of racial discrimination after the Civil War

➤ The Jim Crow South and the ghetto North

➤ The fight over the "separate but equal" doctrine

➤ A first step: the armed forces are integrated

➤ School desegregation

➤ The civil rights movement in full swing

➤ "I have a dream"

By the mid 1950s, there were still plenty of Americans who longed for the "good old days" of "America first"—a time before the United States shouldered the responsibility for "making the world safe for democracy" or serving as the "arsenal of democracy" or rescuing Europe with the Marshall Plan or "containing communism" in Berlin and Korea. But the reality was that isolationism, as government policy, was dead.

The more profound reality was that the United States had never been truly isolated. Ever since the American Revolution, the world had turned its eyes to America, that country Abraham Lincoln called humankind's "last best hope." Looking at a burned-out Europe—overshadowed by Mussolini, Hitler, burdened by its refugees; and haunted by its death camps—Americans could appreciate their nation's unique position as the sweet land of liberty and justice for all.

Well, not quite for all.

Focusing on the United States, this chapter looks at civil rights in the 20th century.

A Dream Deferred

In the middle of the bloodiest war Americans had fought to that time, Abraham Lincoln dedicated a military cemetery with a speech beginning, "Four score and seven years ago...." In those years the country had been an experiment in liberty fatally flawed by its inclusion of nothing less than the negation of liberty: slavery. The Civil War was the explosive result of that flaw.

Century Stats

Racism in the South was more than a matter of discrimination and segregation. Between 1882 and 1951, 4,730 persons were lynched in the United States, of whom 1,293 were white and 3,437 were black—almost all of the latter in the South.

Voice of the Century

"Segregation is not humiliating, but a benefit, and ought to be so regarded by you gentlemen."

—Woodrow Wilson, speech to a group of African-American leaders, 1913

The Civil War brought an end to slavery, and Congress, in the years following Appomattox, sought to hasten the transition of African Americans from slaves to citizens. Tragically, the motives of Congress, controlled by Radical Republicans bent on punishing the South and keeping the Southern Democrats out of their legislative seats as long as possible, were not exclusively focused on the welfare of the "freedmen." Reconstruction legislation brought bitterness and, if anything, deepened the racial divide in the South, fostering the creation of the Ku Klux Klan and other white, racially motivated shadow authorities and vigilante bands.

In 1876, after enduring more than a decade of Reconstruction hardships and outright abuse, the electorate of the South gave Democratic presidential candidate Samuel J. Tilden a narrow majority of the popular vote over Republican Rutherford B. Hayes. In response, the Republicans reversed the electoral vote tally in three Southern states whose governments they still controlled under the provisions of Reconstruction. The stolen election was thus thrown into dispute until both sides agreed to send the results of the election to a special commission.

In the meantime, behind the scenes, a deal was being hammered out. In return for the White House, Republican Hayes promised the Southern Democrats that he would withdraw the federal troops currently enforcing Reconstruction. The commission put Hayes into office, the troops were withdrawn from the South, and, for better and for worse, Reconstruction came to an end.

"IN SELF-DEFENSE."
Southern Chiv. "Ef I hadn't-er killed you, you would hev growed up to rule me."

A Northern view of Southern racism as expressed in a political cartoon from the 1870s. "Ef I had'nt-er killed you," the caption runs, "you would hev growed up to rule me."
(Image from arttoday.com)

Old Jim Crow

The "better" part of Reconstruction's end was the return of the South to civilian government. The "worse" part was the opportunity this gave for Southern state governments to sanction and institutionalize racism. Southern states enacted *Jim Crow laws,* which were aimed at enforcing the strict segregation of blacks and whites. Jim Crow laws included the segregation of public spaces such as bus stations, public accommodations, and movie theaters, and they included restrictions on suffrage such as poll taxes, literacy tests, and the *grandfather* clause, which exempted those whose grandfathers had been free (in the early part of the century, such persons were exclusively white) from meeting the new requirements.

Southerners claimed that their laws provided "separate but equal" service to blacks and whites in all publicly funded areas, such as public schools.

Such services and facilities were certainly separate, they were hardly equal. Facilities provided for blacks were manifestly inferior to those provided for whites, and African Americans were treated as

Talk of the Times

Jim Crow laws were enacted in the South to enforce the discrimination against and suppression of African Americans. The name derived from a derogatory name for a black person. **The grandfather clause** was a provision in many Southern state constitutions exempting from poll taxes, literacy tests, and other qualifications for suffrage those whose grandfathers had been free.

an underclass, and, what is worse, treated this way as a matter of law. Moreover, segregation was enforced beyond publicly funded services and facilities. All public facilities, including nongovernmental, commercial enterprises, such as lunch counters and train and bus waiting rooms, were strictly divided into areas for "colored" and "white."

The Jim Crow separate-but-equal fiction endured in the South, unabated, into the 1950s. Liberal Northerners wagged disapproving fingers, ignoring the reality that segregation was a Northern as well as Southern way of life. True, in the North, segregation was not enforced by law, but it was nevertheless a fact. In legal parlance, segregation was *de jure* (by law) in the South and *de facto* (by fact) in the North.

Talk of the Times

De facto segregation is segregation that actually ("in fact") exists, although it is not sanctioned by law. **De jure** segregation is decreed or supported "by law."

Following the century's world wars, African Americans moved in large numbers from the rural South to the industrial cities of the North. Management welcomed their cheap labor, but many rank-and-file whites, fearing they would lose their jobs to the newcomers, met them with hostility. White managers typically assigned blacks the most menial jobs at the lowest wages, and landlords saw to it that they lived, for the most part, in slum districts that were soon labeled with the European word *ghetto*.

Americans willing to look at the situation honestly had to conclude that the entire United States, North and South, was separate *and* unequal.

This Man's Army

Harry Truman's upbringing, in Independence, Missouri, had been neither more nor less racist than what most children of late 19th-century America had experienced. But Truman had also been imbued with a sense of fair play and justice. An artillery captain in World War I, he had seen African Americans serve their country in battle—always in segregated units commanded by white officers. He was also aware that blacks, still segregated, had served well in World War II. The time had come to do the right thing. On July 26, 1948, President Truman issued Executive Order 9981, which mandated "equality of treatment and opportunity to all persons in the Armed Services without regard to race." The order did not use the word *integration*, but when the president was asked pointblank if that is what the order meant, he replied with his characteristic directness: "Yes."

As commander in chief, Truman had the authority to order the integration of the armed forces, but not to command the integration of civilian society. The president was well aware, however, that his order would reach beyond the military. First, for many soldiers, sailors, and airmen, integration in the Army, Navy, and Air Force (created as a service branch independent from the Army in 1947) would be a first experience in integration—an experience they would carry into civilian life.

Even more immediately, Executive Order 9981 meant that the many private businesses just beyond the gates of military posts in the North and the South had to welcome all military personnel, white and black. If a local lunch counter refused to serve a black soldier, for instance, it would be declared "off-limits" by the post commander—and there would be no soldiers to serve, black or white.

Linda Brown Fights the Board of Education

Truman's order had opened the door, however narrowly, to the integration of American society. But change continued to be slow in coming. The next big step would start with a matter to all appearances much smaller than the structure of the armed forces of the United States.

The Browns were an African American family living in Topeka, Kansas. They lived four blocks from a public school; however, it was reserved for white students. Linda Brown was obliged to walk six blocks to a bus stop and take a bus to an all-black school two miles away. Oliver Brown, Linda's father, didn't think this was right, and he sued the local Board of Education. The court ruled that the Board of Education could indeed compel Linda Brown to attend a segregated school. The principle of separate but equal public facilities had been long established and was upheld by an 1896 Supreme Court decision in the case of *Plessy v. Ferguson*.

This is when Thurgood Marshall, a young attorney working for the NAACP, stepped into the picture. He would appeal the lower court's decision to the U.S. Supreme Court. A suit to make a girl's school days a little easier was now an effort to overturn *Plessy v. Ferguson*, to end the regime of separate but equal, and thereby to end legally sanctioned segregation.

Thurgood Marshall as a young NAACP attorney. (Image from the Collection of the U.S. Supreme Court)

But Marshall faced a sharp uphill climb. The NAACP had repeatedly sued segregated school districts beginning in the 1930s, and, each time, the Supreme Court had upheld its 1896 decision: "Separate but equal" accommodations for blacks were constitutional, provided that all *tangible* aspects of the accommodations were, indeed, equal. In that word *tangible*, Marshall found his argument. He recruited 75 experts in fields as varied as history, economics, and psychology to support the proposition that segregated school systems were inherently unequal because of *intangible* social factors. The high court agreed. On May 17, 1954, it handed down a decision in the case of *Brown v. Board of Education of Topeka, Kansas* that drove a stake through the heart of *Plessy v. Ferguson*.

Integration of the nation's schools now became the law of the land. And, in some places, it was just that simple. Citizens and school boards complied, obeying the law, period. In other places, it was resisted violently. The easygoing administration of Dwight D. Eisenhower was loath to intervene aggressively in these cases, but, in 1957, when Arkansas governor Orval Faubus called out the Arkansas National Guard to "prevent violence" by *blocking* the access of nine black students to Little Rock Central High School, the president was at last moved to act. Eisenhower mobilized 1,200 U.S. Army paratroopers to escort the students into the school.

20th-Century Life

In response to federal legislation mandating the desegregation of public schools, Little Rock, Arkansas, officials admitted just nine African-American students to the all-white Little Rock Central High School. This, they declared, was integration.

The "Little Rock Nine" were subject to threats and harassment, the mildest of which (as student Elizabeth Eckford recalled) were mob chants of "No nigger bitch is going to get in our school!" Arkansas governor Orval Faubus called out the National Guard to block entrance of the Little Rock Nine—claiming that he was doing so to protect them. In response, President Eisenhower ordered 1,200 paratroopers to usher the nine students into the school.

The Little Rock Nine heroically endured a year of tension and hostility, which made possible the gradual greater integration not only of Central High in Little Rock, but of school systems throughout the nation.

Birth of a Movement

The crisis at Little Rock received nationwide television coverage. This shook many Americans, white and black alike, out of their complacency. That it required the spectacle of 1,200 U.S. soldiers, dressed for battle, to defend the rights and lives of nine teenagers—here, in America—was both shocking and sobering.

Upon some other Americans the spectacle had quite different effect. They saw Faubus's stand on segregation as a heroic defense of a way of life. The lines were drawn more clearly than ever before, and in this polarized climate, the modern civil-rights movement was born.

Rosa Parks Sits Down

By the mid 1950s, such figures as Faubus and other Southern governors emerged as the champions of segregation. The period also saw the emergence of the champions of civil rights.

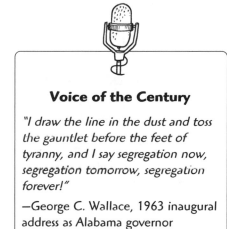

Voice of the Century

"I draw the line in the dust and toss the gauntlet before the feet of tyranny, and I say segregation now, segregation tomorrow, segregation forever!"

—George C. Wallace, 1963 inaugural address as Alabama governor

If student Linda Brown had been an unlikely focus of the civil rights movement in 1954, on December 1, 1955, Rosa Parks, a Montgomery, Alabama, seamstress, was perhaps even less likely. Returning from a hard day's work, she boarded a Montgomery city bus and settled into a seat near the front of the vehicle.

It was an act that should have been too mundane to command the attention of anyone present, let alone the attention of the nation and of history itself. But in Montgomery, in 1955, it was a crime for an African American to sit in the front of a city bus. Instructed to yield her seat to a white person, Rosa Parks found the strength to refuse. For this, she was arrested and jailed.

The arrest triggered a boycott of Montgomery city buses. If the town's African Americans could not ride in the front of the bus, they would not ride at all. For the city's black citizens, most of whom depended heavily on the buses, the boycott was a hardship. But they maintained the action for more than a year, long enough to focus national attention on Montgomery and, more importantly, on the issues of civil rights for African Americans.

Rosa Parks on a Montgomery City Bus.
(Image from the Library of Congress)

The Rise of Martin Luther King Jr.

At the time of the bus boycott, the Reverend Martin Luther King Jr. was pastor of the Dexter Avenue Baptist Church in Montgomery. He had been born on January 15, 1929, in Atlanta, Georgia, the son of a prominent local minister, and was educated at local Morehouse College, Crozer Theological Seminary, and then Boston University, from which he received a doctorate in 1955. With the Reverend Ralph David Abernathy and Edward Nixon, King entered the national spotlight during the Montgomery bus boycott, seizing on it for the symbol that it was.

After Montgomery, King lectured nationally and became president of the Southern Christian Leadership Conference (SCLC). He conducted major voter registration drives, demonstrations, marches, and campaigns in Albany, Georgia (December 1961–August 1962), Birmingham, Alabama (April–May 1963), and Danville, Virginia (July 1963).

The Arsenal of Non-Violence

In 1951, Langston Hughes wrote a poem called "Harlem." "What happens to a dream deferred?" the poet asked. "Does it dry up / like a raisin in the sun?" Does it fester, he continued, or stink like rotten meat, or "crust and sugar over—like a syrupy sweet?" Maybe it just sags, like a heavy load. "Or," Hughes concluded, "does it explode?"

As the civil rights movement gained organization and momentum, the potential for violence, from blacks as well as whites, became increasingly great. King and others realized that violence was not merely destructive, but *self*-destructive. King became an apostle of nonviolent change and would prove so effective in its application that, in 1964, he was internationally recognized with the Nobel Peace Prize.

Lessons from Thoreau and Gandhi

As an advocate and practitioner of nonviolent change, King participated in philosophical movement that reached across time and national boundaries.

King's genius lay in his ability to work on a local level in such a way that local issues assumed national—indeed, international—significance. His further genius was in his ability to apply the lessons of such advocates of peaceful change as the American philosopher Henry David Thoreau and the martyred Indian political activist, Mahatma Gandhi, who had won his nation's independence from Britain. From the example of Gandhi, King learned the principle of satyagraha—"holding to the truth" by nonviolent civil disobedience. It was a bold and courageous alternative to the means of change most pervasive in the century: war.

Sitting In

King and the other civil-rights leaders did not approach the issues with philosophy and words alone. In the struggle for India's independence, Gandhi had used the technique of the *sit-in*, in which demonstrators peacefully entered a business or a public place and remained seated there until they were either evicted by force or had their grievances answered. King adopted the technique first in a segregated Greensboro, North Carolina, lunch counter in 1960, and it became a mainstay technique of the early civil-rights movement.

Talk of the Times

Satyagraha is an Indian word used by Mahatma Gandhi to describe his doctrine of effecting social and political change by "holding to the truth" through nonviolent civil disobedience.

At first glance, the sit-in technique seems rather feeble, perhaps even pathetic, and certainly elementary. Yet King and others saw beyond this. The state, they understood, wielded all the might the law and technology could muster; but such force was never intended to be directed against passive resistance. Gandhi had known the wisdom born of Eastern thought—how effective it is to develop techniques of nonviolent combat, which draw not on one's own strengths, but on the weaknesses of one's opponent. Any attempt to terminate a sit-in would appear brutal, thereby exposing the essential flaws in the position of the opposition while garnering sympathy from liberals, moderates, and even wholly uninvolved individuals.

Talk of the Times

The **sit-in** is a technique of nonviolent civil disobedience in which protesters enter a business or public place and remain seated there until evicted by force or until their grievances are addressed.

The very simplicity of passive resistance was its strength. Sit-ins and other means of nonviolent protest were ways of compelling a complex society to deal directly with human beings in search of justice. Moreover, such protests commandeered the forces of technology, as television crews converged to show the event to the world.

Talk of the Times

Freedom rides occurred during the early 1960s to test federal laws mandating the full integration of vehicles used in interstate transit. Defying angry mobs, African American freedom riders boarded Greyhound and Trailways buses throughout the South and refused to sit in the designated "colored" section at the back of the vehicles.

Freedom Riders

What is not immediately obvious is the great courage passive resistance required. It is one thing to prepare to do battle or to engage in rioting, but quite another to give over one's undefended body to the mercies of heavily armed policemen. But perhaps the most physically dangerous acts of protest during the civil rights era were the *freedom rides*.

The Congress of Racial Equality (CORE), which had been founded in 1942, became especially active during the late 1950s and early 1960s. CORE sponsored "Freedom Riders," African-American men and women who challenged segregation on interstate buses throughout the South. Because interstate transportation was regulated by the federal government, segregated seating and other discriminatory practices were forbidden by federal law, even in places where state law sanctioned these things.

Freedom riders in the South were subject to harassment, arrest, and beating. Their lives were threatened.

March on Washington

The great climax of the early civil-rights movement came when King organized a massive March on Washington. Martin Luther King Jr. spoke from the steps of the Lincoln Memorial, Washington, D.C., on August 28, 1963: Not just the nation, but the world was stirred by the speech King gave.

"I have a dream," the speech began, and it embodied King's remarkable ability to speak on an intensely personal level that was the more universal precisely because it was so personal. The speech crystallized the struggle for civil rights in this nation, and just as Gandhi and others had inspired King, so the speech would inspire others who struggled for freedom in the United States and elsewhere in the world. Most immediately, though, it spoke not just to black Americans or even to liberal white Americans, but to all Americans of conscience. Perhaps more than any other act in the century, the March on Washington and the "I Have a Dream" speech brought the civil rights movement in from what many still perceived as the fringes of society. Now it was irrevocably in the American mainstream.

> *… I have a dream that one day on the red hills of Georgia sons of former slaves and the sons of former slave owners will be able to sit down together at the table of brotherhood. I have a dream that one day even the state of Mississippi, a state sweltering with the heat of injustice, sweltering with the heat of oppression, will be transformed into an oasis of freedom and justice.*

I have a dream that my four little children will one day live in a nation where they will not be judged by the color of their skin but by the content of their character. I have a dream today. …

… Let freedom ring from Stone Mountain of Georgia. Let freedom ring from Lookout Mountain of Tennessee. Let freedom ring from every hill and molehill of Mississippi, from every mountainside. Let freedom ring.

And when this happens, when we allow freedom to ring—when we let it ring from every village and every hamlet, from every state and every city, we will be able to speed up that day when all of God's children, black men and white men, Jews and Gentiles, Protestants and Catholics, will be able to join hands and sing in the words of the old Negro spiritual, "Free at last, Free at last, Thank God A-mighty, We are free at last."

Voice of the Century

"One hundred years of delay have passed since President Lincoln freed the slaves, yet their heirs, their grandsons, are not fully free. They are not yet freed from the bonds of injustice. They are not yet freed from social and economic oppression. And this nation, for all its hopes and all its boasts, will not be fully free until all its citizens are free."

—John F. Kennedy, television address to the nation, June 11, 1963

Martin Luther King Jr. during the march on Washington, 1963. (Image from the National Archives)

JFK Responds

Even before King's speech, President John F. Kennedy responded to the call for civil rights. On June 11, 1963, he made an extraordinary broadcast to the nation, in which he threw the full support of his office behind the cause and urged passage of a sweeping civil-rights act.

The moment was heady and hopeful. But the harsh reality was that Kennedy, who had been elected over conservative Republican candidate Richard M. Nixon in 1960 by the narrowest margin in modern history, lacked the political influence with Congress to gain passage of any such bill. And just hours after Kennedy had made his speech, on the morning of June 12, Medgar Evers, an African American activist who had led many of the voter registration efforts of the NAACP, was ambushed, shot, and killed in front of his home in Philadelphia, Mississippi.

As Kennedy's speech was a prelude to the strides that would yet be made in civil rights, so the murder of Medgar Evers presaged the violence that would increasingly plague the struggle.

The Least You Need to Know

➤ Civil Rights was and remains a worldwide issue, but, precisely because of the avowed democratic principles of the United States, the world focused its attention on civil rights in America.

➤ After the Civil War, racism was protected by law in the South and, although not legally sanctioned, was also rampant in the North.

➤ Segregationists defended their actions with the "separate but equal" doctrine, which was finally overturned by the Supreme Court in the 1954 *Brown v. Board of Education* decision.

➤ Martin Luther King Jr. catalyzed the modern civil rights movement by focusing national and international attention on a variety of local issues, situations, and injustices.

➤ As Gandhi had done, King fashioned the techniques of nonviolent protest into 20th-century instruments of social and political change that were alternatives to the violence that so plagued and marked the century.

Chapter 21

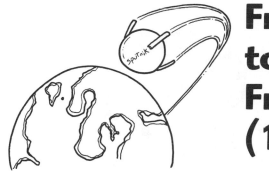

From *Sputnik* to the New Frontier (1955–1963)

In This Chapter

➤ America moves to the suburbs

➤ Science in the fifties: Salk cures polio

➤ Rock 'n' roll, the beats, and youthful rebellion

➤ The changing status of women

➤ The space race

➤ The Kennedy years

Black America made great strides in the 1950s, but had a long way to go. Many white Americans were aware of the inequalities of American society; some were distressed, and a small minority were even outraged. As the 1950s ended and the 1960s began, the awareness and the outrage deepened, but throughout most of the 1950s, the majority basked in the warm glow of complacency, despite the Cold War, despite the bomb, despite social injustice.

It was not simply insensitivity or blindness. The fact is that postwar America was booming and rich with promise—especially if one didn't look too far below the surface.

We Like Ike

There was something about his smile. He had led the Allies to victory in Europe, yet he was far from being a hard-bitten, ramrod-straight military man—a blood-and-guts

Patton or a lordly MacArthur. Dwight David Eisenhower radiated quiet competence and the assurance that, whatever the problems of the decade, they were temporary and would be overcome.

Portrait of Dwight D. Eisenhower by Dorothy Canfield Fisher. (Image from arttoday.com)

Of Suburbs and Interstates

Recession—sometimes even depression—typically follows a major war. When war contracts are canceled, workers are let go. It's that simple. But this didn't happen after World War II. Soldiers returned to their homes, eager to start families. The nation experienced a *baby boom*, and, with it, consumer demand soon more than compensated for the end of wartime production.

One of the consumer items families wanted most was a home of their own. Suburbs grew, and, with their growth, the face of the nation was profoundly transformed. With the mass production of Ford Model Ts and other automobiles in the 1920s, the demand for good roads developed into a passion, and the lion's share of local and state government funding was given over to a frenzy of highway construction. Roads meant prosperity, and automobile production meant jobs—not just in the auto industry, but in everything the automobile made possible: booming steel and oil industries, tourism and related services, roadside restaurants, motels.

Talk of the Times

The **baby boom** was a sharp postwar increase in births in the United States from 1947 to 1961.

World War II had interrupted production of private automobiles, so that the postwar demand skyrocketed. Before the war, all roads had led to the cities from the farms, as America became an urban nation; now, after the war, the roads led out of the cities and to the suburbs. Dwight Eisenhower, presiding over this unprecedented population explosion and demographic expansion, gave his blessing to 1956 legislation funding construction not just of a highway system, but of a system of superhighways—a broad, multilaned, high-speed Interstate Highway System.

The benefits of the system were enormous. All parts of the nation would enjoy access to trade and economic as well as cultural opportunity. Insofar as physical freedom is an expression of spiritual and political freedom, people could feel that much freer. The Interstate Highway System may be seen as a logical step in an evolution that had begun with the canals and railroads in the 19th century (Chapter 2, "A Nation Rises," and 4, "A Nation Torn and Reborn"). America had always offered space, and now the new highway system made that space more available and more accessible. The cost of the system was also enormous—not just in federal dollars, but, many would insist, in social terms as well.

Food, Fast

The new road system tended to homogenize the country, introducing a certain sameness to the landscape. An apt symbol of this transformation is the fast-food restaurant, pioneered by salesman and entrepreneur Ray Kroc, who, in 1955, founded the McDonald's Corporation, which franchised a nationwide chain of drive-in hamburger emporia. While each McDonald's restaurant was independently owned, franchisees had to agree to conform to strictly detailed operating procedures and to build their restaurants according to prescribed plans, which always included the now-familiar Golden Arches.

The uniformity of the McDonald's chain offered advantages to customers. Diners could be confident that their food was being prepared cleanly and with standard ingredients, cooking times, cooking temperatures. A McDonald's burger in Topeka would taste no different from one in Anchorage. Service was generally fast, so that one could get on the road again as quickly as possible. And because high-efficiency preparation methods were used and foodstuffs purchased in bulk (McDonald's still maintains its own beef herds), prices were reasonable—no small consideration in the midst of a baby boom.

Century Stats

By the 1990s, more than 24,500 McDonald's restaurants were operating not only in the United States but in 115 countries. Total sales at the end of the century were somewhere beyond 65 billion burgers.

The Cities Decay

But what was the true price of the homogeneity that the Interstate Highway system, fast food, and suburbia had brought upon the land? Since the beginning of the century, the cities of the United States had been getting increasingly diverse, home to immigrants from various nations as well as African Americans from the rural South. As the suburbs were made accessible by the highway system, middle-class whites tended to leave the cities.

On the one hand, the result was a suburbia characterized by an overall blandness. More sinister, however, was the economic decay of the inner cities, now largely populated by minority groups with limited wealth. These urban ghettoes, especially in the Northern cities, were often economically deprived slums, the breeding grounds of fear and violence. With the rise of the suburbs, the gulf dividing middle-class white America from minority America, chiefly African Americans and Latinos, widened. Not only were these groups now separated from each other by physical distance, but, even more profoundly, by economic distance. A suburb might be 30 miles *and* millions of dollars from center city.

Dr. Salk's Miracle

So amid the optimism of the 1950s, there was a nagging feeling that the nation was suffering from a social malaise, an urban disease. Snug in the suburbs, many had become fearful of the cities. But they also had another, more urgent reason for fear.

Since 1942, parents had come to dread the arrival of summer. The season traditionally associated with vacations and the play of children now brought epidemic poliomyelitis, polio, also called infantile paralysis, because it typically struck infants and young children. A viral disease, it might come and go like a nasty case of the flu, or it might prove fatal—or, in about 20 percent of those infected, it might result in temporary or permanent paralysis.

Century Stats

In the peak epidemic year 1950, 33,344 cases of polio were reported in the United States.

Talk of the Times

Killed-virus vaccines were a medical breakthrough of the 1950s, making possible safe inoculation against such viral diseases as polio. In contrast to inoculation with *live-virus vaccines*, killed viruses confer immunity without the danger of infection.

The spectacle of children either confined to wheelchairs or burdened by heavy leg braces was terrifying enough. In some polio victims, however, the paralysis was much more extensive, involving damage to the nerves that control respiration. For these individuals, life meant confinement in an *iron lung*, a cumbersome respirator that, by alternately increasing and decreasing air pressure around the victim's body, allowed the person's own lungs to expand and contract. Without the machine, the victim would die of asphyxiation.

Come summer, public swimming pools were closed, and parents worried every time they let their children play with others. Nothing more starkly contrasted with the prevailing optimism of the period than the specter of polio. But confidence ran high throughout the nation that had defeated the forces of Germany and Japan that science would also defeat polio. And it did.

Jonas Salk first became intensely interested in vaccines as a student. Instead of going into practice upon graduation from New York University's medical school, he took up research on immunology under Dr. Thomas Francis at the University of Michigan. There scientists had produced the first *killed-virus vaccine* against influenza. Before this vaccine, medical theory held that although vaccines prepared from dead bacteria were effective in immunizing against bacterial infections, immunization against viruses required live-virus vaccines. The trouble with such vaccines is that inoculation with live viruses might well result in infection with the very disease one was trying to prevent. Seizing on the work at Michigan, which proved wrong the theory that killed-virus vaccines were necessarily ineffective, Salk became head of a viral-research laboratory at the University of Pittsburgh and began looking for a way to prepare a polio vaccine from killed polio virus.

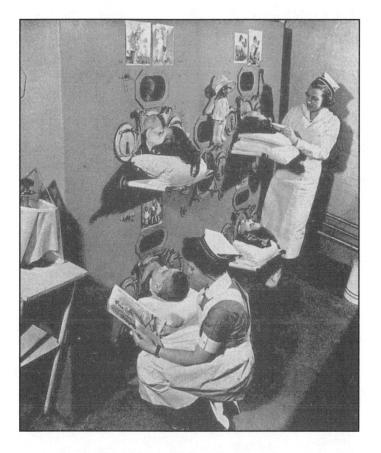

Children, victims of polio, are kept alive in iron lungs.
(Image from arttoday.com)

In 1954, Salk began testing the vaccine, and the following year, the U.S. Food and Drug Administration declared it safe and effective. The "Salk vaccine" was used universally throughout the United States until 1962, when Dr. Albert Sabin persuaded much of the medical community to switch to his live-virus vaccine, which is administered orally rather than by injection. But Salk's pioneering work had ended one of the century's great scourges—the very disease that had afflicted Franklin D. Roosevelt.

The conquest of polio led the public to believe that the 20th century would see "miracle drug" cures for all of humankind's plagues. Even conservative authorities predicted a cure for cancer before the end of the century. That goal, however, has proven elusive.

315

A Whole Lotta Shakin'

Middle-class America could retreat into the suburbs and escape from inner-city cultures they did not understand and of which they were afraid—but they couldn't get away from their own children. Not since the 1920s had parents felt so alienated from their offspring.

Elvis Presley Meets Ed Sullivan

The most visible—and audible—manifestation of youthful rebellion came in the form of music. Most astoundingly, it seemed to come overnight—on a Sunday evening in 1956, to be precise.

Called, with debatable justification, the "golden age" of television, the mid 1950s were without doubt the golden age of the TV variety show. Supreme among such programs was *The Ed Sullivan Show*, which presented a broad range of acts, albeit within the confines of what Mr. Sullivan and the CBS censors deemed "wholesome." It came as a shock, therefore, when the Sullivan show presented the latest teen singing sensation, a young man with dark good looks and a rich, bluesy baritone voice. His name was Elvis Presley.

Elvis Presley appears on The Ed Sullivan Show, *CBS television, in 1956.* (Image from the Frank Driggs Collection)

Presley had already outraged middle America in appearances on lesser TV shows not so much by how he sounded (though, to many, he sounded black, and that was enough to raise eyebrows) as by what he did onstage. The new music he performed had been christened rock 'n' roll, and Presley rocked and rolled, twisting his knees and shaking his hips suggestively, the sensual effect of which detractors sought to dilute by deriding the performer as "Elvis the Pelvis." In a concession to the censors, Elvis was shot onscreen from the waist up. Nevertheless, the effect of the broadcast was stunning.

Elvis Presley was born in Tupelo, Mississippi, in 1935 to a family of sharecroppers. He had grown up in Memphis and was working as a truck driver, but spent his free time in and around Sun Records, Sam Phillips's small Memphis recording studio. Phillips, a white man, had carved out a recording niche by capturing the music of the black country-blues singers who performed in the Beale Street clubs of Memphis.

Tired of the bland sounds of 1950s pop music, Phillips believed that the African-American blues artists were producing the only original, exciting music around. He also understood, however, that *real* money was not to be made in "race records" (as recordings by black artists marketed to black audiences were then called). Phillips was looking for a way to take this music to the mainstream.

For four dollars, anyone could walk into the Sun studio and walk out with their very own voice on a record. In the summer of 1953, Elvis came in and recorded two ballads to give to his mother, he said, for her birthday. Phillips was out, but his assistant manager, Marion Keisker, made a tape of him, along with a note, "Elvis Presley. Good ballad singer." Phillips listened to the tape, but did nothing.

In January 1954, Elvis came in and recorded two more songs. This time Phillips was there. Phillips hooked him up with Scotty Moore, a local guitarist, to see if they could come up with anything. For the next few months, Elvis, Scotty, and bass player Bill Black worked and practiced, looking for something whose name and sound they did not know.

In the studio on a hot evening in July, after another failed attempt to record another weepy country tune, the trio took a break. Elvis started playing "That's All Right, Mama," a blues tune by Arthur "Big Boy" Crudup, playing it too fast, fooling around. Scotty and Bill joined in the racket, and Phillips, who had no idea Elvis knew any blues, rushed into the room to ask what they were doing. They didn't know what they were doing, but Phillips told them to back up and do it again. They quickly worked out the song and rolled the tape—and changed the American musical landscape. "That's All Right, Mama" was up-tempo, unrestrained, and utterly unlike anything Phillips had heard before. In an instant, Sam Phillips knew he had found the white singer he'd been looking for.

But Sam Phillips was a small-time operator, and while he recorded a series of singles many fans still consider Presley's best work, the young man did not rocket to fame until Philips sold his recording contract to recording giant RCA (for $20,000—considered a lordly sum for such a singer from such a label at such a time). Beginning with "Heartbreak Hotel" and boosted by his *Ed Sullivan* appearance, Presley had a string of smash hits from 1956 to 1959.

20th-Century Life

By the late 1960s, the new rock music and culture had overtaken Elvis, and he was in danger of becoming irrelevant. But he made a spectacular comeback on a televised 1968 Christmas special, clad head-to-toe in black leather and recapturing his earlier intensity.

In the '70s, Presley continued to be a highly successful performer, known by his fans simply as "the King," yet he lived a life of miserable seclusion in his gaudy Memphis estate, Graceland. Bloated by alcohol, prescription pills, and binge eating, he died suddenly in 1977, at 42.

In death, Elvis achieved apotheosis as a true idol of popular culture, and Graceland, open to the public, now attracts more visitors annually than George Washington's Mount Vernon. His fans—and most Americans—remain transfixed by a quintessentially American success story: Elvis Presley, a country boy who makes good, achieving success and adulation beyond his wildest dreams, only to be left at the end a hollow husk of a man, in a solitude as wretched as it was magnificent.

Bringing together youthful sensuality and the antithesis of white suburban complacency, Elvis Presley ushered in a musical sound that many adults hoped would depart as suddenly as it had arrived. In fact, rock 'n' roll has proved perhaps the most durable popular music form ever. It would serve as the anthem of youth in the 1950s and would evolve in the 1960s into the music of forthright protest and rebellion before it was slickly co-opted by the record companies in the 1970s and became an increasingly conventional commercial product that will, doubtless, continue to sell far into the 21st century.

Beats and Beatniks

While Elvis Presley was an emblem of youthful rebellion, he was still just an entertainer, with no real artistic or intellectual agenda. The 1950s saw some rebels who took themselves rather more seriously. They called themselves the *"beat generation"* or simply *"the beats."* The word connoted weariness, as in world-weariness or a weariness with mainstream America, but it also suggested their identification with music, especially modern jazz, and the idea of being beatific—spiritually enlightened. Outsiders and other detractors called them *beatniks*.

A number of the beats were serious, innovative poets and prose writers, who lived in and around San Francisco's North Beach, Venice Beach in Los Angeles, and

Manhattan's Greenwich Village. Poets like Allen Ginsberg, Lawrence Ferlinghetti, and Gregory Corso developed powerful free-verse styles that broke dramatically with traditional, academic poetry and, as Walt Whitman had done in the mid-19th century, invigorated poetic expression with the vivid language of the streets. Jack Kerouac, the most famous of the beat novelists, developed a free-flowing, poetically intense prose style intended to convey the emotional immediacy of experience.

Most of the beats labored in relative obscurity, writing primarily for one another, but Ginsberg achieved much wider fame with such poems as *Howl* (1956), a frenetic lament for lost creativity in conformist American society, and Kerouac created a best-selling novel in *On the Road* (1957), a celebration of wandering and rootlessness in an era that valued above all else the white picket fence and a steady job.

With a few brilliant literary exceptions, however, most of the beats were hangers on who enjoyed dressing in dark, threadbare clothes. For men, berets and goatee whiskers were de rigueur, as was a "hip" vocabulary lifted from the world of the black jazz musician. While the free-and-easy lifestyle the beats advocated was in itself a political statement, most were avowedly apolitical, nihilistic, even, and they dismissed the workaday ambition of the I-Like-Ike generation as "square."

Talk of the Times

The **beat generation** (or simply the beats) was a group of writers, musicians, and artists (as well as wanna-bes and hangers-on) who, in the 1950s and early 1960s, rejected the commercial values of mainstream American society and embraced a pose of world weariness and an attitude of emotional, sexual, and aesthetic freedom. Outsiders derided them as beatniks.

Blackboard Jungles

Except for literary works like Ginsberg's *Howl* and Kerouac's *On the Road*, which struck a chord with many Americans, most folk gliding down one of the new interstates simply shrugged off the "beatniks" and their challenge to the values of mainstream American culture, ascribing it all to laziness and the desire for a "free ride." Elvis was harder to dismiss, partly because, more in appearance than in manner, he evoked an identification with a growing outlaw element in American youth—"juvenile delinquency."

The fact was that Americans, especially those over the age of 30, were fearful of the Bomb and the communists, all right, but what scared them most was their own kids. In past generations, Hollywood, always a barometer of the American mood, had portrayed good-natured, earnest, achieving youths, such as the irrepressible Andy Hardy (in a series of films between 1937 and 1944) and *Young Tom Edison* (1940)—both roles played by Mickey Rooney, the beaming, disarming, slightly goofy boy-next-door.

By the mid 1950s, "troubled youth" occupied the screen. In 1954, there was Marlon Brando in *The Wild One*. Leader of an outlaw motorcycle gang, Brando and his gang terrorize a small town.

"Why?" the Brando character is asked. "What are you rebelling against?"

"Whadda ya got?" comes the reply.

The teenage rebel theme was continued in *Rebel Without a Cause* (1955), starring James Dean, more sensitive and vulnerable than Brando, but still sullen, explosive, uncontrollable. That same year, 1955, *Blackboard Jungle* was released. A grittier look at juvenile delinquency in a tough New York City high school, it featured the first rock 'n' roll music used as a movie theme, "Rock Around the Clock" by Bill Haley and the Comets. The music sounds innocent enough now. In 1955, adults found it downright sinister.

Studio publicity still from The Blackboard Jungle. *At the left are a youthful Vic Morrow and Sidney Poitier. Third from the right is a boyish Jamie Farr, known to fans of TV's* M*A*S*H *as Corporal Klinger.*
(Image from the author's collection)

A Woman's Place

If images of rebellious youth became too disturbing, one could always switch on the television for quick comfort. TV families of the 1950s were white and suburban, the children mischievous, perhaps, but ultimately obedient and respectful of their prosperous fathers who worked in non-specific white-collar jobs.

And then there were the TV mothers. In such popular series as *Father Knows Best* and *Leave it to Beaver*, they were strictly homemakers who never raised their voices and who cooked, cleaned, and cared for their children without assistance from the outside—and always, it seemed, while attired in a freshly laundered and starched dress. Fonts of non-demonstrative affection and sage advice for their kids, sources of reassuring strength for their husbands, they were supremely contented.

Not that television didn't offer an alternative to these household paragons. If you grew weary of Barbara Billingsley as June Cleaver in *Leave it to Beaver* or Jane Wyatt as Margaret Anderson in *Father Knows Best*, you could tune into Joan Davis playing Joan Stevens in *I Married Joan* or Lucille Ball as Lucy Ricardo in *I Love Lucy*. In these shows, the lady of the house was not a serene and supremely competent homemaker, but a ditzy blonde (Joan) or scatter-brained redhead (Lucy). Her mission in life was strictly to get into humiliating jams, often involving embarrassment to her husband and always requiring, by way of solution, his long-suffering intervention. Unquestionably, the stars of *I Married Joan* and *I Love Lucy* were the wives, yet the titles focused, in the first person, on the husbands, as if to assure televiewers that the man of the house was and always would be the person who really mattered.

Of course, television hardly portrays the full reality of life in any time and place, but it *does* portray the popular perception of reality or, at least, the way most people would like reality to be. Yet by the end of the 1950s, reality—as well as its perception—was changing. With increasing national consumerism came a need for additional family income, which sent many women out of the house and into the workplace. In the past, the course of a woman's life had been determined in large part by biology. A woman would marry then get pregnant, and any thought of a career was put on indefinite hold or forsaken altogether. In 1960, however, the *birth-control pill*—often known simply as "the pill"—was introduced. By altering the hormone-regulated cycle of ovulation, the pill made it possible for a woman to have sex without getting pregnant. Not only could married couples now determine when (and if) to have children, women could also more safely decide whether or not to have sex before or without marriage.

By the early 1960s women were not only liberating their bodies, they were, in greater and greater numbers, expanding their minds as well, attending and graduating from college.

One such graduate was a freelance magazine journalist, Betty Friedan, who decided to write a book based on her graduating class from Smith College. She sent questionnaires to her classmates, soliciting descriptions of their lives since leaving school. Friedan's hypothesis, revolutionary for the times, was that middle- and upper-class women were not satisfied with their roles as wives and mothers, but were victims of what she called the *"feminine mystique,"* the ubiquitous notion that normal women could gain genuine satisfaction only through marriage and children.

Friedan's 1963 book, *The Feminine Mystique*, created an instant sensation among women who suddenly recognized that they were not alone in their all-but-submerged feelings of dissatisfaction. Friedan went on, in 1966, to become a founder of the National Organization for Women, NOW, which campaigned for liberalized abortion laws, equality in the workplace, and passage of an Equal Rights Amendment to the Constitution.

Talk of the Times

The Feminine Mystique, title of a 1963 book by Betty Friedan, describes the socially ubiquitous belief that "normal" women can achieve genuine satisfaction only through marriage and children.

New Moon

Despite racial, generational, and incipient sexual conflicts, the 1950s struggled to be an era of good feelings. With industry and technology booming, at least we could rest easy that our scientists were, stride by stride, mastering the physical world—and doing so faster and more boldly than the scientists of any other nation.

A Triumph of Soviet Science

Then came October 4, 1957. From a site deep within the interior of the USSR, the Soviets launched a rocket that lofted into space a metal sphere containing nothing more than a radio transmitter. It was called *Sputnik I*, and it was the first human-made object sent into orbit around the earth. The Soviets had created a new moon.

Each of the innocuous electronic beeps *Sputnik* beamed to radio receivers on earth hit the United States like detonations. How could this *communist* dictatorship beat us into space? It seemed a vindication of the Soviet system, of Soviet technology, of Soviet science, of Soviet brains. As many saw it, *Sputnik* also portended military disaster. Everyone from general down to buck private knew the strategic importance of gaining the high ground. But who knew what kinds of weapons could be wielded from this new high ground of orbit above the Earth?

Talk of the Times

Sputnik, the Russian word for satellite, was the name of the first artificial satellite rocketed into orbit, by the Soviet Union, on October 4, 1957.

Stumbling in the Space Race

Both the United States and the Soviet Union had initiated rocket-development programs after World War II, both sides having captured a number of the V-1 and V-2 rockets German scientists had developed as weapons to use primarily against London. Both nations also appropriated a share of those scientists, who formed the core of the new space programs.

Talk of the Times

The **space race** was the familiar name Americans applied to the U.S. space program after the USSR successfully launched Sputnik in 1957. The space race was "won" in 1969, when Apollo 11 landed two American astronauts on the moon.

The launch of *Sputnik* signaled the start of a *space race*, which Americans stumbled into more or less without questioning its value. And stumble they did. The first several U.S. launches following *Sputnik* were miserable failures. When, on December 6, 1957, a *Vanguard* rocket fizzled, toppled, and burst into flame on its launch pad, newspapers christened it Flopnik and Kaputnik.

Finally, in January 1958, the United States succeeded in orbiting *Explorer I,* and other successful satellite projects followed. But Americans could not rest easy for long. On April 12, 1961, the Soviets not only launched the first man into space, cosmonaut Yuri Gagarin, but they also sent him into a single orbit around the earth.

Beaten again, the U.S. space program followed a month later with the successful launch of Alan B. Shepard—albeit in a brief, 15-minute suborbital flight. It would be a full nine months before John Glenn made the first U.S. orbital flight, circling the globe three times.

Superpowers

As the dust of World War II settled, it was clear that the world was now dominated by two opposed *superpowers*, the United States and the Soviet Union. After the USSR developed its own nuclear and thermonuclear weapons, the two powers engaged in an arms race, each side vying with the other to stockpile more missiles and bombs, each capable of delivering sufficient destructive power to wipe out a city. After *Sputnik*, the arms race was joined by the space race, which became a kind of nonviolent equivalent of war, with both sides trying to demonstrate the superiority of hardware that could send a warhead against a city just as readily as it could loft an astronaut into orbit.

The Torch Is Passed

The popular Ike Eisenhower had served two terms as president, and he anointed his vice president, Richard Milhous Nixon, to run for the office in 1960. His opponent was a dashing young senator from Massachusetts named John Fitzgerald Kennedy.

Why Kennedy Won

With his good looks, great personal charm, and World War II record as a naval hero (he saved most of his crew when his PT boat was cut in two by a Japanese destroyer), Kennedy was an attractive candidate—although many thought that Americans would never put a Catholic in the White House.

Richard Nixon had served the Eisenhower administration well, having made his political reputation as an anti-communist crusader during the McCarthy era while managing to avoid the fate of the senator from Wisconsin.

The election was the closest in modern history, but, in the end, JFK emerged victorious. Some ascribed his victory to his performance in a televised series of debates. Although it was a toss-up as to which candidate came out ahead strictly on the issues, there was no doubt that Kennedy looked very good on TV, and Nixon did not. Kennedy appeared dynamic, forthright, and self-confident; Nixon sweated profusely and appeared unshaven, shifty-eyed, even rather haggard.

Century Stats

Of more than 69 million votes cast, Kennedy squeaked to victory with a margin of only 113,057 votes. 502,773 votes went to minority party candidates, including U.S. Sen. Harry F. Byrd Jr. (D-VA), who captured 15 electoral votes. Nixon received 219 electoral votes to Kennedy's 303.

More important, however, JFK's victory suggested that Americans were ready to leave behind the complacency of the Eisenhower years. Whereas Nixon was associated with the status quo, Kennedy spoke of a "New Frontier," into which he was prepared to lead the American people (as he would say) "with vigah." At 43, the youngest *elected* president in the nation's history (Theodore Roosevelt was only 42 when he assumed office after the assassination of William McKinley), JFK projected a virile idealism that promised to lead America to victory in the space race and the arms race, as well as in the effort to make the nation a more socially just place.

But there was more. The president and his beautiful wife, Jacqueline—Jackie—brought a new grace, elegance, and even an enchantment to the White House. It was the closest the American presidency had ever seemed to royalty.

President Kennedy shakes hands with Soviet premier Nikita Khrushchev during a 1961 meeting in Vienna. (Image from the John Fitzgerald Kennedy Library)

Disaster: The Bay of Pigs

While much of the nation adored Jack Kennedy, he faced a Republican Congress that blocked passage of most of the social programs he advocated, including those related to civil rights, that interested him.

Early in his administration, Kennedy also suffered a serious foreign-policy blow. Relations between the United States and the island-nation of Cuba, just 90 miles off the Florida coast, had been uneasy since the Spanish-American War (Chapter 5, "Through the Golden Door"), which had gained Cuba's independence from Spain. Although the United States did not attempt to annex Cuba, the Platt Amendment, enacted in 1902, effectively made the small country a U.S. protectorate. In 1934, this arrangement formally ended, but, economically, Cuba remained a virtual satellite of the United States.

American foreign policy supported a series of Cuban regimes that were friendly to the United States, especially American business interests, but also thoroughly corrupt, creating conditions that left the majority of islanders in poverty. Among the most corrupt administrations was that of Fulgencio Batista, who acted ruthlessly to suppress a growing popular movement to topple him. At last, in 1959, a young lawyer-turned-guerrilla, Fidel Castro, succeeded in ousting Batista and assumed the presidency. Initially, Castro was friendly to the United States, but within the first six months of his regime, he entered into an increasingly intimate alliance with the Soviet Union and took frequent opportunity to express hostility toward the United States.

The prospect of a Soviet client state so close to America was intolerable, and, in the closing months of the Eisenhower administration, the Central Intelligence Agency (CIA) devised a plan to overthrow the new Cuban leader. JFK, who inherited the plan, authorized action, and, on April 17, 1961, a force of some 1,500 anti-Castro Cuban refugees, trained and equipped by the CIA, landed at the Bay of Pigs on Cuba's southwestern coast.

The operation was a disaster. The CIA had been confident that the Cuban people would rise up to join the invaders. Instead, they repelled them, and Kennedy declined to risk open warfare by sending the U.S. air support that had been promised the invaders. The Bay of Pigs was a major embarrassment to the new administration. It hardened Castro's stance against the United States and sent Cuba deeper into the Soviet camp.

Danger: Missiles in Cuba

In October 1962, an American U2 spy plane photographed some curious construction on the island. After studying the photographs, experts determined that they were seeing missile bases—Soviet missile bases taking shape.

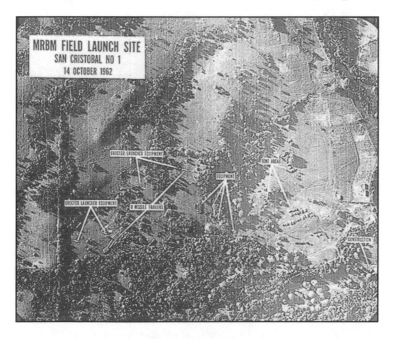

U2 surveillance photograph of a Soviet missile launch installation at San Cristobel, Cuba, 1962. (Image from the John Fitzgerald Kennedy Library)

On October 24, President Kennedy announced the discovery to the American people in a televised speech, and he further announced a naval blockade of Cuba. Ships approaching the island would be subject to search, and, if they were found to be carrying missiles or materials for the construction of bases, they would be turned back.

Not only Americans but the people of the entire world held their breath as each day of the ensuing crisis dragged by. Never before had two thermonuclear powers stood toe-to-toe in this way. In schools all across America, air-raid drills became a part of each day. Students were instructed to "duck and cover" beneath the meager shelter of their desks.

The standoff in the Caribbean was at last ended on October 28, when Soviet premier Nikita Khrushchev (who had emerged victorious in the bloody power struggle that followed the death of Josef Stalin in 1953) offered to remove the missiles under United Nations supervision, in exchange for the secret commitment to withdraw U.S. missiles stationed in Turkey, and the public commitment that the U.S. would never invade Cuba. On the following day President Kennedy suspended the blockade, and, by November 2, the missile bases were being dismantled.

The Cuban Missile Crisis was a triumph for JFK and did much to redeem the Bay of Pigs fiasco. It was, indeed, a major U.S. victory in the Cold War, but it came at the hair-raising expense of contemplating what might well have been the end of the world.

Reaching Out: A "Peace Corps"

Flushed with victory over the Cuban missiles, JFK sought to build American international influence on a more positive basis. In August 1961, the Kennedy administration sponsored creation of the Alliance for Progress, an international economic development program with 22 Latin-American countries. The purpose of this economic assistance program was to encourage the maintenance of democratic governments throughout the region.

A similar purpose on a broader international scale was envisioned in the creation of the Peace Corps. Staffed by volunteers, the Peace Corps would provide skilled workers in such fields as education, agriculture, health, trade, technology, and community development to work in the underdeveloped nations of the world, bringing immediate practical benefits to local people while acting as de facto ambassadors of goodwill on behalf of the United States.

Century Stats

In 1961, the year of its establishment, the Peace Corps consisted of 900 volunteers serving in 16 countries. Its peak strength came in 1966, when 15,556 volunteers served in 52 countries. Today, some 5,000 volunteers serve in about 90 countries, including some in eastern Europe.

Dallas, November 22, 1963, 12:30 P.M.

In November 1963, President Kennedy decided to visit Texas in an effort to bolster his support, which had always been weak there. He was preparing for what promised to be a tough reelection campaign in 1964.

Air Force One touched down at Dallas's Love Field on the morning of the 22nd, and the president was gratified by the warm welcome he received. Kennedy reveled in politics and enjoyed wading into crowds to press the flesh. The Secret Service couldn't persuade him to ride beneath the bullet-proof bubble top that was normally mounted on the armored presidential limousine. JFK wanted to see and to be seen.

The presidential motorcade made its way through downtown Dallas, greeted by friendly crowds lining the route. As it passed by a warehouse building known as the Texas School Book Depository, shots rang out, the second of which ripped into the president's head, fatally wounding him. Texas governor John Connally, riding in the front seat of the car, was also grievously wounded, but recovered.

It was one of those moments that would be forever burned into the consciousness of those old enough to know what had happened. For years afterward, conversations would roll around to the question, "Where were you when you heard JFK was shot?" and the answer was always precise. People remembered exactly.

The accused assassin, captured later in the day (but not before murdering Dallas police officer J.D. Tippett) was Lee Harvey Oswald, a misfit who had lived for a period in the Soviet Union, having renounced his U.S. citizenship. On November 24, as he was being transferred from the city to the county jail, Oswald was himself murdered by Dallas nightclub owner and small-time mobster Jack Ruby.

Jackie Kennedy, whom the nation would now see in the president's televised funeral, caring with great dignity and tenderness for her two children, Caroline and John, later enjoyed recalling how her husband liked to listen to a recording of *Camelot*, the popular 1960 Lerner and Loewe musical about the noble magic of King Arthur's realm. Many Americans would likewise look back on the Kennedy years—no more than a thousand days—as a vanished Camelot of lofty dreams, high ideals, and noble purposes.

The Least You Need to Know

➤ The postwar baby boom, increased automobile production, and the development of the Interstate Highway System contributed to the suburbanization of America in the 1950s.

➤ The decade witnesses a newly rebellious younger generation, whose rock 'n' roll music and tendency to delinquency vexed parents.

➤ Salk's polio vaccine reinforced Americans' faith in science, but early Soviet victories in the "space race" created anxiety over the nation's ability to compete technologically.

➤ While mainstream culture identified the woman of the 1950s as a happy home-maker, increasing numbers of women sought fulfillment elsewhere, especially in careers of their own.

➤ The Kennedy years signified a change in the nation's attitude from complacent acceptance of the status quo to a restless desire to confront the "New Frontier."

Chapter 22

"The Great Society" (1964–1967)

With his long, droopy face, good-natured but hang-dog, and his down-home Texas drawl, Lyndon Baines Johnson made a stark contrast to John Kennedy. It was a contrast that had been apparent to Johnson himself as well as to Kennedy. Insiders knew that Kennedy's choice of Johnson as vice president had been strictly political, that, temperamentally, the president and vice president had little in common and didn't even like each other. Aboard Air Force One, the plane that had taken JFK to Dallas and that now would take his body back to Washington, LBJ was sworn in as the 36th president of the United States.

What would he do, how would he do it, and how would it affect the world in the 20th century?

A Martyr's Causes

There is no debating that John F. Kennedy was a remarkable man. Subsequent years—and many, many books—also reveal that he was a deeply flawed man, driven not just by high ideals and a desire to see his nation excel and prevail, but by a prodigious and

Voice of the Century

"A piece of each of us died at that moment."

—Senator Mike Mansfield, shortly after the JFK assassination

reckless sexual appetite more suited to a Roman emperor than an American president. In the days, months, and even years following Kennedy's assassination (it was frequently called a martyrdom), JFK was beatified by a genuinely grief-stricken public, who compared his greatness to that of another martyred president, Abraham Lincoln.

More objectively considered, however, the presidency of John F. Kennedy was less than a triumph. Elected by a razor-thin majority, he had never secured the cooperation of Congress, and very few of the liberal social programs he proposed were enacted.

President Kennedy's family leaves the Capitol, where his body lies in state. Jacqueline Kennedy holds the hands of Caroline and John Jr. Robert Kennedy is beside Jean Kennedy Smith. In the back, Peter Lawford can be seen. (Image from the John Fitzgerald Kennedy Library)

"Let Us Continue"

President Johnson was a consummate politician, which meant, in part, that he was a consummate national psychologist. Johnson not only believed in JFK's program of social reform, he wanted to accomplish reform on an even broader scale, comparable to Roosevelt's New Deal. But Johnson understood that his best leverage in selling such a program was not his own power of persuasion, but the spirit of the "martyred" president.

"Let us continue," LBJ declared to the nation and to Congress, by which he really meant let us accomplish, after Kennedy's death, what Kennedy had been unable to accomplish in life.

Lyndon Baines Johnson in an official White House photograph.
(Image from the Wisconsin Historical Society Collection)

The Civil Rights Act of 1964

The single greatest piece of unfinished business from the Kennedy presidency was comprehensive civil rights legislation. In 1964, LBJ engineered passage through Congress of a sweeping Civil Rights Act, which banned segregation and discrimination in public accommodations such as restaurants, theaters, and hotels, and barred employers from discriminatory hiring practices based on race. For years, during the long struggle for civil rights, recalcitrant whites as well as pessimistic blacks had claimed that, whatever one believed or didn't believe, it was just not possible to "legislate morality." Here was legislation that aimed to do just that.

As many saw it, the Civil Rights Act of 1964 was the fulfillment of the promise of liberty made by the Declaration of Independence, but never fully realized in a Constitution that had originally condoned slavery. A great step had been taken, many felt, to make the nation whole.

Launching a Great Society

Today's middle-aged generation, the baby boomers, remember growing up at a time when liberalism was considered the norm. It was the policy of Kennedy and, even more, of Lyndon Baines Johnson. That LBJ was in tune with the liberal mood of the nation was proven by his landslide victory in the 1964 election over the conservative Republican candidate, Arizona Senator Barry M. Goldwater.

Presidential candidate Barry M. Goldwater, about 1964. Many feared that, if elected, he would use nuclear weapons against North Vietnam. LBJ supporters wore lapel buttons proclaiming BURY GOLDWATER.
(Image from the Wisconsin Historical Society Collection)

Desperate Neighborhoods

Americans celebrate their nation as a land of abundance, and, compared to most other parts of the world, they do so with justification. Yet poverty has always been a fact of American life. Many Americans have lacked the resources to clothe, feed, and shelter themselves and their families. In the course of the 20th century, the level of American poverty has declined; however, by the mid 1960s, the *white flight* to the suburbs had economically drained the nation's *inner cities*. In terms of gross national product and average income levels, the United States was wealthier than ever, but its cities had rarely looked poorer, and pride in them was at a low point.

With the poverty came an increasing sense of desperation in the inner cities. Ghetto residents felt neglected and abandoned. Those businesses that remained in inner-city neighborhoods were rarely locally or minority owned, and residents were routinely exploited by outsider merchants who charged exorbitant prices for inferior goods.

Despite federal legislation, racial and ethnic discrimination in housing and employment enforced ghetto boundaries and limited opportunity. Urban police forces, in the North as well as the South, typically included few minority officers, and ghetto residents were often treated in ways that ranged from humiliating incivility to outright physical abuse.

Talk of the Times

White flight described the mass exodus of the white middle class from the nation's cities to its suburbs. The oldest—and most decayed—neighborhoods of a city were collectively called the **inner city**, a euphemism for ghetto.

Increasingly disaffected ghetto youth turned to crime and the use of illegal drugs. Yet no drug could deaden the growing sense of outrage in the nation's cities. The collective anger simmered through the early 1960s. By mid decade, it began boiling over.

Despite the passage of the Civil Rights Act of 1964, vindicating the nonviolent teachings of such leaders as Martin Luther King Jr., the decade witnessed racial unrest of unprecedented scope and violence. In the South, Medgar Evers had been assassinated (Chapter 21, "From *Sputnik* to the New Frontier"). Four little girls were killed when white segregationists hurled a bomb into a black church in Birmingham, Alabama, and civil-rights workers were brutally murdered in Mississippi while working to register black voters. On March 7, 1965, the Southern Christian Leadership Conference began a march from Selma, Alabama, to the state capital, Montgomery, but marchers were attacked by police at the Pettus bridge on the outskirts of Selma. Many were injured by tear gas and billy clubs in what came to be called Bloody Sunday. That very evening, white segregationists killed a northern white minister, the Reverend James Reeb, who was active in the civil-rights movement. Bloody Sunday and the death of Reeb helped prompt passage of another piece of LBJ legislation, the Voting Rights Act of 1965, which was aimed at ensuring that local officials could not deny African Americans the right to vote.

Black Power

In the North, racial violence took a different turn as many African Americans began to regard King's approach to civil disobedience as too passive. Black leaders such as Malcolm X, prominent in the Nation of Islam, a black nationalist movement commonly known as the Black Muslims, urged a more aggressive approach. Rejecting integration and racial equality, Malcolm X called for black separatism, black pride, and black self-dependence. He also advocated the use of violence—albeit for self-protection—a position that frightened and outraged many whites, even those sympathetic to the civil rights movement, who wrote off Malcolm X and other black nationalists as dangerous fanatics.

By the mid 1960s, however, Malcolm X had split with the Nation of Islam and had begun to take a more conciliatory view toward racial relations. With ironic tragedy, it was at this point in his development as a leader that he was assassinated, gunned down on February 21, 1965, while giving a speech in Harlem's Audubon Ballroom. Nation of Islam extremists were subsequently convicted of the murder.

Still, thousands of young African Americans were turning away from King and the SCLC to more militant organizations, such as the Congress for Racial Equality (CORE), organized by Floyd McKissick, and the Student Nonviolent Coordinating Committee, led by Stokely Carmichael, who called for "Black Power" and an end to white involvement in the civil rights movement. By the summer of 1965, the civil-rights movement was severely split, and violence was in the air.

20th-Century Life

Malcolm X and the Nation of Islam advocated black nationalism, a movement to empower African Americans politically and economically but independently from whites. Whereas civil-rights leaders such as Martin Luther King Jr. sought racial equality and integration, the black nationalists promoted a separate identity of proud African ancestry. Extreme black nationalists advocated the creation of a separate black nation by African Americans.

While black nationalism reached its peak in the 1960s, it had its origins in the movement led by Marcus Garvey (1887–1940) in the early '20s. He spoke of creating an independent black nation. Garvey created the Universal Negro Improvement Association, promoting his cause in the association's newspaper. He founded the Negro Factories Corporation and the Black Star Line in 1919, as well as a chain of restaurants and grocery stores, laundries, a hotel, and a printing press. Unfortunately, Garvey's business methods were "unconventional," and he was indicted for fraud in connection with the sale of Black Star stock. He served two years in prison before President Calvin Coolidge commuted his sentence to deportation to his native Jamaica.

The first major explosion came on August 11, 1965, in the Watts ghetto of Los Angeles. A white policeman patrolling the neighborhood stopped a young black man on suspicion of drunken driving. What should have been a simple arrest became a major confrontation. Police reinforcements arrived, and the gathering crowd began hurling stones, cinder blocks, and bottles at the officers. The police responded by sealing off the neighborhood, which sealed in the violence. That night, thousands roamed the streets, hurling Molotov cocktails and looting stores. The governor called in National Guard troops, but the riot continued over the next six days. Thirty-five people were killed and more than a thousand injured. Property damage totaled approximately $200 million.

Voice of the Century

"Violence is as American as the Fourth of July and cherry pie."

—Black activist H. Rap Brown, "We Burned Detroit Down and Put America on Notice," *Open City*, August 17, 1967

Watts seemed to signal a shift in attitude among African Americans. The next summer, riots broke out in New York and Chicago. In 1967, Newark and Detroit were the scenes of deadly riots. Throughout urban America, summer became a season of dread, and news commentators spoke gravely of the approach of yet another "long, hot summer."

A War on Poverty

In this atmosphere of unrest, President Johnson accelerated his stewardship of what he was now calling the Great Society. Not only was additional civil-rights legislation passed, but a variety of social and welfare programs were also enacted.

In 1965, Medicare was created to help all Americans over the age of 65 pay for medical treatment. The following year, medical coverage was expanded by Medicaid to include welfare recipients. Great Society legislation also profoundly affected American education. The 1965 Elementary and Secondary Education Act provided federal funds to poor school districts across the country. The Higher Education Act of 1965 gave tuition assistance to college and university students, ensuring that millions could now earn a college degree, the traditional ticket into the American middle class.

Under the multiple umbrellas of the Great Society, the Department of Housing and Urban Development, the Department of Transportation, the National Endowments for the Humanities and the Arts, and the Corporation for Public Broadcasting were all created. Most dramatic among the Great Society laws were those passed in the name of Johnson's declared War on Poverty. In 1964 came the Economic Opportunity Act, which created the Office of Economic Opportunity to oversee the numerous community programs, including the Job Corps, the Volunteers in Service to America (VISTA), the Model Cities Program, Upward Bound, the Food Stamps program, and Project Head Start.

Nor was urban America the only beneficiary of the Great Society. During this period, a host of major environmental legislation was enacted, including creation of the National Wilderness Preservation System and the Land and Water Conservation Act in 1964 and the National Trails System and the National Wild and Scenic Rivers System in 1968.

A Domino Leans

President Johnson, who had come of age politically during the New Deal era of Franklin Roosevelt, reveled in his role as architect of the Great Society. He believed that he was creating a permanent positive legacy for the United States.

What was not clear, in 1964, was that developments in a small Asian nation, thousands of miles from Watts, or Detroit, or Newark, would drag down LBJ's plans and tear apart the Great Society before it got under way.

French Indochina

It was not only Europe that the end of World War II left unstable. Southeast Asia, largely colonized by European powers but occupied by the Japanese during the war, was now ripe for change. During the 19th century, France had colonized Laos, Cambodia, and Vietnam. When France caved in to Germany in 1940, the Japanese allowed French colonial officials puppet authority in the region until the Allies liberated France in 1945. Japan then seized control, purging the French police agencies and soldiery that had kept various local nationalist groups in check.

In Vietnam, Ho Chi Minh (1890–1969) led the most powerful of these independence-seeking groups, the Viet Minh, founded in 1941 as successor to the Indochina Communist Party, which Ho had established in 1930. Despite its communist ties, the Viet Minh was aided by U.S. Office of Strategic Services (OSS) personnel in a guerrilla war against the Japanese occupiers. When the war in Europe ended, Allied forces were free to turn their attention to Vietnam and the rest of Southeast Asia. Chiang Kai-shek's Nationalist Chinese troops occupied northern Vietnam, while the British secured southern Vietnam preparatory to re-entry by the French, who vigorously acted to "neutralize" supporters of Ho Chi Minh. From this point, a chronic state of guerrilla warfare developed, which escalated sharply when Chiang Kai-shek, hoping to checkmate communist ambitions in the region, withdrew from northern Vietnam and turned that region over to French control.

Chiang Kai-shek was not alone in his fear of communist inroads in Southeast Asia. The United states began to supply French colonial troops with funding, military equipment, and—on August 3, 1950, the first contingent of U.S. military "advisors." By 1953, the United States was funding 80 percent of the cost of France's war effort.

Ike's Assessment

The French assigned General Henri Eugene Navarre to strike a decisive blow on the strategically located plain of Dien Bien Phu, near Laos. On the eve of this strike, President Eisenhower stepped up military aid, presenting to reporters, on April 7, 1954, his rationale for that aid to a foreign power fighting a colonial war in a far-off place.

Talk of the Times

The **domino theory** is the argument that, if one small nation is allowed to fall into communist hands, others will follow like the chain reaction of a row of dominoes.

"You have a row of dominoes set up," Ike explained, "you knock over the first one, and what will happen to the last one is the certainty it will go over very quickly." It was an off-hand metaphor, but one that was immediately christened the *domino theory*. It would became the basis for some 30 years of escalating American involvement in Vietnam.

Despite Navarre's massing of troops, Dien Bien Phu fell to the forces of Ho Chi Minh on May 7, 1954. This disaster was followed by a succession of Viet Minh victories, and, in a July peace conference in Geneva, Switzerland, the French and the Viet Minh agreed to divide Vietnam along the 17th parallel and concluded a cease-fire.

The "Advisory" Years

A central condition of the Vietnam armistice was that the divided nation was to hold elections within two years with the object of reunification under a popularly chosen leader. South Vietnam's President Ngo Dinh Diem not only feared, but assumed that Ho Chi Minh would win the election; Diem therefore declined to abide by the Geneva accords, refusing to hold the promised elections. The United States was more concerned with "containing" communism than with seeing democracy practiced in Vietnam. Eisenhower backed Diem's position, and, under Ike's successor, John F. Kennedy, the number of military "advisors" sent to Vietnam steadily rose.

JFK, determined to stop the falling dominoes in Asia, turned a blind eye to the thoroughly corrupt, brutal, and unpopular regime Diem had created. All that mattered was that the president of South Vietnam was not a communist.

But what happened next was impossible to ignore. Not only did Diem install his cronies and relatives into high civil and military positions, channeling money into the cities while keeping the nation's farmers in dire poverty, he zealously practiced religious persecution. A Catholic, Diem rigorously supported Vietnam's Catholic minority at the expense of the Buddhist majority, which he often insulted and abused. In protest, several Buddhists monks doused themselves with gasoline and set themselves ablaze in the streets of Saigon. These human conflagrations were covered worldwide by news photographers and newsreel cinematographers.

By mid 1963, the Kennedy administration could no longer stomach Diem. President Kennedy secretly allowed the CIA to plot the assassination of the South Vietnamese president in a U.S.-backed military coup that overthrew him on November 1, 1963.

Regardless of the immorality of JFK's action, it was a strategic disaster. Diem's death unleashed a series of coups that made South Vietnam even more unstable over the next two years, encouraging the communists to escalate a war that was now fueled by increasing Soviet and Chinese aid.

Century Stats

In June 30, 1962, before most Americans had even heard of the country, there were 6,419 American military "advisors" in South Vietnam.

Gulf of Tonkin

Recent scholars have discovered and discussed evidence that, in the closing weeks of his presidency, Kennedy, desiring to avoid further escalation of a war he did not believe could be won, was contemplating a pull-out from Vietnam. His assassination prevented the pull-out, and a legion of *conspiracy theorists,* including filmmaker Oliver Stone (in his 1991 blockbuster *JFK*), have tried to link the Kennedy assassination to forces within the United States who did not want to see America's involvement in Vietnam ended.

Talk of the Times

Conspiracy theorist is the term applied to anyone who speculates on secret government involvement in any number of events, including political assassination and especially that of John F. Kennedy.

Whatever Kennedy's plans were or would have been, Lyndon B. Johnson was determined to move vigorously to oppose the North Vietnamese insurgents. He authorized the CIA to oversee diversionary raids on the northern coast while the Navy conducted electronic espionage in the Gulf of Tonkin. The new president also named General William Westmoreland to head the Military Assistance Command, Vietnam (MACV) and increased the number of military "advisors" to 23,000.

President Johnson believed that he could win the war in Vietnam if he had a free hand to deploy troops and other military aid as he saw fit. The trouble was, not all of Congress could be counted on to agree, and Congress ultimately controlled the purse strings.

Johnson saw his opportunity to seize the power he wanted when, on August 2, 1964, the U.S. destroyer *Maddox,* conducting electronic surveillance in the Tonkin gulf, was fired on by North Vietnamese torpedo boats. Two days later, the destroyer *Turner Joy* reported having been attacked as well—although there actually was no second attack. Without explaining to Congress the provocation for the attacks—that the ships were actually supporting a clandestine raid on the North Vietnamese coast by South Vietnamese gunboats—LBJ secured passage of the Gulf of Tonkin Resolution on August 7, giving him virtual carte blanche to expand the war.

War and Protest

Although armed with the Gulf of Tonkin Resolution, LBJ recognized the inherent weaknesses of a succession of Saigon governments and had second thoughts about escalating the war. In February 1965, he sent his personal advisor, McGeorge Bundy, to Saigon on a fact-finding mission. Johnson might have decided to reduce U.S. involvement in the war—had the Viet Cong not forced his hand. On February 7, these North Vietnamese troops attacked U.S. advisory forces and the headquarters of the U.S. Army 52d Aviation Battalion, near Pleiku, killing nine Americans and wounding 108. Bundy, Gen. Westmoreland (commanding U.S. forces in Vietnam), and U.S. Ambassador Maxwell Taylor recommended a strike into North Vietnam.

Talk of the Times

Body count was a grim term frequently heard during the Vietnam War. It was a measure of the effectiveness of battle, a method of keeping score by counting the dead.

Operation Flaming Dart retaliated against a military barracks near Dong Hoi, provoking a Viet Cong counterstrike on February 10 against a barracks at Qui Nhon. The next day, U.S. forces struck back with Rolling Thunder, a series of air strikes deep into the North. Beginning on March 2, 1965, Rolling Thunder was the start of a major escalation in which 50,000 new ground troops were sent to Viet Nam—to "protect" U.S. air bases.

Johnson's strategy was to continue a gradual escalation of the war, bombing military targets in a war of attrition that would grind down the North Vietnamese—without provoking overt intervention from China or the USSR.

This proved to be a no-win strategy that only prolonged the war. In an aggressive military campaign, success is measured by objectives attained—cities captured, military targets eliminated—but in a war of attrition, the only measure of success is *body count*. To be sure, American forces produced a massive body count among the enemy, but, just as Buddhist monks were willing to set themselves aflame, this enemy was prepared to die.

Enduring tremendous military losses, the North Vietnamese nevertheless continued not only to infiltrate the South militarily, but politically as well. Special "political cadres" secured support from the rural populace of the South, which the Saigon government had always neglected. With this support, the Viet Cong achieved great mobility throughout the country, often fighting from a complex network of tunnels that were all but invisible. Using stealth, courage, and sheer ingenuity, the "VC" continually disrupted and terrorized U.S. and South Vietnamese operations. It was a war without front lines. The enemy could appear anywhere, even to attack bases and positions far to the south.

Not that U.S. troops were failing. Indeed, they were increasingly successful in "clearing" enemy territory. But the numbers of troops were never great enough to *occupy* the territory that had been cleared. No sooner were battle zones secured than they were again overrun.

President Johnson and his advisors began to recognize that the war could not be won by U.S. intervention. The only route to victory was *Vietnamization*, giving the ARVN (Army of the Republic of Vietnam) the tools and training it needed to take over more and more of the fighting, so that U.S. forces could be reduced and, ultimately, withdraw.

In the early stages of American involvement in Vietnam, President Kennedy had spoken of the need to win the "hearts and minds" of the Vietnamese people. Yet it was becoming increasingly apparent that the hearts and minds of the South Vietnamese, our allies, were not committed to victory. We could give them weapons and training, but not the will to fight on behalf of a government unpopular with most of the people.

Something else was becoming apparent as well. The hearts and minds of the American people were also at stake, and, as the war ground on, as televised reports of useless battles in nameless places took the place of conversation around American dinner tables, and as more and more body bags

Century Stats

In 1965, 75,000 Americans were fighting in Vietnam. In 1966, the number jumped to 375,000.

Talk of the Times

Vietnamization was the process of turning over to the South Vietnamese responsibility for the conduct of the Vietnam War.

came home, many of those hearts and minds were turning against the war. Voices of protest were now being heard—at first mainly on college campuses, but soon elsewhere. And the voices would grow louder and larger as the Vietnam War drained precious national resources from the Great Society.

The Least You Need to Know

➤ In death, JFK was widely perceived as a heroic martyr to the cause of social justice; LBJ used this perception to promote passage—in Kennedy's memory—of his program of social reform, the Great Society.

➤ Even as LBJ instituted social change, America's cities suffered decay, and racial tensions exploded into a series of urban riots summer after summer.

➤ The origin of the Vietnam War was the collapse of the French colonial empire coupled with the "domino theory," a belief that allowing one Asian nation to fall to communism would lead to the fall of other nations, one after the other.

➤ As the Vietnam War expanded, funding and support for the Great Society dwindled.

Chapter 23

Vietnam, the Moon, and a Nation Called Woodstock (1968–1969)

In This Chapter

➤ The Vietnam War becomes increasingly unpopular

➤ Antiwar protest fuels the creation of the counterculture

➤ LBJ takes his hat out of the ring

➤ Policy under Nixon and Kissinger

➤ Assassinations: Martin Luther King Jr. and Robert F. Kennedy

➤ Americans walk on the moon

➤ Woodstock

The monks and other scholars who chronicled medieval times labeled a year noteworthy for disasters or for wonders an *annus mirabilis*—a wondrous year. For America, and for much of the world, 1968 was such a year, a year of great social upheaval, political murder, and other horrific violence. The following year, 1969, might well merit the same label, but more for its wonders than for its horrors. The year saw, in the midst of war and a society fraying at the edges, a festival of love and hope and a flight from this troubled blue world to one that is lifeless, gray, cold, but beautiful nonetheless. This chapter chronicles two of the century's most remarkable years.

"Hell, No! We Won't Go"

By 1968, it was clear that American policy in Vietnam had not only failed to win the hearts and minds of the Vietnamese, it was losing the hearts and minds of many

Americans as well. President Johnson increasingly relied on the *Selective Service system*—the draft—to supply troops for the conflict. But the Selective Service was routinely more "selective" than fair. Moderately well-off young people could put off or avoid conscription through "student deferments" (college enrollment skyrocketed during the war) and by other means. Less-privileged youth, especially African Americans and Latinos, bore the brunt of the draft. This fact—along with the perception that the war was generally unjust—merged the increasingly strident struggle for civil rights with the movement protesting the war in Vietnam.

Not that antiwar sentiment was confined to black America. The antiwar movement began on college campuses, which had become staging areas for mass protest demonstrations, including a series of marches on Washington starting in 1965 and continuing through 1968 and again in 1971. Demonstrators would publicly burn their Selective Service registration cards—"draft cards"—and would chant such slogans as "Ho, Ho, Ho Chi Minh! The NLF is going to win!" (the NLF was the National Liberation Front, the Viet Cong) and "Hell, no! We won't go!" Many not only protested the war, but resisted the draft, often by fleeing to Canada or other countries when called up.

In the 1950s, as Chapter 21, "From *Sputnik* to the New Frontier," pointed out, the generations seemed to lose touch with one another. Now, in the late 1960s, people were speaking of a *generation gap*, which pitted "young people" against "anyone over 30." The single greatest issue dividing the generations was the war.

By the end of 1967, it was apparent that the Vietnam War was grimly stalemated. In an effort to counter this impression, President Johnson repeatedly assured the nation that there was "light at the end of the tunnel," but the mounting U.S. casualties created a *credibility gap* between what the administration claimed and what the public believed.

Talk of the Times

The **Selective Service System**, a system by which young men between the ages of 18 and 45, were subject to conscription into the U.S. armed forces, was adopted in 1917 and renewed and revised throughout the century. On July 1, 1973, "induction authority" ceased—the military draft ended, and the era of an all-volunteer armed forces began.

Century Stats

African Americans made up 11 percent of the U.S. population during 1967–1968, but accounted for 16 percent of the army's casualties in Vietnam during 1967 and 15 percent over the course of the entire war.

Soldiers of the 9th Cavalry, 1st Cavalry Division (Airmobile), search a Viet Cong tunnel, 1967. (Image from the National Archives)

Antiwar protesters in Wichita, Kansas, 1967. (Image from the National Archives)

343

Talk of the Times

The 1960s were full of "gaps." The **missile gap** was the difference between the number of intercontinental ballistic missiles (ICBMs) in the U.S. arsenal versus the Soviet arsenal, the **generation gap** described the gulf between young and old, and the **credibility gap** came to describe the difference between what the administration presented as the truth and what everyone else believed.

Voice of the Century

"I feel like a hitchhiker on a Texas highway in the middle of a hail-storm. I can't run, I can't hide, and I can't make it go away."

—Lyndon B. Johnson, on the Vietnam War

Tet Offensive

It was squarely in this period of deepening doubt that Hanoi launched a series of massive offensives, first along the border, with attacks against the U.S. base at Khe Sanh, and then on South Vietnamese provincial capitals and principal cities, beginning on January 30, 1968, the Vietnamese lunar holiday, Tet. The offensive, which included an assault on the American embassy in Saigon, was hard on U.S. and ARVN forces, but was far more costly to the Viet Cong. Nevertheless, the three-week campaign was a clear psychological victory for the communists. Tet persuaded many Americans—politicians and policy makers among them—that the Vietnam War was unwinnable.

Now that American casualties had topped a thousand a month, Tet hardened popular opposition to the war and sharply divided congressional lawmakers into "hawks" (war supporters) versus "doves" (peace advocates).

A haggard, careworn Lyndon Johnson appeared on television on March 31, 1968, to announce, first, that he would restrict bombing above the 20th parallel—a clear signal to Hanoi that he wanted a negotiated settlement to the war. Then he stunned his audience by announcing that he would not seek another term "as your president."

Johnson had seen his Great Society plans dismantled and then destroyed by the war. Having entered the White House to carry out and improve upon JFK's program of national social reform, LBJ realized that his advocacy of the war was tearing the nation apart.

Peace Talks and Escalation

Cease-fire negotiations began in May, only to stall over Hanoi's demands for a complete bombing halt and NLF (National Liberation Front) representation at the peace table. At first Johnson resisted, but, in November, he agreed to these terms. Although this hopeful glimmer of an end to the war boosted the sagging presidential campaign of Democrat Hubert Humphrey, Richard Milhous Nixon (whom many had counted out of politics—and in fact retired—after he lost the race for California governor in 1962) emerged victorious.

Those who knew Nixon understood that he was a fierce competitor, who believed in winning at any cost. To ensure victory in the 1968 elections, he repeatedly (albeit vaguely) promised to end the war. Yet, once elected, he promptly *expanded* the war into Laos and Cambodia, Vietnam's neighbors. In conjunction with his brilliant foreign-policy advisor, former Harvard professor Henry Kissinger, Nixon formulated a strategy to improve relations with the Soviets (through trade and an arms-limitation agreement) with the object of disengaging Moscow from Hanoi. To divorce Chinese interests from those of North Vietnam, Nixon also sought to normalize relations with Mao's government. Improved relations with the Soviets and the Chinese would not only make the world a safer place, Nixon and Kissinger reasoned, it would also put the United States in a position to negotiate with North Vietnam what Nixon repeatedly called "peace with honor."

Talk of the Times

Officers who ordered their men into dangerous situations risked being **fragged**—that is, being killed or wounded by their own troops, typically by fragmentation grenade.

20th-Century Life

No event in the Vietnam War was uglier that what occurred on March 16, 1968. An infantry company commanded by Lieutenant William L. Calley marched into the South Vietnamese hamlet of My Lai, supposedly a Viet Cong stronghold, and massacred 347 unarmed civilians, including women, old men, and children, herding many of them into ditches and shooting them. The action was recorded by Army photographers.

The "My Lai Incident" was not made public until 1969, through the efforts of veteran Ronald Ridenhour, who threatened to go to the media if the U.S. Army failed to initiate an inquiry. That resulted in the court martial of several soldiers, of whom only Calley was convicted.

My Lai seemed to reveal the Vietnam War as a conflict in which the defenders of democracy were the butchers of innocent women and children. However, some saw Calley himself as a victim, thrust into a war in which everyone was a potential enemy. Sentenced to life imprisonment, Calley was released in September 1974 when a federal court overturned the conviction.

Unfortunately, the Soviet strategy failed: The USSR announced recognition of the Provisional Revolutionary Government (PRG) formed by the NLF in June 1969. Peace talks, in Paris, between the United States and the North Vietnamese now drifted.

In the meantime, Nixon continued to probe for ways to extricate the United States from the conflict without, in effect, simply giving up. Despite the continued poor performance of ARVN forces, the president accelerated the "Vietnamization process," withdrawing increasing numbers of U.S. troops. American casualties were thereby reduced, but the morale of U.S. troops disintegrated. Nobody wanted to be among the last soldiers killed in a losing war. Drug use among U.S. combat soldiers assumed epidemic proportions, and many elements of the Army were chronically on the verge of mutiny. Officers who were in the least zealous to lead their men into harm's way risked being *fragged* by their own men.

Talk of the Times

The **counterculture** was a term applied to those—mainly young people—who rebelled against the perceived values of mainstream American culture.

Voice of the Century

"Do your thing. Be what you are. If you don't know what you are, find out. F**k leaders."

—1967 statement in a San Francisco underground newspaper

The Making of a Counterculture

As we read in Chapter 21, Marlon Brando, as the young motorcycle gang leader in *The Wild One*, replies to the question, "What are you rebelling against?" with "Whaddya got?" In 1968, however, the focus of youthful rebellion was much sharper. Youth was the heart of the antiwar movement, which, in turn, became associated with a general *counterculture movement*.

Rebellion against the prevailing culture, perceived as dominated by the twin evils of the pursuit of money and the violent pursuit of power, involved embracing alternative values of a more spiritual nature. In practice, the rebellion was often a desire to be free from all constraint and rule, to be at liberty to "do your own thing." Despite this happy anarchy, the counterculture movement developed a familiar uniform: long hair (for both sexes) and disheveled clothing that, to the over-30 generation, suggested the lifestyle of the gypsy or the hobo.

"Turn On, Tune In, and Drop Out"

The gypsy-hobo uniform marked its wearers as *hippies,* and many of them also openly indulged in the use of "recreational" drugs (such as marijuana and the hallucinogenic LSD) and "recreational" sex. Government officials assumed that the entire peace movement was backed by communists and used the FBI and (illegally) the CIA to infiltrate antiwar organizations. True, some organizations associated with the movement were undoubtedly subversive; however, most protestors were "mainstream" individuals, aged 20 to 29, who were simply disgusted and outraged by the war.

The "reckless youth" of the 1920s were awash in bootleg gin, but the pattern of drug use associated with the counterculture of the 1960s was something entirely new. From the earliest years of the century, illicit drug use had been common on the criminal fringes of society, and, by the 1950s, addiction to such narcotics as heroin was becoming a major and highly visible problem in many American cities. At that time, a new class of criminal emerged—the *junkie*, who would commit any crime to get the money needed for his next "fix."

But by the mid 1960s, the hippies, a new generation of middle-class youth, who enjoyed relative affluence and the advantages of education, had become passionately dedicated to forms of music and other types of popular art that expressed a turning away from much that had been accepted as the "American dream." For many of these young people, marijuana and LSD became as integral a part of everyday life as rock music.

Talk of the Times

Hippie came into use in the 1960s to describe members of the counter-culture. It was derived from *hip*, an adjective originally used by African American jazz musicians to describe people, music, and ideas in tune with the advanced styles and trends of the time.

Marijuana may be seen as just one more form of protest and escape (all rolled up into a cigarette called a "reefer" or "joint"). LSD was a rather more complex matter. Formally called D-lysergic acid diethylamide and familiarly known as "acid," LSD is a hallucinogenic drug that was discovered in 1943 by Swiss chemist Albert Hofmann. It produces powerful sensory distortions, with visual (and sometimes auditory) hallucinations. In 1966, Harvard psychologist Timothy Leary began passionately advocating LSD use as a way of expanding one's consciousness. Some years earlier, the British novelist and essayist Aldous Huxley had experimented with hallucinogenic drugs, claiming that they "opened the doors of perception." Now Leary proclaimed, "If you take the game of life seriously, if you take your nervous system seriously, if you take your sense organs seriously, if you take the energy process seriously, you must turn on, tune in, and drop out."

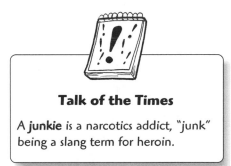

Talk of the Times

A **junkie** is a narcotics addict, "junk" being a slang term for heroin.

By taking drugs—"turning on"—one could "tune in" to what was really worthwhile in life and, as a consequence, be prompted to "drop out" of life in the hollow mainstream. The phrase became the banner slogan of a generation: *Turn on, tune in, drop out.*

The use of marijuana and LSD were part of a desire to get beyond conventional beliefs and morality, which stifled self-expression. Sex was another route to the expansion of self, as was adherence to various forms of Eastern religious belief. The later 1960s spawned a series of spiritual leaders, or *gurus*, including the Maharishi Mahesh Yogi, who introduced a generation to transcendental meditation and who gained renown as spiritual counselor to a bevy of celebrities, including the Beatles. Cynics would say that the Maharishi marketed enlightenment.

Campus Ferment

Nowhere was the 1960s counterculture more visible than on the nation's college campuses. At its best, during this period, the campus was a place of productive social and intellectual ferment, of the intense and free exchange of ideas. Often, however, campuses of late 1960s were full of the sound and fury of protest, some of it fruitful, but much of it signifying nothing more than rebellion against authority, whatever its form. Student "activists" stormed administration buildings, ransacked academic records, staged sit-ins, occupied offices of deans, even closed down schools from time to time. All over the country, campus ROTC (Reserve Officer Training Corps) facilities, regarded as breeding grounds for war, became the targets of student vandals and arsonists.

Blood in Memphis, Blood in L.A., Blood in Chicago

The mid 1960s, with an increasingly strident civil rights movement, had been disturbing enough to many Americans. Now, however, more or less violent protest was becoming routine. Blacks were angry. Students were angry. The cop on the beat who used to wear a cap, now donned a helmet. Social commentators spoke of the nation as "polarized," sharply and violently divided between what President Nixon like to call the "silent majority," supporters of the status quo, and the hippies, the radicals, or what Nixon's vice president, Spiro T. Agnew, dubbed the "radical liberals."

Voice of the Century

"Somehow this madness must cease. I speak as a child of God and brother to the suffering poor in Vietnam and the poor of America who are paying the double price of smashed hopes at home and death and corruption in Vietnam.... The great initiative in this war is ours. The initiative to stop it must be ours."

—Martin Luther King Jr., Riverside Church, New York City, 1967

King Is Slain

Where were the voices of moderation? Martin Luther King Jr., still an advocate of non-violence, had nevertheless outraged some supporters by embracing the antiwar movement. He had come to believe that the cause of black civil rights was seamlessly joined to the twin causes of peace and justice. Yet he did not lose his focus on his original constituency.

In early April 1968, King went to Memphis to address and support the city's striking sanitation workers. On the evening of April 3, he made a speech remembered as second in importance only to the "I have a dream" given in Washington in 1963. "I have been to the mountaintop," King said in Memphis, "and I have seen the Promised Land." Emotionally, seeming almost haunted, King told his listeners that he might not reach that land with them. It was as if he were foretelling his own death, even as he spoke of the triumph that was close at hand.

The next day, April 4, as King stood on the balcony outside his room at the Lorraine Motel, he was cut down by a sharpshooter's rifle. (The confessed assassin, a white drifter named James Earl Ray, was tried, convicted, and sentenced to life imprisonment—although he later repudiated his confession and claimed innocence. Ray died, in prison, of liver cancer in 1998.)

The violent death of the apostle of nonviolence triggered riots in more than a hundred cities across the United States, as grief-stricken, outraged, and hopeless men, women, and youths set ablaze the ghettos to which America had consigned them.

Another Kennedy Dies

To some, the nation seemed to have crossed the verge into full-scale civil insurrection. To others, it appeared instead to be on the threshold of wholesome revolution and rebirth. LBJ had taken himself out of the presidential race. The antiwar Democrat Senator Eugene McCarthy had made a strong showing in the New Hampshire primary, but even more promising was the candidacy of Robert F. Kennedy.

Attorney general in his brother's administration (and, for a time, in Johnson's), and now a U.S. senator from New York, Bobby Kennedy combined the personal magnetism and idealism of John Kennedy with the antiwar pedigree of a 1960s liberal. Even to his supporters, wide-eyed with hope, he seemed a long shot, but on June 6, 1968, RFK won a stunning victory in the all-important California presidential primary. The dream seemed within reach.

Senator Robert F. Kennedy with Lyndon Johnson in the Oval Office, 1966. (Image from the Lyndon Baines Johnson Library)

Millions watched his televised impromptu victory speech at a Los Angeles hotel, which ended with his flashing the two upraised fingers that had signified V-for-victory during World War II and now, in the 1960s, expressed a desire for peace. Minutes later, as he and his entourage made their way out of the hotel ballroom through a back passageway, Robert Francis Kennedy was shot in the head, from close range, by a self-professed Arab nationalist named Sirhan Sirhan.

The Democrats Meet in Chicago

Bobby Kennedy had been the Democratic party's "most electable" antiwar candidate. With Kennedy's assassination, Hubert H. Humphrey, vice president under Johnson, emerged as the most likely candidate, a fact that outraged many liberals, especially those of draft age and others who objected to the war on moral grounds. They favored another antiwar candidate, Eugene McCarthy, a Minnesota senator and former college professor who had trailed RFK in four out of five primaries. Unlike either Kennedy or McCarthy, Humphrey was a mainstream Democrat who neither pledged nor favored an immediate end to the war.

The Democratic National Convention took place during August 26-29, 1968, in Chicago—typically referred to, at the time, as "Mayor Daley's Chicago." Daley, an old-style political boss, was a major force in the national Democratic party. He had no tolerance for the more than 10,000 protesters who had massed in Grant and Lincoln parks along Chicago's lakefront, to demonstrate against the war and against the nomination of Humphrey ("Dump the Hump!" they chanted in unison), and generally to disrupt the convention. The protestors also aimed invective against Mayor Daley, whom they derided as a racist and even a fascist.

Chicago's Richard J. Daley greets Richard Nixon during a 1970 visit to the city. These two men, one a Democrat, the other a Republican, were equally despised by liberals. (Image from the National Archives)

At first, the mayor deployed the Chicago police force—"pigs," the protestors called them—with restraint. The officers endured much verbal and physical provocation. At last, however, Daley gave the officers license to move against the demonstrators, which they did so violently that journalists and other eyewitnesses called what happened next a "police riot." Daley's policemen—"Chicago's Finest"—viciously clubbed and gassed demonstrators and journalists in dramatic clashes in the street, which were broadcast into everyone's living rooms. It was nothing short of open combat, as if the country was at war from within. It was the quintessential "confrontation" (to use the word then current) of the 1960s, a clash between the symbols of the Establishment and those of the counterculture.

In the end, Humphrey did run against Nixon—and suffered a decisive defeat. Now the Establishment had in the White House a vestige of the Eisenhower years, resolutely anti-communist and pro-business, a conservative who always wore an American flag pin in his lapel. Now the counterculture had somebody in the White House they could despise much more fiercely than they could ever have despised Hubert Horatio Humphrey.

A Lunar Promise Kept

The world—and Americans in particular—breathed a sigh of relief with the passage of 1968, a year of riots and assassins. But 1969 didn't promise to be much better. Vietnam raged on, America remained deeply divided, and the world was still a very dangerous place.

Small Steps

After the United States lofted into orbit its first satellite, *Explorer 1*, on January 31, 1958, a series of unmanned satellites and probes followed. Then, on May 5, 1961, about three weeks after the Russians put a man into a single orbit, U.S. Navy commander Alan B. Shephard was launched on his 15-minute sub-orbital flight. Just 20 days later, on May 25, President John F. Kennedy spoke to Congress: "I believe this nation should commit itself to achieving the goal, before the decade is out, of landing a man on the moon and returning him safely to earth. No single space project in this period will be more impressive to mankind, or more important for the long-range exploration of space, and none will be so difficult or expensive to accomplish."

Voices were raised in protest, both in the political and scientific communities. Why put men on the moon, when unmanned probes could tell as much or more—and accomplish the mission with far less expense and danger? But the dream of actually setting foot on the lunar surface was just too compelling to resist.

The Russians had successfully launched their first unmanned lunar probe, *Luna 2*, on September 12, 1959, and the United States launched a series of probes beginning in 1961. In 1966 and '67, the five *Lunar Orbiter* missions mapped much of the lunar surface in 1,950 wide-angle and high-resolution photographs. These images were used to select the five primary landing sites for the manned *Apollo* missions.

In the meantime, the USSR and the United States continued to send cosmonauts and astronauts into space, in the Soviet *Vostok* series (1961–63, which included *Vostok 6*, carrying the first woman, Valentina V. Tereshkova, into space) and the U.S. Mercury series (1961–63). America's *Gemini* program came next, 12 two-man space flights launched between 1964 and 1967 and specifically designed to prepare for the manned lunar missions by testing the ability of astronauts to maneuver their spacecraft, to develop techniques for orbital rendezvous and docking with another vehicle—essential procedures for the subsequent *Apollo* moon-landing program—and to endure long space flights (the eight-day *Gemini 5* mission, launched August 21, 1965, was the longest space flight to that time).

A Giant Leap: July 20, 1969

The *Apollo* program, the manned mission to the moon, was not only the most complex space exploration program ever conceived, it was the biggest, most complex, and most daring scientific and technological venture in the history of humankind. A *Saturn V* multistage booster (rocket) would lift the three-man *Apollo* spacecraft on a $2^1/_2$-day voyage to the moon. The craft would assume lunar orbit, then the Lunar Module, with two men aboard, would separate from the orbiting Command Module and land on the moon. After a period of exploration on the lunar surface, the astronauts would climb back into the Lunar Module, lift off, and dock with the orbiting Command Module, which would blast out of lunar orbit and carry the three astronauts back to earth.

The *Apollo* program began with catastrophe when a fire broke out inside the *Apollo 1* spacecraft during a launchpad test on January 27, 1967. Astronauts Virgil I. "Gus" Grissom, Edward H. White, and Roger B. Chaffee were killed. National Aeronautics and Space Administration (NASA) officials had to persuade an angry Congress to press on with the program, and, after several preliminary missions, including earth- and moon-orbital flights, Apollo 11 was launched on July 16, 1969, manned by Neil A. Armstrong, Edwin E. "Buzz" Aldrin Jr., and Michael Collins.

While the spacecraft was in lunar orbit, Armstrong and Aldrin entered the Lunar Module, which separated from the Command Module and took the two men to a landing on the surface of the moon while command pilot Collins remained in orbit in the Command Module. The landing came on July 20, at 4:17 Eastern Daylight Time (8:17 P.M. Greenwich Mean Time).

"That's one small step for [a] man," Armstrong declared as he jumped off the module's ladder, "one giant leap for mankind."

Armstrong and Aldrin spent 21 hours and 36 minutes on the moon, collecting lunar soil and "moon rocks" and setting up various scientific experiments. But Armstrong's words best expressed the rationale for an effort that reached beyond science and to speak of and to the human spirit. The landing brought to the United States—and to all the world—a moment of human triumph in a time of great bitterness, doubt, and despair.

Voice of the Century

"Here men from the planet Earth first set foot on the moon, July 1969 A.D. We came in peace for all mankind."

—Plaque left on the moon to mark the site of the first lunar landing

Astronaut Neil Armstrong snapped this photo of Edwin "Buzz" Aldrin descending the ladder to the lunar excursion module. Aldrin was the second man to walk on the moon.
(Image from NASA)

Woodstock Nation

Apollo 11 was one act of humanity in an often inhumane time. Another came the very next month, during August 15–17, on a farm near the village of Woodstock, New York. The Woodstock Festival was to be an open-air rock concert, with the top musical acts of the day scheduled to perform, but no one expected half a million young people to converge on Max Yasgur's dairy farm.

From Hobos, to Beats, to Beatniks, to Hippies

Who were these hippies, and what were they about? Americans, for the most part, like to think of themselves as achievers, and this has never been truer than in the 20th century, often called the "American Century." Yet, if the desire to achieve, to excel, to make money, to be *doing things* is very American and very much of the 20th century, so is a kind of counter-desire—a desire *not* to be doing, but simply *to be.*

The majority of Americans may have scoffed at the hippies, just as they had derided the beats as beatniks, and, in earlier days, chased the hobos from their towns. Yet, somewhere within, these scoffers also envied the hobo, the beatnik, and the hippie. Here were people who had found contentment outside of the American mainstream in which, to be sure, one might prosper, but in which one might also simply drown.

The most famous Woodstock poster, advertising "3 Days of Peace & Music." (Image from the author's collection)

Voice of the Century

We Are the People Our Parents Warned Us Against

—Title of a book by social commentator Nicholas von Hoffman, 1968

Why Woodstock Mattered

A half million people went to Woodstock, but if a survey were taken today, surely millions of aging baby boomers would *claim* to have been there.

Woodstock mattered because it was the symbol of a generation's solidarity in rebellion against the Establishment and its war in Vietnam. Woodstock was a collective wish to be better than the past—to be more loving, more generous, more *alive*. It was a gesture toward remaking America spiritually. It was the expression of a generation that didn't want to die in Vietnam or drown in the American mainstream.

The Least You Need to Know

➤ The period of 1968–69 saw some of the most intense, disturbing, and yet hopeful change American society ever experienced.

➤ The antiwar movement energized and was driven by a more general counterculture movement, a mass protest against the American status quo.

➤ The year 1968 saw some American dreams crushed by the murders of Martin Luther King Jr. and Robert F. Kennedy, but much of the nation and the world united in wonder at the landing of U.S. astronauts on the moon in 1969.

➤ For many Americans, Woodstock, a three-day rock festival on a muddy dairy farm in upstate New York, expressed and symbolized the hopes and aspirations of a generation that did not want to die in Vietnam nor waste life in the blind pursuit of empty economic goals.

Part 6
A New World: 1970–1989

Talk to anyone who lived through the '60s, and you'll get conversation filled with nostalgia punctuated by the observation that "they were scary times." Few people feel the same intensity of emotion about the 1970s, which, while less socially turbulent than the '60s, were also a harsher, more cynical time.

In this section, we will see America painfully extricated from Vietnam amid diplomatic breakthroughs with the Soviets and the Chinese engineered by Richard Nixon and his secretary of state, Henry Kissinger, and see the president go down in the flames of Watergate. We will take America through a disquieting identity crisis that began with the "energy crisis" of the early 1970s, when the "oil sheiks" of the Middle East seemed to dictate the price of freedom and the U.S. economy became mired in "stagflation," a wicked one-two punch compounded of inflation and recession.

We will pass through the Iran hostage crisis and the deeds of other fanatics, then enter the era of Ronald Reagan, who made many Americans feel good again with the promise that prosperity would "trickle down" to all. The 1980s were years of plague, in the form of a mysterious virus called HIV, and years of hope, as the Cold War rapidly thawed and the Iron Curtain imprisoning Eastern Europe simply rusted away.

Chapter 24

Truces and Terrorists (1970–1975)

In This Chapter

➤ The violent "peace process" in Vietnam

➤ Nixon's breakthrough with China

➤ The U.S. and USSR talk arms limitation

➤ Rise of terrorism

➤ Watergate and the fall of Richard Nixon

➤ Decade of liberal environmental and social reforms

No sooner had the last chords of Woodstock died and the last muddy reveler departed the Yasgur farm than rock promoters were eager to repeat the magic of the festival. At the end of their 1969 tour, the Rolling Stones decided to stage a free concert outside of San Francisco. A third of a million fans converged on the Altamont Speedway, about 40 miles southeast of the city whose Haight-Ashbury district became the mecca of the hippie movement, but was once again settling back into the down-at-the-heels neighborhood it had been before the 1960s.

But Altamont had none of the good feelings, let alone the romantic aura, of Woodstock. If Woodstock had been a hippie dream, Altamont was a counterculture nightmare. Poorly planned, the "festival" was a disaster. Malfunctioning sound systems and a dearth of sanitation facilities for 300,000 fans created anger, while "security" was provided by members of the notorious Hell's Angels motorcycle gang, allegedly hired by the Stones and the Grateful Dead for $500 in beer. In the worst among many acts of violence, Hell's Angel members knifed to death a young man who had pulled a gun. Other deaths, apparently drug-related, also occurred.

Observers of the social scene pronounced Altamont the last gasp of the counterculture—the end of the '60s. While many were relieved by this prospect, others saw it as the sad finish to an era of high hopes.

"Peace with Honor" and Death from Above

Richard Nixon was hard to like and easy to hate. He had already been known for years as "Tricky Dick" in part because he gave the impression of shiftiness (apparent, perhaps fatally so, back in the 1960 televised debates with JFK) and in part because he was a wily politician who was always willing to take a cheap shot at his opponents, and a leader who never seemed to approach issues straightforwardly or without an array of ulterior motives.

Voice of the Century

"Cambodia is one country where we can say with complete assurance that our hands are clean and our hearts are pure."

—Secretary of State William P. Rogers, testifying to the Senate in March 1970, a year after he had helped formulate a plan for secretly bombing that neutral nation

His approach to Vietnam was typical. On the one hand, he needed to give the American people the impression that the war was winding down, and he did withdraw troops, promote "Vietnamization," and bring the North Vietnamese to the conference table. On the other hand, he needed to increase the pressure on the communists to negotiate a favorable peace, a "peace with honor"; so he figured out ways to escalate the war, even as he wound it down.

When the Paris peace talks faltered in 1970, Nixon expanded the war into Cambodia, striking at communist supply and staging areas in that country. This incursion did not go unnoticed at home. Waves of angry protests again swept American college campuses, including one at Kent State University in Ohio, where protesters set fire to the ROTC building. In response, the governor called out 900 National Guardsmen, "weekend warriors," many of them no older than the students, and woefully inexperienced at handling anything like a riot.

Amid taunts and jeers, 28 of the guardsmen "overreacted" (a word much used during the period) and fired into the students, killing four and wounding nine.

Life magazine published a photograph of a young woman, face upturned in uncomprehending horror, kneeling beside the body of a slain student. It was one of many images the war in Vietnam produced. Earlier, there had been photographs of naked children horribly burned by napalm, and an unforgettable image, captured by news photographer Eddie Adams, of a South Vietnamese police chief discharging his handgun into the head of a bound North Vietnamese prisoner. But here was an image of an American boy, killed by other American boys, and grieved over by an American girl.

In the wake of Kent State, some 100,000 demonstrators converged on Washington in the largest, most dramatic antiwar protest yet. Congress got the message. It was getting harder and harder to be a hawk, and the legislative body voted to rescind the Tonkin Gulf Resolution, which ended executive authority to continue prosecuting the war at will.

Under pressure, Nixon withdrew ground troops from Cambodia, but he simultaneously stepped up the bombing raids there. The determined communist guerrillas continued to infiltrate South Vietnam, however, and the president now ordered U.S. air support for an ARVN invasion of Laos in February 1971. Simultaneously, the withdrawal of American troops was stepped up, an action that tended to placate some of the protest at home, even as it completed the destruction of the long-deteriorating morale of front-line troops.

The Easter Offensive

In March 1972, communist forces launched a new invasion of the South, readily routing ARVN troops. The American president responded by authorizing augmented U.S. air attacks, by mining Haiphong harbor, and by establishing a naval blockade of the North. Following this communist "Easter Offensive" and Nixon's harsh response to it, Henry Kissinger and North Vietnamese representative Le Duc Tho at last formulated an agreement for withdrawing U.S. troops, returning POWs, and for laying the foundation of a political settlement through the establishment of a special council of reconciliation.

Voice of the Century

"I refuse to believe that a fourth-rate power like North Vietnam does not have a breaking point."

—Henry Kissinger, as Nixon's national security adviser, 1969

"Peace Is at Hand"

Now Kissinger was able to go before the world and announce that "peace is at hand." This assured Nixon's reelection in 1972, over the well-meaning, mild-mannered, and utterly uninspiring Democratic candidate, South Dakota senator George McGovern.

Once in office, Tricky Dick came to the fore yet again. Because they permitted Viet Cong forces to remain in place in the South, South Vietnamese president Nguyen Van Thieu had rejected the peace terms Kissinger and Tho formulated. Announcing his support for Thieu, Nixon repudiated his own envoy Kissinger and ordered massive B-52 bombing raids north of the 20th parallel.

Sure enough, the Christmas bombings brought North Vietnam back to the negotiating table, but the agreement hammered out after the bombing was not very different from what had been concluded in October. This time, however, the wishes of President Thieu were ignored. At last, on January 31, 1973, the United States and North Vietnam signed the Paris Accords, which brought U.S. withdrawal and the return of the POWs, some of whom had been languishing in North Vietnamese prisons for nearly a decade. A four-party Joint Military Commission and an International Commission of Control and Supervision supervised the cease-fire.

The war was over—but, in the world created by the Nixon White House, it wasn't *really* over. The Paris agreement notwithstanding, the Nixon administration continued to send huge amounts of military aid to the Thieu government. For their part, the communists also freely violated the accords, and Nixon seized on this fact to reenter the war more overtly. The United States Air Force once again started bombing Cambodia.

Congress Acts

But the America of 1973 was not that of 1964. Congress was as weary of the war as the American people were, and, in November 1973, lawmakers passed the War Powers Act, by which the president was required to inform Congress within 48 hours of deployment of U.S. military forces abroad. In the absence of congressional approval, troops were to be withdrawn within 60 days. The following year, Congress slashed U.S. aid to South Vietnam from $2.56 billion to $907 million, and then to $700 million in 1975.

20th-Century Life

The reunification of North and South Vietnam as the Socialist Republic of Vietnam was officially proclaimed on July 2, 1976. The new nation faced staggering problems after more than a generation of war. Millions were left homeless by the war, and, in the south, fully one-seventh of the population had been killed or wounded. Figures for the north are not available, but, doubtless, the costs were even higher. To make matters worse, the nation suffered floods followed by drought during the late 1970s. In early 1978, hundreds of thousands—mostly ethnic Chinese—fled Vietnam on foot or by boat. These refugees were popularly called "the boat people."

Except for relations with the Soviet Union, Vietnam was politically and economically isolated, the United States and most other Western countries having imposed economic embargoes. Under pressure Vietnam backed away from strict Marxist doctrine and launched a reform program patterned after the USSR's *perestroika* policy. By the late 1990s, the nation's trade relations gradually increased, and, in 1997, President Bill Clinton reestablished diplomatic relations with Vietnam, sending the first ambassador to the country since the Saigon embassy was evacuated in 1975.

As we will see before this chapter ends, by this time, the 37th president of the United States, facing the specter of impeachment for high crimes and misdemeanors, was as embattled as the Vietnamese. Nixon resigned in August 1974, after which the pace of South Vietnamese military defeat steadily accelerated. By early 1975, the situation was desperate. Congress rejected President Gerald Ford's request for $300 million in "supplemental aid" to South Vietnam, prompting Nguyen Van Thieu to resign his office and turn over leadership of his nation to Duong Van Minh. Minh performed a single official act as president of the Republic of South Vietnam. He surrendered unconditionally to the North on April 30, 1975. The Vietnam War was over.

Nearly 60,000 young Americans had been killed in this, the longest war in our history. Now, its closing moments turned an interminable tragedy into tragic farce. Television camera crews beamed to America and the world images of frenzied evacuation. United States and some South Vietnamese personnel were airlifted by helicopter from the roof of the U.S. embassy in Saigon. The spectacle was as humiliating as it was heartbreaking. If victory were strictly a matter of body count, the United States had won the war. But South Vietnam had ceased to exist, and the Asian nation was now united under a communist regime. By this measure, the war surely had been lost. At least it was over.

Portraits of anxiety: President Gerald R. Ford and Secretary of State Henry Kissinger during the evacuation of Saigon, 1975. Ford listens to a briefing. Kissinger gets the latest information by telephone.
(Images from the Gerald R. Ford Library)

Nixon and Kissinger

In contrast to President Johnson, Nixon never let his administration get entirely bogged down by Vietnam. He focused foreign policy not just on the war, but on what he saw as the nations and conditions that provided the ideological force behind North Vietnam and every other "domino" that might fall to communism. Not since Woodrow Wilson had a president so thoroughly insisted on claiming for the United States a leading role in shaping the world of the 20th century. But whereas Wilson had taken upon himself alone the task of remodeling the political world, Nixon had an ally.

His name was Henry Kissinger. Born in Germany in 1923, he immigrated to the United States with his family in 1938 to escape the Nazi persecution of Jews. Kissinger was naturalized as a citizen in 1943, studied accounting at City College, New York, then served in the U.S. Army during World War II and in the U.S. military government of Germany. In 1954, he received a Ph.D. from Harvard University, then joined its faculty. Kissinger became a professor of government in 1962 and served as director of the Defense Studies Program from 1959 to 1969. From the mid 1950s to 1968, he was called on by the administrations of Eisenhower, Kennedy, and Johnson to consult on security matters. Richard Nixon appointed him assistant for national security affairs in December 1968, then head of the National Security Council (1969–75), and, finally, secretary of state (1973–1977), under Nixon and Ford.

Century Stats

Between August 4, 1964 and January 27, 1973, 8,744,000 U.S. military personnel served in Vietnam, of whom 47,369 died in battle and 10,799 died from non-battle causes. An additional 153,3030 suffered non-fatal wounds. In current dollars, the U.S. cost of the war was approximately $140,600,000,000.

Talk of the Times

In the United States, hardline anti-communist politicians were typically called **cold warriors** because of their aggressive stance in the Cold War.

A Visit with Mao

Nixon had made his early political reputation as a hardline *cold warrior*, and, in 1969, when he took office as president, relations with no nation were icier than with communist China. But Nixon immediately began sending signals to Beijing through French president Charles de Gaulle and Yahya Khan of Pakistan. In December 1970, Yahya Khan returned from the Chinese capital with an invitation for an American envoy to discuss the status of Taiwan, the island nation to which the non-communist, "nationalist" Chinese had retreated after Mao assumed power in 1949.

A diplomatic breakthrough came in April 1971. One thing the Chinese took most seriously was table tennis—Ping-Pong—so it was no frivolous gesture when the

Chinese government invited an American team to participate in a championship tournament in Beijing. On this so-called *Ping-Pong diplomacy*, the fate of U.S.-Chinese relations—and, therefore, much of the safety and security of the world—depended.

Following the tournament, Kissinger was dispatched to China for secret talks with the Chinese premier Zhou en-Lai and with Mao himself. Kissinger pledged the removal of U.S. forces from Taiwan in return for Chinese support of a negotiated settlement in Vietnam, and Mao agreed to invite President Nixon to China for a state visit in February 1972.

Talk of the Times

Ping-Pong diplomacy was the term popularly applied to the breakthrough in U.S.-Chinese relations that occurred in 1971, when communist China invited a U.S. team to participate in a championship table-tennis tournament played in Beijing.

President Nixon meets with Mao Tse-tung. (Image from the National Archives)

A Grain of SALT

In itself, normalization of relations between the United States and the most populous nation on earth was a momentous step. It was also crucial to ending the war in Vietnam, and it made the Soviet Union more willing to achieve *détente* with the United States. Once staunch allies, China and the Soviets were now rivals in the communist world, and the USSR was not comfortable with the increased coziness between the United States and China.

In 1972, the United States was engaged in Strategic Arms Limitation Talks (SALT) with the Soviets. The

Talk of the Times

Détente is a French term signifying an easing of tension between rivals through increased diplomatic, commercial, and cultural contact.

Chinese situation not only hastened the signing of SALT agreements, which limited the nuclear stockpiles of the two superpowers, it also sparked a second, more comprehensive round of talks, SALT II, from 1972 to 1979. The U.S. Senate ultimately declined to ratify the SALT II treaty, but the Soviets and the United States nevertheless generally abided by its more extensive arms-reduction provisions.

Mission to the Holy Land

Thanks in large part to Kissinger's efforts behind the scenes, the politician derided as Tricky Dick entered the ranks of the most important and effective presidential diplomats. In 1973, much as Theodore Roosevelt had brokered peace in the Russo-Japanese War in 1905 (Chapter 7, "Rising and Sinking"), Nixon, again through Kissinger, mediated a cease-fire and troop disengagement following the Arab-Israeli War. Kissinger also helped lay the foundation for more lasting accords between these hitherto irreconcilable foes.

Talk of the Times

Terrorism is the use of force or violence by an individual or group against persons or property, usually with the purpose of coercing some desired political action.

Talk of the Times

Unaligned nations was a term applied to countries, typically small and relatively impoverished, which had declared political affinity with neither the United States nor the Soviet Union. Collectively, such nations were often referred to as the **Third World**, a term still used to describe developing countries.

Acts of Terror

The Nixon-Kissinger diplomacy consisted of bold steps and sweeping agreements, sometimes negotiated in secret, but ultimately executed on the world stage. Indeed, the 20th century was an era of increasingly global action, whether in war, diplomacy, or trade. Yet, in contrast to the great public gestures of the century, the conclusion of momentous treaties, and the actions of great armies, there was an increasing incidence of action by individuals and groups whose size and influence in the world was small.

Working in the context of mighty world powers and powerful states, leaders such as Gandhi and Martin Luther King proved the effectiveness of collective non-violence, through which the chronically powerless and oppressed might become empowered. Working in this same context, certain individuals and groups turned from non-violence to *terrorism*.

Third-World Warriors

The postwar world came to be divided into three major "camps." There were the Western powers, including the United States and its allies, which liked to refer to themselves as the "free world." There were the Eastern powers, the Soviet Union and China, along with their allies. This left a great many other nations, the majority of them small and poor, which were aligned with neither the West nor the East. These *unaligned nations* were collectively called the Third World.

In the 19th century and the early 20th, the nations that would become the Third World were mostly colonies belonging to the empires in Europe. Two world wars, however, disassembled most of the old colonial structure, the nations of the Third World emerged, replete with problems of poverty and instability, as well as animosity toward and fear of the major powers.

Although the U.N. gave all nations a voice in the international community, the Third World became a fertile field on which a new form of expression—terrorism—came into ugly blossom. Third World governments, as well as political factions within typically unstable Third World nations, knew that conducting conventional warfare against the great powers was useless. But acts of violence directed against political figures and private citizens could deliver the powerful message that, for all their strength, for all the megatonnage in their nuclear arsenals, for all the troops in their armies, for all the wealth in their treasuries, the great powers of the West were ultimately powerless to defend their citizens against the determined acts of a few skilled and daring terrorists. If conventional politics was the art of international persuasion, terrorism was the art of international blackmail.

Interrupted Journeys

On May 1, 1961, a passenger forced a commercial airliner en route from Miami to Key West, Florida, to detour and land in Cuba. By the end of the year, three more planes had been hijacked to Cuba, and, throughout the 1960s, a number of *skyjacked* aircraft, in the United States or elsewhere in the Western Hemisphere, were flown to Cuba. The skyjackers were sometimes homesick Cubans, but, more often, they were extreme leftists, who expected an open-arms welcome from the Castro regime. A number of skyjackings were acts of piracy, with the skyjackers demanding large sums of money in return for the release of the passengers.

Skyjackings to Cuba became almost routine in the 1960s and, while frightening, rarely resulted in anything more than delay for the unfortunate passengers. Beginning in the fateful year of 1968, however, skyjackings became more sinister and dangerous as politically motivated Palestinians or other Arabs commandeered aircraft in flight and deliberately used passengers and crews as hostages, threatening executions or even suicidal bombings unless certain of their comrades were released from jail, usually in Israel.

The most outrageous act of 20th-century piracy took place in September 1970, when a coordinated sequence of skyjackings over an 11-day period resulted in the taking of 300 passenger hostages and the destruction of four jet aircraft—on the ground.

The issue of "air piracy" underscored the unique dangers of terrorism. One or more individuals, either acting at the behest of a government or on their own, could take advantage of the century's

Talk of the Times

Skyjacking is a coinage from *hijacking* and describes "air piracy," the seizure of aircraft and kidnapping of passengers and crew.

367

unparalleled access to international mobility and high technology to commit a crime so ancient that it had afflicted the very first seafaring civilizations.

The prevalence and dangers of skyjacking caused the U.S. Federal Aviation Administration to institute a program of systematic searches of each airline passenger and his or her luggage. Metal detectors, X-ray units, and other devices were soon installed in all airports. In addition, through the United Nations, a series of treaties and international conventions against air piracy have been signed by many countries.

Black September

The Olympic games were first played in Greece some 3,500 years ago and were revived at the end of the 19th century through the efforts of Baron Pierre de Coubertin. Coubertin intended that the first games be held in Paris, in 1900, to inaugurate the new century, but the honor of hosting the first Olympics fell instead to Greece in 1896.

The Olympic games were intended to foster an appreciation of human achievement and international amity. This was particularly important when the games were resumed after World War II, and the summer Olympics of 1972, held in Munich, West Germany, were especially intended to be characterized by a spirit of friendship and openness. The presence of Israeli athletes on the soil of the nation that had perpetrated the Holocaust was a singularly healing gesture. Trusting to the good feelings that animated the games, security was kept to the lowest possible level. Even the dormitory buildings in the Olympic Village were unlocked.

The stage was set for perhaps the cruelest act of "peacetime" terrorism the 20th century had yet witnessed. Black September was an extremist unit of the Palestine National Liberation Movement, called al-Fatah, which was dedicated to recovering the homeland the Palestinians believed the Israelis had stolen from them. An hour before dawn on September 5, 1972, eight members of al-Fatah easily climbed the low fence surrounding the Israeli Olympic Village compound, entered Building 31 on Connollystrasse, walked up to its second floor, and knocked on the door that led to the Israelis' rooms.

Immediately, two Israelis were killed, but others managed to warn their countrymen, many of whom escaped. Nine athletes, however, were taken hostage and bound, one to another, on a sofa. The Black Septemberists demanded the release of 200 Palestinian guerrillas imprisoned in Israel and safe passage for themselves back into the Arab world. They set a noon deadline, announcing that, come noon, they would begin executing the hostages, one by one. Terrorist and guerrilla tactics were not new, but worldwide television coverage of them was. Satisfying the public's need to know, the media gave the tiny group of terrorists center stage in world events.

Although the Israeli government refused to meet the Palestinians' demands, adhering to a policy of not negotiating with terrorists, German officials offered "unlimited" ransom; some, with great heroism, even offered themselves in exchange for the captive Israelis. These negotiations bought a little more time, and German antiterrorist units took up positions to lay siege to Building 31. Against the surreal—but all too real—background of the hostage crisis, Russia and Poland continued to play Olympic volleyball not a hundred yards from the besieged dormitory.

Because the hostages were bound together, storming the building was out of the question. Authorities permitted the terrorists and their captives to board a bus for a short ride to three helicopters waiting to take them to the airport, where, as they had demanded, a Lufthansa 727 was waiting. The plan was for a sharpshooter ambush at the airport, but the plan soon fell apart. Too few sharpshooters had been positioned, and they opened fire prematurely. Although two of the terrorists were killed by the snipers and another wounded, the surviving Black Septemberists summarily executed their hostages. German police killed another three terrorists and captured the remaining three. A German police officer was also slain.

As typically happened, violence begot violence. Israel launched Phantom and Mirage jet fighter attacks against guerrilla bases and naval installations in Lebanon and Syria, and a fresh cycle of Middle Eastern violence was under way.

Dirty Tricks and Dirty Lies

Even those who sympathized with the Palestinian cause deplored the Munich assault, which not only cost innocent lives, but defiled the spirit of the Olympics. Black September deepened the spiritual malaise many felt during the period.

Pentagon Papers

For many Americans, the Nixon administration, despite its formidable diplomatic achievements, was part of this malaise, for it had created a crisis of trust. Many people were always uneasy with Nixon, but the first big jolt came in June 1971, when the *New York Times* published a series of articles on a secret government study popularly called *The Pentagon Papers*. Running to 47 volumes, the 1967–1–69 report of Defense Department analysts revealed in agonizing detail how the federal government had systematically deceived the American people with regard to its policies and practices in Southeast Asia. Revealed, among many other things, was the CIA's role in the assassination of South Vietnamese president Diem and the fact that the Gulf of Tonkin Resolution had been drafted months before the attacks on American destroyers supposedly prompted the resolution.

The top-secret study had been *leaked* in 1971 by Daniel Ellsberg, an MIT professor and high-level government consultant who had become disgusted with the Vietnam War. The Department of Justice attempted to block publication of the document, but the Supreme Court upheld freedom of the press and ruled in favor of the *Times*. Ellsberg, whom some hailed as a hero and others condemned as a traitor, was indicted for theft, espionage, and conspiracy, but the charges were dismissed in 1973 because the government had illegally obtained evidence against him—even, at the behest of the Nixon administration, burglarizing the office of his psychiatrist to collect material to embarrass him.

Bungled Burglary

The intrusion into the office of Ellsberg's psychiatrist was not the only burglary in which the president would be directly implicated. Few Americans doubted that President Nixon would achieve reelection in 1972, yet Nixon was taking no chances. He directed his reelection organization, the Committee to Re-Elect the President—familiarly known by the remarkable acronym CREEP—to ensure victory through a campaign of espionage against the Democratic party and a program of "dirty tricks" aimed at smearing Democratic challengers.

On June 17, 1972, in the midst of the presidential campaign, five burglars were arrested for having broken into the headquarters of the Democratic National Committee at the exclusive Watergate office building in Washington, D.C.

As it was soon revealed, these were no ordinary burglars, but operatives the White House called "Plumbers," assigned the mission to plug any leaks—security breaches—that might develop in the aftermath of the publication of *The Pentagon Papers*. Beyond this mission, they served Nixon as a kind of private palace guard, assigned tasks that lay well beyond the chief executive's constitutional mandate, including planting bugs (electronic listening devices) at the headquarters of the political opposition. It was yet another "dirty trick" intended to assure Nixon's reelection.

Among the Plumbers were three anti-Castro Cuban refugees (veterans of the ill-fated Bay of Pigs invasion, discussed in Chapter 21, "From Sputnik to the New Frontier") and James McCord Jr., former CIA agent and now "security" officer for CREEP. McCord reported directly to the head of CREEP, Nixon's campaign manager, none other than U.S. Attorney General John Mitchell—the chief law-enforcement agent in the country.

The entire episode would have seemed more sinister had the burglars not seemed like the gang that couldn't shoot straight. In the pocket of one of the plumbers was an address book that included the name of E. Howard Hunt, a former CIA agent (he'd been in charge of the Bay of Pigs fiasco) and writer of spy of novels who was assistant to Charles Colson, special counsel to President Nixon. What was Hunt's address? "The White House."

The Nixon administration scrambled to cover up the implications of the Watergate break-in. Attorney General Mitchell flatly declared that the "White House has had no involvement whatever in this particular incident." But, over the succeeding months, investigation resulted in the arrest, one after the other, of top Nixon aides. In September, the burglars and two coplotters—Hunt and former FBI agent G. Gordon Liddy, another CREEP operative—were indicted on charges of burglary, conspiracy, and wiretapping. After their convictions, Nixon's aides, one after the other, started talking.

A Cancer on the Presidency

What they said pointed to constitutional corruption at the very highest levels of government, yet President Nixon won reelection. Not that this put an end to the "Watergate crisis."

In February 1973, the Senate created an investigative committee headed by North Carolina Senator Sam Ervin Jr. and, as the Army-McCarthy Hearings had two decades earlier, so the Watergate Hearings riveted a nation to their television sets. As the committee uncovered the guilt of conspirator after conspirator, the president announced the resignation of one key aide after another. John Ehrlichman and H.R. Haldeman, his closest advisors, were compelled to step down. Nixon's counsel, John W. Dean III, was dismissed.

The Ervin committee discovered crimes far beyond the break-in. It was revealed that Attorney General Mitchell controlled secret monies used to finance a campaign of forged letters and false news items intended to damage the Democratic party. The extent to which major U.S. corporations had made illegal campaign contributions was revealed in detail. The burglary of Ellsberg's psychiatrist was exposed as an administration operation, as was a plan to assault Ellsberg physically. Witnesses testified that the president himself promised the Watergate burglars clemency and even bribes in return for their silence, and it was found that L. Patrick Gray, Nixon's nominee to replace the recently deceased J. Edgar Hoover as head of the FBI, had illegally turned over FBI records on Watergate to White House counsel John Dean.

The list of presidential "high crimes and misdemeanors" ground on: that two Nixon Cabinet members, Mitchell and Maurice Stans, took bribes from shady financier John Vesco; that illegal wiretap tapes were in the White House safe of Nixon advisor John Erhlichman; that Nixon directed the CIA to instruct the FBI not to investigate Watergate; that Nixon used $10 million in government funds to improve his personal homes; that during 1969–1970, the United States had secretly bombed Cambodia without the knowledge (let alone consent) of Congress.

Voice of the Century

*"I don't give a s**t what happens. I want you all to stonewall it, let them plead the Fifth Amendment, cover-up or anything else, if it'll save it—save the plan. That's the whole point."*

—Richard M. Nixon, remark to White House aides, tape recorded in the president's office at the Executive Office Building, March 1973

Voice of the Century

"I think we ought to let him hang there. Let him twist slowly, slowly in the wind."

—Telephone call from presidential adviser John Ehrlichman to John Dean, on the fate of acting FBI director L. Patrick Gray

As the Watergate crisis relentlessly rose in crescendo, the vice president of the United States, Spiro T. Agnew, was suddenly indicted for having accepted bribes when he was Maryland's governor. He resigned as vice president in October 1973 and was subsequently replaced by Congressman Gerald Ford of Michigan.

Throughout the hearings, President Nixon had managed, just barely, to avoid being decisively and directly implicated. But, at last, it was revealed that the president had covertly taped White House conversations. When special prosecutor Archibald Cox subpoenaed the tapes, Nixon claimed "executive privilege" and withheld them. He then ordered Elliot L. Richardson (who had replaced the disgraced John Mitchell as attorney general) to fire Cox. On October 20, 1973, Richardson refused and resigned in protest; his deputy, William Ruckelshaus, likewise refused and was fired. It fell to Nixon's solicitor general, Robert H. Bork, to discharge Cox, and this so-called "Saturday night massacre" seemed to prove that Nixon had a great deal to hide.

Early in the crisis, John Dean had warned Richard Nixon that there was "a cancer on the presidency." It was now about to prove fatal. Having no alternative, the president released transcripts of some of the White House tapes (containing 18$\frac{1}{2}$ minutes of highly suspicious gaps), and on July 27–30, the House Judiciary Committee recommended that Nixon be impeached on multiple counts of three charges: obstruction of justice, abuse of presidential powers, and attempting to impede the impeachment process by defying committee subpoenas. Nixon now released the remaining tapes, which clearly revealed the steps he had taken to block the FBI's inquiry into the Watergate burglary.

On August 9, 1974, Richard Milhous Nixon made a national television address. "Good evening," he began.

> This is the thirty-seventh time I have spoken to you from this office, where so many decisions have been made that shaped the history of this Nation. Each time I have done so to discuss with you some matter that I believe affected the national interest. …

> I have never been a quitter. To leave office before my term is completed is abhorrent to every instinct in my body. But as president, I must put the interests of America first. America needs a full-time president and a full-time Congress, particularly at this time with problems we face at home and abroad…. Therefore, I shall resign the presidency effective at noon tomorrow.

Voice of the Century

"My fellow Americans, our long national nightmare is over. Our Constitution works. Our great republic is a government of laws, not of men."

—Gerald R. Ford, August 9, 1974, following Nixon's resignation, his own succession to office, and a month before announcing his controversial pardon of the former president for "any offenses he may have committed" against the United States

He was the first president in American history to resign.

The Liberal Backlash

Richard Milhous Nixon had been counted out of the political picture back in 1962, when he lost a bid for the California governorship. At that time, he told perpetually hostile reporters that they wouldn't "have Dick Nixon to kick around anymore." But, of course, he did return—as president. After his resignation, many expected him to shrink into obscure retirement, but, once again, he gave the lie to the doomsayers, becoming a prolific author and consultant, whose counsel as an elder statesman was sought by subsequent presidents of both parties.

The rehabilitation of Nixon's reputation was just one of the many paradoxes that had characterized the man and his administration. A hardline anti-communist, he achieved détente with China and the Soviet Union. A diplomat with a strikingly modern world view, he was a chief executive with an archaically imperial attitude toward power, acting like an emperor as much as a president.

Triumph of the Environmentalists

A conservative Republican strongly backed by industrial and business interests, President Nixon was surely no friend of the environmental movement, which had grown to major proportions in America since the first bold federal environmental legislation of the era of Theodore Roosevelt (Chapter 8, "The World Reshaped"). Nevertheless, the late 1960s and early '70s launched what many have called the "environmental decade."

Although President Nixon did not block environmental legislation, he certainly didn't go out of his way to endorse it and, at one point, even requested from White House counsel John Ehrlichman a "plan for cooling off the excesses" in the field of environmental legislation. Nevertheless, the Nixon years saw the establishment of a Commission on Population Growth and the American Future; legislation blocking construction of a jetport in the Florida Everglades and a halt to construction of the Cross-Florida Barge Canal; enactment of the National Environmental Policy Act, a sweeping set of environmental laws; and the establishment of the Council on Environmental Quality and the very powerful Environmental Protection Agency (EPA). This body of environmental legislation, collectively the most significant passed by any nation in the century, may be an unlikely aspect of the Nixon legacy, but it is part of that legacy nonetheless.

Out of the Closet

The president had nothing to do with another issue that rose on the liberal national agenda during this period: the greater social and legal acceptance of homosexuality, the lifestyles of gay men and lesbian women. The single most significant breakthrough came in 1973, when the American Psychological Association, a highly influential professional body, voted to remove homosexuality from its standard diagnostic manual of psychological diseases.

This move was the culmination of a struggle for gay rights that, before the end of the 19th century, would have been unimaginable. The first major step toward recognition of homosexuality as something other than an illness, sin, or outright abomination was made in 1897, when a homosexual Scientific-Humanitarian Committee was founded in Berlin. The committee sponsored rallies and campaigned for legal reforms on behalf of homosexuals throughout Germany, Austria, and the Netherlands. The committee's founder, Magnus Hirschfeld, was a prime mover behind the World League of Sexual Reform, which sponsored international congresses from 1921 to 1935, when Adolf Hitler's regime put an end to the movement.

Although other gay-rights groups appeared after the war, an organized movement for gay rights did not reach the United States until Henry Hay founded the Mattachine Society in 1950 in Los Angeles; however, the movement did not achieve a truly high profile until 1969. On June 28, at about 3:00 in the morning, New York City police officers raided a gay bar, the Stonewall Inn, at 53 Christopher Street in Greenwich Village. In the past, bar patrons would have taken such harassment in stride, but, this time, some 200 gay men fought back, igniting a 45-minute riot that was repeated on succeeding nights, ultimately crystallizing into a series of organized protest rallies.

After Stonewall, gay-rights organizations proliferated, gradually succeeding in gaining the repeal of many laws against homosexuality and in securing civil rights protection for gay men and lesbians.

Roe v. Wade

If any sex-related issue has been more inflammatory during the century than homosexuality, it is abortion. We saw in Chapter 9, "Sarajevo Shooting," that birth-control activist Margaret Sanger campaigned for legalized abortion beginning in the 1910s, but the issue exploded onto the American scene in 1973, when the Supreme Court, in the case of *Roe v. Wade*, decided that a woman's constitutional right to privacy includes the right to abort a fetus, albeit only during the first trimester of pregnancy. (Beyond three months of gestation, the fetus is "viable"—capable (with medical intervention) of living outside the womb—and the Supreme Court also ruled that, after the first trimester, the state has the responsibility of protecting the unborn child.)

The Supreme Court ruling immediately gave rise to opposing movements, a "pro-choice" movement, dedicated to preserving women's right to have abortions, and a "right-to-life" movement, opposed to abortion. By the early 1980s, the right-to-lifers were calling for a constitutional amendment to ban all abortions, except in cases of rape, incest, or threat to the mother's life. The National Organization for Women (NOW) took up defense of *Roe v. Wade*, and has consistently supported pro-choice candidates for public office while the right-to-lifers have endorsed anti-abortion advocates.

From the 1973 decision onward, many political campaigns have succeeded or foundered on the single issue of abortion, an issue that has also occasioned acts of terror directed at abortion providers, including the murder of physicians and the bombing of abortion clinics. In a decade freighted with extremely complex and frustrating issues of domestic and international policy, abortion figured as an intensely human issue, which has often overshadowed all others.

The Least You Need to Know

➤ The Nixon administration attempted to achieve "peace with honor" in Vietnam through a combination of troop withdrawals and intense aerial bombing raids, including over "neutral" Cambodia and Laos.

➤ Nixon and Kissinger engineered diplomatic breakthroughs with China and the Soviet Union, and also brokered a semblance of peace between Israel and the Arab nations.

➤ The early 1970s saw a sharp rise in terrorism as a violent tool of Third World "diplomacy."

➤ Despite the conservatism of the Nixon administration, the 1970s were a decade of environmental, social, and sexual reforms.

➤ Caught in the web of the Watergate conspiracy, Richard M. Nixon became the first president of the United States to resign from office.

Hostage Situations (1974–1980)

Taking office immediately after Nixon's resignation, President Gerald R. Ford declared that "our long national nightmare is over," and he did his best to create an atmosphere of reconciliation. The affable Ford was personally far more open and likable than Nixon had been, but he received little respect from the press and public. His blanket pardon of Nixon smacked of a backroom deal, and television comics such as *Saturday Night Live*'s Chevy Chase delighted in caricaturing Ford as accident-prone and slow-witted. ("Did you hear about the power failure? President Ford was stuck on an escalator for four hours!")

The attitude toward Ford—in reality a highly intelligent and rather graceful man—was, at bottom, a symptom of how the country was feeling about itself. Just *how* was it feeling? Sick, tired, disappointed, and scared. This chapter discusses how we came through a discouraging time.

The Nation Has a Birthday

The federal government sponsored a Bicentennial Commission to mount and coordinate events celebrating the 200th anniversary of the signing of the Declaration of Independence. Back in 1876, the centennial had been a joyous national event. In 1976, however, planners found it difficult to generate much enthusiasm.

Identity Crisis

The Vietnam War was ended, but its effects continued to hover over the American spirit. Whereas troops returning from previous wars had been welcomed as heroes, Vietnam vets were regarded either as emotionally damaged or as potentially psychopathic killers who could never wash the blood of women and children from their hands. While most vets, in fact, adjusted well to a return to civilian life, a significant and highly visible minority became drug addicts, petty criminals, and "street people"—homeless misfits.

Even the best-adjusted Vietnam vets suffered from a kind of identity crisis, torn between the knowledge that they had answered their country's call, yet, in so doing, had, at the very least, wasted sacrifice in a futile and hollow endeavor and, at worst, had even made themselves hateful to many.

But, then, the entire nation was suffering from a crisis of identity. Twentieth-century Americans had become accustomed to thinking of themselves as citizens of the most powerful, the richest, the freest, and the most just nation of earth. Now, however, they weren't so sure.

Voice of the Century

Col. Harry G. Summers: "You never defeated us on the battlefield."

Anonymous North Vietnamese colonel: "That may be so, but it is also irrelevant."

—quoted in Stanley Kranow, *Vietnam: A History*, 1983

A Lack of Energy

A big part of American identity has always been bundled with the notion of abundance—an abundance of land, an abundance of treasure, and abundance of energy.

Americans used energy not just to heat and cool their homes and to operate industry, but to drive their cars. Ever since Henry Ford turned out his first Model T in 1908 (Chapter 8, "The World Reshaped"), ownership of an automobile had increasingly come to seem like an American right. Except for rationing during World War II, neither government nor world events had impinged on this right, and, through the 1960s, gasoline was plentiful and cheap. *Too* cheap, as it turned out.

At the start of the '60s, American and European oil producers, facing a glut on the market, slashed their prices. This prompted the key oil nations of the Middle East—Iran, Iraq, Kuwait, and Saudi Arabia, in addition to the Venezuela in South America—to band together as the Organization of Petroleum Exporting Countries (OPEC) on September 14, 1960, with the object of preventing a price free fall. (Qatar, Indonesia, Libya, Abu Dhabi—now part of the United Arab Emirates—Algeria, Nigeria, Ecuador, and Gabon joined later; Ecuador subsequently withdrew.)

Century Stats

With 6 percent of the world's population, the United States consumes a third of the world's energy, much of it in the form of petroleum.

For the first decade of its existence, OPEC had modest, defensive aims—to head off further reductions in the price of oil. Beginning in 1970, however, OPEC seized the offensive by pushing for price hikes. OPEC also discovered itself as a political force. On October 17, 1973, the cartel temporarily embargoed oil exports to nations, including the United States, that had supported Israel in its recent war with Egypt.

The OPEC embargo hit Americans where they lived. In 1973, gas prices were pegged at an average of 38.5 cents per gallon. By June 1974, they were up to 55.1 cents—*if* you could get gas at all. In many parts of the country, motorists were stalled in "gas lines," queues of cars extending from the pumps and round the block. Throughout the rest of the decade, OPEC held the United States and the other nations of the West hostage, exercising strict control over the supply and price of oil from the Middle East.

From Peanuts to the Presidency

In the 1976 presidential elections, voters rejected Ford's bid to stay in the White House and elevated instead Jimmy Carter. Ford was a warm and earnest man, who had nevertheless worked uncooperatively with Congress and was perceived by many as nothing more than a caretaker chief executive. Worse, a significant portion of the electorate was uncomfortable with his blanket pardon of Richard Nixon (for crimes he "may have" committed), which smelled of back-room deal making.

Governor of Georgia, Carter passed himself off as a simple peanut farmer, but, in fact, was a savvy politician who had also enjoyed a career in the Navy as a reactor engineer and assistant to Admiral Hyman Rickover, regarded as the father of the nuclear Navy. Carter understood energy, and he wanted Americans to begin conserving it, to get used to "doing with less." He endorsed a new national 55-mile-an-hour speed limit, which saved lives even as it reduced gasoline consumption. (But motorists hated it.) He appeared on television, giving speeches from the White House dressed in a cardigan sweater: He had turned down the White House thermostat; Americans should follow his example. Carter even dispensed with the customary floodlighting of the White House and its lighted Christmas decorations.

Jimmy Carter's message got through. Americans managed to reduce oil consumption by a respectable, if not spectacular, 7 percent, which was sufficient to prompt some OPEC oil-price rollbacks by the early 1980s.

Yet Americans didn't like it. They didn't like being told to do without. And most liked even less Jimmy Carter's gentle-but-stern lectures.

Stagflation

So many things just didn't seem right in the 1970s. Vietnam had cast the United States in the "wrong" role, as an aggressor and as a loser. OPEC, coming out of the Third World, suddenly had a stranglehold on the planet's premier superpower. Next, the economy went sour—but in a particularly galling way.

Economics has long been known as the "dismal science," chiefly because the realities it deals with are grim and intractable. If demand for something is high, its price will be high, and, if sufficiently high, demand will drop, depressing prices. When employment is high, inflation usually rises. If inflation is low, however, employment is generally depressed.

These are the hard trade-offs of economic life. It is almost impossible to have two good things going simultaneously—low unemployment and a low rate of inflation (although this was precisely the case in the late 1990s). Imagine, then, the feelings of a people gripped by stagflation. *Stagflation* combines the worst of a stagnant economy, in recession, with the worst of an overheated economy, suffering from inflation. A stagflated economy offers aspects of recession and inflation: high unemployment, relatively low demand, *and* high prices.

The economists, theoreticians, and economic political advisers of the late 1970s and early 1980s were vexed and frustrated. Here was an economic situation that just wasn't supposed to happen. Of course, their frustration was as nothing compared with the emotions of the ordinary working man and woman, stuck in a low-paying job—or unemployed—and paying inflated prices for everything from food to cars.

Talk of the Times

Stagflation is an economic state characterized by high unemployment and inflation—usually two mutually exclusive conditions.

For professionals, however, the frustration wasn't just academic. The economic policy measures that are used to cope with inflation are generally hard on employment and vice versa. How, then, is a government supposed to cope with a combination of inflation and recession, when the steps taken to relieve the one tend to exacerbate the other?

Ultimately, stagflation was relieved in the normal course of the business cycle and also by renewed confidence generated during the first years of Reaganomics, as we will see in Chapter 26, "Years of Plague, Years of Hope." But, in the '70s, no end was in sight.

The Right to Die and the Nature of Life

If stagflation torpedoed conventional ideas about the economy, scientific developments were calling into question traditional ideas about life as well as death.

The Karen Ann Quinlan Story

Karen Anne Quinlan was a 21-year-old New Jersey woman who, on April 15, 1975, downed a few gin-and-tonics and, perhaps, made the mistake of taking some narcotic drugs as well. She fell into unconsciousness, then lapsed into a full-blown coma from which she failed to awaken. Her doctors pronounced her condition a "persistent vegetative state" and declared that, while her most basic life processes could be kept going artificially, including respirators and intravenous nourishment, she had, for all practical purposes, ceased to be a human being.

Or had she? Had Quinlan's misfortune occurred even a few years earlier, there would be no question about her fate. The technology to sustain her life would not have existed. Even more important, nor would the technology to detect any life within her. Her coma was profound, her brain was damaged beyond recovery. To all appearances, she was dead; however, a piece of advanced medical equipment, an electroencephalograph (EEG), did detect traces of electrical activity in her brain. The activity was insufficient to produce consciousness, let alone movement or speech, but the machine said that she was not "brain dead." For most physicians and for the legal system, this meant that Karen Anne Quinlan was technically alive, even if her life was detectable only by a machine.

Quinlan's parents, deeply religious, consulted their parish priest and struggled with their consciences. At length, they determined that their daughter, tethered to an array of machines, had a *right* to "die with dignity." Physicians, medical ethicists, and jurists came down on both sides of the question, some arguing that life, whatever its state, was sacred and had to be preserved at all costs, while others agreed with the Quinlans. The 20th century had come to this: Just where was the boundary separating life and death? No one knew for sure anymore.

20th-Century Life

Karen Ann Quinlan lived a full decade after she was removed from life support, succumbing to pneumonia in 1986. By the 1980s, advocates and opponents of the "right to die" had turned from the Quinlan case to Dr. Jack Kevorkian, a retired pathologist who saw his life's mission as helping terminally ill patients to die by their own hand.

Kevorkian earned his medical degree in the 1950s. Even as a medical student, he distanced himself from accepted medical practice by advocating the establishment of suicide clinics ("obitoria") for the terminally ill.

Dubbed "Dr. Death" by the press, Kevorkian gained attention in 1990 when he enabled 54-year-old Janet Adkins of Portland, Oregon, in the early stages of Alzheimer's disease, to kill herself by using a lethal-injection machine he had devised. Kevorkian has been implicated in the deaths of at least 46 persons, frequently prosecuted for assisting suicides, and even served brief jail terms. In 1999, he was found guilty of second-degree murder for the death of Lou Gehrig's disease patient Thomas Youk. Sentenced to a long prison term, he vowed to appeal and even to starve himself to death in protest of laws against assisted suicide.

The Quinlans embarked on a precedent-setting legal battle. Karen had been on a respirator for seven months when the New Jersey Superior Court rejected their plea to have the machine turned off. "This is not a court of love, of compassion," Karen's court-appointed guardian declared, "but a court of law. You can't just extinguish life because it is an eyesore."

The New Jersey Supreme Court overturned the lower court's ruling, however, and, on March 31, 1976, the respirator was disconnected. To the surprise of all, Karen Anne Quinlan did not lapse into brain death, but persisted in a profound coma for years, as has the debate over what constitutes life and death and the point at which life becomes so painful that it is no longer endurable.

Test-Tube Babies

If the century created the conditions in which death was no longer clearly defined, it also pushed the frontiers of life to new scientific extremes—and to new ethical limits.

Throughout history, kings and commoners alike have confronted the devastating reality of infertility. Usually, this condition is the result of blocked fallopian tubes in women or low sperm count in men. Before 1978, infertility was essentially hopeless.

But, on July 25, 1978, Lesley Brown, of London, gave birth to a child conceived *in vitro*—that is, outside of the womb.

So-called "test-tube babies," such as Mrs. Brown's, are actually conceived in another piece of laboratory glassware, the culture dish. Using a surgical instrument called a laparoscope, a mature egg is removed from the mother's ovary and transferred to a culture dish containing the father's sperm and a nutrient solution. The fertilized egg is then placed in another solution, where it begins to divide. When it has divided into eight cells, it is returned to the uterus through the cervix, using a plastic tube called a cannula. With luck, the growing ball of cells implants itself in the uterine wall and develops into a fetus.

Although *in vitro* fertilization was widely hailed as a modern miracle of science, especially by infertile couples, others objected to "playing god." The Roman Catholic Church opposed in vitro fertilization on the grounds that embryos not used for implantation were destroyed; that someone other than the husband could serve as a sperm donor, thereby removing conception from the marital context; and that severing reproduction from the conjugal act is inherently sinful. Still others worried that in vitro fertilization would lead to Frankensteinian genetic experimentation.

Talk of the Times

In vitro fertilization is a medical procedure in which fertilization of an ovum takes place outside of the mother's body.

Talk of the Times

Eugenics is the practice of selectively breeding human beings with the purpose of producing offspring with certain desired traits and without other, non-desired traits.

As it turned out, "test-tube babies" were merely a first step beyond the boundaries of "natural" life. Soon, the technology became available for freezing ova, sperm, or even embryos for future implantation. It became possible for a prospective mother to be inseminated with the sperm of a man she never met, but whose genetic characteristics had been evaluated by professionals at the "sperm bank." The issue of *eugenics*, breeding human beings as if they were prize animals, came to the fore.

By century's end, techniques of *cloning*—reproduction by entirely nonsexual means—had been perfected and practiced on various mammalian species, including sheep. The only thing keeping experimenters from attempting the process with human beings was a thin membrane called ethics.

Talk of the Times

Cloning is a method of propagating a plant, animal, or even human being in the laboratory by asexual means.

Life on the Small Screen

As Chapter 18, "A War Served Cold," discussed, the technology of television was being cobbled together by the 1920s, but the medium wasn't launched as a viable commercial enterprise until the vaudeville antics of Milton Berle parted enough people from their money to put a lot of televisions in a lot of homes. A mediocre vaudeville comic, Berle had a genius for television. He hardly offered entertainment of much *cultural* value, but he clearly gave the people what they wanted, and, from then on, television was criticized for rarely reaching above the lowest common denominator.

Roots: *A Shared Experience*

In a 1961 speech to the National Association of Broadcasters, Newton Minow, chairman of the Federal Communications Commission, invited his listeners "to sit down in front of your television set when your station goes on the air ... and keep your eyes glued to that set until the station signs off. I can assure you that you will observe a vast wasteland."

The FCC chairman's damning phrase was widely quoted. It wasn't so much that people were tired of low-quality entertainment or shows so inconsequential as to be lighter than air, or even that they were concerned about how the "boob tube" was "rotting the brains" of their children. (Studies by social psychologists in the early 1960s revealed even worse effects: Televised violence prompted violent behavior and insensitivity to violence in children.)

No, what was galling about the technological wonder called television was that so much of its potential was going unrealized. Marshall McLuhan, an influential media theorist of the 1960s, predicted that television would interconnect the peoples of the world, transcending international borders and political divisions to create a *global village*.

It was a nice idea, but typical 1970s programs like *Charlie's Angels* (about three gorgeous female crime fighters) and *The Gong Show* (a bizarre reincarnation of old-time amateur-night entertainment) appealed more to the mentality of the village idiot than to citizens of a global village.

More than a glimmer of hope came during eight nights in 1977, when ABC aired *Roots*, a "mini-series" based on a novel in which African-American writer Alex Haley explored the roots of his family in slavery. One Harvard sociologist called *Roots* a "television event" and compared its impact to the televised aftermath of JFK's assassination, while a number of civil-rights leaders said that the broadcast was the most significant civil-rights event since the 1965 march on Selma, Alabama. Vernon Jordan, director of the National Urban League, called *Roots* "the single most spectacular educational experience in race relations in America."

Talk of the Times

Global village was a phrase coined by media theorist Marshall McLuhan to describe how television would bring together the diverse peoples of the world.

Roots commanded an unprecedented viewing audience of 130 million, about half the U.S. population, attracted not only by a magnificently told story and the intensity of our collective past, but by the power of television itself. By the 1970s, TV was no longer a guest in our homes, but a member of the family. The product of mass production and the conduit of mass entertainment, television is nevertheless an intimate and personal medium, the focal point of families and individuals alike. Given ambitious and meaningful material to broadcast, the medium really did take a major step toward fulfilling McLuhan's prophecy that it would create a global village.

Talk of the Times

Personal computer was a phrase coined by IBM in 1981 to describe its first desktop computer, small enough and cheap enough to be purchased and used by an individual rather than a corporation or institution.

The PC Begins a Revolution

While all of America got into *Roots* in a big way in 1977, a small segment of that public was getting involved with a brand-new product called the *personal computer*. Like *Roots*, however, this curious new appliance was destined to extend the boundaries of the nascent global village.

Chapter 18 talked about the first computers, which cost millions, weighed many tons, required a room-size environment, and called for an army of technicians to operate. In 1975, an article in the premiere issue of *Popular Electronics* announced that "the era of the computer in every home—a favorite topic among science-fiction writers—has arrived!"

The subject of the article was the Altair 8800, a computer kit that was programmable not through software, but by an array of switches, and which produced its output not on a monitor screen, but by illuminating light-emitting diodes (LEDs) on the front panel. Whereas today's desktop PC may contain 128 megabytes (128 million bytes) or more of random-access memory (RAM), Altair maxed out at eight kilobytes (8,000 bytes). Really, Altair wasn't of much immediate practical use—but, to the intelligent hobbyist, it opened the door to the potential of personal computers.

The Altair proved very popular, and by 1977, new companies such as Apple and Commodore were producing more sophisticated personal computers that employed a relatively simple programming language (originally developed for large "mainframe" computers) called BASIC, which could be readily harnessed for practical calculating and word-processing tasks.

The established computer companies, most notably IBM, at first dismissed the idea of such small, inexpensive machines. But in 1981, IBM introduced a product it dubbed the personal computer—a "PC"—and the revolution got under way. For IBM, the PC was a mixed blessing. Invested heavily in "mainframes"—the big, expensive traditional computers—IBM was often half-hearted in pushing the new product. Other manufacturers jumped in to fill the vacuum, and IBM found itself trailing the very market it had created. Competition, however, accelerated development of the PC, which grew prodigiously in memory and capability.

But the next big step came when the PC was linked to a vast network of computers called the Internet, which we will look at in Chapter 28, "Prosperity and Scandal." In the workplace, the desktop PC gave the humblest middle manager access to much of the information formerly available only to those closeted in the board room. By the end of the century, more than half of the homes in America had personal computers, which plugged ordinary people into unimaginably vast sources of instant information. McLuhan seemed more on the money than ever before.

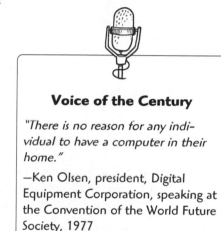

Voice of the Century

"There is no reason for any individual to have a computer in their home."

—Ken Olsen, president, Digital Equipment Corporation, speaking at the Convention of the World Future Society, 1977

Peacemakers, Fanatics, and Revolutionaries

The *Roots* phenomenon and the PC were about solidarity and personal empowerment—themes that, for better as well as worse, dominated the late 1970s and early 1980s.

Temple of Doom: The Jonestown Massacre

Americans have long both celebrated and feared individualists. Even today, for example, history teachers wrestle with how to present a man like John Brown, the abolitionist whose raid on the federal arsenal at Harpers Ferry heralded the Civil War. Was he a bold individualist and revolutionary in the American tradition? Or was he simply a dangerous deviant?

Similarly, there was much to admire about James Warren Jones. Born on May 13, 1931, in Lynn, Indiana, he dedicated himself in the 1950s and '60s to an independent ministry to the poor of Indianapolis. In 1967, however, he moved his church to California, settling first in Ukiah and then, in 1971, in San Francisco. He called it the People's Temple and attracted a following who came to believe that Jim Jones was the messiah. Jones did nothing to discourage this belief.

The press did not portray Jones as a minister to the poor, but as the leader of a cult, who was not only ruling the minds of his congregation, but who was also embezzling temple funds. Under intense pressure and facing certain criminal investigation, Jones moved his temple again—this time to Guyana, South America. Guyana had no extradition treaty with the United States, and its jungles were among the most remote places on earth. Jones set up a communal compound he called Jonestown and, away from the interference of press and the law, seized control not only of his followers' minds, but of their passports, assets, and, in the case of attractive women, their bodies as well.

The families of the Jonestown cultists prevailed on California congressman Leo Ryan to investigate Jonestown, and on November 14, 1978, Ryan and a group of journalists and relatives of the cultists, arrived in Guyana. Although Jones, by this time heavily addicted to narcotics, stage-managed the appearance of a happy community, 14 residents begged Ryan for rescue.

On November 18, Ryan and his party, including the defectors, prepared to leave from an airstrip near the compound. Jones dispatched a group of assassins, who opened fire on those about to leave. Ryan and four others, including three journalists, were killed, but others escaped. Rather than face what would come next, Jones executed what was clearly a well-rehearsed plan of mass suicide. Cyanide-laced Flavor-Aide punch was distributed to all, men, women, and children. Most drank it willingly, but those who didn't were compelled at gunpoint. A total of 913 human beings, 276 of them children, died. Jones apparently shot himself.

Men of Good Will: The Camp David Accords

Jim Jones had no corner on 20th-century fanaticism, of course. Ever since Israel had been carved out of Arab land in 1948, the Middle East seemed to be animated by fanatical passions rather than any rational effort to achieve peaceful coexistence.

It took the extraordinary courage of Egypt's president, Anwar Sadat, to make the first move toward peace. Sadat, formerly a high-ranking army officer and protégé° of Gamal Abdel Nasser, implacable enemy of Israel, took, on November 19-21, 1977, the unimaginable step of making a state visit to Israel and addressing the Knesset (Israeli parliament). The result of this gesture was a series of negotiations between Sadat and Israeli prime minister Menachem Begin (who, like Sadat, had been a hardline military officer). When talks reached a deadlock in 1978, President Jimmy Carter invited both heads of state to Camp David, the rural Maryland retreat established by Franklin Roosevelt as Shangri-La in 1942 and renamed Camp David in 1953 by Dwight Eisenhower after his grandson.

Having concluded the Camp David Accords, on September 17, 1978, Egypt's Anwar Sadat shakes hands with Prime Minister Menachem Begin of Israel as President Jimmy Carter looks on. (Image from the Israeli National Photograph Collection)

With great determination and skill, Carter mediated negotiations between Sadat and Begin, and, after 12 days of talks, the three emerged with a framework for a peace treaty between Israel and Egypt and an outline of a program for peace throughout the Middle East.

20th-Century Life

Together with Menachem Begin, Sadat was awarded the Nobel Prize for Peace in 1978, and, after continued negotiations, the two concluded a treaty of peace between Egypt and Israel on March 26, 1979. It was the first between Israel and any Arab nation.

The price of peace for Sadat was high. On October 6, 1981, as Sadat was reviewing a military parade commemorating the Arab–Israeli War of 1973, he was assassinated by Muslim extremists.

Khomeini in Iran

In 1979, the *Ayatollah* Ruhollah Khomeini, who, from exile in Paris, had long led a movement against Muhammad Reza Shah Pahlavi, the Shah of Iran, returned to Iran after the shah fled the country. It was an all-too-familiar 20th-century story. The shah had been a faithful anti-communist U.S. ally, but had also ruled his nation as a tyrant, enforcing his authority with the brutal and much-hated Savak, a secret police force.

Yet Khomeini was no communist, and the revolution that had been wrought in Iran was a matter of religion rather than of secular politics; it was an Islamic revolution. But even if Iran was not yet another domino falling to the communists, the United States would be drawn into the struggle. The shah fled into exile in January 1979. In October, he fell desperately ill with cancer and was granted permission to come to the United States for medical treatment. In response to this gesture, on November 4, 500 Iranians stormed the U.S. embassy in Tehran and took hostage 66 U.S. embassy employees, demanding the return of the shah.

Talk of the Times

An **ayatollah** is a religious leader among the **Shiite** Muslims, whose religious zeal and orthodoxy is often compared to that of Christian "fundamentalists."

President Carter refused to betray America's ally. The shah voluntarily left the United States in early December, but this did not bring the release of the hostages (except for 13, either black or female, who were let go during November 19–20). In frustration, Carter authorized an Army Special Forces unit to attempt a rescue on April 24, 1980. The mission miscarried and had to be aborted. Fortunately, its failure did not result in harm to the hostages, but it seemed just one more humiliating defeat for a militarily and economically humbled superpower.

At last, in November 1980, the Iranian parliament proposed conditions for the release of the hostages, including an American pledge not to interfere in Iranian affairs, the release of Iranian assets frozen in the United States by President Carter, the lifting of all U.S. sanctions against Iran, and the return of the shah's property to Iran. An agreement was signed early in January 1981, but Khomeini purposely delayed the release of the hostages until January 20, the day Ronald Reagan, having defeated Jimmy Carter in his reelection bid, was inaugurated as the 40th president.

In an act of justice and grace, the new president asked Carter to serve as his special envoy to greet the returning hostages at a U.S. base in West Germany. Nevertheless, the Iran hostage crisis was seen by many Americans as a failure of the Carter administration, and it certainly ensured that he would not be reelected.

The End of a Banana Republic

As the longtime alliance with the Shah of Iran demonstrated, the United States, self-proclaimed defender of democracy and human rights throughout the world, often supported tyrants, whether to block communism, to reap the profits of big business, or both. Such was the case with the regime of the Somoza family in Nicaragua.

As we saw in Chapter 5, "Through the Golden Door," beginning in the 19th century, giant American-owned fruit companies exerted great influence on the fate of "banana republics" such as Nicaragua. From 1909 to 1925, a detachment of U.S. Marines was stationed there to back the authority of the conservative government, which acted harshly toward Nicaraguan peasants, but was friendly to American business. When the

Marines were withdrawn, civil war immediately broke out, and the Marines returned. An election was conducted under U.S. supervision, which resulted in the installation of liberal party presidents in 1938 and 1932. Before they again left in 1933, the Marines trained the Nicaraguan National Guard and handpicked Anastasio Somoza Garcia to command it.

Although the liberal government of the 1930s was less repressive than the conservative government had been, Nicaraguan radicalism was not dead. The radical Cesar Augusto Sandino continued to lead resistance against both the government and the U.S. presence and influence. Somoza Garcia invited Sandino to a peace conference, then treacherously assassinated him—doing so in the confidence that the United States would not object. In 1936, Somoza Garcia assumed power, inaugurating the long Somoza dynasty, which exploited Nicaragua's meager wealth, while serving the interests of American business.

Voice of the Century

"Somoza may be a son of a bitch, but he's our son of a bitch."

—Attributed to Franklin D. Roosevelt, about 1936

Opposition to the Somoza regime intensified in the 1970s, culminating in the overthrow of Anastasio Somoza Debayle in 1979 and the installation of a Sandinista government (named in honor of Sandino). The Sandinistas established close ties with Cuba, an action that President Reagan interpreted as a falling domino in Central America. The new American president authorized some $20 million to arm former members of Somoza's national guard, now counter-revolutionaries, or *contras*—"Freedom fighters," Reagan called them—living in exile in Honduras and El Salvador. The consequences of this action we will explore in Chapter 26.

The Soviets in Afghanistan

The United States was not the only superpower mired in violent Third World politics. Late in December 1979, the Soviet Union sent troops into Afghanistan, with which it shared a border, to install and support a Marxist government under Prime Minister Babrak Karmal. The Soviet objective was to create an economically dependent client state to serve as a buffer against Pakistan, which now enjoyed cozy relations with China—by now a dangerous rival to Soviet power.

More than 100,000 Soviet troops, including air and ground forces, sought to deliver a quick and crushing blow to the anti-Marxist resistance led by the *mujahadin*, "Islamic warriors."

Like the Viet Cong in America's Vietnam War, the mujahadin were poorly equipped, while the Soviets had all the weaponry of a modern superpower. But, also like the Viet Cong, the mujahadin were skilled guerrillas, fighting on their home territory, in a cause to which their devotion was absolute. Repeatedly, they prevailed against the vastly superior Soviet forces, steadily eroding the morale and resolve of the Russian soldiers and command.

20th-Century Life

Following the Soviet invasion of Afghanistan in December 1979, President Jimmy Carter called for a boycott of the 1980 Olympics, which were to be held in Moscow. Sixty nations joined the United States in the boycott; however, Great Britain, France, Italy, and Sweden, all prominent Western nations, did not stay away, although several nations refused to attend the opening ceremony. The games were marred by bad feelings, violent behavior from spectators, cheating by officials, and Soviet security so intrusive that winners in track events were physically prevented from taking the traditional victory laps.

The 1980 boycott was not the first. Only 49 nations—including the United States—chose to attend the 1936 Olympics in Berlin. Others boycotted the games in protest of Nazi racism. An alternative set of games, the "People's Olympics," was scheduled for Barcelona, Spain, but was aborted because of the outbreak of the Spanish Civil War.

Indeed, Afghanistan became the Soviet Vietnam and was among the many pressures that helped bring about the eventual collapse of the Soviet Union (Chapter 27, "Red Sunset and Desert Flames"). The Soviets withdrew during 1989, leaving behind, however, not the democracy the West had hoped for, but a power vacuum in which various religious factions—none particularly friendly to the West—continued to fight.

Solidarity

Simpler and more straightforward was the struggle against communism that took shape in Poland during the 1970s and 1980s. The world's communist revolutions were driven by the world's workers because they felt that communism would serve their needs as capitalism had not. But when communism failed the workers, it was the workers who started the movement to end communism.

In Europe, the anticommunist revolution began with the Workers' Defense Committee formed in Poland in 1976. In 1979, the committee published a Charter of Workers' Rights, which sparked general strikes throughout Poland the following year. The most intense activity was in Gdansk, where some 17,000 workers struck the Lenin Shipyards, barricading themselves within the vast facility.

They were led by an electrician named Lech Walesa, a naturally charismatic leader who not only directed the local action but formed an Interfactory Strike Committee, which coordinated the movement throughout the country. On August 30, 1980, Walesa elicited from General Wojciech Jaruzelski, the Polish head of state, consent to the right of unions and strikes, as well as concessions in the areas of political and religious expression. The following month, a national labor party, Solidarity, was formed, with a membership of 10 million—virtually the entire labor force of Poland.

Solidarity was not only a viable national party, it inspired a following worldwide. Teenagers in the United States and western Europe took to wearing t-shirts bearing the Solidarity banner. Nevertheless, Solidarity almost became a victim of its own success. Walesa, a strong leader, was a moderate, who believed in achieving change incrementally. Against his wishes, Solidarity became increasingly imperious in the demands it made, and Jaruzelski, bowing to his Soviet handlers, imposed martial law on Poland on December 31, 1981. He outlawed Solidarity and began arresting its leaders.

At this point, Solidarity went underground, diligently organizing a new wave of strikes, which swept Poland in 1988. The following year, the government recognized and reinstated Solidarity, allowing it to participate in free elections. The party took 99 out of 100 Senate seats and all 161 seats in the Sejm (the lower house of the Polish parliament). Solidarity's Taduesz Mazowiecki was named prime minister, Jaruzelski resigned, and, in 1990, Walesa was elected to the office of president.

Poland had its first non-communist government in four decades, and it signaled the impending collapse of communism throughout Europe and, ultimately, the end of the Soviet Union.

Made in Japan

Since the end of World War II, Americans had been resigned to losing a certain amount of ground to the communists. Now they breathed an exhilarated sigh of relief as communism itself began to shrivel and contract.

It seemed like a vindication of Western capitalism. The only trouble was that Western capitalism wasn't doing all that well, either.

Things Fall Apart

Gripped by stagflation, Americans were also depressed by the conditions they saw around them. Many things seemed down at the heels, shabby, in disrepair. The national system of highways, for example, the pride of 1950s America, were pitted with potholes. The nation's bridges were a national disgrace—many so deteriorated that they were in imminent danger of collapse. The "white flight" from the inner cities, which had begun in the '50s, continued unchecked, and street crime became a major concern.

Then there was New York. Traditionally the cultural and economic capital of the United States, it had become an unwilling emblem not of the

Century Stats

President Ford signed a $2.3 billion loan to New York City on December 9, 1975, exactly two days before the city would have defaulted on its loans. The city made all of its loan repayments on time, and the U.S. Treasury cleared a modest profit on the so-called "bail out."

nation's greatness, but of its decay. Everything was bigger and badder in Gotham: poverty, decay, crime, and corruption. In 1975, Mayor Abe Beame announced the stunning news that his city could not pay its creditors. New York City was broke.

Many Americans saw the financial state of New York as both symbol and symptom of urban America's spiritual bankruptcy, and President Gerald Ford did not help matters when he steadfastly refused to extend federal aid to avert default. The *New York Daily News* trumpeted an instantly famous headline:

FORD TO NY: DROP DEAD!

Through the efforts of such Democratic leaders as Texas representative Jim Wright, Congress ultimately voted emergency loans, and the city avoided bankruptcy.

Who Drives an American Car?

Then there was the U.S. auto industry. In 1981, Detroit turned out 6,200,000 passenger cars—a 20-year low. American cars had earned a reputation as junk—poorly designed, poorly engineered, poorly made. All over the world, including right here in the United States, people were passing over the long-familiar names of Chevy and Ford to buy Toyotas, Datsuns, Hondas, and other imports from Japan, the nation we had defeated in World War II, and which now was producing products of all kinds, more cheaply, with better engineering, and higher quality than in America.

Meltdown at Three-Mile Island

Potholes were hell on tires and suspensions, and urban economic meltdown was bad enough. But there was worse to come. During the late 1950s and early 1960s, Americans were subject to an intense publicity campaign to sell them on the peaceful use of the atom. Nuclear power was touted as the key to cheap and virtually limitless energy. At staggering cost, nuclear power plants were built across the nation, but by the 1970s, environmentalists and others were questioning the safety of atomic power. Not only did effluent water from the plants raise the temperature of river water, thereby endangering life in these streams, but no one had ever devised a workable plan for disposing of the radioactive waste products the plants produced. Most of all, what would happen if something just plain went wrong?

Adding to the woes of the nuclear-power industry was the reality that the plants were proving far more costly than anyone had ever imagined. By the end of the 1970s, nuclear power was under serious and sustained assault.

Issues surrounding nuclear power were sufficiently popular that Hollywood made a movie around the theme. *The China Syndrome* was about a nuclear accident

Voice of the Century

"A nuclear power plant is infinitely safer than eating because 300 people choke to death on food every year."

—Dixy Lee Ray, chair of the Atomic Energy Commission, 1977

in a California power plant. The film's title came from the theory that a full-scale *meltdown* of a reactor's core (caused by a chain reaction gone out of control) would burn so intensely that the radioactive core material would, in effect, sear its way deep into the earth—down to China, experts grimly joked.

On March 28, 1979, days after the movie hit the theaters, a combination of mechanical and human error at the Three Mile Island electric generating plant, near the Pennsylvania capital of Harrisburg, caused one of the reactors to lose coolant water, exposing the reactor core and initiating a partial meltdown.

A badly shaken Pennsylvania governor Richard Thornburgh appeared on television to warn residents to remain indoors and advised pregnant women to evacuate the area. The accident had already released an amount of radioactive gases into the atmosphere, and experts disagreed about the dangers of an explosion posed by the accumulation of hydrogen gas in the reactor containment building.

There is ample evidence that plant officials improperly delayed notifying public authorities of the accident. Nevertheless, the plant's backup safety features did successfully prevent a major disaster of the proportions of the April 26, 1986 meltdown at Chernobyl in the Ukraine, which would kill 31 persons immediately and untold additional numbers as a result of radioactive contamination of an area that is home to millions.

But Three Mile Island was bad enough. It capped the growing American impression that Americans had somehow lost the ability and wherewithal to do anything right.

Talk of the Times

Meltdown is a condition in which the radioactive material at the core of a nuclear reactor becomes superheated as a result of a runaway chain reaction. The end result may be an explosion, as the core material melts down through the earth then contacts ground water.

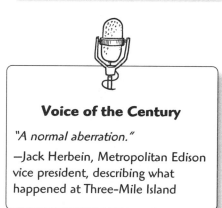

Voice of the Century

"A normal aberration."

—Jack Herbein, Metropolitan Edison vice president, describing what happened at Three-Mile Island

Hostage Crisis

The Iranian hostage crisis of 1979–81 was no mere metaphor. It was real, and, with each passing day, the nation feared for the well-being of those held captive. Nevertheless, as time went on, the crisis also came to seem a symbol of the state of the nation. We saw ourselves as a mighty power held hostage by Third World strife, by a cruelly "stagflated" economy, and, most of all by our own loss of confidence, spirit, and positive national identity.

The Least You Need to Know

➤ The post-Vietnam era was plagued by a bad economy ("stagflation") and a general crisis of American confidence.

➤ The late 1970s brought radical new perspectives on the nature of life (with "test-tube" babies) and death (dramatized by the case of Karen Ann Quinlan).

➤ By the end of the 1970s, television and the advent of the personal computer were helping to transform the world into what Marshal McLuhan had called a "global village."

➤ The 1970s saw a host of extremists and fanatical actions, ranging from the Jonestown tragedy to the Iranian hostage crisis, as well as the heroism of men of goodwill—the Sadat–Begin peace accords in the Middle East.

Chapter 26

Years of Plague, Years of Hope (1980–1989)

In This Chapter

➤ The appeal of Reagan and Reaganomics

➤ A decade of buyout, merger, and acquisition

➤ The AIDS crisis

➤ Some consequences of Reaganomics

➤ Cold War victory

➤ The communist world shrinks

We think of history as being made up of great events and movements. Certainly, no century offered more of these than the 20th. Yet history, the direction and fate of a people at a particular time and in a particular place, is also shaped by feelings, and in 1980, the nation was feeling low. No one doubted the earnestness and essential decency of President Jimmy Carter. A low-key leader, he believed in leveling with the people, even if that meant telling them unpleasant truths. It was an admirable approach to the office of president, but it was not very inspiring. And, in 1980, Americans were ready to be inspired.

Why Reagan?

For generations, American boys—and, more recently, girls as well—have been told by parents and teachers that "anyone can be president of the United States." The remarkable thing about this old saw is that it's *true*. In most other nations, even republics and democracies in which governance is not inherited, there is a sort of ruling class, a set of young people who are, in effect, brought up and educated to assume the reins of government. Such is not always the case in America. Our presidents have come from all walks of life: soldiers, lawyers, tailors, farmers, haberdashers, college professors.

Ronald Wilson Reagan had been a sports announcer, film actor (even costarring with a chimp named Bonzo), and a minor television personality before he was elected governor of California in 1966, defeating the popular Democrat Pat Brown and earning a reputation as a ruthless Republican tax-cutter.

Voice of the Century

"I used to fantasize what it would be like if everyone in government would quietly slip away and close the doors and disappear. See how long it would take for the people of this country to miss them.... We would get along a lot better than we think."

—Ronald Reagan, on the campaign trail, 1980

The "Great Communicator"

In his 1980 bid for the White House, Reagan would trade heavily on what he had done in California, how he had slashed state taxes and reduced the size of state government. The national electorate liked the sound of this—and they did not seem to hear the other side of the Reagan tax cuts: How county and city governments more than commensurately increased taxes to make up for reduced state support. The people also liked the idea of cutting "big government" down to size—a leading Reagan theme—since, after all, big government had failed both to end stagflation and to extricate the hostages from Iran. All big government did was tax, tax, *tax*.

Official photograph of Ronald Reagan. (Image from the White House Photograph Collection)

Ronald Reagan had a B-movie actor's talent for reducing complex issues to simple messages and for reviving hope and pride in America. One of his best-known film roles had been as George Gipp, Notre Dame's star football player better known as "the Gipper," in the 1940 *Knute Rockne, All American*. Older now, Reagan no longer saw himself as the Gipper, but as Rockne himself, the legendary Notre Dame coach, now willing and able to inspire America to victory in the big game. An enthusiastic press dubbed President Reagan the "Great Communicator."

Supply Side, Trickle Down, and Something Called the Laffer Curve

Whereas President Carter was clearly uncomfortable making speeches, reading his material deliberately, slowly, and with an awkward sense of timing that often made his messages difficult to follow, Reagan was smooth, confident, and incisive—a pleasure to listen to, even when he said stunningly stupid things. When, for example, environmentalists pointed to a need for more regulation of automobile pollution, candidate Reagan responded incongruously that trees were responsible for more air pollution than cars. Shortly before his inauguration, the president-elect paid a courtesy call on the Democratic speaker of the House, Thomas "Tip" O'Neill in O'Neill's office. When the speaker remarked to Reagan that his desk had once belonged to Grover Cleveland, the president-elect replied that he "played him once in a movie." "No, Mr. President," O'Neill gently countered, "you played Grover Cleveland Alexander, the baseball player."

And so it went. But it hardly mattered. The new president's popularity knew no bounds. Nothing negative stuck, so that the press often referred to him as the "Teflon president." The president called upon all his powers of persuasion to sell the nation on his economic agenda, which he set about installing with a speed that recalled FDR during the "100 days" (Chapter 13, "The Party Ends").

Heading up the Office of Management and Budget (OMB) was director David Stockman, a young man whose unsmiling appearance seemed to signal his enthusiasm as a slasher of taxes and domestic social-welfare spending. Stockman executed a conservative economic policy called *supply-side economics*. Ever since John Maynard Keynes had

Voice of the Century

"Approximately 80 percent of air pollution stems from hydrocarbons released by vegetation, so let's not go overboard in setting and enforcing tough emission standards from man-made sources."

—Candidate Ronald Reagan, 1980

Talk of the Times

Supply-side economics is an economic approach aimed at achieving efficiency by using government policies to stimulate production.

Talk of the Times

Trickle down, a catch phrase of the Reagan years, described the belief that reducing taxes on the wealthy and on businesses would stimulate investment, thereby increasing employment opportunities and improving the economy, the benefits of which would eventually "trickle down" to the majority of Americans.

called for government intervention to stimulate the economy out of the doldrums of the Great Depression (Chapter 13), the dominant approach to the economy had been to support consumers—the working stiffs and ordinary citizens. In contrast, the idea now was to stimulate the production of goods and services (the "supply side") in the belief that supply creates demand: Make it, and people will buy it. In this scheme, the proper role of government is to spur production by reducing taxes as well as reducing the regulation of industry.

There was, however, a catch. Even as taxes were reduced, conservative supply-side economics also called for operating the government on a balanced budget, because deficit spending encourages destructive inflation. In fact, what came to be called *Reaganomics* rested on three legs:

➤ Reducing government regulation of commerce and industry

➤ Slashing government spending

➤ Cutting taxes

20th-Century Life

The Teflon president seemed immune not only to political attacks, but to a far more serious attack. Reagan had been in office two months when he left the Washington Hilton Hotel on March 30, 1981, after a speech. Six shots issued from a .22-caliber revolver loaded with explosive "Devastator" rounds. Secret Service agent Timothy J. McCarthy and Washington police officer James Delahanty were wounded, as was White House press secretary James S. Brady, who was shot in the head.

Secret Service agents bundled the president into his limousine, which sped away. At first it appeared that the president was unhurt, but he had been wounded in the chest. The bullet, lodged in his lung, had failed to explode and was removed in an emergency surgical operation.

The shooter was 25-year-old John Warnock Hinckley Jr., the drifter son of a wealthy Denver oil engineer. Hinckley had a bizarre obsession with actress Jodie Foster, who had made a sensation as a teenaged prostitute in the 1976 film *Taxi Driver*, a film dealing in part with political assassination. Hinckley apparently decided to kill the president to impress Foster. A jury found Hinckley not guilty by reason of insanity, and he was confined to a psychiatric hospital. All of his victims fully recovered, except for Brady, who was left partially paralyzed. Brady became a highly effective advocate of federal regulation of handguns, a policy President Reagan himself opposed.

The president had quite a sales job ahead of him. The tax cuts he proposed would not directly benefit middle- and lower-income individuals—the vast majority of Americans—but the wealthiest minority, and business. Reagan had to persuade the people that reducing the tax burden on the rich would free up more money for investment, the benefits of which would ultimately *trickle down* to the less well-off in the form of more and better jobs.

Even more difficult was persuading the American people that taxes could be cut *and* the budget balanced. Reagan insisted that cutting taxes would actually increase government revenue—a notion so fantastic that Vice President George Bush had called Reagan's idea "voodoo economics" when he ran against him in the Republican primaries. But Reagan called on conservative economist Arthur Laffer to explain that tax cuts would stimulate increased investment and savings, thereby ultimately increasing taxable income and generating more revenue. The president frequently alluded to the "Laffer Curve" as proof of this theory.

The fact was that a majority of Americans were prepared to take any economic leap their new president proposed, and, in 1981, a bold program was hurried through an often bewildered Democratic Congress. It included a major tax cut, a staggering $43-billion cut in domestic programs, broad cutbacks in environmental and business regulation, but dramatic increases in defense spending.

In Praise of Greed

The drastic first steps of Reaganomics were designed to "jump-start the economy," and, in fact, a relatively small number of people became very wealthy very quickly.

Money, Money Everywhere

Critics of Reaganomics pointed out that the new wealth came not as a result of increased production and consumption, but by a frenzy of corporate acquisitions and mergers. It wasn't so much that more products were being made and sold, but that more money was changing hands. Companies were acquired and merged for efficiency—with a resulting loss of jobs—or they were dismantled, their component parts and assets sold at a profit for happy stockholders—again with a resulting loss of jobs.

The unemployment produced by the high-level financial activity of the 1980s was hard on the man and woman in the street, but the movement of huge blocks of capital enriched the few who could afford to invest in the right companies at the right time.

Voice of the Century

"Greed is all right, by the way ... I think greed is healthy. You can be greedy and still feel good about yourself." —Ivan Boesky, address to the graduating class of the School of Business Administration at the University of California, Berkeley, May 18, 1986

"The point is, you can't be too greedy." —Donald Trump, *The Art of the Deal*, 1987

Shell Games

For generations, Americans had been raised to believe that businesses existed to make products and to provide employment. The 1980s brought a different view. Financial movers and shakers insisted that companies existed first and foremost to enrich investors, and they would play any game to achieve this end. If destroying a company, breaking it up, would put money in the investors' pockets, so be it.

In the words of Gordon Gecko, a fictional tycoon based on real-life Wall Street financier Ivan Boesky, played by Michael Douglas in the popular movie *Wall Street* (1987): "Greed is good. Greed is right. Greed will save the USA."

The Down and the Out

Out of the gate, confidence in Reaganomics was high, but it soon faltered as the recession of the Nixon-Ford-Carter years deepened even further. But when inflation at last began to roll back, the public was willing to grasp at that single straw, and support for Reagonomics remained high, despite continued high interest rates and high unemployment.

Talk of the Times

Homeless people became a ubiquitous euphemism for those formerly described as indigent, derelicts, or bums.

In the meantime, the money moving back and forth on Wall Street was just too seductive to ignore. Of course, it was also becoming difficult to ignore the legion of *homeless people* living on the city streets. Not since the Great Depression had the down-and-out and desperate been so much in evidence.

The homeless were the tip of the economic iceberg. For every homeless person, there were many, many Americans who still had roofs over their heads, but who were nevertheless running out of time and money. Chronically unemployed or underemployed; unable to service heavy household debt; certainly unable to save, let alone invest, any portion of their income; they struggled along, the walking wounded of Reaganomics.

The "Gay Plague"

Yet life went on, and the Great Communicator still managed to make more people feel better about themselves and their nation than they had in a long time.

But not everyone was feeling well. Late in the 1970s, certain rare cancers and gravely serious infections were suddenly appearing in previously healthy young individuals. By the end of the decade, it had become clear that these people had a single fact of life in common: they were either gay or bisexual, or intravenous drug users who shared dirty needles. In 1981, acquired immune deficiency syndrome, AIDS, was formally described by physicians.

And the Band Plays On

As "gay cancer" or the "gay plague," AIDS began to draw a great deal of attention, even as mainstream heterosexual America breathed a sigh of relief that the terrible and universally fatal disease seemed confined to homosexuals. With that feeling of immunity came apathy and, in some cases, cruel moralism, as if AIDS were a biblical plague visited upon the sinful. As for President Reagan, he didn't even mention the subject of AIDS until 1987—despite the growing numbers of victims, including intravenous drug users, hemophiliacs, and others (such as transfusion recipients) who might receive contaminated blood or blood products.

Grass Roots

Despite a dearth of government funding of AIDS research, scientists in France (led by Luc Montagnier at the Pasteur Institute) and the United States (led by Robert Gallo at the National Institutes of Health) identified the human immunodeficiency virus (HIV), which causes AIDS by attacking certain white blood cells, T4 lymphocytes, thereby greatly compromising the body's immune system and leaving it vulnerable to a variety of fatal infections.

The discovery of the cause of this baffling disease was a great scientific breakthrough, but it did not provoke concerted government action to combat the disease. Instead, gay men and lesbian women, already politically sophisticated, quickly banded together in grass-roots organizations to fight AIDS with whatever tools were currently available, chiefly providing AIDS education and medical care.

Organizations such as the Gay Men's Health Crisis (GMHC) and AIDS Coalition to Unleash Power (ACT UP) were vehement in criticism of the Reagan administration's failure to respond to an epidemic perceived to affect socially "marginal" groups: homosexuals and intravenous drug abusers. Largely through the efforts of AIDS activists, the national consciousness and political conscience were raised, so that federal funding was increased from $5.6 million in 1982 to more than $2 billion a decade later.

Century Stats

By the close of the 1990s, there had been more than 8 million cases of AIDS worldwide, resulting in 6 million deaths. About 750,000 victims were in the United States, and some 23 million individuals throughout the world were infected with HIV, the virus that causes AIDS.

Bhopal and Chernobyl

If the American mainstream was able to turn a blind eye toward the epidemic in their own country, it was even easier to ignore deplorable conditions in the rest of the world.

First-World Industry, Third-World Consequences

Twentieth-century civilization offers many products and benefits that come with unseen dangers. If we want a cheap, reliable, and plentiful supply of food, then pesticides are a necessary evil.

But just how evil? In the United States, as a result of decades of environmental legislation, the manufacture and use of such potentially lethal substances as pesticides are strictly regulated. Such regulation is expensive, and many large chemical manufacturers regularly look elsewhere for places to set up shop.

Many nations of the Third World, desperate to relieve their chronic poverty by rapidly industrializing, welcomed such companies with open arms, offering an abundance of cheap land and cheap labor and an absence of government regulation. Such was the case with India and a town called Bhopal. Here the American-based multinational chemical giant Union Carbide built a pesticide plant, which loomed over the workers' shantytown that sprouted in its shadow.

The night of December 3, 1984 was unusually cold for central India, when a worker reported that an indicator was showing dangerously high pressure in a storage tank holding MIC, methyl isocyanate, a deadly concentrated pesticide ingredient. The worker alerted his supervisor, who sounded an alarm, but it was already too late. A cloud of white gas, 45 tons of poison, had escaped and was spreading over Bhopal.

"It was like breathing fire," one survivor recalled. People panicked, choked, vomited, defecated, collapsed, died. Before the cloud dissipated, more than 2,500 people were dead and at least 200,000 more had been injured, perhaps half of them permanently, suffering such ills as blindness, sterility, kidney disease, liver infections, tuberculosis, and brain damage.

The plant at Bhopal was all too typical of Third World industrial installations: understaffed and operating with few safety procedures. The 1984 disaster was not the first accident at the plant. On October 5, 1982, a flange joining two pipes split, releasing gas and touching off a minor riot. Indeed, leaks were routine, reported in 1983 and in January 1984, resulting in the death of a worker. The Indian government, unwilling to close the plant even temporarily, ignored these incidents. It was 1989 before the Indian Supreme Court ordered Union Carbide to pay $470 million in compensation.

Deadly Metaphor in Russia

As many saw it, Bhopal was a horrible metaphor for how the industrialized world—the "First World"—routinely exploits the Third World. But, by the 1980s, it was getting more difficult to divide the geopolitical planet neatly into a First World and a Third. The Soviet Union, as we will see later in this chapter, was buckling under the weight of an artificial economic system it could no longer sustain. It still had the technological trappings of a mighty superpower, but it no longer had the financial wherewithal to support all of that hardware. The consequences of such a situation could be deadly.

Chernobyl, 80 miles from Kiev, third largest city of the Soviet Union, was the site of a major nuclear power plant. It was only three years old, but it had been built on the cheap, following an already outmoded design. On April 26, 1986, engineers were performing an experiment with the plant's reactor number 4. Because of a miscalculation, the atomic chain reaction suddenly went out of control, producing a power surge that created an explosion of radioactive steam, which blew the roof off the reactor. The initial explosion was followed by a chemical explosion, and fragments of superheated reactor material ignited many fires at the plant.

The year before, Mikhail Gorbachev had become general secretary of the Communist Party of the Soviet Union, promising to lead the nation into a new era of *glasnost*—openness—which would contrast with the secrecy that had traditionally characterized communist Russia. Nevertheless, it was only after several days of evasion that Soviet authorities began to own up to the scope of the disaster. Thirty-one persons had been killed in the initial blasts, and at least 500 more had been injured. The explosions had been so powerful that radioactive material was sent high into the atmosphere and was now drifting across the Northern Hemisphere. Authorities throughout the Soviet Union and northern Europe scrambled to protect water and food sources from radioactive contamination.

Century Stats

Fifty tons of radioactive material were released at Chernobyl, 10 times the amount of fallout at Hiroshima. Ten years after the accident, the "official" death count as a result of the explosion was still given as 33, but the consensus among scientists is that as many as 10,000 may now have died as a result of the accident. It is believed that cancer deaths resulting from Chernobyl will be as much as 11 times those that resulted from the combined 1945 bombings of Hiroshima and Nagasaki.

Abandoned building near the Chernobyl nuclear power plant, Chernobyl, Ukraine.
(Image from russiatoday.com)

403

All residents living within 19 miles of Chernobyl were quickly evacuated, but millions more were still living on ground contaminated to some degree. Throughout the 1990s, the incidence of thyroid cancer, leukemia, and other radiation-related disorders was abnormally high.

The lesson seemed starkly simple: The 20th-century industrial standard of living is a high-maintenance proposition and is not tolerant of error. Yet the Soviet authorities seemed heedless of the lesson and, arguing that the region's power requirements could be served in no other way, put two of the facility's remaining three reactors back on line, keeping them fired up even after a series of minor accidents prompted a public outcry.

Black Monday, October 19, 1987

In the wake of Chernobyl, the American nuclear industry assured citizens that U.S. reactors were far more advanced than the Soviet facilities and incorporated many more safety features. There would be no Chernobyl-style meltdown in this country, we were told. But there are meltdowns, and then there are meltdowns.

When trading opened on the New York Stock Exchange on the morning of October 19, 1987, the Dow Jones average was pegged at 2,246.73. When trading ended, it had melted down to 1,738.41, a loss of 508 points, just about double the fall that had occurred in the crash of 1929 (Chapter 13).

Much as Herbert Hoover had assured the American public that "prosperity was just around the corner," President Reagan dismissed the 508-point plunge as "some people grabbing profits." Indeed, the market did gradually recover, but the crash of 1987 signaled an end to the high-flying era of Reagonomics.

The House That Junk Built

What went wrong? Seasoned investors traditionally look at the "fundamentals" of the companies they invest in: profits, business practices, debt, the nature of the market and the industry, and so on. In the high-flying 1980s, fundamentals typically took a backseat to whatever quick profits could be made in buying out—then, often, disman-tling—companies. To finance the buyouts, traders turned to *junk bonds*, high-risk investments in firms without established earnings histories or burdened by poor credit. Junk bonds could be acquired cheaply and paid a high rate of interest. Often, junk bonds were purchased with very little hope that the issuing company would ever be able to repay the loan, but, in the short run, the interest payments made were so high that the underlying worthlessness of the bond hardly seemed to matter.

Talk of the Times

Junk bonds are low-cost, high-yield bonds issued by new, typically risky, ventures or by companies with poor credit ratings.

Until investors decided that it *did* matter. And then the junk hit the fan. A sell-off frenzy swept the financial markets, and the Dow plummeted.

The National Debt

No one in the Reagan administration would dare shake a disapproving finger at the junk-bond traders, however. Reagonomics had stirred the national economy from its doldrums, all right, and the president had reduced taxes—at least, for some—but the cost of it all was astounding. During the Reagan years, the national debt rose from a staggering $1 trillion to a stupefying number that easily topped $4 trillion. It was a crippling debt load.

Bailing Out

If the government couldn't wag a finger, there were plenty of "ordinary" and "sensible" people who could—people who didn't try to "get rich quick," who believed in working hard and *saving* whatever they didn't absolutely have to spend. Traditionally, these down-to-earth types put their money in savings and loan associations, sometimes called "thrifts."

The thrifts were known for their safety and their neighborhood folksiness. But when interest rates went through the roof in the late 1970s, the 5.5 percent rate ceiling mandated by law for these institutions became intolerably puny. Depositors left the thrifts in hordes. Fearing that this important segment of the banking industry would collapse, the federal government, in 1980, decided to allow S&Ls to pay whatever interest rate was necessary to compete. The government also raised the federal insurance on deposits from $40,000 to $100,000. Then, in 1982, the Federal Home Loan Bank Board allowed the thrifts to accept unlimited deposits from brokerage firms, and the S&Ls were transformed, almost overnight, from neighborhood savings places to aggressive, big-time financial institutions. They were shining examples of the heights that could be reached once government regulation was laid to rest.

In the absence of regulation, competition among the S&Ls became cutthroat as institutions vied with one another in offering the highest rates of return on savings. Soon, firms were paying double-digit rates while earning only single-digit rates on the long-term home loans that still constituted the bulk of their assets.

The government pressed on with deregulation, passing, in 1982, the Garn-St. Germain Act, which allowed S&Ls to make high-risk acquisition, development, and construction loans. Moreover, rules concerning appraisal of the projects on which loans were made were radically liberalized; S&Ls were now allowed to loan 100 percent of the appraised value—which, depending on the appraiser, often meant something closer to 150 percent.

Century Stats

By the end of the 1990s, the cost of the S&L bailout was expected to surpass $300 billion over 30 years. The funds Congress committed in 1989 added about $3,000 to the income tax bill of each and every American taxpayer.

The deregulated S&L industry was headed for a disaster that was hastened by a general decline in the real-estate market. Nationwide, reckless loans were made on what became all-but-worthless property, and by the mid 1980s, savings and loan institutions all over the country found themselves buried under mounting debt.

Various interim steps were taken to shuffle and shift losses in order to keep the industry afloat, but the burden of cleaning up what news commentators liked to call the "S&L mess" fell not to President Reagan, but to his successor, George Bush. At the new president's urging, Congress committed $166 billion to bail out the S&Ls.

Star Wars and the Evil Empire

Ronald Reagan had built his early political career as a staunch anti-communist. His sentiments in this regard were sincere. In response to proposals for a freeze on the size of the U.S. nuclear arsenal, the president warned that the nation was dealing with "an evil empire" and that we were locked in a "struggle between right and wrong, good and evil."

The Strategic Defense Initiative

While slashing government spending in the domestic and social sectors, President Reagan increased defense spending dramatically. He acted aggressively to meet perceived military threats throughout the world, sending U.S. Marines in the summer of 1982 to Lebanon as a peacekeeping force. On October 23, 1983, more than 200 Marines were killed as they slept when a truck packed with 25,000 pounds of TNT was crashed into the troops' Beirut headquarters. Just two days after this disaster, Reagan ordered an invasion of the tiny (population 110,000) island nation of Grenada in the West Indies. Cuban troops had been sent to Grenada at the behest of its anti-American dictatorship, and the president was determined to protect the approximately 1,000 American citizens there. As many saw it, the president also regarded a successful "liberation" of the country as a kind of emotional compensation for the massacre of the Marines in Beirut.

But the president's most ambitious project was the Strategic Defense Initiative (SDI), dubbed by its detractors "Star Wars," after the popular George Lucas science-fiction movie of 1977. The idea was to create a shield against incoming intercontinental ballistic missiles by attacking and destroying them, from orbiting weapons systems, before the missiles began their descent.

The catch was that the weaponry involved was indeed the stuff of science fiction and included x-ray and particle-beam devices that weren't even in development yet. When they weren't pointing out the unworkability of "Star Wars," critics also worried that the system was a violation of the 1972 ABM (antiballistic missile) treaty and was, in fact, a temptation to thermonuclear war, because it promised to make such a war survivable. Then there was the cost. The system would drain $100 to $200 billion from the nation's coffers, a sum that might permanently cripple America.

The many objections notwithstanding, both Presidents Reagan and Bush pursued Star Wars to the tune of $30 billion.

20th-Century Life

In 1993, anonymous SDI researchers revealed that at least one major test of a part of the "Star Wars" system in development had been rigged to yield falsely positive results. Caspar Weinberger, who served as President Reagan's secretary of defense, at first denied these charges, but later explained that the test in question—and perhaps the entire SDI program—had been a $30 billion ruse designed with the sole purpose of duping the Soviet Union into spending money it could not afford on its own version of "Star Wars." Weinberger claimed that U.S. policy makers knew the plan was unworkable.

If what Weinberger says is true, SDI was certainly the most expensive Trojan Horse in history. Perhaps ironically, plans for some version of a strategic defense initiative were revived in 1999, to be implemented as soon as the technology might become available.

Ollie, Iran, and the Contras

Star Wars was not the only grand plan Ronald Reagan had for tipping the balance of power in the world. In November 1986, the president confirmed reports that the United States had secretly sold arms to Iran, the very nation that had kidnapped American embassy personnel at the end of the Carter years (Chapter 25, "Hostage Situations"). Reagan initially denied reports that the purpose of the arms sale was to obtain the release of Americans held by terrorists in war-torn Lebanon, but, later, he admitted an arms-for-hostages swap.

Then, incredibly, the plot became even thicker. Attorney General Edwin Meese learned that a portion of the proceeds from the arms sale had been diverted to finance the Contras, the men President Reagan called "freedom fighters," who were working to overthrow the democratically elected Sandinista government of Nicaragua. Congress had explicitly prohibited aid to the Contras, and the secret diversion of the secret arms profits was illegal and unconstitutional.

Under congressional investigation, the plot slowly unfolded. In 1985, a cabal of Israelis had approached National Security Adviser Robert MacFarlane with a scheme in which Iran would use its influence to free the U.S. hostages in Lebanon in exchange for arms. Secretary of State George Schultz and Secretary of Defense Caspar Weinberger objected to the plan, but (MacFarlane testified) President Reagan agreed to it—and then Oliver ("Ollie") North, a U.S. Marine colonel, proposed the plan to funnel arms money to the Contras.

Talk of the Times

Iran–Contra Affair is the label applied to the arms-for-hostages plot hatched during President Reagan's second term, whereby funds obtained from selling arms to Iran would be channeled to the Contra "freedom fighters" in Nicaragua.

The congressional investigation evoked memories of Watergate, as the search for the origin of the plot led higher and higher up the rungs of the White House ladder. At the end of the investigation, few were left believing that President Reagan had been ignorant of the scheme, but, if he had been, the implications were perhaps even more disturbing: Here was a passive chief executive who blindly delegated authority to his staff.

In the end, the president's Teflon coating remained intact. He was charged with no offense. Colonel North was convicted on 3 of 12 criminal counts against him, but the convictions were subsequently set aside on appeal. Other high officials were indicted or convicted, but none served prison time, and all were subsequently ultimately pardoned by President Reagan's successor, George Bush.

"Mr. Gorbachev, Tear Down This Wall!"

It is easy to be hard on Ronald Reagan, and some historians and scholars of government have numbered him among the very worst American presidents. But one truth is inescapable. During his administration, the long, costly, and dangerous Cold War wound down and, during the Bush years, it ended—without a shot having been fired—at least, not between the two main combatants.

Those reluctant to attribute this "victory" to Reagan and Bush point out that communism is inherently flawed (as the humorist Will Rogers said in 1927, "Communism is like Prohibition, it's a good idea but it won't work,") and the Soviet Union collapsed under the weight of its own economic stagnation. Others, however, insist that Reagan's hard line kept the pressure up, and his faith in "Star Wars" did, in fact, push the Soviets over the precipice of bankruptcy and dissolution.

Whatever the causes or combination of causes, the Cold War *did* end as the government of the Soviet Union was first liberalized under Mikhail Gorbachev and then fell apart altogether amid the clamor of the masses calling for democratic capitalist reform.

The first tangible symbol of the end to Soviet power came at the ugly site of the most tangible evidence of that power. In 1987, standing near the Berlin Wall, the president made a stirring speech calling out to the Soviet leader: "Mr. Gorbachev, open this gate! Mr. Gorbachev, tear down this wall!" And just two years later, ordinary Berliners spontaneously began chipping away at the wall that had so long divided East from West Berlin, the communist world from the free world. Not long before, such an action would have been met by hails of gunfire. Now, the East German guards merely looked on.

GENERAL SECRETARY GORBACHEV, IF YOU
SEEK PEACE /- IF YOU SEEK PROSPERITY FOR
THE SOVIET UNION AND EASTERN EUROPE /-
IF YOU SEEK LIBERALIZATION/ COME HERE,
TO THIS GATE.

MR. GORBACHEV, OPEN THIS GATE.

MR. GORBACHEV, TEAR DOWN THIS WALL.

Portion of the actual text of Ronald Reagan's 1987 speech in front of the Berlin Wall.
(Image from the Ronald Reagan Library)

Human Rights

The long assault on the Berlin Wall gave hope to the entire world. There were other bright developments as well, some lasting, some not.

Deng's China

Deng Xiaoping had fallen victim to the purges of the Mao Tse-tung's Cultural Revolution in 1967–1969 and was stripped of power in the government of China. In 1973, he was reinstated by Premier Zhou Enlai and made deputy premier. Two years later, he became vice-chairman of the Chinese Communist Party's Central Committee, a member of its Political Bureau, and chief of the general staff. But he was purged again by the Maoist "Gang of Four" in 1976—although, with Mao's death, he was soon once again returned to power.

Throughout the 1980s, Deng worked toward liberalizing China politically and economically. As the world's most populous nation apparently moved closer to democracy, the free world looked on hopefully.

The Tragedy of Tiananmen

There was an air of unreality to it all. Not only were America's implacable adversaries becoming far less adversarial, they were embracing, it seemed, a whole new attitude toward the individual, a respect for human rights.

Deng's program of reforms led to a popular desire for more. For two months in the spring of 1989, students and other pro-democracy protesters demonstrated in a number of Chinese cities. The focal point of these demonstrations was Beijing's Tiananmen Square, where the world media covered the ongoing nonviolent protests.

At length, Deng declared martial law, but the protests continued, students even bringing to the Square a "Goddess of Liberty," essentially a replica of the Statue of Liberty fashioned from plaster and Styrofoam. On June 3, unarmed soldiers waded into the crowd at Tiananmen, in an effort to disperse the demonstrators peacefully. Pelted by rocks, the troops retreated, only to return—this time with tanks. The protesters escalated the violence, assaulting the tanks with rocks and Molotov cocktails. On June 4, shortly after midnight, the army returned once again, and, this time, opened fire. Perhaps as many as a thousand protesters were killed. The pro-democracy dream was bloodied, but not killed.

Deng Xiaoping is seen at a state dinner, given by President Jimmy Carter, in January 1979. Deng was vice premier of China at the time. President Nixon was among the guests. (Image from the Jimmy Carter Library)

There would be no magical transformation in China, but, from 1989 onward, the leadership increasingly endorsed economic reform. While Deng and the other leaders maintained a hard line against political dissent, the West continued to hold out hope that, with a liberalized economy, democracy would inevitably, quietly come.

The Least You Need to Know

➤ Ronald Reagan rose to power by reviving hope in American greatness and the American dream.

➤ Reaganomics, a conservative revolution in U.S. economic policy, brought great wealth to a few, temporarily lifted the economy out of the doldrums, but also created enormous national debt and set the stage for a stock market crash and the costly collapse of the savings and loan industry.

➤ Although the federal government was slow to respond to the national and worldwide AIDS pandemic, grass-roots organizations did much to curb the spread of the disease and to relieve the suffering of its victims.

➤ The Reagan and Bush years saw a happy ending to the Cold War and the collapse of the Soviet Union and the retreat of communism throughout the world, as well as halting steps toward democracy in China.

Part 7
Unfinished Century: The 1990s

The death of communism did not inevitably bring with it the birth of democracy. From Africa to Europe, as old governments collapsed, a kind of tribalism replaced them, resulting in mass deportation and mass murder.

At home, despite a popular triumph over Saddam Hussein in the Middle East, President George Bush lost his reelection bid to the governor of Arkansas, Bill Clinton. Under the Clinton administration, unprecedented economic prosperity returned to the United States, and an unprecedented sexual scandal engulfed the White House. Americans focused on their new wealth and the new scandal, as well as the racially charged murder trial of football star O.J. Simpson and the brief life and sudden death of Britain's Princess Di, rather than on the political anarchy raking Africa and South America and the economic anarchy threatening Russia and Asia.

Like the other decades of the century, the 1990s were packed with despair as well as hope, with ancient enmities and remarkable reconciliations, with instances of intolerance born of ignorance and incredible scientific advances. Taking these together, this section ends with a look to the future.

Chapter 27

Red Sunset and Desert Flames (1990–1992)

In This Chapter

➤ The rise and fall of Mikhail Gorbachev

➤ The Berlin Wall falls

➤ An end to the Soviet regime

➤ Tribal warfare in Africa—and Europe

➤ The Persian Gulf War

Leaf through the pages of any book on European history, and you will find an assortment of wars with names like the Hundred Years' War, the Eighty Years' War, the Thirty Years' War. What a terrible thought: to be born into a generation whose reality was such a war, a generation that entered and left life in a time unrelieved by true peace.

Ancient history? Well, it is a fact that the wars just mentioned were all fought in the Middle Ages and the Renaissance, but, here in America, in our own century, the Baby Boom generation was likewise born and raised in what might be called our own Forty Years' War. It was the Cold War, and for four decades, it was reality.

Then it ended. This chapter tells what happened.

The God That Failed

Born in 1931, the son of Russian peasants in the Stavropol district of southwestern Russia, Mikhail Gorbachev knew only one world, the very hard world of Stalinist communism. Young Gorbachev joined the Komsomol (Young Communist League) in 1946 and drove a combine harvester on a state farm for the next four years. He rose through the ranks of the Komsomol, and in 1952 was sent to the law school of Moscow State University. There he became a member of the Communist Party, and, after graduating with his law degree in 1955, he began a steady rise through the party and the government.

His was the ideal Communist Party success story. The Soviet system suppressed traditional religion because it wanted no "false gods" to interfere with the worship of Marx, Lenin, and Stalin. But, worship these faithfully, and your reward might well be earthly power and prosperity.

It worked for Gorbachev, who became a member of the Central Committee of the Communist Party of the Soviet Union in 1971, and was appointed a party secretary of agriculture in 1978. When he became a candidate member of the *Politburo* in 1979 and a full member in 1980, he joined the ranks of the inner circle of Soviet power and was positioned to succeed Konstantin Chernenko as general secretary of the Communist Party of the Soviet Union when Chernenko died in 1985.

Talk of the Times

The **Politburo** was the chief executive and political committee of the Communist Party of the Soviet Union.

Since the death of Stalin in 1953, leadership of the Communist Party (which amounted to leadership of the Soviet government) had been the exclusive preserve of old men, thoroughly hardened in the ways of orthodox communism. At 54, Gorbachev was not only the youngest party head ever, he was the youngest member of the Politburo. Unlike his older predecessors, he was willing to face the fact that the Soviet economy was stagnant. He called for a program of rapid technological innovation and increased productivity from a work force that, guaranteed an income, had become apathetic. He also moved to streamline the moss-encrusted Soviet bureaucracy.

Soviet Tremors

Gobachev's initial reforms, while ambitious, were ultimately superficial. The leader realized that nothing less than a total revision of almost three-quarters of a century of communist policy had to be undertaken. Without such a revision, the Soviet Union would wither and die, just like the old men who had been running the nation.

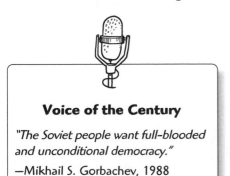

Voice of the Century

"The Soviet people want full-blooded and unconditional democracy."
—Mikhail S. Gorbachev, 1988

During 1987–1988, Gorbachev instituted *glasnost* ("openness") and *perestroika* ("restructuring"). Under traditional communism, culture and government had been closed and secretive, with all news carefully filtered through the party's official channels, including the *Pravda* ("The Truth") newspaper. Suddenly, the press was given vastly expanded access to information and was encouraged to report the news with candor. For the first time in Soviet history, certain elections were opened to multiple candidates, not just the individuals handpicked by the party. Perhaps the most profound changes came in opening, however tentatively, the Soviet economy to private enterprise and free-market mechanisms.

The majority of Soviet citizens welcomed Gorbachev's reforms, and, outside the Soviet Union, in the West, he was hailed as a hero. President Reagan, in particular, welcomed his overtures toward warmer, saner East-West relations.

But the fact was that the Communist Party and the Soviet government were still dominated, especially at the middle and lower levels, by hard-line communists, who did not suffer gladly the tremors of a proposed democratic rebirth. They were fearful that giving up any degree of central control over information, power, and money would mean the inevitable collapse of the Soviet Union.

Talk of the Times

Glasnost, Russian for openness, describes a reform in policy, instituted by Mikhail Gorbachev in the late 1980s, aimed at ending the Soviet habit of hiding the nation's activities in a cloak of secrecy. *Perestroika,* another of Gorbachev's policy reforms, means restructuring. It refers mainly to economic reforms, intended to move the Soviet Union toward a free-market economy.

Mikhail Gorbachev and Ronald Reagan sign the Intermediate-Range Nuclear Forces (INF) Treaty, 1987.
(Image from the National Archives)

Germany: The Rush to Reunify

Since the end of World War II, Germany had been divided into a communist East and a democratic West. East Germany was universally regarded as a puppet of Moscow. Erich Honecker, the communist functionary who assumed leadership of East Germany in 1971, was at first content to maintain strict subservience to the Soviets, but after East Germany achieved recognition as a sovereign nation by the western democracies—including, ultimately, West Germany—Honecker began to steer a more liberal course. Trade with the free world was opened, and, while East Germans were still rarely allowed to visit West Germany, Honecker freely permitted West German citizens to visit the East.

Century Stats

The Berlin Wall stood from 1961 to 1989. Between 1949 and 1961, some 2.5 million East Germans fled from East to West. After 1961, about 5,000 East Germans managed somehow to overcome the wall and reach West Berlin safely. At least 5,000 more were captured, and 191 were killed while attempting to cross the wall.

But with increased contact, it became ever more obvious to the East Germans that they were living miserably compared to citizens of the West. Consumer goods were hard to come by; housing was in short supply and in very poor condition; public works, roads, and railroads were grossly inadequate. Indeed, East Germany had never been completely rebuilt after World War II. Honecker now sought to limit the influx of West German visitors by raising fees charged for visas. When that failed to stanch the flow, he classified some two million of its citizens as "bearers of secrets," forbidding their personal contact with Westerners.

Still, the voice of dissent was rising in the East. Honecker cracked down, imprisoning protesters and even "banishing" some to West Germany. In 1974, he pushed through constitutional amendments that defined the nation not as German but as a socialist state irrevocably tied to the Soviet Union.

These were acts of desperation, and, in the 1980s, Honecker did an about-face, inching policy in the opposite direction. Now he even allowed East Germans to visit the West. At last, in 1987, West German chancellor Helmuth Kohl responded to the liberalization of East German policy by receiving Honecker in an official state visit.

But just as East Germany was being accorded the trappings of legitimacy by the West, its own citizens had come to see the government as an empty shell. In 1989, the reformist government of Hungary began allowing East Germans to escape to the West through Hungary's newly opened border with Austria. Gorbachev refused to respond to this situation, and Honecker was powerless to prevent the emigration. The Berlin Wall had been, in effect, breached.

West German Foreign Minister Hans-Dietrich Genscher presents President George Bush with a piece of the Berlin Wall, 1989.
(Image from the George Bush Library)

One after another, the USSR's satellite nations were leaving the Soviet orbit. Now East German refugees could escape through Hungary, Poland, or Czechoslovakia, all of which had achieved freedom from Soviet domination during the remarkable year of 1989. In October, the East German politburo replaced Honecker with another hard-line communist, Egon Krenz, who decided that, since it was impossible to control the flow of refugees through the former nations of the Soviet bloc, it was best to avoid further embarrassment by allowing those who wished to travel to the West to do so directly from East Germany.

Krenz's government had specified that such travel required official permission, but wildly enthusiastic East Berliners took the November 9 order as a decision to open the Berlin Wall. Crowds demanded passage into West Berlin, and the border guards, unprepared, allowed tens of thousands of East Germans through. Once in West Berlin, they celebrated in the streets.

The opening of the Berlin Wall was the end of East Germany. Krenz was replaced by a more liberal regime, and within a year a unification treaty was drawn up. It was ratified by the Bundestag and the People's Chamber (the West German and East German parliaments) in September and went into effect on October 3, 1990. Germany was again one land. The Berlin Wall and the Iron Curtain had both collapsed, and the Cold War was over.

The End Comes

Among the most sweeping change Mikhail Gorbachev introduced into Soviet policy was his repudiation of the so-called "Brezhnev Doctrine." Promulgated by Leonid Brezhnev, president of the Soviet Union from 1977 to 1982, the doctrine declared the USSR's right to intervene militarily within the *Warsaw Pact* nations—essentially, the Iron Curtain countries—whenever deemed necessary. This meant the Soviets could freely crush any incipient rebellion in these satellite countries. Once Gorbachev ended this policy, many of the Soviet republics declared themselves sovereign or independent. Gorbachev scrambled to renegotiate relations with the 15 Soviet republics, nine of which agreed to a new union treaty.

For many hard-line Soviet communists, the very idea of negotiating with the republics was abhorrent. On August 19, 1991, while Gorbachev was taking a break from these negotiations at his *dacha*—his summer home—KGB and army conservatives moved against him. The president and his family were placed under house arrest, and tanks rolled through Moscow, laying siege to the parliament building of the Russian republic.

Talk of the Times

The **Warsaw Pact** was the Soviet response to the establishment of NATO. Established in 1955, it was ostensibly a mutual-defense alliance, but, in reality, gave the Soviet Union military power over its satellite nations. The pact was dissolved in 1991.

Most of the international community of the West, which had so recently seen democracy violently quashed at Tiananmen Square, assumed that the coup would succeed, sending the Soviet Union back along the communist road. French President François Mitterrand even made a television announcement acknowledging coup leader Gennady Yanayev as the "new leader" of the Soviet Union, and he promptly assured his countrymen that France could "do business" with the new hard-liners.

20th-Century Life

Boris Yeltsin was born in 1931 and rapidly rose through the Communist Party hierarchy as Gorbachev's special protégé. He became head of the Moscow Communist party organization in 1985, but, even more liberal than his mentor, he broke with Gorbachev in 1987 and was removed from the party leadership.

But the burly Yeltsin had a common touch that appealed to the man and woman on the street. In 1989, he achieved election to the Congress of People's Deputies, a position from which he quickly built a new and independent political power base. After resigning from the Communist Party—an action that would have been unthinkable just a few months earlier—he was elected president of the Russian Republic in May 1990.

In Moscow, however, Boris Yeltsin, president of the Russian republic, had barricaded himself and his followers in the parliament building. Improvised barricades were quickly erected around the building by construction workers sympathetic to the cause of reform. Then, incredibly, thousands of ordinary Soviet citizens joined hands around the building, forming a human chain.

As liberal as Gorbachev was, Yeltsin had achieved his own power by advocating even faster and further-reaching reforms. His differences with Gorbachev were deep and bitter. Nevertheless, Yeltsin now focused on obtaining the release and safe return of the Soviet president. As Yeltsin hunkered down in the parliament building, the human chain around the parliament rapidly grew in depth as more and more people joined it. Many army units had refused to participate in the coup to begin with, and, now, others were defecting from its ranks, including the crews of the tanks that had been sent into the capital's streets. The Moscow militia (the local police force) openly sided with the parliament's defenders, distributing gas masks to those surrounding the building and administering to them a crash course on the tactics of civil disobedience.

Despite lack of faith outside of the Soviet Union, the hard-line communist coup collapsed within days of its beginning. Gorbachev was released and returned to Moscow.

Television images of Gorbachev were beamed across the USSR and the world. He appeared profoundly shaken, in contrast to the robust Yeltsin, and, from this point forward, Yeltsin steadily eclipsed Gorbachev. Russia and most of the other republics voted to dissolve the Union of Soviet Socialist Republics and to create in its place the Commonwealth of Independent States. Mikhail Gorbachev was now a president with neither a party nor a nation. He resigned on December 25, 1991, leaving the new "commonwealth" in the hands Boris Yeltsin, his savior and rival.

And now America and the rest of the West found themselves in a world suddenly without the USSR. Not only had the Cold War come to an end, but the "enemy" had ceased to exist.

Reflections on the Communist Experiment

In a speech of November 18, 1956, Nikita Khrushchev, then premier of the Soviet Union, declared to the West: "Whether you like it or not, history is on our side. We will bury you." America and its allies were shocked by so blatant a toss of the gauntlet. Never mind that the infamous and often-quoted phrase "we will bury you" was actually a bad translation of a Russian proverbial saying that meant nothing more aggressive than "we will live to dig your grave"—that is, our system will outlast yours. Instead, it was taken as a threat of war as well as an affront.

Now, in 1991, the phrase, however translated, rang hollow. The Soviet System had lasted about 75 years. Yet few Americans found enduring cause for celebration. To begin with, there was no assurance that Yeltsin would be able to prevent another communist coup. He faced the daunting task of balancing the need for a certain degree of authoritarian rule with the democratic reforms he himself had fought for.

Few people called the Commonwealth of Independent States by that new name. For most of the world, it was "the former Soviet Union." And therein lay the problem. Soviet institutions had been dismantled, but nothing yet existed to replace them. For three-quarters of a century, the giant nation had existed according to an artificial economy created by dictatorial decree. How could it now maneuver itself into a free-market economy without starving the people and bringing about a massive reactionary backlash?

Then there was the issue of the former Soviet Union's immense stockpile of thermonuclear

Century Stats

In 1988, on the very eve of the dissolution of the Soviet Union, its stockpile of nuclear and thermo-nuclear weapons reached its historic peak of some 33,000 warheads.

Voice of the Century

"Capitalism in [post-communist] Russia has produced far more Al Capones than Henry Fords.... In fact, the economy hardly merited the name of capitalism at all, since it operated largely outside the framework of law."
—David Remnick (historian), 1997

weapons, much of it distributed throughout now-independent states. What would become of it? Who would control it?

In January 1993, Yeltsin met with U.S. President George Bush to conclude the epoch-making START II arms-reduction treaty, but just three months later, Yeltsin barely survived a motion for impeachment in the Congress of People's Deputies. After securing the support of 58 percent of the electorate in a national vote of confidence, he dissolved the Congress and called for new elections. When his opponents refused to dissolve the legislature, Yeltsin sent troops and tanks against the very parliament building he had recently defended.

Why had the Russian people rushed from communism to chaos such as this?

The short answer is that communism failed. But how did it fail? We can point to its economic failure: People did not live as well under communism as they did under capitalism. We can point to its political failure: Most people remained communists only at the point of a gun.

Voice of the Century

"Communism terribly overestimated how much humanity could be engineered from the top down through enforced social engineering."

—Jim Wallis (historian), 1994

The failure of communism was even more basic, however. Communism failed to address the humanness of humanity. Founded on uncompromising rationality, it failed to address the basic irrationality of human beings: the all-consuming need they have to compete, to struggle, to be free, even if all of these things bring a degree of pain, failure, inefficiency, and injustice.

Return to Tribalism

In a 1954 speech before the Harvard Club of Los Angeles, film mogul Dore Schary observed that "America is a 'happy-ending' nation." Many Americans, observing the remarkable transformation of Eastern Europe, the reunification of Germany, and the end of the Soviet Union, assumed that the failure of communism automatically meant the success of democracy.

Not necessarily. In some parts of the world, the end of repression did not bring liberty, but terror, as government gave way to something more primitive, which can only be described, even at the close of the 20th century, as tribalism.

Civil War in Rwanda

For most of the century, few Americans gave any thought to Rwanda, a small nation in east-central Africa, claimed by Germany in 1890 and occupied by the Belgians beginning in 1916. With the blessing of the League of Nations, Belgian colonial authorities initially ruled through the traditional kings of the dominant Tutsi tribe, but later sought to bring a measure of democracy to the country and encouraged the rise of the Hutu people, traditionally the lower classes of Rwanda.

During the late 1950s and early 1960s, much of old colonial Africa was in turmoil, and, in 1959, civil war erupted between the Tutsi and the Hutu. The Tutsi ruler Kigeri V was forced into exile, along with thousands of other Tutsi. Two years later, Rwanda declared its independence under Hutu leadership. The decade was stormy, as fighting between the Hutu and Tutsis grew increasingly bloody. At last, in 1981, free elections were held, but any stability this might have brought was offset by severe economic hardship as world coffee prices fell and a severe drought produced massive crop failure.

In October 1990, rebel forces consisting mostly of Tutsis who had fled Rwanda during the 1960s and 1970s invaded from exile in Uganda. A tentative peace was concluded between the predominantly Tutsi rebels and the Hutu-controlled government in 1993, but extremist Hutu leaders refused to share power. Then, on April 6, 1994, the presidents of Rwanda and Burundi were killed when their plane crashed—apparently shot down by the extremist Rwandan presidential guard. During this period, several moderate Hutu politicians were assassinated.

Then the Hutu-led army, the presidential guard, and extremist Hutu militia forces unleashed their full fury on the land, killing as many as a half-million civilians, most of them Tutsi. The Tutsi rebel forces responded in kind, sending hundreds of thousands of Hutu as well as Tutsi fleeing into neighboring countries. By the summer of 1994, it was estimated that more than 2 million persons, out of a population of 5.5 million, were refugees.

Civil War in Yugoslavia

It was difficult for Americans and other westerners to comprehend the enormity of what was happening in Rwanda. It was the worst possible combination of modern warfare and ancient tribal hatreds. But, of course, that was Africa. Tribalism in 20th-century Europe? Impossible! Or so most of the world believed.

The country of Yugoslavia was a 20th-century invention. It came into being after the dissolution of the Austro-Hungarian Empire at the end of World War I. However, until World War II, Yugoslavia was not so much a single nation as it was a collection of strongly nationalistic, ethnically diverse and irreconcilable factions. What brought them together into something resembling genuine nationhood was their mutual opposition to German-Italian invasion.

The military leader of these diverse people was Josip Broz, known as Tito. After brilliantly leading the *partisan* resistance against the Fascists in World War II, Tito instituted a Marxist dictatorship over Yugoslavia. But Tito's Yugoslavia, while communist, was not a Soviet satellite. Indeed, it was unique in Eastern Europe in that it was maintained independently of Soviet military and economic support. Tito stood up to Josef Stalin, who could do nothing more than expel Yugoslavia from the communist bloc in 1948. For his part, without betraying his essential Marxism, Tito opened up remarkably cordial relations with the West, and, of all communist nations, Yugoslavia became the most forward-looking and economically successful.

It all ended with the dictator's death in 1980. Observers of Yugoslavia had warned that the glue holding the nation together was the personality of Tito and Tito alone. After Tito's death, the Croatians and Slovenes, the largest nationalist groups in the country, developed separatist movements. In January 1990, the Communist Party voted to relinquish its constitutional monopoly on power in Yugoslavia—a move that came too late to satisfy the Slovenes and Croatians, who declared their independence from Yugoslavia and proposed a new, decentralized union.

Slobodan Milosevic, communist leader of Serbia, another of the Yugoslav republics, opposed the new plan of union. Urged on by Milosevic, the Serbian minority in Croatia rebelled against the Croatian government, and Milosevic sent the Serbian-led Yugoslav army into Croatia to support the Croatian Serbs. Almost instantly, this civil war ceased to be a political struggle and emerged as what it really was—the reemergence of violent, ancient ethnic allegiances. Twentieth-century Europe was experiencing tribal warfare among the Serbs, the Croats, and the Moslems of what had been Yugoslavia.

In January 1992, the United Nations imposed a truce on the region, but it proved short-lived when Bosnia seceded from Yugoslavia in March 1992. Now the Serb population of this republic rebelled, and Bosnia was reduced to bloody, bitter anarchy. Its capital city, Sarajevo, scene of the 1914 assassination that had triggered World War I, emerged as a symbol of modern warfare—modern weapons used in primal causes.

It was warfare that recalled the days of Adolf Hitler, as civilian populations were targeted in the name of *ethnic cleansing*, the Serbs' systematic expulsion of Muslims and Croats from Serb-controlled areas.

The struggle in "the former Yugoslavia" was another lesson in post-communist reality. Americans weaned on movies tend to see the world according to simple oppositions of good versus evil. But the death of what President Reagan had called the "evil empire" of communism did not bring a wave of democratic bliss. Instead, the world that emerged was both more complex and more primitive.

Rwanda and Bosnia, as well as other "hot spots," such as perpetually troubled Somalia and Haiti, offered no evil empire to oppose. If "good guys" were in notably short supply, the "bad guys" were plentiful on all sides—though not nearly as abundant as the victims, men, women, and children. With the implosion of communism, the foreign policy of western nations, including the United States, had lost its rudder.

Talk of the Times

Ethnic cleansing is the Serbian policy of expelling or otherwise eliminating non-Serbs (Muslims and Croats) from the Serb-controlled areas of the former Yugoslavia.

Century Stats

By the end of 1993, ethnic cleansing had created some 700,000 refugees, who clogged the cities of western Europe.

Desert Shield and Desert Storm

Despite his Teflon coating, Ronald Reagan suffered the fate of many two-term presidents, beginning with Thomas Jefferson. His second term failed to live up to the promise of his first. Despite the erosion of his popularity, however, and a gloomy economic picture, his vice president, George Bush, handily defeated Massachusetts governor Michael Dukakis in 1988. Although Dukakis enjoyed a wide margin of popularity in early polls, the gap soon closed. The Democrat was a colorless and uninspiring candidate.

The New World Order

Bush shared the average American's wonder and hopefulness over a world from which the stain of communism was fast fading. He spoke of the United States leading a "new world order," and most Americans gave his administration high marks for its conduct of foreign policy.

But as recession stole over the country, as unemployment climbed, and as a national real-estate boom began to fall apart, Bush's success in international matters began to weigh against him. He was increasingly perceived as overly absorbed in the affairs of the world, and ineffective, even indifferent, to domestic problems, especially the crisis of the economy. Moreover, in contrast to the "Great Communicator," President Bush often seemed testy and on the verge of whining. The magic was missing.

Dealing with Saddam

George Bush's popularity declined daily, and he seemed doomed to a one-term presidency. Then, on August 2, 1990, Saddam Hussein, president of Iraq, invaded his neighbor, the small, oil-rich state of Kuwait. If ever a dictator looked the part of evil, it was Saddam Hussein, whose ample mustache recalled Josef Stalin and whose ruthless actions—not only in Kuwait, but against the Kurdish people within his own country—invited comparison with Adolf Hitler.

A tense diplomatic crisis was created. The Middle East has long been of immense strategic importance to the West. To allow Saddam Hussein to control more oil than he already did would deepen the economic crisis in the United States by reproducing the kind of situation OPEC had created in the 1970s (Chapter 25, "Hostage Situations"). Beyond this, Saddam had acted in utter violation of international law, and President Bush saw the crisis as a test of America's new role as the planet's sole superpower, the leader of the new world order.

Century Stats

The Persian Gulf coalition included Argentina, Australia, Bahrain, Bangladesh, Belgium, Canada, Czechoslovakia, Denmark, Egypt, France, Greece, Hungary, Italy, Kuwait, Morocco, the Netherlands, New Zealand, Niger, Norway, Oman, Pakistan, Poland, Qatar, Saudi Arabia, Senegal, South Korea, Spain, Syria, the United Arab Emirates, United Kingdom, plus the United States.

While some voices were raised in protest of even thinking of shedding "blood for oil," the president acted aggressively but also with careful planning. His administration brilliantly used the United Nations to sanction acting against Iraq, and, with masterful diplomacy, President Bush assembled a remarkable coalition of nations to oppose the invasion.

A special challenge was securing the support of the Arab countries in opposition to an Arab nation while keeping Israel, the target of attacks by Iraqi *Scud missiles*, out of the fighting. No Arab nation would support a situation in which Israel attacked Iraq.

Although the coalition was impressive, the greatest commitment of troops and equipment was by far that of the United States. The largest force since Vietnam was now assembled in the region bordering Iraq: more than a half-million troops, 1,800 aircraft, and some 100 ships. Vietnam: The comparisons were uncomfortably plentiful. Were we about to be sucked into another unwinnable war? A quagmire of conflict?

Talk of the Times

Scud is the NATO code name for the relatively short-range, Soviet-made surface-to-surface missiles used by Iraq during the Persian Gulf War. The chief advantage of the Scud is that it may be launched from transportable launchers, which can be hidden from attack.

20th-Century Life

If the Persian Gulf War offered a melodramatic villain in Saddam Hussein, it also produced a genuine American hero in General H. Norman Schwarzkopf, overall commander of operations Desert Shield and Desert Storm.

Born in Trenton, New Jersey, on August 22, 1934, Schwarzkopf graduated from West Point in 1956 and served with distinction in numerous staff strategic and personnel-management assignments, as well as in field command in Vietnam and in the 1983 invasion of Grenada. During the Persian Gulf War, Schwarzkopf commanded a combined U.S.-coalition force of 530,000 troops opposed to 545,000 Iraqis and achieved overwhelming victory. Schwarzkopf appeared frequently on television press conferences during the conflict, always impressing viewers with his military competence combined with a kind of plain-spoken humanity.

"Any soldier worth his salt," Schwarzkopf declared, "should be antiwar. And still there are things worth fighting for." Much honored, Schwarzkopf retired after the war.

Operation Desert Shield officially began in early August 1990, when King Fahd of Saudi Arabia invited American troops into his country to protect the kingdom against possible Iraqi aggression. In January 1991, the U.S. Congress voted to support military operations against Iraq in accordance with a U.N. Security Council resolution, which set a deadline of January 15, 1991, for the withdrawal of Iraqi forces from Kuwait. When that deadline expired, Operation Desert Shield became Operation Desert Storm.

It was a massively coordinated lightning campaign against Iraq from the air, the sea, and on land. After continuous air attack beginning on January 17, the ground war was launched at 8:00 on the night of February 23 and lasted exactly 100 hours before Iraqi resistance collapsed and Kuwait was liberated.

The Economy, Stupid

Months and years afterward, Americans would reevaluate the success of the Persian Gulf War. Unquestionably, the Iraqi military had been devastated, yet Saddam Hussein's government remained intact, and Saddam himself as belligerent as ever. Also disturbing were widespread outbreaks of mysterious ailments among troops who had served in the Gulf—Gulf War Syndrome, many called it—and it evaded identification and diagnosis. Many believe the syndrome was caused by contamination with chemical weapons agents that Saddam either used or that had been blown up (and, therefore, inadvertently released into the air) by coalition forces.

Nevertheless, immediately following the war, Americans felt good about themselves. The military success of the operation, together with the very low U.S. casualty rate, proved the effectiveness of the all-volunteer army and seemed to say that the military no longer suffered the stigma of Vietnam. Bush's sagging popularity ratings soared. "If the election were held today," many TV news commentators remarked, "President Bush would be assured of easy reelection."

But the election would not come until November 1992, and, by then, the euphoria had worn off. What seemed far more relevant than the recent victory was the reality that the American dream, insofar as it translated into financial well-being, was drifting farther and farther away.

The incumbent Bush was opposed by the young governor of Arkansas, Bill Clinton, whose campaign manager, a high-strung smart aleck named James Carville, identified the key issue of the campaign. "It's the economy, stupid," he said.

Century Stats

Combined U.S. and coalition forces in the Gulf War amounted to 530,000 troops opposed to 545,000 Iraqis. U.S. and coalition losses were 149 killed, 238 wounded, 81 missing, and 13 taken prisoner (they were subsequently released), whereas Iraqi losses have been estimated in excess of 80,000 men, with overwhelming loss of materiel.

The Least You Need to Know

➤ Mikhail Gorbachev moved boldly to reform the Soviet government and economy, in the process dismantling communism and dissolving the Soviet Union.

➤ The fall of the Berlin Wall symbolically marked the end of Soviet hegemony in Europe.

➤ The fall of communism did not automatically bring about the rise of democracy; much chaos, including war and genocide, has come in the wake of the Soviet collapse.

➤ The late 20th century has seen a resurgence of what can only be described as tribal warfare, both in Africa (especially Rwanda) and Europe (in the region of the former Yugoslavia).

Chapter 28

Prosperity and Scandal (1993–)

In This Chapter

➤ The Clinton victory

➤ The chaos of Third World politics

➤ The Princess Di story

➤ The "trial of the century"

➤ Homegrown terrorism

➤ The future

Ask an astronomer what is the *most* difficult galaxy to see, and the answer will come back unequivocally: the Milky Way. We can't see it—not all of it, anyway—precisely because we live within it. We're imprisoned within our own perspective. And so it is with the present time. We're in it. We can't take in the full meaning of this or that event, or know what a series of events might add up to. We're just too close to the action.

If the first 27 chapters of this book are a kind of movie of the 20th century, this final chapter, a victim of perspective, is more like a series of snapshots.

The Comeback Kid

Back in the 1988 Democratic primaries, Colorado senator Gary Hart was more than 20 percentage points ahead of the field when he was photographed on a Bahama-bound yacht with Donna Rice, a Miami model, sitting on his lap. The ensuing scandal ended Hart's presidential aspirations.

Voice of the Century

"When I was in England [as a Rhodes scholar], I experimented with marijuana a time or two, and I didn't like it, and I didn't inhale, and I never tried it again."

—Bill Clinton, 1992

In 1992, it looked as if Bill Clinton's presidential campaign would similarly self-destruct when Gennifer Flowers, a nightclub singer and later a Little Rock TV reporter, announced that she had had a 12-year sexual affair with Clinton, had become pregnant by him in 1977 (she aborted the baby), and had smoked marijuana and used cocaine with him. The affair, according to Flowers, did not end until 1989.

Candidate Clinton denied the accusations, and his wife, Hilary Rodham Clinton, voiced her faith in her husband. Defying pollsters and pundits, the Clinton candidacy not only survived the scandal, but the Arkansas governor went on to defeat George Bush in his reelection bid.

The Reagan-Bush Era Ends

It was, as Clinton campaign strategist James Carville had put it, "the economy, stupid." Now, Ronald Reagan had also successfully run on economic issues, but he had relied on the Republicans' traditional base of support among conservative wealth and business interests—the "supply side" of the economy. Clinton turned the focus back on the "consumer side." Economic well-being, he proposed, was not a matter of helping the rich get richer by promising that their augmented wealth would "trickle down" to the rest of us. Rather, economic recovery depended on empowering the great middle class as well as helping the poor.

Why did America embrace Clinton's message? In part, it appealed to the traditions of justice and generosity that are, when all is said and done, very much a part of the American character. The greed-is-good ethic of the Reagan-Bush years had been an appealing aberration and might well have endured—if it had worked. But it didn't. People felt the American dream slipping from their grasp. Worse, *candidate* Bush offered no alternative to business as usual. He spoke of creating a "kinder, gentler" America, but the words rang as hollow as his broken campaign promise of 1988 to introduce no new taxes.

Voice of the Century

"Read my lips: no new taxes."

—George Bush, campaign speech, 1988. *(Major income tax increases were enacted during the Bush presidency.)*

For all his flaws—perhaps *because* of them—Bill Clinton seemed more human and more humanly credible that George Bush. Obtaining the Democratic nomination, he called himself the "Comeback Kid," and won a decisive victory in the November 1992 elections.

The Centrist Strategy

Clinton did not ride to victory on the wings of revolution. Clinton offered only his humanity and a move not to the liberal left (the traditional Democratic affinity) but toward the center. He proposed to give the nation back to the people—not meaning the "disadvantaged," but the middle class. Clinton came close to being an American everyman. Born in poor circumstances, he identified with the poor, but his aspirations and achievements were solidly middle class. He had not achieved patrician wealth, but he had achieved prosperity. He was connected to American society on many levels. Moreover, he had the youth of JFK without imposing the challenge of a New Frontier on an unwilling nation.

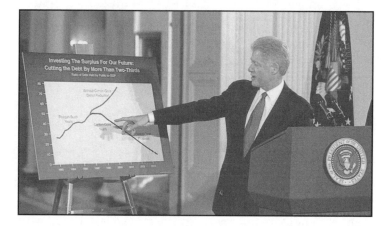

President Bill Clinton. (Image from the White House Collection)

Portraits of Anarchy

As voters saw it, the United States needed no turmoil. The rest of the world offered plenty.

Somalia

Somalia, on the easternmost projection of the African continent, was one of many African nations once under the colonial control of Europe and now independent—but beset by such poverty that independence had hardly set its people free.

In 1960, the independent Republic of Somalia was created, but, after its president, Cabdirashiid Cali Sherma'arke, was assassinated in 1969, a military coup led by Major General Maxamed Siyaad Barre replaced parliamentary government with a dictatorial Supreme Revolutionary Council. The new military dictatorship allied itself with the Soviet Union and invaded the Ogaden region of Ethiopia in an attempt to annex the territory. The Soviets rapidly shifted support to Ethiopia, defeating Siyaad's armies and creating chaos in Somalia. At last, in 1991, Siyaad was ousted by an alliance of clan-based rebel groups, which, however, never succeeded in creating a new government. Instead, anarchy reigned in a country of 8 million, now shattered into regions controlled by various clans. Warfare became a way of life, and agricultural production, already reeling under a protracted drought, ceased almost entirely.

In 1992, President Clinton announced the U.S.-led and U.N.-sanctioned Operation Restore Hope, to bring humanitarian aid and order to Somalia. By the end of March 1993, much food had been delivered, but U.S. and U.N. troops had not succeeded in disarming the militias of the various warlords. When the most prominent and intractable of them, Muhammad Farah Aydid, stepped up violence, which resulted in the deaths of eighteen U.S. soldiers and the capture of others, American politicians rethought the U.S. presence in the country. No one could argue against the humanitarian purpose of Operation Restore Hope, but who could win a war in which there was no order to restore?

United Nations and United States troops withdrew from Somalia in 1995, sparking fears that civil war would be general throughout the land. But, unpredictably, Somalia seemed to return to some semblance of normality, especially after the death of General Aydid in a 1996 battle.

Century Stats

By the early 1990s, some 1.5 million Somalis were starving or close to starvation.

Economies Awry

The violent anarchy in Somalia was one type of chaos afflicting the end of the century. Less immediately violent, but no less chaotic, was the economic turmoil many nations were suffering at the end of the century.

The United States enjoyed an extraordinary resurgence in the mid to late 1990s, with unemployment hovering a fraction above 4 percent, interest rates (and, therefore, inflation) very low, and productivity soaring. In the spring of 1999, the Dow Jones average, a traditional barometer of stock-market performance, broke through the 10,000 mark. In much of the rest of the world, however, economies were in severe crisis.

Century Stats

In March 1999, U.S. unemployment was 4.2 percent, just two-tenths of a percentage point below what economists define as "full employment." Economic theory holds that 100-percent employment is a practical impossibility, because, under the very best circumstances, 4 percent of the workforce will be technically out of work—in the process of changing jobs, acquiring new training, briefly laid off, and so on. This is known as "frictional unemployment."

Most shocking of all the 1990s economic crises was the decade-long depression that had settled over Japan. Following World War II, the Japanese rebuilt and recovered rapidly, producing and exporting huge amounts of cheap goods—often shoddy imitations of more costly Western products. In the 1960s, however, Japanese manufacturers, especially in electronics, began producing innovative, high-quality goods. By the late 1960s, Japanese heavy industry, especially steel producers and automobile manufacturers, was making great strides in the world marketplace. Envious American firms spoke of the "Japanese miracle." Through the 1970s and 1980s, the Japanese economy boomed, while the American economy drifted. As Japanese business leaders had once studied American methods, U.S. executives now threw themselves into intensive study of Japanese models of management.

Led by Japan, the Asian economy generally soared. The only worry on the horizon was the impending transfer of the commercial center of Hong Kong, a British crown colony, to China. In July 1997, the 99-year lease by which Great Britain held Hong Kong, would expire, and there would be no choice but to return control of this bastion of capitalism to the biggest communist nation on earth. (By the time of the transfer, China itself had shed its Maoist economic isolationism and had become a major world importer and exporter. Chinese authorities announced their intention to maintain Hong Kong as a "special administrative region," a booming zone of free enterprise.)

But Japan fell victim to its own success. The cost of living outstripped productivity, and the costs of production priced many products out of the market. With setbacks in the Japanese economy, the rest of Asia followed Japan into crisis. By the close of the 20th century, the problem of *Asian debt*—the gargantuan sums Asian producers owed to Western business and financial interests— loomed ominously.

Talk of the Times

Asian debt is the term used to describe the collective debt created by the Asian economic crisis of the close of the 20th century.

Annus Horribilis

Strangely, most Americans remained more or less indifferent to the economic crisis gripping so much of the world's population. Inevitably, the tremors in the Asian economy would be felt here, but no one was holding his or her breath. U.S. productivity remained high, unemployment low, and stock market returns robust.

Great Britain's First Family

Rather than focus on the Asian money crisis, many Americans found themselves riveted by the soap opera unfolding within the British royal family. Politically, this could have no effect on America, but, as the playwright George Bernard Shaw had once observed, the Americans and British were one people, separated only by a common language. Americans were irresistibly drawn to the lives of the British royal class.

Born in 1961, Diana Spencer was the youngest daughter of Edward John Spencer, Viscount Althorp, heir to the 7th Earl Spencer, and his first wife, Frances Ruth Burke Roche, who was daughter of the 4th Baron Fermoy. After a finishing-school education in England and Switzerland, Diana

Talk of the Times

The **heir apparent** is the person whose right to inheritance cannot be denied, provided he or she survives an ancestor. Contrast **heir presumptive**, whose right to inheritance can be defeated by the subsequent birth of a relative closer to the ancestor.

taught kindergarten at a fashionable school in London and renewed her social ties with the British royal family. On February 24, 1981, her engagement to Prince Charles, *heir apparent* to the British throne, was announced, and, on July 29, 1981, the couple was married in St. Paul's Cathedral. The globally televised ceremony was viewed by an audience numbering in the hundreds of millions.

It had about it the aura of a fairy tale—made the more appealing by the highly publicized marital turmoil among other members of the royal family. Diana was a beautiful young woman who enthusiastically worked on behalf of charitable causes, including AIDS and, later, the international movement to ban the use of land mines—buried explosive antipersonnel weapons, which, in the aftermath of many conflicts across the world, are left behind until touched off by some innocent civilian.

Diana's marriage to Charles produced two boys—"an heir and a spare," as Britishers called them—but also produced much unhappiness. To make matters worse, the couple's marital discord and, ultimately, infidelities were covered in detail by tabloid journalists. The worldwide public, it seemed, could not get enough of the popular princess—and of the ongoing saga of the dissolution of her marriage.

Talk of the Times

Annus horribilis *is Latin for "year of horrors."*

Death of a Princess

In 1992, Charles and Diana were separated. That same year, Sarah Ferguson, Duchess of York, was divorced from Charles's younger brother, Prince Andrew, and a destructive fire broke out in one wing of Windsor Palace, ancient seat of the royal family. In an address to Parliament, Queen Elizabeth II referred to 1992 as an *annus horribilis*.

After the divorce, Princess Diana nevertheless maintained a high profile in various charitable pursuits, her continued popularity often a source of annoyance to the royal family. At last, in 1996, she and Charles were divorced, Diana receiving a substantial settlement.

Talk of the Times

Paparazzi (singular, *paparazzo*), from an Italian word denoting journalists, describes a class of photographers who specialize in the invasion of celebrity privacy, taking intrusive and embarrassing photographs, which are published in sensationalist tabloid newspapers.

She began a relationship with Dodi Fayad, the son of the owner of (among other investments) the Ritz Hotel in Paris and Harrod's, the landmark London department store. On August 31, 1997, the couple left dinner at the Ritz in a chauffeured Mercedes, which sped away in an effort to evade the ever-present, ever-pursuing *paparazzi*. Traveling at high speed, the Mercedes struck a supporting pier in a street tunnel near the Seine River. The driver and Fayad were killed instantly. Diana was fatally injured. A body guard, severely hurt, recovered.

Two Trials in L.A.

Amid the many triumphs and terrors of the 1990s, the world mourned the death of Diana with unprecedented intensity. This was in part a tribute to the woman herself, a decent and charming human being who was sincere in her charitable work and who responded to the public with great warmth. It was also, however, the product of media technology. Television, the medium through which most Americans—and much of the world—gathered information about events, thrived on personal stories even as it shunned more abstract, intellectual, and issue-based material.

The Beating of Rodney King

After the death of Martin Luther King Jr. in 1968, no single great personality of King's stature arose to focus leadership of the civil rights movement. By the early 1990s, the movement seemed to have receded into the background. Then, the peculiar intimacy of television suddenly brought it front and center once again. On March 3, 1991, Rodney King, an African American motorist, was pulled over for speeding on a California freeway. By sheer chance, a witness carrying a camcorder videotaped the arrest: a brutal beating by four nightstick-wielding Los Angeles police officers. The tape was broadcast nationally, creating an outcry from coast to coast.

Incredibly, the officers were acquitted on April 30, 1992, by an all-white jury in the upscale California community of Simi Valley. The verdict touched off five days of rioting, arson, and looting in Los Angeles, especially in the city's predominantly black South Central neighborhood. (In a subsequent trial on federal civil rights charges, two of the officers were convicted.)

Despite the initial acquittal of the officers and the ensuing riot, the videotaped beating ultimately compelled Americans, including those of middle-class white backgrounds, to come to grips with the issues of racism that remained unresolved in America.

Voice of the Century

"People, I just want to say, you know, can we all get along? Can we get along? Can we stop making it, making it horrible for the older people and the kids?"

—Rodney King, during the Los Angeles riots, May 2, 1992

The O.J. Show

Another media experience took such issues to a new, even more disturbing level.

O.J. Simpson was an old-fashioned football hero, an African American who had made it big in sports and gone on to become a sports broadcaster and television and movie personality.

On June 12, 1994, Simpson's ex-wife, Nicole Brown Simpson and a friend, Ronald Goldman, were stabbed to death outside Nicole Simpson's home in Los Angeles. A shocking celebrity murder in an exclusive Los Angeles neighborhood, it received national attention immediately, but it quickly jumped to surreal heights. Within a few days, the investigation centered on Simpson himself, and when police came to make the arrest, Simpson "escaped" in his white Ford Bronco, driven by a friend. Police pursued him onto the freeway, careful not to force the Bronco to high speeds, talking to him via cellular phone as he cowered in the backseat with a gun to his head. The slow-motion chase was followed by news helicopters and broadcast live, nationwide, as crowds gathered along overpasses to gawk and "encourage" the former NFL star with signs and cheers. It was perhaps the most bizarre shared media experience since Orson Welles's "War of the Worlds," and it was only the beginning.

The nation's attention was now not merely focused—it was riveted. O.J. Simpson was arrested, charged, indicted, and became the focus of what was billed as the *"Trial of the Century."* For 266 days, the televised trial riveted a sizable portion of the population, becoming, all by itself, a minor television industry.

Talk of the Times

The phrase **"Trial of the Century"** was frequently used to describe the trial of O.J. Simpson. Previously, the 1935 trial of Richard Bruno Richard Hauptmann, for the kidnapping and murder of the infant son of Charles Lindbergh and Anne Morrow Lindbergh, had been dubbed the "trial of the century."

L.A.P.D. mug shot of O.J. Simpson, June 17, 1994. (Image from author's collection)

On October 3, 1995, after deliberating for less than four hours, and despite what prosecutors described as a "mountain of evidence" against Simpson, the Los Angeles jury found the defendant not guilty. Simpson's highly paid defense team had successfully impugned the work of the Los Angeles Police Department, suggesting that, motivated by racism, certain officers had framed Simpson.

Once again, television had united the nation in focus on a single event. But the televised verdict also revealed the depth of the nation's continued division along racial lines. Whites overwhelmingly deemed the acquittal a miscarriage of justice, whereas a majority of African Americans believed Simpson had been the victim of a racist frame-up.

An Age of Rage

To declare our century violent is both understatement and anticlimax. What still has the power to surprise us, though, is the degree to which violence—rage—permeates life today. Automobile bumpers became display space for angry slogans, enraged *sound bites* continually issue from such confrontational television trash as *Jerry Springer* and *Jenny Jones*, and a new breed of radio personality, the *shock jock*, makes the rhetoric of intolerance his bread and butter.

Right to Life

The issues surrounding abortion, as mentioned in Chapter 24, "Truces and Terrorists," often usurp the dialogue of political campaigns. As the 20th century wound down, the anti-abortion—or self-proclaimed "right-to-life" movement—sometimes turned violent. In the name of halting the "murder" of babies, some anti-abortion zealots have threatened, intimidated, and even murdered physicians and other medical personnel. Abortion clinics have been the target of bombings.

Terrorism Hits Home

The attacks on abortionists and abortion clinics are examples of a new kind of terrorism, the source of which is not Third World, but homegrown.

On April 19, 1993, agents of the FBI and the U.S. Treasury Department's Alcohol, Tobacco, Firearms Unit (ATF) moved to end a 51-day standoff with David Koresh (his real name was Vernon Howell) and his followers, members of a religious cult called the Branch Davidians, who were holed up in a fortified compound outside of Waco, Texas. They had been resisting the intrusion of the federal agents, who were sent to investigate reports of an illegal arsenal at the compound as well as rumors of child abuse. When ATF officers had advanced on the compound on February 28, the cultists opened fire, killing four agents. Koresh was wounded in the exchange, and at least two of his followers were killed.

Voice of the Century

"All these niggers in L.A. city government ... all of 'em should be lined up against a wall and f**king shot."

—Mark Fuhrman, taped remark to screenwriter Laura Hart McKinney, revealed during the O.J. trial. Fuhrman, a lead detective investigating the murder, was offered as an example of the racist mentality of the Los Angeles Police Department.

Talk of the Times

Shock jock describes radio personalities ("disc jockeys") who specialize in outrageous talk, often of a sexually obscene or otherwise socially objectionable nature.

When the FBI and ATF made their decisive move on April 19, the Branch Davidians responded by setting fire to their own compound. Both the February 28 shootout and the April 19 inferno were televised to millions.

Exactly two years later, on April 19, 1995, television audiences saw the bloody aftermath of the bombing of the Alfred P. Murrah Federal Office Building in Oklahoma City, in which 169 persons, including many children housed in the building's daycare center, were killed.

Century Stats

Eighty cultists, including 24 children, were killed in the blaze that engulfed the Branch Davidian compound in Waco, Texas. It was the worst cult incident since the Jonestown mass suicide of 1978 (Chapter 25). On March 26, 1997, in Rancho Santa Fe, near San Diego, California, 39 members of a millennial cult called Heaven's Gate decided to "shed their containers"—their earthly bodies—and get on a "companion craft" hiding in the tail of the Hale-Bopp comet. Twenty-one women and 18 men, ages 26 to 72, died together.

Talk of the Times

Militia movement describes militant right-wing groups opposed to what they perceive as government oppression ranging from taxation, to gun control, to the promulgation and enforcement of civil rights laws.

Timothy McVeigh and Terry Nichols, the two young men tried and convicted in connection with the bombing, were associated with the *militia movement*, a phrase describing militant groups organized in several states after the Branch Davidian raid and a 1992 government assault on Randy Weaver, a white supremacist, and his family in Ruby Ridge, Idaho. The incidents at Waco and Ruby Ridge, together with passage of relatively mild federal gun-control legislation, inspired the formation of armed cadres opposed not only to what they deemed excessive government control of everyday life, but also to what they saw as a United Nations plot to take over the United States in a drive toward "One World Government."

A Place Called Kosovo

In the United States, homegrown terror was shocking. Elsewhere in the world, it was a way of life. As the century came to an end, the civil war in the former Yugoslavia became increasingly bloody.

In the breakup of the states that had formed Communist Yugoslavia, Kosovo was accorded the ambiguous status of autonomous province within Serbia. Ethnic Albanians—mostly Muslim—make up 90 percent of Kosovo's population. Serbs make up 10 percent. The Albanian majority protested against Serbia's taking control of Kosovan administration, and, in 1992, Kosovo voted to secede from Serbia and Yugoslavia, with the intention of merging with Muslim Albania. The government of Yugoslavia, under the leadership of Slobodan Milosevic, first tightened its control of Kosovo, then, in 1999, waged full-scale war against the Albanian majority.

Despite the overwhelming Albanian majority there, the Serbs consider Kosovo the cradle of Serbian culture. The small province was caught between the violent passion of Serbia and the opposition of world powers, which fear that independence will trigger a wider war in the Balkans—that hatchery of conflict, in which World War I began.

In search of a solution, President Clinton proposed wider autonomy for Kosovo, just short of independence. The ethnic Albanians accepted the compromise plan, but Slobodan Milosevic rejected it. Beginning in February 1998, Milsovic launched an offensive against the Kosovo Liberation Army, which has resulted in the deaths of at least 2,000 people and the forced exodus of some 300,000 more. In response to the offensive, NATO, with the United States leading, launched massive air strikes against Serbian forces.

Century Stats

Kosovo occupies an area of 4,203 square miles and, before invasion by Serb forces, contained a population of 1,954,747.

And an Age of Reconciliation

If the closing years of the century were filled with rage, they also offered episodes of remarkable, even miraculous reconciliation.

Israel and the PLO

Since 1988, when the Palestine Liberation Organization proclaimed the State of Palestine, a government in exile, there had seemed no way to resolve the differences between the Palestinians and Israel, no alternative to the chronic state of war that had been under way since 1948. But in April 1993 began secret negotiations with Israel in an effort to reach a settlement. On September 13, 1993, Arafat and Israeli prime minister Yitzhak Rabin shook hands on an agreement that included mutual recognition and outlined a gradual transfer of governing authority to the Palestinians of the West Bank and Gaza Strip over a five-year period. On the very next day, Jordan's King Hussein signed the preliminaries to a peace treaty with Israel as well.

Palestinian leader Yasir Arafat and Israeli prime minister Yitzhak Rabin, after signing a preliminary agreements on Israeli-Palestinian peace.
(Image from the Israeli National Picture Collection)

Like Egypt's great peacemaker, Anwar Sadat (Chapter 26, "Years of Plague, Years of Hope"), Rabin would pay a heavy price for his work. While attending a peace rally in November 1995, he was assassinated by a Jewish extremist.

President Mandela of South Africa

In a century of so much change, one grim reality seemed destined to outlast what many had supposed the eternal enmity between Israel and the Arab world. And that was the permanence of oppression in South Africa, where a black majority lived separate from and under the perpetual domination of a white minority. This situation had begun with the conclusion of the Second (Great) Boer War, as we saw in Chapter 6, "First Years," and it endured even after the late 1950s and 1960s, when the former European colonies of sub-Saharan Africa all gained their independence and achieved black self-rule.

Although the white Afrikaners had ruled South Africa since the beginning of the century, the nation's program of absolute racial segregation, *apartheid*, was codified into law in 1948. In 1952, the African National Congress (ANC) began advocating passive resistance to apartheid. In 1959, under political and moral pressure from the outside world, Afrikaner prime minister Hendrik Verwoerd promoted passage of the Bantu Self-Government Act, which assigned blacks to so-called "homelands." This was presented as a move toward decolonization, but, in fact, it was the equivalent of what the United States had done with the Indians during the 19th century. Black Africans were, in effect, herded onto reservations—poor lands that made up 13 percent of South Africa. On the homelands, there was no place to make a living. Outside of the homelands, blacks would have virtually no rights.

Talk of the Times

Apartheid, an Afrikaans word meaning "separateness," was the long-standing policy of absolute racial segregation that guided South African politics for most of the 20th century.

Through the rest of the 1950s and '60s, the government's defense of apartheid became increasingly violent. In 1962, ANC leader Nelson Mandela was arrested and imprisoned—for what would be 30 years. By 1977, southern Africa's remaining white-ruled countries, Rhodesia, Angola, and Mozambique, had finally come under black-majority rule (with Northern Rhodesia now called Zambia, and Southern Rhodesia renamed Zimbabwe). Only South Africa held out, entrenching itself more and more in white supremacy.

Rioting was chronic, most significantly in Soweto, a sprawling black shanty town outside of Johannesburg. The world watched, and the world heeded the lessons of Soweto. International corporations, including many based in the United States, divested themselves of all South African holdings. The American and British governments levied economic and trade sanctions against South Africa in 1985, which became an international pariah, an outlaw nation strangling on its own racial hatred.

Gradually, the bonds of apartheid were loosened, and then, in 1991, Prime Minister F.W. de Klerk sponsored the creation of a new constitution, which brought an end to apartheid entirely. He also freed Nelson Mandela, whose long imprisonment had been a spiritual focus of the anti-apartheid struggle. On May 9, 1994, Mandela was elected president of South Africa. It was another miracle of reconciliation between forces so long opposed that their opposition had seemed absolute and impossible to change.

Of Genetic Engineering and Cyber Surfing

If the century taught us one great lesson, it was that many things considered absolute and unchangeable were neither.

Weaving the Threads of Life

The debate between "nature" and "nurture" is probably as old as humanity: How much of a person's self is determined by absolute heredity and how much by changeable experience? By the 1980s, however, scientists were changing the "nature" half of this equation by altering the possibilities of heredity itself.

In 1944, a Canadian-born American bacteriologist, Oswald Avery, discovered deoxyribonucleic acid, DNA, and demonstrated that this is the most basic genetic material, a complex molecule that is, in effect, the key to life. In 1953, the English physicist Francis Crick and the American biochemist James Watson deciphered the structure of the DNA molecule, describing it as a two chains of nucleotides arranged in a double helix, which would separate as an organism cell underwent reproduction, each separated strand building up a complementary strand on itself. Thus the DNA molecule would be replicated without changing its structure (except for accidental mutation), and the characteristics of an organism were passed on from generation to generation.

As the mechanisms by which DNA operates became more fully understood, scientists developed *recombinant DNA*, in which DNA molecules from two or more sources were artificially combined and then inserted into host organisms, in which they could propagate. This gene *cloning* could produce, at will, new genetic combinations that might result in organisms with desirable qualities—perhaps bacteria that could be used to fight disease, new crops resistant to insects and parasites, or even human beings possessed of "desirable" traits.

In 1980 and 1986, the U.S. Department of Agriculture approved the sale of the first living genetically altered organism—a virus, used as a pseudorabies vaccine—and, since then, hundreds of patents have been issued for genetically altered bacteria and

Talk of the Times

Recombinant DNA is genetically engineered DNA, in which DNA molecules from two or more sources are artificially combined and then inserted into host organisms to create **cloned** genes. The purpose of such a procedure is to produce offspring organisms with certain desirable traits or without certain undesirable ones.

plants. Then, in 1997, the world was stunned by photographs of a quite ordinary-looking lamb named Dolly.

Ordinary *looking*. Unlike any mammal that ever lived, Dolly had no father and was an exact duplicate of her mother, having been cloned. Nuclei from various sheep cells had been implanted into unfertilized sheep eggs from which the natural nuclei had been removed using microsurgery techniques. The transfer gave the recipient eggs a complete set of genes, just as if the eggs had been fertilized by sperm. These eggs were cultured, then implanted into sheep. One of these implantations was carried to term, resulting in Dolly. Of particular significance is the fact that the transferred cell nuclei came not from embryonic cells, but from mammary cells. That is, the cloning process did not use sex cells—just body cells. Biologists had long believed that an animal cell could not be coaxed to regenerate an entire organism. This belief was shattered.

Even more disquieting was the realization that, genetically speaking, a sheep is not very different from a human being. The moral, legal, and ethical frontiers posed by the prospect of human cloning are enormous. No research institution is funding human cloning research, and, publicly, at least, numerous governments have condemned the idea.

The Internet Revolution

The end of the 20th century saw the crossing of many frontiers. Throughout the later 20th century, political boundaries receded in importance as commerce became truly international. By the early 1990s, with the explosive development of the Internet, many of these boundaries dissolved utterly. Companies, organizations, and individuals were interconnected, whether they were physically separated by the length of an office corridor or by an ocean.

The Internet is not so much an entity as it is a fact, a fact of the interconnectedness of millions of computers and computer networks. Physically, its origin may be found in ARPANET, the Advanced Research Projects Agency Network, a communications network established by the U.S. Department of Defense in 1969. Soon after ARPANET was established, researchers not only in defense, but in other academic fields made use of the network, which expanded steadily. As personal computers, equipped with *modems*, became increasingly affordable, the Internet exploded beyond the confines of governments, corporations, and institutions, and entered the households of the world.

Today, just about any human activity involving communication—the exchange of information—may be conducted via the *information superhighway* known as the Internet.

Talk of the Times

Millions log onto the Internet through a **modem (modulator-demodulator)**, a computer peripheral device that enables the computer to communicate digital information over telephone lines.

Sex, Lies, and the White House

On September 11, 1998, the United States Congress published on the Internet the full text of a report written under the direction of Kenneth Starr, an "independent counsel" appointed to investigate allegations of possibly impeachable offenses committed by President Bill Clinton. Millions of Americans were free to read the laboriously detailed accounts of the president's sexual liaison with a White House intern, Monica Lewinsky.

The Starr report was the culmination of a four-year, $40 million-dollar investigation into Clinton's conduct—initially focusing on financial matters. Starr's investigation cleared Clinton of all wrongdoing, except in the matter of Lewinsky.

Although the zealous Starr (a conservative jurist who once told an interviewer that, as a youth, his chief Saturday-evening recreation was polishing his father's shoes) meticulously documented the sexual details of Clinton's affair with Lewinsky, he and others involved in the investigation insisted that sex was not at issue. The issue, they insisted, was that the president had violated his oath of office by lying about the affair in a sworn deposition he had given in a sexual-harassment lawsuit brought against him by a former Arkansas state employee, Paula Jones. It was alleged that the president also lied about the affair to a grand jury. Based on the Starr report, the Congress voted, along strict party lines, to *impeach* President Clinton, and, for the first time since Andrew Johnson was impeached in 1868, the United States Senate was the scene of an impeachment trial.

Although Republicans held a majority of Senate seats, removal of a president requires a two-thirds Senate vote, which no one believed would be forthcoming. For months during the Congressional proceedings, many had argued that, even if true, the charges leveled against the president did not "rise to the level" of impeachment. Polls gave the president his highest approval ratings ever. The people generally deplored his behavior and criticized his character, but, with a booming economy, they overwhelmingly approved of his performance as president—and many deplored the aggressive, invasive tactics of Starr and his deputies.

Heedless of public sentiment, the Republican-controlled Congress pressed on with what they called their "constitutional duty." On February 12, 1999, to no one's surprise, the Senate acquitted the president.

Talk of the Times

To **impeach** is to charge an office holder with offenses that, if proven, warrant removal from office. Impeachment is not synonymous with such removal.

A Look Ahead

The impeachment of President Clinton bewildered most of the world, which could not fathom what was seen as an obsession with the chief executive's private life, and it seemed surreal to many Americans. As the first impeachment in 131 years, its historical importance was obvious—yet, just as obvious to most Americans, was the feeling that all of it was utterly unnecessary and uncalled for.

The partisan impeachment of a president who may or may not have committed adultery (depending on one's definition of sex) and who certainly lied about his misbehavior, but who may or may not have committed perjury (depending on how one defined perjury versus merely lying and, once again, how one defined sex) was depressing and distressing. But, to most Americans, it also seemed silly and irrelevant. Certainly, it was a sorry way to end a century filled with so many events of so much greater moment.

So much of the talk and attention of the closing years of the century were commanded by events whose historic importance can only fade: the O.J. trial, the death of Princess Di, the trial of William Jefferson Clinton.

What issues will endure into the next century? Perhaps we can divide them into three major categories.

What We'll Buy

An old saying goes something like this: People have few needs, but many wants. Most likely, the 21st century will see a continued expansion in the variety of consumer goods available, but perhaps the most important of these will be drinkable water and breathable air. Despite advances in environmental technology, pollution of natural resources remains a critical issue.

If we will need to add air and water to our 21st-century shopping lists, we will also probably find ourselves shopping for what might be called "foodaceuticals," an emerging product line that combines medicine with food for the purpose of maintaining health and preventing disease rather than curing existing ailments. Related to this, and based on further developments in genetic engineering and *gene therapy*, will be likely advances in essential life-prolonging technologies, including anti-death drugs.

Century Stats

President Andrew Johnson was impeached in 1868. He was acquitted by a single vote in the Senate. President Clinton was acquitted by a wider margin. Two articles of impeachment were brought against him. On Article I, he was acquitted 55 to 45; on Article II, the vote was evenly split, 50 for acquittal, 50 for conviction.

Talk of the Times

Gene therapy describes procedures that may be used to alter or repair "defective" genes in order to prevent disease—or aging.

What We'll Know

In addition to further decoding the mechanisms of genetics to improve our physical lives and longevity through gene therapy and genetic engineering, it is likely that we will also achieve a goal physicists have long set for themselves: the creation of a *unified field theory*—a full understanding of how the forces of the universe are tied together.

Yet the most complex discoveries likely to be made will be those relating to the inner universe, a greater understanding of the processes of the human mind, of how we think.

How We'll Live

Extrapolating from present trends, we may find ourselves continuing the process that "futurist" Faith Popcorn called *cocooning*, concentrating more and more of our lives in our homes. Although crime rates in the United States have declined, reversing a century-long trend, personal security remains a hot-button issue. Each year, more and more homes install "security systems," ranging from elaborate locks and burglar alarms to full-scale video surveillance systems. It is likely that homes of the 21st century will come increasingly to resemble fortresses: miniature, high-tech versions of the moated castle. Not only will the comings and goings of people be monitored and controlled, but, increasingly, homes will develop independence in terms of their physical plant. The water we drink will be individually filtered and processed, as will the air we breathe. Individual production of electric power may become commonplace.

Talk of the Times

Unified field theory is the Holy Grail of physics—a theory of the universe that fully explains the relation among all forces of the universe.

The trend toward *telecommuting* and generally merging the workplace with the homeplace will likely continue. Positive effects may include strengthened family life and less pollution and congestion produced by commuter traffic. But how will a home-centered life affect the social structure of our society?

The homes in which we "cocoon" will not be cut off from the rest of the world. We can expect the interconnectedness of the Internet, already prodigious, to become even more extensive. More and more of our personal business—even such things as routine medical check-ups—will be conducted electronically, without regard to municipal, state, or even national boundaries.

Talk of the Times

Cocooning, a term coined by futurist Faith Popcorn, describes a late 20th-century trend toward centering one's life in and around one's home. **Telecommuting** describes the practice of working from one's home rather than in a central office.

Boundaries: It has been the overall trend of the 20th century to dissolve existing boundaries rather than to create new ones. Will the 21st century see humankind reaching beyond the boundaries of our planet to colonize other worlds? Many scientists believe that small colonies will be created on the moon and on Mars before the 21st century ends.

Many scientists also predict that we will soon move outside of the boundaries of our own bodies. Cloning has already been demonstrated in mammals, but will ectogenic birth, literally the creation of "test-tube babies," become a reality? And if we can learn to create life outside of our bodies, can we reincarnate life after the body containing it has expired? Futurists currently see artificial reincarnation, the biotechnology of physically perpetuating life far beyond a normal lifespan, as an area that will be developed in the not-too-distant future.

Will We Live Better?

It would be fun to write a *Complete Idiot's Guide to the Future*, for there are many more extrapolations to make and much more imagination left to exercise. But let's end with the question about the future that matters most. Maybe it is the only question that, finally, matters at all.

Will we live better? That is, will we live more happily? More generously? More gently? More wisely? The answer will certainly depend on politics, the economy, and technology. And all of these things are tied to the passage of time and the evolution of ideas. But the answer also depends on aspects of the human spirit, which, if not truly timeless, are nevertheless highly durable. They are the very aspects on which the great American experiment in democracy was founded, and if we can cling to them *despite* time, while also continuing to develop them *through* time, the answer may well be *yes*.

The Least You Need to Know

➤ Plagued by sexual scandal, President Clinton has managed to survive and prosper in office, largely because, at century's end, the United States seemed immune from the economic crises plaguing much of the rest of the world.

➤ While violence and economic crisis tore much of the Third World, Americans tended to focus on the life and death of a British princess and on sensational court trials at home.

➤ "Homegrown terrorism," violent expressions of an "age of rage," was a disturbing trend in the United States by the end of the century.

➤ In the Middle East and South Africa, irreconcilable enemies made great strides toward reconciliation.

➤ The last decade of the 20th century saw extraordinary advances in genetics and electronic communication—cloning and the Internet.

Who Was Who in the 20th Century

Addams, Jane (1860–1935)   Pioneer of social work; founded Hull House (1889) to educate and care for Chicago's poor.

Arafat, Yasir (1929–)   Leader of al-Fatah and the Palestine Liberation Organization (PLO); led the struggle for Palestinian nationhood, but ultimately sought accord with Israel.

Armstrong, Louis "Satchmo" (1900–1971)   Cornetist and trumpeter who was the first great soloist in jazz, "America's classical music."

Armstrong, Neil (1930–)   American astronaut who was the first human being to walk on the moon (1969).

Baekland, Leo Hendrik (1863–1944)   Belgian-born chemist who created Bakelite, thereby launching the age of plastic, perhaps the most important manufacturing material of the century.

Begin, Menachem (1913–1992)   Zionist leader instrumental in the establishment of Israel, Begin shared the 1978 Nobel Prize with Anwar Sadat for working to resolve the Arab-Israel conflict.

Bell, Alexander Graham (1847–1922)   Inventor of the telephone.

Berle, Milton (1908–)   "Mr. Television"—pioneering TV entertainer whose popularity was instrumental in establishing television as the century's most pervasive communications medium.

Bush, George (1924–)   Forty-first president of the United States.

Capone, Al (1899–1947)   Italian-born American who became the century's archetypal gangster.

Carnegie, Andrew (1835–1919)   Scottish-born American steel magnate, who ultimately used his enormous wealth for the public benefit.

Carter, Jimmy (1924–)   Thirty-ninth president of the United States.

Castro, Fidel (1927–)   Revolutionary leader who overthrew the regime of Fulgencio Batista and instituted communism in Cuba.

Chiang Kai-shek (1887–1975)   Leader of the Chinese nationalists against the Chinese communists; president of nationalist China (Taiwan) from 1949 until his death.

Churchill, Winston S. (1874–1965)   British prime minister who led his nation to victory in World War II and who wrote some of the most distinguished histories of the century.

Clinton, Bill (1946–) Forty-second president of the United States.

Coolidge, Calvin (1872–1933) Thirtieth president of the United States.

Crick, Francis H. (1916–) With James D. Watson, formulated the spiral double-helix model of the DNA molecule, laying the foundation of modern genetics.

Darwin, Charles (1809–1882) Naturalist whose theory of evolution by natural selection would profoundly shape much of 20th-century scientific and social thought.

Deng Xiaoping (1904–1997) Leader of communist China who liberalized the nation's political and economic policy, but also cracked down on the Tiananmen Square democracy movement.

Duchamp, Marcel (1887–1968) French-born artist whose *Nude Descending a Staircase* made a sensation at the 1913 Armory Show and helped transform modern conceptions of art.

Eastman, George (1854–1932) Inventor of dry-plate photography, flexible photographic film, and the Kodak box camera, which brought photography to the masses.

Edison, Thomas Alva (1847–1931) U.S. inventor of the incandescent electric light and the phonograph, as well as basic inventions of the movie industry and the electric power industry.

Einstein, Albert (1879–1955) German-born American physicist whose theories of relativity transformed our conception of the universe and laid the foundation for the exploitation of atomic energy.

Eisenhower, Dwight D. (1890–1969) Supreme Allied Commander of Europe during World War II and, later, 34th president of the United States.

Fermi, Enrico (1901–1954) Italian-born American physicist who directed the creation of the first sustained nuclear chain reaction (1942), a step in the development of the atomic bomb.

Fitzgerald, F. Scott (1896–1940) American novelist who became literary spokesman for what he called the "Jazz Age" in the 1920s.

Fleming, Alexander (1881–1955) Discoverer of penicillin, the first important antibiotic.

Ford, Gerald (1913–) Thirty-eighth president of the United States.

Ford, Henry ((1863–1947) Designed the first truly popular automobile, the Model T, and created a system of mass production to manufacture it, profoundly transforming the way of life in the 20th century.

Freud, Sigmund (1856–1939) Viennese physician whose psychoanalysis became the century's most influential explanation of human behavior.

Friedan, Betty (1921–) American feminist whose *The Feminine Mystique* (1963) transformed attitudes of and about women; in 1966, she was a founder of the National Organization for Women (NOW).

Gagarin, Yuri (1934–1968) Soviet cosmonaut who became the first person in space (1961).

Gandhi, Mohandas (1869–1948) Leader of the Indian independence movement, prime minister of India, and architect of nonviolent civil disobedience, which influenced Martin Luther King Jr., Nelson Mandela, and others; assassinated in 1948.

Garvey, Marcus (1887–1940)   Jamaican-born American black nationalist leader, who sought to establish economic and political self-reliance for African Americans.

Goddard, Robert H. (1882–1945)   American pioneer of rocketry, who established the basis for modern rocket science.

Gorbachev, Mikhail (1931–)   Soviet leader whose liberal reforms brought an end to the Cold War and, ultimately, led to the dissolution of the Soviet Union.

Graham, Billy (1918–)   American evangelist, popular American religious leader, and "spiritual adviser" to presidents.

Harding, Warren G. (1865–1923)   Twenty-ninth president of the United States.

Hearst, William Randolph (1863–1951)   American newspaper and magazine publisher who built the world's largest publishing empire, which used to influence American public opinion.

Hemingway, Ernest (1899–1961)   Nobel Prize-winning American fiction writer recognized as among the most influential literary figures of the century.

Hirohito (1901–1989)   Emperor of Japan during World War II and the postwar recovery.

Hitler, Adolf (1889–1945)   Absolute dictator of Germany and would-be architect of world conquest, he perpetrated genocide against Europe's Jews (and others) and, more than any other figure, was responsible for World War II.

Ho Chi Minh (1890–1969)   Communist revolutionary leader of North Vietnam, who achieved independence from French colonial rule and led the war against the U.S.-supported government of South Vietnam.

Hoover, Herbert (1874–1964)   Thirty-first president of the United States.

Hoover, J. Edgar (1895–1972)   Controversial director of the Federal Bureau of Investigation from 1924 until his death.

Johnson, Lyndon Baines (1908–1973)   Thirty-sixth president of the United States.

Kennedy, John F. (1917–1963)   Thirty-fifth president of the United States; assassinated in Dallas, Texas, by Lee Harvey Oswald.

Kerensky, Alexandr (1881–1970)   Russian revolutionary who came to power after the overthrow of Czar Nicholas II, but who was in turn ousted by the Bolsheviks.

Keynes, John Maynard (1883–1946)   British economist whose ideas formed the basis of Franklin Roosevelt's New Deal policies and who was, generally, the most influential economist of the century.

Khomeini, Ayatollah (1900–1989)   Iranian revolutionary and Shi'ite religious zealot who led (from Parisian exile) the overthrow of the shah, installed an Islamic government in Iran, and refused to free American diplomatic hostages.

Khrushchev, Nikita (1894–1971)   Soviet premier during the height of the Cold War.

King, Martin Luther Jr. (1929–1968)   Most influential African American civil rights leader of the 1950s and 1960s; a leading exponent of nonviolent civil disobedience.

Kissinger, Henry (1923–)   German-born U.S. diplomat who, as national security adviser and then secretary of state in the Nixon and Ford administrations, helped engineer an end to the Vietnam War and bring détente with China and the Soviets.

Lenin, Vladimir I. (1870–1924)   Chief architect of the Bolshevik Revolution.

Lindbergh, Charles A. (1902–1974)   American aviator who made the first solo trans-Atlantic flight (1927).

Malcolm X (1925–1965)   Dynamic African American activist and founder of the Organization of Afro-American Unity.

Mandela, Nelson (1918–)   South African black political leader, jailed for 30 years, who became the first black president of South Africa.

Mao Tse-tung (1893–1976)   Principal leader of the Chinese communist revolution and communist China's head of state.

Marconi, Guglielmo (1874–1937)   Principal inventor of radio.

Marshall, George C. (1880–1959)   U.S. Army chief of staff in World War II and secretary of state to Harry S Truman; architect of the Marshall Plan for the recovery of Europe following World War II.

McCarthy, Joseph (1908–1957)   Wisconsin senator who presided over the communist "witch hunts" of the early 1950s.

McKinley, William (1843–1901)   Twenty-fifth president of the United States; assassinated in office.

Milosevic, Slobodan (1941–)   President of Serbia who waged an ethnic war against the Albanian majority in the Serbian province of Kosovo beginning in the late 1990s.

Mussolini, Benito (1883–1945)   Italian dictator and founder of Fascism.

Nicholas II (1868–1918)   Last czar of Russia; presided over the disastrous Russo-Japanese War of 1905 and Russian participation in World War I; overthrown in the Revolution of 1917 and subsequently executed with his family the following year.

Nixon, Richard M. (1913–1994)   Thirty-seventh president of the United States; the first to resign from office.

Oppenheimer, J. Robert (1902–1967)   American physicist who directed the Manhattan Project, which produced the nuclear weapons dropped on Hiroshima and Nagasaki, Japan, ending World War II.

Parks, Rosa (1913–)   Civil rights leader whose refusal to "go to the back of the bus" in Montgomery, Alabama, touched off a bus boycott that marked the beginning of the modern civil rights movement.

Pétain, Henri Phillipe (1856–1951)   French World War I hero who cooperated with Nazi Germany as leader of the Vichy government of unoccupied France in World War II.

Picasso, Pablo (1881–1973)   Most famous painter of the 20th century; one of the modernist art vanguard.

Pickford, Mary (1893–1979)   "America's Sweetheart"; silent-film sensation and first American woman to earn a million dollars.

Presley, Elvis (1935–1977)   American rock 'n' roll pioneer, who revolutionized 1950s mass culture.

Rabin, Yitzhak (1922–1995)   Israeli leader who negotiated peace agreements with the PLO and with Jordan; he was assassinated by a Jewish extremist.

Reagan, Ronald (1911–)   Fortieth president of the United States.

Roosevelt, Franklin D. (1882–1945)   Thirty-second president of the United States for an unprecedented four terms.

Roosevelt, Theodore (1858–1919) Reform politician, Spanish-American War hero, environmentalist, and 26th president of the United States.

Ruth, George Herman "Babe" (1895–1948) Single most famous baseball player of all time; the "Sultan of Swat."

Sadat, Anwar (1918–1981) President of Egypt who shared the 1978 Nobel Peace Prize with Israeli Prime Minister Menachem Begin for his efforts toward Israeli-Egyptian peace; assassinated by Islamic fundamentalists.

Salk, Jonas (1914–1995) American medical researcher who discovered the first effective vaccine against polio (1954).

Sartre, Jean-Paul (1905–1980) French writer and philosopher associated with existentialism; the most influential philosophy of the century.

Somoza, Anastasio Debayle (1925–1980) Nicaraguan strongman dictator (1963-1979), supported by the United States, and overthrown by the Sandinista National Liberation Front.

Stalin, Josef (1879–1953) Absolute dictator of the Soviet Union from 1922 until his death.

Stein, Gertrude (1874–1946) Avant-garde American writer and art collector living in Paris; friend and mentor to Hemingway, Fitzgerald, and others; credited with coining the phrase "a lost generation."

Stravinsky, Igor (1882–1971) Considered the quintessential 20th-century composer; combined radical modernism with a taste for the primitive.

Sullivan, Louis (1856–1924) American architect who brought to artistic maturity the skyscraper—*the* architectural form of the 20th century.

Sun Yat-sen (1866–1925) A leader of the Chinese Revolution that overthrew the Manchus in 1911; served briefly as China's provisional president.

Taft, William Howard (1857–1930) Twenty-seventh president of the United States and, later, chief justice of the Supreme Court.

Teller, Edward (1908–) Hungarian-born American physicist who spearheaded development of the hydrogen (thermonuclear) bomb.

Tito, Josep Broz (1892–1980) Leader of Yugoslav partisan resistance against Hitler in World War II; as longtime communist president of Yugoslavia, maintained the nation's independence from the Soviet Union.

Truman, Harry S (1884–1972) Thirty-third presient of the United States.

Turing, Alan (1912–1954) British mathematician who established the theoretical basis of computer science.

Victoria I (1819–1901) Queen of England and, for many, personification of 19th-century European values.

Walesa, Lech (1943–) Polish labor leader instrumental in achieving Polish independence from the Soviet bloc; awarded the Nobel Peace Prize (1983); elected president of Poland (1990).

Watson, James D. (1928–) With Francis H. Crick, formulated the spiral double-helix model of the DNA molecule, laying the foundation of modern genetics.

Wilhelm II (1859–1941) Kaiser (emperor) of Germany (1888–1918); led his nation into World War I.

Wilson, Woodrow (1856–1924)   Twenty-eighth president of the United States.

Wright, Orville (1871–1948) and Wilbur (1867–1912)   Ohio-born brothers who designed and built the first successful heavier-than-air craft (1903).

Yeltsin, Boris (1931–)   Pro-democracy Russian leader who led resistance to a hard-line communist coup in 1991 and presided over the establishment of the Commonwealth of Independent States, which replaced the Soviet Union in December 1991.

Zworykin, Vladimir (1889–1982)   Russian-born American physicist and inventor who developed the iconoscope (1923), heart of television technology.

Talk of the Times

Afrikaners See *Boers*.

Annus horribilis Latin for "year of horrors."

Anschluss The so-called "union" of Germany and Austria in March 1938; actually, the German annexation of Austria, which was unopposed by any European power.

antibiotic See *penicillin*.

apartheid An Afrikaans word meaning "separateness"; the long-standing policy of absolute racial segregation that guided South African politics for most of the 20th century.

appeasement Term used by British prime minister Neville Chamberlain to describe the British policy toward German expansionism in the late 1930s. By "appeasing" Hitler—making certain territorial concessions to Germany—Chamberlain hoped to secure "peace for our time." The policy helped create World War II.

Asian debt The collective debt created by the Asian economic crisis at the close of the 20th century.

atomic energy Also called *nuclear energy*. The energy released by nuclear fission (the splitting of an atomic unit into fragments) or nuclear fusion (the joining of atomic nuclei).

ayatollah A religious leader among the Shi'ite Muslims of Iran, whose religious zeal and orthodoxy is often compared to that of Christian "fundamentalists."

baby boom The sharp postwar increase in births in the United States from 1947 to 1961.

Balkans, the Frequently heard in the first quarter of the 20th century, *the Balkans* described a geographical area including Albania, Montenegro, Serbia, Bosnia and Herzegovina, Greece, Bulgaria, and Rumania. It was a flashpoint of conflict and the cauldron from which World War I would emerge.

barnstormer From the 1910s through the early 1930s, an itinerant exhibition aviator who performed stunts and took curious passengers aloft.

battle fatigue An emotional breakdown caused by the unrelieved stress of combat. In World War I, it was called *shell shock*. Today, it is often called *post-traumatic stress syndrome*. An intolerant General George S. Patton called it cowardice.

beat generation   Or simply *the beats*. A group of writers, musicians, and artists (as well as wanna-bes and hangers-on) who, in the 1950s and early 1960s, rejected the commercial values of mainstream American society and embraced a pose of world weariness and an attitude of emotional, sexual, and aesthetic freedom. Outsiders derided them as *beatniks*.

beatniks   See *beat generation*.

black list   The phrase functioned both as a noun and a verb to describe the roster of those accused of communist affiliation during the McCarthy era. Black-listed individuals were, in effect, off limits to employers—unemployable.

blitzkrieg   German word meaning "lightning war." The doctrine of strategy and tactics developed by German military planners after World War I designed to attack an enemy with great speed and violence, penetrating his front lines while encircling and destroying him.

body count   Grim term frequently heard during the Vietnam War. It was a measure of the effectiveness of battle, a method of keeping score by counting the dead.

Boers   Also called *Afrikaners*. Dutch colonists and their descendants in South Africa.

bootlegger   One who made, smuggled, or sold liquor during Prohibition. The term originated in the 19th century, from the practice of hiding a whiskey flask in the upper part of one's boot.

box camera   A simple, cheap, fixed-focus camera for casual picture takers. Designed for average-light and average-distance situations, neither its shutter speed, aperture, nor focus is adjustable, as they are on more sophisticated cameras.

celluloid   The first practical form of plastic. It is made by treating cellulose nitrate with camphor and alcohol. Celluloid was thought of as a "miracle substance" because it could be fashioned to imitate a host of costly materials.

charge plate   Early term for what is now called a credit card. Early in the 20th century, many department stores issued metal plates stamped with the customer's name. These were used to imprint vouchers for items bought on credit. The name "charge plate" remained in common usage long after the metal plates had been replaced by plastic cards.

cloning   Method of propagating a plant, animal, or even human being in the laboratory by asexual means.

cocooning   Term coined by futurist Faith Popcorn, *cocooning* describes a late 20th-century trend toward centering one's life in and around one's home.

Cold War   Coined in 1947 by journalist Herbert Bayard Swope in a speech he wrote for financier Bernard Baruch, referring to the postwar strategic and political struggle between the United States (and its western European allies) and the Soviet Union (and communist countries). A chronic state of hostility, the Cold War was associated with two major "hot wars" (in Korea and Vietnam) and spawned various "brushfire wars" (small-scale armed conflicts, usually in Third World nations), but was not itself a shooting war. Its end was heralded in 1989 by the fall of the Berlin Wall.

Cold Warrior   Hard-line anti-communist U.S. politicians, who took an aggressive stance in the Cold War.

collectivization   The policy and process by which Lenin and, later, Stalin forcibly nationalized agriculture in the Soviet Union.

Comintern   A "local" branch of *the* Comintern, an association of international communist parties established by Lenin in 1919 (and dissolved by Stalin in 1943).

computer   See *programmable computer*.

concentration camp   Phrase apparently first used during the period immediately preceding the Spanish-American War to describe camps in Cuba to which Spanish authorities consigned those active in the Cuban independence movement. The phrase resurfaced in World War II to describe the "deportation" and death camps of the Nazi regime.

conspiracy theorist   Anyone who speculates on secret government involvement in any number of events, including political assassination and especially that of John F. Kennedy.

containment   United States foreign policy during the *Cold War* years, calling for confronting the Soviet Union whenever and wherever it attempted to expand its ideological influence.

cosmology   The study of the origin, nature, and fate of the universe.

counterculture movement   Phrase applied to those—mainly young people—who rebelled against the perceived values of mainstream American culture.

credibility gap   The 1960s were full of "gaps." The "missile gap" was the difference between the number of intercontinental ballistic missiles (ICBMs) in the U.S. arsenal versus the Soviet arsenal, the *generation gap* described the gulf between young and old, and the credibility gap came to describe the difference between what the administration presented as the truth and what everyone else believed.

critical mass   The smallest mass of fissionable material that will sustain a nuclear chain reaction.

cruise missiles   See *smart bombs*.

D-Day   A term that has come to be identified exclusively with the Normandy invasion, *D-Day* is general military jargon for the day on which an operation commences. *H-hour* is the specific hour of that day appointed for commencement of the operation.

de facto segregation   Segregation that actually ("in fact") exists, although it is not sanctioned by law. *De jure* segregation is decreed or supported "by law."

de jure segregation   See *de facto segregation*.

détente   French term (borrowed into English) signifying an easing of tension between rivals through increased diplomatic, commercial, and cultural contact.

domino theory   The argument that, if one small nation is allowed to fall into communist hands, others will follow like the chain reaction of a row of falling dominoes.

doughboys   The British called their soldiers *Tommies*, the French *poilus*—literally, "hairy ones." American troops were familiarly known as *doughboys*, a term of obscure origin. Some believe that the word comes from the dusty appearance of troops who served in the American West—they looked as if they had been dusted with flour— while others believe the term is a reference to resemblance between the buttons of the infantry uniform and a piece of bread dough rolled thin and fried in deep fat, also called a "doughboy."

élan (or *élan vital*)   French word meaning, roughly, spirit; however, as used by the philosopher Henri Bergson (1859-1941), it connoted an unconquerable life spirit— which the French military believed was inherent in every French soldier and would lead inevitably to victory.

453

ethnic cleansing   The Serbian policy, during the 1990s, of expelling or otherwise eliminating non-Serbs (Muslims and Croats) from the Serb-controlled areas of the former Yugoslavia.

eugenics   The practice of selectively breeding human beings with the purpose of producing offspring with certain desired traits and without other, non-desired traits.

evangelist   Zealous, missionary-style preacher, who takes the Word out of the church and to the people.

fascism   A form of totalitarian government in which the state is the focus of life and, governing the state, is an absolute leader, whom the people are to follow, unquestioningly, to greatness.

Feminine Mystique, The   Title of a 1963 book by Betty Friedan; describes the socially ubiquitous belief that "normal" women can achieve genuine satisfaction only through marriage and children.

fission   A nuclear reaction in which an atomic unit splits into fragments, thereby releasing energy. Given a sufficient amount of fissionable material, the split-off fragments collide with other nuclei, causing them to fragment as well, until a self-sustaining chain reaction is under way.

flak   An acronym for the German *Fliegeraabwherkanone*, "antiaircraft gun"; it describes ground-based antiaircraft fire.

flapper   Label for the "liberated" young woman of the 1920s, whose interests were unabashedly worldly and whose inhibitions were few or none. The origin of the term is obscure, but may refer to the wild flapping gestures associated with such '20s dances as the Charleston.

Forbidden City   The Imperial Palace complex within the Inner City of Beijing (formerly Peking), China. It is surrounded by a 35-foot-high wall and contains hundreds of buildings—a total of some 9,000 rooms, which housed the entire imperial court.

fragging   Officers who ordered their men into dangerous situations risked *fragging*—that is, assassination by their own troops, typically by fragmentation grenade.

freedom rides   During the early 1960s, a demonstration to test federal laws mandating the full integration of vehicles used in interstate transit. Defying angry mobs, African American freedom riders boarded Greyhound and Trailways buses throughout the South and refused to sit in the designated "colored" section at the back of the vehicles.

führerheer   A German word roughly translated as "army of leaders." It referred to the small, highly professional army Germany developed in accordance with the restrictions of the Treaty of Versailles.

gene therapy   Medical procedures that may be used to alter or repair "defective" genes in order to prevent disease.

generation gap   Coined in the 1960s, the phrase describes the emotional, intellectual, and social distance perceived between the younger and older generations. Also see *credibility gap*.

ghetto   Borrowed from Italian, *ghetto* was originally applied to the Jewish quarter in Venice during the Middle Ages. In World War II, it took on a new, horrific meaning, as the city districts in which the Nazis confined Jews before "deporting" them to death camps. Over the years, the word has been applied to any urban neighborhood—usually run-down and crime-plagued—in which minority groups are compelled, by social pressure and economics, to live.

glasnost   Russian for openness; describes a reform in policy, instituted by Mikhail Gorbachev in the late 1980s, aimed at ending the Soviet habit of hiding the nation's activities in a cloak of secrecy. *Perestroika*, another of Gorbachev's policy reforms, means restructuring. It refers mainly to economic reforms, intended to move the Soviet Union toward a free-market economy.

global village   Phrase coined by media theorist Marshall McLuhan in the early 1960s to describe how television would bring together the diverse peoples of the world.

gradualism   Program of social change advocated by Booker T. Washington, who believed that social and political equality was less necessary to African Americans than economic self-determination, and that such equality would come, gradually, after economic self-determination had been achieved.

guerilla warfare   During the 17th century, the French in frontier Canada used the phrase *la petite guerre* ("little war") to describe small-scale, stealthy combat. The phrase evolved into the single word *guerrilla* to describe a limited, covert style of warfare as well as the combatants who fight such wars. Guerrilla warfare figured importantly throughout the 20th century.

H-hour   See *D-Day*.

hallucinogen   A drug or other substance that produces hallucinations and distorts the perception of reality often in extravagantly fantastic form.

Hapsburgs   The ruling dynasty of Austria-Hungary until the Treaty of Versailles (1919). They had held power since about A.D. 950.

heir apparent   The person whose right to inheritance cannot be denied, provided he or she survives an ancestor. Contrast *heir presumptive,* whose right to inheritance can be defeated by the subsequent birth of a relative closer to the ancestor.

heir presumptive   See *heir apparent.*

hippie   Coined in the 1960s to describe members of the *counterculture*. It was derived from *hip*, an adjective originally used by African American jazz musicians to describe people, music, and ideas in tune with the advanced styles and trends of the time.

Holocaust   The genocide of European Jews at the hands of the Nazis during World War II.

homeless people   Euphemism for those formerly described as indigents, derelicts, or bums.

Hoovervilles   Depression-era shanty towns built by the homeless and unemployed. The name is an ironic reference to President Herbert Hoover.

impeach   To charge an office holder with offenses that, if proven, warrant removal from office. Impeachment is not synonymous with such removal.

impressment   The British naval practice of boarding foreign vessels, identifying (often doubtfully) British nationals, and "pressing" them into involuntary service in the Royal Navy.

in vitro fertilization   Medical procedure in which fertilization of an ovum takes place outside of the mother's body.

Indian removal   The federal policy, inaugurated by the Indian Removal Act of 1830, of "relocating" Indians living east of the Mississippi to "Indian Territory" reserved for them in the West.

inner city See *white flight*.

Iron Curtain The term Winston Churchill used to describe the extent of the Soviet sphere of influence and domination in the postwar period. The term was popularized in a March 5, 1946, speech at Westminster College in Fulton, Missouri, but it was first used by Churchill in a May 12, 1945 telegram to President Harry Truman.

island hopping The U.S. World War II strategy for regaining the initiative in the Pacific and ultimately achieving victory. The idea was to retake one Japanese-held island after another, always closing in on the Japanese mainland.

isolationism National policy of avoiding political ties with other nations.

jazz Highly improvisational form of music primarily developed by African Americans who combined European harmonic structures with African rhythmic complexities. These are, in turn, overlaid with European and white American dance and march rhythms and with elements borrowed from the blues tradition. The word is probably derived from a slang term for sexual intercourse.

jet propulsion The principle behind modern jet aircraft. Oxygen is rapidly mixed with fuel and burned, producing a jet of hot exhaust gases, which provide tremendous forward thrust.

Jim Crow laws Legislation enacted in the Southern states to enforce the discrimination against and suppression of African Americans. The term derived from a derogatory name for a black person, which was in turn derived from the title of a popular 19th-century blackface minstrel show song.

junk bonds Low-cost, high-yield bonds issued by new, typically risky, ventures or by companies with poor credit ratings.

junkie A narcotics addict; "junk" is a slang term for heroin.

killed-virus vaccines Medical breakthrough of the 1950s, making possible safe inoculation against such viral diseases as polio. In contrast to inoculation with *live-virus vaccines*, killed viruses confer immunity without the danger of infection.

laissez-faire capitalism An economic system in which the marketplace is left to balance and correct itself, regardless of "temporary" consequences and without government intervention.

limited warfare War strictly confined in order to avoid creating a larger (presumably nuclear) conflict.

live-virus vaccine See *killed-virus vaccine*.

malaria One of the world's most prevalent infectious diseases. Marked by severe cycles of chills and high fever, it is caused by infection of red blood cells by a protozoan (of the genus *Plasmodium)*, transmitted by the bite of an infected female anopheles mosquito.

Manchu Also called the Qing. Last of the Chinese imperial dynasties. The Manchus came as invaders from the northeast and seized power in 1644. They were overthrown in the revolution of 1911.

Manifest Destiny Phrase coined by *New York Post* editor John L. O'Sullivan in 1845, which came to describe the sense, shared by most 19th-century Americans, that the United States was divinely destined to encompass the entire continent.

margin To purchase a stock "on *margin*" is to pay a small percentage of the value of the stock and to finance the remainder of the purchase price through the stock brokerage.

meltdown   Condition in which the radioactive material at the core of a nuclear reactor becomes superheated as a result of a runaway chain reaction. The result may be an explosion, as the core material melts down through the earth then contacts ground water.

militia movement   Organization and activities of militant right-wing groups opposed to what they perceive as government oppression ranging from taxation, to gun control, to the promulgation and enforcement of civil rights laws.

mobilization   Putting a nation's military forces on a full war footing; preparing for immediate war. A word that echoed through the summer of 1914.

muckraker   First used by President Theodore Roosevelt to describe the social-reform writers and journalists of the 1910s. Roosevelt took the word from *Pilgrim's Progress*, a Christian allegorical novel written by John Bunyan in the 17th century. The book was a fixture in many 19th-century homes and was widely taught in the schools, so most of the public was familiar with Roosevelt's reference to one of the characters, who used a "muckrake" to clean up the (moral) filth around him, as he remained oblivious to the "celestial" beauty above.

musical comedy   Also called the musical. A form of popular theater in which the dialogue and action are interspersed with song. More colloquial and popular in tone than either opera or operetta, musical comedy developed to maturity on the American stage during the 1920s to 1950s.

mutual deterrence   Strategic policy assumption that the possession of nuclear weapons by ideologically opposed states will prevent war, because each nation understands that such war would ultimately be self-destructive. This is related to the doctrine of Mutually Assured Destruction, "MAD," the understanding that a nation's use of nuclear weapons will be met with nuclear retaliation, thereby assuring the destruction of both nations—and, presumably, most of civilization.

mutually assured destruction (MAD)   See *mutual deterrence*.

NATO   North Atlantic Treaty Organization. Formed in 1949 by the United States and 11 other Western nations as an anti-communist military alliance.

natural selection   The principal vehicle of species evolution; the operation of random variation that enables a species to survive in its environment. Proposed as a theory of evolution by the 19th-century biologist Charles Darwin.

Northwest Passage   Water route mistakenly believed to exist across the North American continent, joining the Atlantic and Pacific. Many expeditions of American exploration were formed in the 17th through 19th centuries in search of this illusory passage.

Okies   The popular (and often derisive) term for victims of the Dust Bowl who traveled—mostly to California—in search of a better life or even better prospects for survival.

overachiever   A person who habitually works too hard and demands too much of himself or herself. The word did not appear in dictionaries before the 1970s, but is frequently heard today.

paparazzi   Singular, *paparazzo*. From an Italian word denoting journalists, *paparazzi* describes a class of photographers who specialize in the invasion of public figures' privacy, taking intrusive and embarrassing photographs, which are published in sensationalist tabloid newspapers.

penicillin   First important antibiotic, a drug that destroys harmful microorganisms, inhibiting the synthesis of murein, the substance that makes bacterial cell walls strong. Since the cell walls of nonbacterial cells do not contain murein, penicillin can destroy bacterial cells without harming body cells.

perestroika   See *glasnost.*

personal computer   Phrase coined by IBM in 1981 to describe its first desktop computer, small enough and cheap enough to be purchased and used by an individual rather than a corporation or institution. See also *programmable computer.*

phonograph   Like *telephone*, the word *phonograph* was used before the invention of the device that bears the name. Earlier in the 19th century, *phonograph* was used as a synonym for hieroglyphs or other written characters that represented sounds. It was also the name of an 1863 device that electromagnetically transcribed notes played on a piano or other keyed instrument.

Ping-Pong diplomacy   Term popularly applied to the breakthrough in U.S.-Chinese relations that occurred in 1971, when communist China invited a U.S. team to participate in a championship table-tennis tournament played in Beijing.

plow   An implement for breaking up the ground and cutting the furrows in which seeds may be sown. A *reaper* harvests the mature crop.

poilus   See *doughboys.*

Politburo   The chief executive and political committee of the Communist Party of the Soviet Union.

political patronage   The use of lucrative political appointments in return for political support and to pay off political debts.

population explosion   Term coined in the 1950s to describe the great increase in population worldwide following World War II.

post-traumatic stress syndrome   See *battle fatigue.*

Proclamation of 1765   Promulgated by England's King George III, a decree forbidding settlement west of the Appalachian Mountains. This outraged and alienated frontier colonists and helped create the political climate in which the independence movement was born.

programmable computer   A "universal" device capable of performing a great many different calculational and logical operations, depending on the instructions (the program) presented to it. This is in contrast to simple calculators, for example, which can perform limited operations, such as addition, multiplication, and so on.

progressivism   An American political philosophy that favored an array of reforms aimed at establishing "clean government" and giving the electorate more power—though it stopped short of anything approaching radicalism. Progressive ideas figured importantly from the beginning of the 20th century through the administrations of Theodore Roosevelt, William Howard Taft, and Woodrow Wilson.

propaganda   The systematic and persuasive use of selected truths (typically by government authorities) in order to further a cause. The word is rooted in the Catholic church, in which it refers to the official body charged with regulating missionary preaching.

psychoanalysis   Sigmund Freud's theory of mind; also applies to the clinical procedures for understanding mental processes and treating mental disorders.

quantum mechanics   Branch of physics that deals with the emission and absorption of energy by matter and with the motion of subatomic particles in matter. It did not exist before 1900, and is now a cornerstone of our understanding of the universe and our ability (for better or worse) to release the enormous energy of the atom.

reaper   See *plow*.

recombinant DNA   Genetically engineered DNA, in which DNA molecules from two or more sources are artificially combined and then inserted into host organisms to create cloned genes. The purpose of such a procedure is to produce offspring organisms with certain desirable traits or without certain undesirable ones.

Relativity, Theory of   Proposed by Albert Einstein; describes a universe in which the only absolute is the speed of light and in which matter and energy are ultimately equivalent. It demonstrates that the commonsense model of the universe proposed by Isaac Newton is valid only for our particular ("local") frame of reference.

salient   Fortified enemy area that comes closest to one's own lines.

satyagraha   An Indian word meaning "holding to the truth." It was used by Mohandas ("Mahatma") Gandhi to describe his doctrine of effecting social and political change through nonviolent civil disobedience.

Schlieffen plan   Formulated and repeatedly revised by Germany's brilliant chief of staff Count Alfred von Schlieffen (1833-1913); prescribed a strategy for fighting a decisive two-front war against France and Russia. Deviation from the plan in the opening month of World War I stalemated the war for four unprecedentedly bloody years.

scorched-earth policy   The practice of destroying crops and other resources in order to keep them from falling to an invading enemy.

scud   *NATO* code name for the relatively short-range, Soviet-made surface-to-surface missiles used by Iraq during the Persian Gulf War. The chief advantage of the Scud is that it may be launched from transportable launchers, which can be hidden from attack.

Selective Service System   System by which young men between the ages of 18 and 45, were subject to conscription into the U.S. armed forces. Adopted in 1917 and renewed and revised throughout the century. On July 1, 1973, "induction authority" ceased—the military draft ended, and the era of an all-volunteer armed forces began.

shell shock   See *battle fatigue*.

shock jock   Radio personalities ("disc jockeys") who specialize in outrageous talk, often of a sexually obscene or otherwise socially objectionable nature.

sit-in   Technique of nonviolent civil disobedience in which protesters enter a business or public place and remain seated there until evicted by force or until their grievances are addressed.

skyjacking   A coinage from "hijacking"; describes "air piracy," the seizure of aircraft and kidnapping of passengers and crew.

skyscraper   A word that goes back to the 18th century, when it referred to a lofty sail high on a ship's mast. Beginning in the early 19th century, the word was also used as a synonym for an exaggeration —a "tall story"—a high-standing horse, a very tall man, and even a rider on a high-wheel ("penny-farthing") bicycle. In 1891, *skyscraper* was first used (by a Boston newspaper) to describe a new, multistory building.

smart bombs   Weapons that may be electronically controlled or programmed to find their designated targets. *Cruise missiles* are essentially pilotless aircraft, steerable to their targets by remote guidance.

snapshot   Before 1900, a hunting term that meant a quick shot fired without taking careful aim. After the introduction of the Brownie, however, the word was universally applied to photographs casually taken with a handheld camera, and the original meaning of the word was largely forgotten.

Social Darwinism   The use of Charles Darwin's concept of survival of the fittest in nature to justify—in society—the economic success of one class at the expense of another.

sodbuster   Nineteenth-century settlers of the American prairie, who typically built their first houses out of the material most readily available: the prairie sod.

Soviet   Any popularly elected legislative assembly in Russia and, later, the Soviet Union. Soviets existed on local, regional, and national levels.

space race   Familiar name Americans applied to the U.S. space program after the USSR successfully launched *Sputnik* in 1957. The space race was "won" in 1969, when *Apollo 11* landed two American astronauts on the moon.

sphere of influence   Territorial area over which political or economic influence is wielded by a nation.

Sputnik   Russian word for satellite; the name of the first artificial satellite rocketed into orbit, by the Soviet Union, on October 4, 1957.

stagflation   An economic situation characterized by high unemployment and inflation—usually two mutually exclusive conditions.

strategic bombing   The practice of massive bombing of civilian and industrial targets in order to diminish the enemy's overall capacity for war. Contrast *tactical bombing*, which is the smaller-scale bombing of specific military targets directly involved in combat.

supply-side economics   An approach to economic policy aimed at achieving efficiency by using government policies to stimulate production.

tactical bombing   See *strategic bombing*.

telecommuting   The practice of working from one's home rather than in a central office.

telegraph   Derived from the Greek, meaning "distant writing," or writing over distance. The word was coined by Samuel F.B. Morse to describe his 1844 invention, which revolutionized communication in the United States and the rest of the world.

telephone   Made up of Greek roots meaning "afar" and "voice"; the word was actually in use before Bell's invention. As early as 1835, it described any megaphonelike instrument.

terrorism   The use of force or violence by an individual or group against persons or property, usually with the purpose of coercing some desired political action.

Third World   Underdeveloped nations politically aligned neither with more developed capitalist nor communist powers.

Tommies   See *doughboys*.

total war   The policy of waging war against an entire people, combatants and non-combatants alike, with the object of destroying the enemy's will to fight.

transistor   A semiconductor device that uses very low voltages to regulate higher voltages. It functions as both a control and amplification device in electronic circuits and is the heart of all modern electronic devices. Replaced the *vacuum tube*.

"Trial of the Century"   A phrase frequently used to describe the 1994 trial of ex-football star and television personality O.J. Simpson for the murder of his ex-wife and her friend. Previously, the 1935 trial of Richard Bruno Hauptmann, for the kidnapping and murder of the infant son of Charles Lindbergh and Anne Morrow Lindbergh, had been dubbed the "trial of the century."

trickle down   Catch phrase of the Reagan years; described the belief that reducing taxes on the wealthy and on businesses would stimulate investment, thereby increasing employment opportunities and improving the economy, the benefits of which would eventually "trickle down" to the majority of Americans.

turing machine   Not a physical machine at all, but a theoretical construct proposed in 1936 by British mathematician Alan Turing (1912–1954), which forms the basis of modern computer theory and technique.

unaligned nations   Countries, typically small and relatively impoverished, which declared political affinity with neither the United States nor the Soviet Union. Collectively, such nations were often referred to as the *Third World*, a term still used to describe developing countries.

unconscious, the   Part of the mind that is normally not available to conscious perception and that contains repressed memories, desires, and drives.

unified field theory   The Holy Grail of physics—a theory of the universe that would fully explain the relation among all forces of the universe.

universal manhood suffrage   The right of all male citizens, above a certain minimum age, to vote.

vacuum tube   An electron tube that acts to amplify weak electric currents or to use low-voltage currents to control higher-voltage currents. It is the basis of all electronic circuitry before the invention of the *transistor* in 1948.

Vietnamization   The process of turning over to the South Vietnamese responsibility for the conduct of the Vietnam War.

Warsaw Pact   The Soviet response to the establishment of *NATO*. Established in 1955, it was ostensibly a mutual-defense alliance, but, in reality, gave the Soviet Union military power over its satellite nations. The pact was dissolved in 1991.

Weimar Republic   So called because it was established pursuant to a constitution drawn up in the city of Weimar, Germany, in 1919; the Weimar Republic governed Germany from 1919 to 1933.

white flight   The mass exodus of the white middle class from the nation's cities to its suburbs, beginning in the 1950s. The oldest—and most decayed—neighborhoods of a city were collectively called the *inner city*, a euphemism for *ghetto*.

witch hunt   Term derisively applied to the reckless investigation of Communist infiltration in American government and industry led by Senator Joseph McCarthy from 1950 to 1954. In 1953, the playwright Arthur Miller wrote *The Crucible*, ostensibly about the witch trials in 17th-century Salem, Massachusetts, but really a devastatingly effective allegory criticizing the witch hunts of his own time.

xenophobia   Exaggerated fear of foreigners.

Y2K Bug   Also called the Year 2000 Problem. A glitch in certain computer programs and computer hardware incorporating imbedded programming code that records years with only two digits and, therefore, cannot recognize whether the date "00" is 2000 or 1900. Y2K problems may cause massive breakdowns in computer systems.

yellow fever   Also called Yellow Jack. An infectious tropical disease caused by a virus transmitted by mosquitoes of the genera *Aedes*. This debilitating, often fatal disease, is characterized by high fever, jaundice, and dark vomit resulting from gastrointestinal hemorrhaging.

Recommended Reading

Asimov, Isaac. *Asimov's Chronology of Science and Discovery*. New York: Harper and Row, 1989.

Atkinson, Rick. *Crusade: The Untold Story of the Persian Gulf War*. Boston: Houghton Muffin Company, 1993.

Axelrod, Alan. *The Complete Idiot's Guide to American History*. New York: Alpha Books, 1996.

———. *The Complete Idiot's Guide to Jazz*. New York: Alpha Books, 1999.

Axelrod, Alan, and Charles Phillips. *What Everyone Should Know About the 20th Century: 200 Events That Shaped the World*. Holbrook, Mass.: Adams Communications, 1995.

Baker, Carlos. *Ernest Hemingway: A Life Story*. New York: Macmillan, 1988.

Belz, Carl. *The Story of Rock*. New York: Oxford University Press, 1969.

Blair, Clay. *The Forgotten War: America in Korea—1950–1953*. New York: Random House, 1987.

Bohr, Niels. *Atomic Physics and Human Knowledge*. New York: Wiley, 1958.

Branch. Taylor. *Parting the Waters: America in the King Years, 1954–1964*. New York: Simon & Schuster, 1988.

Bulliet, Richard W., ed. *The Columbia History of the 20th Century*. New York: Columbia University Press, 1998.

Bullock, Alan. *Hitler and Stalin: Parallel Lives*. New York: Alfred Knopf, Inc., 1991.

Carruth, Gorton. *What Happened When: A Chronology of Life and Events in America*. New York: Penguin Books, 1989.

de Leon, David. *Everything Is Changing: Contemporary U.S. Movements in Historical Perspectives*. New York: Praeger, 1988.

Dickstein, Morris. *Gates of Eden: American Culture in the Sixties*. New York: Viking Penguin, 1989.

Dockrell, Michael. *Atlas of Twentieth Century World History*. New York: Harper Perennial, 1991.

Douglas, Ann. *Terrible Honesty: Mongrel Manhattan in the 1920s*. New York: Farrar, Straus and Giroux, 1995.

Duggan, Stephen, and Betty Drury. *The Rescue of Science and Learning*. New York: Macmillan, 1948.

Dyson, Freeman. *Disturbing the Universe.* New York: Harper and Row, 1979.

Einstein, Albert and Leopold Infield. *The Evolution of Physics.* New York: Simon and Schuster, 1966.

Elliot, Emory. *Columbia Literary History of the United States.* New York: Columbia University Press, 1988.

Ellis, John. *The Social History of the Machine Gun.* New York: Pantheon, 1976.

Emery, Fred. *Watergate: The Corruption of American Politics and the Fall of Richard Nixon.* New York: Times Books, 1994.

Fell. Joseph. *Heidegger and Sartre.* New York: Columbia University Press, 1978.

Foner, Eric, et al. *The Reader's Companion to American History.* Boston: Houghton Muffin, 1991.

Friedman, Jon and John Meehan. *House of Cards: Inside the Troubled Empire of American Express.* New York: G. P. Putnam's Sons, 1992.

Friedrich, Otto. *Before the Deluge: A Portrait of Berlin in the 1920s.* New York: Harper & Row, 1992.

Gabler, Neal. *An Empire of Their Own: How the Jews Invented Hollywood.* New York: Anchor Books, 1988.

———. *Winchell: Gossip, Power; and the Cult of Celebrity.* New York: Alfred A. Knopf, 1994.

Gamow. George. *The Thirty Years That Shook Physics.* New York: Doubleday. 1966.

Garraty, John A. *The Great Depression.* Garden City, NJ: Anchor Books, 1987.

Gentry, Curt. *J. Edgar Hoover: The Man and the Secrets.* New York: W. W. Norton, 1991.

Gilbert, Martin. *A History of the Twentieth Century: 1900–1933.* New York: William Morrow, 1997.

———. *A History of the Twentieth Century: 1933–1951.* New York: William Morrow, 1999.

Glaser, Nathan, ed. *Clamor at the Gates: The New American Immigration.* 1985.

Gordon, Michael R. and General Bernard E. Trainor. *The Generals' War: The Inside Story of the Conflict in the Gulf.* Boston: Little, Brown and Company, 1995.

Gordon, Linda. *Woman's Body, Woman's Right: A Social History of Birth Control in America.* Madison, WI: University of Wisconsin Press, rev. ed., 1990.

Gould, Lewis L. *The Presidency of Theodore Roosevelt.* Lawrence: University of Kansas Press, 1991.

Graham, Davis. *The Civil Rights Era: Origins and Development of National Policy.* 1990.

Greenville, J. A. S. *History of the World in the Twentieth Century.* Cambridge, MA: Belknap Press. 1994.

Groves, Leslie. *Now It Can Be Told.* New York: Harper and Row, 1962.

Henderson, Robert. *D.W. Griffith: His Life and Work.* New York: Oxford University Press, 1972.

Hentoff, Nat and Albert J. McCarthy, eds. *Jazz: New Perspectives on the History of Jazz.* New York: Da Capo, 1975.

Hersh, Barton. *The Old Boys: The American Elite and the Origins of the CIA.* New York: Charles Scribner's Sons, 1992.

Hobsbawm, Eric. *The Age of Extremes: A History of the World, 1914–1991.* New York: Pantheon Books, 1994.

Howard, Michael Eliot, and William Roger Louis, eds. *The Oxford History of the Twentieth Century.* New York: Oxford University Press, 1998.

Keegan, John. *The Second World War.* New York: Viking, 1989.

Kenner, Hugh. *The Pound Era.* Berkeley and Los Angeles: University of California Press, 1971.

Knight, Arthur. *The Liveliest Art: A Panoramic History of the American Movies.* New York: New American Library, 1957.

Kolko, Gabriel. *Anatomy of a War: Vietnam, the United States, and the Modern Historical Experience.* New York: Pantheon, 1985.

Lasch, Christopher. *The New Radicalism in America, 1889–1963.* New York: W.W. Norton & Co., 1965.

Mandela, Nelson. *No Easy Walk to Freedom.* London: Heineman, 1965.

Manchester, William. *The Arms of Krupp, 1587–1968.* Boston: Little, Brown & Co., 1964.

Montgomery, David. *The Fall of the House of Labor.* Cambridge, England: Cambridge University Press, 1987.

Nieman, Donald G. *Promises to Keep: African Americans and the Constitutional Order, 1776 to the Present.* Oxford, England: Oxford University Press. 1991.

Nye, Russell. *The Unembarrassed Muse: The Popular Arts in America.* New York: Dial Press, 1970.

O'Brien, Conor Cruise. *The Siege: The Saga of Israel and Zionism.* New York: Simon and Schuster, 1989.

Orfield, Gary. *Public School Desegregation in the United States, 1968–1980.* New York: Ford Foundation, 1983.

Parmet, Herbert S. *JFK: The Presidency of John F. Kennedy.* New York: The Dial Press, 1983.

Posner, Gerald. *Case Closed: Lee Harvey Oswald and the Assassination of JFK.* New York: Random House, 1993.

Reimers, David, ed. *Still the Golden Door: The Third World Comes to America.* New York: Columbia University Press, 1985.

Reisner, Marc. *Cadillac Desert: The American West and Its Disappearing Water:* New York: Penguin Books, 1986.

Rhodes, Richard. *The Making of the Atomic Bomb.* New York: Simon and Schuster, 1986.

Ross. Walter S. *The Last Hero: Charles A. Lindbergh.* 1964.

Sergeant, Harriet. *Shanghai: Collision Point of Cultures, 1918–1939.* New York: Crown Publishers, Inc., 1990.

Shepard, Alan and Deke Slayton. *Moon Shot: The Inside Story of America's Race to the Moon.* Atlanta: Turner Publishing, 1992.

Sifakis, Carl. *The Mafia Encyclopedia.* New York: Facts on File, 1989.

Speer, Albert. *Inside the Third Reich.* New York: Macmillan Co., 1970.

Takaki, Ronald. *A D4fferent Mirror: A History of Multicultural Americans.* Boston: Little, Brown and Company, 1993.

Teller, Edward. *The Legacy of Hiroshima.* New York: Doubleday, 1962.

Thelen, David, and Frederick E. Hoxie, eds. *Robert La Follette and the Insurgent Spirit.* Madison, WI: University of Wisconsin Press, 1976.

Tice, Panicia M. *Altered States: Alcohol and Other Drugs in America.* Rochester, NY: Strong Museum, 1992.

Tuchman, Barbara. *The March of Folly: From Troy to Vietnam.* New York: Ballantine Books, 1984.

———. *The Guns of August.* New York: Ballantine Books, 1962.

Volkman, Ernest and Blame Baggett. *Secret Intelligence: The Inside Story of America's Espionage Empire.* New York: Doubleday, 1989.

Williams, Juan. *Eyes on the Prize: America's Civil Rights Years, 1954–1965.* New York: Penguin, 1987.

Woodward, C. Vann. *The Strange Career of Jim Crow.* New York: Oxford University Press, 1966.

Yourdon, Edward, and Jennifer Yourdon. *Time Bomb 2000: What the Year 2000 Crisis Means to You.* 2d ed. Upper Saddle River, NJ: Prentice Hall PTR, 1999.

Zieger, Robert H. *American Workers. American Unions, 1920–1985.* Baltimore: Johns Hopkins University Press, 1986.

Zinn, Howard. *The Twentieth Century: A People's History.* New York: Perennial Library, 1980.

Index

J

M

Q-R

X-Z